MINIMALIST LIVING
5 BOOKS IN 1

Minimalist Home, Minimalist Mindset, Minimalist Budget, Minimalist Lifestyle, Minimalism for Families, Learn How to Declutter & Simplify Your Life

Jenifer Scott

TABLE OF CONTENTS

MINIMALIST HOME

Learn How to Quickly Declutter Your Home, Organize Your Workspace, and Simplify Your Life to Have a Minimalist Lifestyle Using Minimalism Mindset & Habits

Introduction 3
Chapter 1 *What Minimalism Is & Isn't*..5
Chapter 2 *Make A Plan* 8
Chapter 3 *Declutter & Organize The Kitchen* 14
Chapter 4 *Declutter The Dining Area* 17
Chapter 5 *Declutter & Organize The Bath Areas*.............................. 19
Chapter 6 *Declutter The Living Room* 22
Chapter 7 *Revamp The Office & Your Budget* 26
Chapter 9 *For Kids Only — Minimalism*... 44
Chapter 10 *Declutter Laundry Spaces* 48
Chapter 11 *Clean & Organize Spare Storage Areas* 49
Chapter 12 *Methods Of Containment & Removal*............................ 51
Chapter 13 *Benefits Of A Minimalistic Home*...................................54
Chapter 14 *The Minimalist Mindset*... 58
Chapter 15 *The Minimalist Plan For Home Maintenance* 60
Chapter 16 *Natural Cleaning Supplies*... 64
Chapter 17 *Super-Clean — Specific Spaces*....................................... 75
Conclusion *Maintain A Minimalistic Viewpoint* 87
Description 88

MINIMALIST MINDSET

Minimalism Habits & Mindsets to Declutter Your Life, Retake Your Personal and Financial Discipline, and Make Your Passions A Priority to Achieve A Better Life!

Introduction 91
Chapter 1 *Minimalism And Happiness* 92
Chapter 2 *Living Life By Principles* 100
Chapter 3 *Reality Check* 108
Chapter 4 *Getting Started* 116
Chapter 5 *Financial Freedom Through Minimalism* 123
Chapter 6 *Decluttering The Digital* 131
Chapter 7 *Living With A Non-Minimalist* 138
Chapter 8 *Traveling Light* 146
Conclusion 154
Description 155

MINIMALIST BUDGET
Save Money, Avoid Compulsive Spending, Learn Practical and Simple Budgeting Strategies, Money Management Skills, and Declutter Your Financial Life Using Minimalism Tools & Essentials

Introduction 158
Chapter 1 *Minimalist Budget Essentials: Entering The Minimalist Mindset* 159
Chapter 2 *Defining Goals And Priorities* 164
Chapter 3 *Budgeting And Money Management Strategies* 167
Chapter 4 *Minimalist Budget Tools* 178
Chapter 5 *Dealing With Compulsive Spending, Setbacks, And Unexpected Expenses* 190
Chapter 6 *The Interaction Of Your Minimalist Budget With Your Family And Friends* 199
Bonus Chapter *Minimalist Budget Meets Frugality* 208
Conclusion 223
Description 224

MINIMALIST LIFESTYLE
How to Become a Minimalist, Declutter Your Life and Develop Minimalism Habits & Mindsets to Worry Less and Live More

Introduction 227
Chapter 1 *Hello, New Minimalist You* 228
Chapter 2 *What's Life Like As A Minimalist Anyway?* 235
Chapter 3 *Where It All Begins* 242
Chapter 4 *The Rulebook To Living With Less* 249
Chapter 5 *Can I Minimize Other Areas Too?* 257
Chapter 6 *Shifting Your Mindset* 264
Chapter 7 *Goal Setting* 271
Chapter 8 *Success Tips For Your New Way Of Life* 278
Conclusion 287
Description 288

MINIMALISM FOR FAMILIES
For Families Who Want More Joy, Health, and Creativity In Their Life by Decluttering Their Home, Learning Simple and Practical Budgeting Strategies to Save Money & Worry Less!

Introduction 291
Chapter 1 *Definition* 292
Chapter 2 *Mindset Of Minimalism* 297
Chapter 3 *Factors To Consider* 302
Chapter 4 *Things That Clutter* 306
Chapter 5 *Questions To Consider* 309
Chapter 6 *Important Places And Items* 314

Chapter 7 *Furnitures And Other Items* 321
Chapter 8 *Confessions And Steps* 325
Chapter 9 *Decorations And Decluttering*... 330
Chapter 10 *Aspects To Embrace*...333
Chapter 11 *Humanity*.. 338
Chapter 12 *Recap* 341
Chapter 13 *Reasons And Guidelines* 346
Conclusion 352
Description 353

MINIMALIST HOME

Learn How to Quickly Declutter Your Home, Organize Your Workspace, and Simplify Your Life to Have a Minimalist Lifestyle Using Minimalism Mindset & Habits

By
Jenifer Scott

Copyright 2019 by Jenifer Scott - All rights reserved.

This book is provided with the sole purpose of providing relevant information on a specific topic for which every reasonable effort has been made to ensure that it is both accurate and reasonable. Nevertheless, by purchasing this book you consent to the fact that the author, as well as the publisher, are in no way experts on the topics contained herein, regardless of any claims as such that may be made within. As such, any suggestions or recommendations that are made within are done so purely for entertainment value. It is recommended that you always consult a professional prior to undertaking any of the advice or techniques discussed within.

This is a legally binding declaration that is considered both valid and fair by both the Committee of Publishers Association and the American Bar Association and should be considered as legally binding within the United States.

The reproduction, transmission, and duplication of any of the content found herein, including any specific or extended information will be done as an illegal act regardless of the end form the information ultimately takes. This includes copied versions of the work both physical, digital and audio unless express consent of the Publisher is provided beforehand. Any additional rights reserved.

Furthermore, the information that can be found within the pages described forthwith shall be considered both accurate and truthful when it comes to the recounting of facts. As such, any use, correct or incorrect, of the provided information will render the Publisher free of responsibility as to the actions taken outside of their direct purview. Regardless, there are zero scenarios where the original author or the Publisher can be deemed liable in any fashion for any damages or hardships that may result from any of the information discussed herein.

Additionally, the information in the following pages is intended only for informational purposes and should thus be thought of as universal. As befitting its nature, it is presented without assurance regarding its prolonged validity or interim quality. Trademarks that are mentioned are done without written consent and can in no way be considered an endorsement from the trademark holder.

INTRODUCTION

Congratulations on purchasing *Minimalist Home: Learn How to Quickly Declutter Your Home, Organize Your Workspace, and Simplify Your Life to Have a Minimalist Lifestyle Using Minimalism Mindset & Habits*, and thank you for doing so!

This book contains proven steps and strategies on how to become a truly excellent organizer in a short time period. I'm not so sure about the "short" part, but the process does work. For example, how many times have you misplaced your keys? It's probably more times than you care to admit! Why not place a hook next to the door as the designated home for your keys?

Here's an inescapable fact: there's nothing worse than coming home from a hard day at work to view your home as a disaster area. You'll be surprised how easy it really is to get your home organized, where everything is in its proper spot.

It truly begins with a blueprint of what you plan will be to become a minimalist. It can start as simple as gathering and maintaining the inflow of clutter! Give yourself a 2-week cleanup excursion. You can always add a few days, but getting motivated is the first step.

If you need to have the carpets cleaned, you will need to add more time to your plan. However, since you have taken the incentive to get your home truly organized, why not have the professionals do the job for you?

Ask yourself a couple of questions: How long since you used the item—a week, a month? Where does the item belong, and does it have a specific space where it belongs? Does the item have a purpose not covered by another belonging? While it may seem that reducing clutter in your life is an impossible task, you unquestionably *can* do it.

Start right now by addressing your personal belongings—using baby steps. Conduct your research for a supportive community, and stay motivated by anticipating the conclusion you desire.

Does the item get in your way? Do I have space for the item? Your feelings are important, but they shouldn't trump the fact that you don't have the space to accommodate them. By overcrowding, you are causing the things you love to suffer.

Does the item in question bring you joy? You must be the one to decide, as a minimalist. Don't get lost in the fear and anxiety.

Do you find yourself saying, "But what if I need this someday?" Instead, think of it this way: "What do I need now?" At that point, "I know that I can't predict the future, and I also don't want to carry around every item imaginable for the next thirty years on the off chance I end up needing it. I put my trust in the universe that I will be able to get what I need, when I need it, from this moment onward."

Remember that simplifying the way you live, as well as minimizing the number of items in your living space, is just the first step for minimalist living. The process is not one to make you feel deprived—but to make you see the satisfaction you can derive with a less cluttered space.

It is essential as a minimalist to evaluate and adjust your style. In a nutshell, always remember true joy and contentment is what you desire—not a bunch of stuff that has no special space in your life. Continue the process and adjust the target goals as they develop over time. Do what you can at the moment using the tools you have acquired.

You will be cleaning and clearing the clutter using natural cleaning products—no more worrying about whether it's safe or not. Make it yourself, and you will know for sure. You will also find a couple of pleasing aromas throughout the book using essential oils.

Each segment is full of information to inform you of how to become a professional in terms of minimalism. I hope each method of organization will help you enjoy your home to its fullest.

"As you simplify your life, the laws of the universe will be simpler; solitude will not be solitude, poverty will not be poverty, nor weakness weakness."
—Henry David Thoreau

CHAPTER 1
What Minimalism Is & Isn't

Minimalism is having a vivid perception of what you value most in your life. You could believe it relates to items consuming your space and time. Minimalism is an *intentional* way that you live and allowing just what coordinates with your essential values to engulf your time and space. Minimalism is an individual choice. Each value is personal and unique to you. You must decide what's most important—and then discard anything that does not support those values.

Kill the Myths

Minimalism means you need to get rid of everything you own.

This is very untrue. It is about making more room for more of what matters in life—more space, more time, more freedom, and more peace.

Minimalism and frugality are just alike.

Frugality involves seeking opportunities to save money as you use caution to purchase less and shop with intentions of not overspending. At the same time, the primary intention of minimalism revolves around being frugal as well.

However, they are similar since both uphold the *intention* of how your money is spent. Minimalism is about living with less. Therefore, you have the essential space and time for everything else, which is most important in your life. Not all minimalists are focused on being frugal since they're willing to purchase higher quality items, which results in costing more money than other choices.

Minimalism makes life harder with its restrictions.

Many believe you need to get rid of all belongings except for the bare essentials, which would indeed make life harder. Not true! Life as a minimalist, you will spend much less time cleaning, looking for lost items, picking up, maintaining your stuff, organizing your stuff, and the list continues. Why? Because you do not have the additional stuff.

After you adopt a minimalist mindset, you will see that the belongings you believed made life simpler, are occupying essential space. Minimalism isn't centered on the removal of your items *if they* make your life easier and also are frequently used items. It's about removing all of the clutter of non-useful items.

Minimalism means an uninviting home.

Generally, minimalist design is aesthetic, and many times is symbolized by all-white rooms using minimal furniture or décor. There is another side to the coin. You can decorate with colorful pillows, throw blankets, books, candles, and other decorative items you *cherish*.

Make the spaces personal and unique to you. Once again, your ideas will be different, allowing you to find the right amount of stuff for *you*. You set the limits of what limitations you place on the items. The key is just to keep what adds value to your life. Discard the remainder of the clutter. That's minimalism!

Minimalism only applies to your belongings.
Minimalism can be applied to all spheres of your life. Once you have a firm grasp of the idea of minimalism; you'll see how a minimalist lifestyle exceeds the decluttering your house. It can be applied on the basis of how you spend your time as well as what you eat.

You can't have a hobby with collections if you're a minimalist.
As a minimalist, you don't need to discard all of your belongings. You just become more intentional about what you keep by eliminating your possessions down to only the items you love and use.

Simply stated, learn moderation. Instead of owning 20 collections, just settle for two that you have a true passion for and enjoy. Stock only items you will use—be honest with yourself.

You must follow specific rules or standards as a *true* minimalist.
Create your own set of rules and alter the guidelines as your life changes. Be prepared for the challenging experience. It can open your mind to new ideas but don't be turned off or restricted by these rules. Work at it and discover the methods that work for you; not what doesn't. Remember, minimalism is identifying what you value most and removing all of the junk that doesn't match your new values.

What to Avoid — The Reasons You May Fail

1. *Procrastination*: Don't put off today and wait until tomorrow. The problems in your budget will not go away unless you stay on top of them constantly, and neither will the clutter created by the purchases. Stop finding excuses to deal with it later.
2. *No Perspective*: Some individuals do not think of his/her spending habits in the long-term. You begin to believe retirement is in the distant future, and the month-to-month money is sufficient. Unfortunately, this isn't the case. You lose perspective when you begin keeping all of your valuable possessions. Once again, you are making excuses for why the items are in such disarray.
3. *You Possess Poor Management Skills:* It is possible to reach an imbalance in your daily scheduling and many times overcommit your time.
4. *Short-Term Perspective*: Some people don't think of daily spending habits as wrong. He/she is not thinking of 20 to 30 years from now. Remember, more is less, and that includes your freedom instead of more objects in your life.
5. *Not Educated On Finances:* Many just do not know the difference between living day-to-day and saving for the future. The money is in

the here and now; have fun! You can still have fun by planning your budget limitations.
6. *Living in the Past*: You need to remove the yearning for holding onto objects because they envelop you into a special memory. You have become sentimental to many attachments that are otherwise worthless to anyone else. Take a snapshot and let the item leave the house. Don't have an unbreakable bond or obligation for that pair of pants because it was a gift or keeping that beat up purse because it belonged to your Grandmother.

Let's make a blueprint of the future!

"It is a preoccupation with possession, more than anything else, that prevents men from living freely and nobly." —Bertrand Russell

CHAPTER 2
Make A Plan

Before making a plan, get your family onboard.

Create a Record of Your Goals

Remember balance and a simple budget can lower your stress, and that is another plus that cannot be ignored in the scheme of budgeting. Use a worksheet such as this one:

Short-Term Goals (Under 6 months)	Cost (Estimated)	Target Date	Save Weekly (Amount Needed)

Medium-Term Goals (6 months-1 year)	Cost (Estimated)	Target Date	Save Weekly (Amount Needed)

Long-Term Goals (Over 1 Year)	Cost (Estimated)	Target Date	Save Weekly (Amount Needed)

Estimate the costs to reach each of the goals. If you are not sure, do some research. You need to set a reasonable date. Don't set a date that will send your budget in a direction you cannot achieve. Determine the amount you need to make by dividing the estimated cost of your first goal by the number of weeks. That is the amount required. You must be ruthless when you make the cuts. Prioritize when you make the budget, but the planning starts here.

Create the Plan

You will create a long-lasting space for your belongings and follow techniques to help you return an item back where it belongs after it's used.

Before you get going, you should first understand the importance of decluttering.

Clutter is paralyzing. Many folks are paralyzed in their tracks when looking at the stacks of paper on a desk or a messy pantry. The answer is; those individuals have *no idea* what to do next. As a result, many of the times, nothing is done. Your brain has difficulties differentiating between what's important and what's not. Generally, clutter will impede your ability to focus.

Decluttering will make you more efficient. You can move forward with your day quickly if you know where all your possessions are located when needed. For example, if your desk is organized with just what you need, tasks such as paying bills will consume much less time. Remember the formula, "Decluttering = More Time."

Clutter can create stress. Studies have indicated that those who walk into a cluttered environment (women in particular); his/her cortisol, your stress hormone levels will zoom. Therefore, you might not consciously realize it, but the disastrous cluttered space is causing anxiety.

Clutter will cause you to waste your time. Eliminating clutter could reduce household cleaning by approximately 40%. Your brain reads the cluttered environment signals that your work is never done. Subconsciously, your mind is preparing a huge to-do list that will continue to play over and over again in your mind.

There Is a Huge Link Between Physical Clutter and Mental Clutter

Clutter comes in all sizes and shapes, including the monstrous mental clutter which can be caused by the overstimulation created by the cluttered space you occupy.

Help Resolve Your Mental Clutter: Use L.I.V.E (List, Internal Organization, Vision and External Organization)

- **List**: Write it down, or you take a huge chance of forgetting it.
- **Internal Organization**: You must begin the organization process inside yourself first.
- **Vision**: You must be absolutely clear about what you want for your life in conjunction with your goals and all elements you want to attract into your lifetime.
- **External Organization**: You now may be organized internally and know where you are going and why. The next step in the process will be to start organizing your external environment.

For many, a daily calendar is essential for accurate time management. Schedule everything in your planner, including personal time events. Write down all of your to-do items on paper and make it a priority to keep it updated. Set the goals for one week, one month, and so forth.

Set limits and stick with it! Consider using some of the time you cut out for getting chores done. Ask for answerability from someone you trust if you're having issues concerning procrastination and getting tasks done.

You have made a huge step toward having a minimalistic home because you have decided; it is time to declutter your entire living space. You have noticed your closet is overstuffed. Your living spaces are cluttered with toys, books, and magazines. The bathroom cabinet is confusing, and the cabinets are totally cluttered. But, the question arises of where to start. Start at the top and work to the bottom.

Where to Begin

This guide will enable you to understand the process better. The professionals suggest preparing three boxes before you begin—one for articles to toss—one to donate—and one for the small items you wish to keep. Prepare a laundry basket for the relocation of gathered the items throughout the house.

The process begins by organizing each room. It's impossible to organize your items when you don't have a clue where to search. You can use a clothes basket or a box to move items from one room to the next. You can save many steps using this process.

It is best to remove all of the items you no longer use or need any more proceeding room by room before you begin to think about cleaning. It isn't unusual to find a Christmas decoration hiding until July.

Pull all of the throw rugs, floor mats, and runners throughout the house, and decide what can be washed and which ones need further cleaning. Even if you don't allow shoes in the house, a lot of dirt travels no matter what. These are some of the ways to start the new journey for the rest of your life:

Tip 1: The Honest Policy: Begin with honesty about what expenses are essential and the ones that are the 'like' or 'want' category. If you can remove a car payment or reduce rent/mortgage – now is a good time to start. Do you need all of the insurance premiums? Can you survive with one car or one that can be purchased outright with cash? Be Honest!

Tip 2: Seek Free Entertainment: Many of the local libraries offer free videos and books for your enjoyment. Consider using them versus the expense of visiting the theater. Go online, either at home or the library and find free community events you and your family can enjoy. Go to the local museum and search for programs and events in your town. Find a walking trail and spend time walking. Besides, it is excellent for your health! Volunteer as an usher at local plays and concerts to have a free ticket. All it will take is a short training period. Visit the zoo during the off-season or look for free days.

Tip #3: Prepare for the Unexpected. If you can take a second job for the short term, you could remove your debts much faster. It does not need to be a fast-paced position. Consider delivering pizza or online positions whereby you could use the Internet, which would justify the additional expense of the Internet. It would be useful and considered a 'need' instead of an entertainment item.

Paint the Picture: What the Minimalist Home Looks Like

- *You will see just essentials in the home.* Always be critical and ask yourself if the item (from a vase to furniture) is essential or if you can live without it. Go ahead, and strip the room down to the basics. Remove it from the space and enjoy the extra breathing room.
- *You will see quality over quantity as a minimalist trait*: Instead of having many items in your house, you would see items used most frequently. A comfortable, nice chair is better than six units of pressboard furniture.
- *Select one room to decorate at a time.* Make one room the center of calm. Use it as an inspiration to move onto the next room and the next.
- *Clear all of the floor space.* Don't stack any crates or boxes in the space. Once your furniture is down to the bare essentials, go ahead and remove everything else. Toss it into the trash or donate it. Just remove it from eyesight.
- *Furniture Usage Should Be Minimal:* You will only see a few essential items of furniture in a minimalist home. A living room may have a couch or loveseat, end tables, a couple of lamps, a minimalist entertainment stand, and a television. It could even contain less. A bedroom might have a functional bed (nothing fancy), a dresser, and perhaps a nightstand, and discard the rest of the clutter.
- *Clear surfaces are evident in a minimalistic home.* Flat surfaces are clear, except for a couple of special decorations.
- *Clear walls do provide serenity.* Display two or three favorite items of nice artwork. A minimalist will indulge in a simple photo, painting, or drawing framed with a solid color on each wall to eliminate boredom. It's perfectly fine to leave some of the walls bare.
- *Accent On Decorations.* Display a few items on a coffee table or have a clear desk with just a have a family photo.
- Turn on some music to get you motivated and get your adrenaline pumping. This is a basic guideline of how to proceed:

How to Declutter Any Room?

Step 1: Choose a space, preferably in the middle of the room. If you are in a room with tables or any other surface, you can also use that for placing items.
Step 2: Start on one side of the room and work around the entire room.
Step 3: Don't jump around! Do one shelf, drawer, or closet section at a time.
Step 4: Pull everything out/off of the drawer/shelf in the designated space.
Step 5: Clean the drawer/shelf and set it aside.

Step 6: Sort into the keep, donate or toss pile. Make quick choices but look at each item. Be honest: when is the last time you used the item?

Tip: When in doubt, throw it out is a good logic to maintain as you declutter your living spaces. However, seasonal items are the exception to the logic of not keeping items if you have not used them at least once in six months.

Step 7: Move to the next shelf or drawer or segment of the floor.

With an organized movement during the sorting stage, you will appreciate the touch-up day. Use each chapter of this book for its designed use. The plans are based on a room to room method, just as a basis of how you could do the whole house without missing a single area. You may choose to perform the clean and decluttering process at the same time.

After cleaning, and discarding the clutter from just one space should give you a feeling of euphoria involved with the minimalistic way of living.

Benefits of Keep-Toss-Donate Containers

The containers keep the plan organized. During the sorting process, give yourself just a few seconds to consider your choice. If it takes longer than that time, you probably don't need the item. Another great tip; use dark trash bags, so you aren't tempted to retrieve any of the items.

Consider how much you can be helping others by donating items. You could be providing a coat for someone who doesn't have a coat for winter or a child that doesn't have any toys. What about donating some of the items your family doesn't use to a homeless shelter?

Don't think about how sad you might be by eliminating so many knick-knacks and books. Look at the amount of time you will save by not needing to pick up and dust them every week. Spend that time with your family and friends.

Items Are Just Items

If you are holding onto items because someone you care about gave them to you; you can still get rid of them. Take a picture to save the memory and let the object go. Keep the items you believe are heirlooms but let the rest leave home. It will clear the space for contentment. You will always share the memory in your mind and in the photo.

Here is a list of some of the items many people don't believe are clutter:
- Broken sunglasses
- Outdated eyeglasses
- Pens without ink (never checked)
- Poor-fitting clothes
- Mismatched socks
- Poor-fitting shoes
- Condiment packages of ketchup, mustard, etc.
- Plastic silverware
- Rubber bands
- Magazines over 2 months

- Week old newspapers
  The list can go on for an eternity of the items you 'might' need. Did you see anything in there that you recognized? The rule of thumb is; if you haven't used it within the last year, it should be donated, consigned, or trashed.

Appraise the Item's Value

Sometimes, sentiments take over, but take a picture and remove the clutter! Try the box and banish routine. If you are tugging with certain items; place them in a box and label them with destroy; tape and date the box. One year later, if you haven't opened the box—take it to a donation center without opening the seal. If you believe later you made a mistake, it is done, and you had claimed the sentiment already when you sealed the box.

You are probably asking, 'what about the true value?' In that case, you need to learn the rules for value by example. An associate has some old computers that he/she believes are valuable. You must consider a computer is not going to be valued even close to what you paid for it when it was new. If you believe you have something of monetary value, set it aside, and ask the dealer. If that is your only excuse (it's valuable), it is time to be placed into the donation box or trash bin.

"Simplicity is the ultimate sophistication." —Leonardo da Vinci

Let's continue!

CHAPTER 3
Declutter & Organize The Kitchen

It is a pretty good chance your kitchen cabinets can use a good clean out. Before you get started, it's a good idea to have the kitchen space in somewhat of an ordinary state.

Fill the dishpan with hot, soapy water for a quick clean-up or removal of dust from some of the items. Also, empty the dishwasher for the dirty items found in the cabinets. Save a step, place the dirty item directly into the dishwasher or dishpan.

As you collect items into the different boxes of the 'keep' items, try to sort them accordingly in groups so it will be simpler after you finish the cleaning to replace them to the proper space or area. Use some of these tips to get you going:

Declutter & Clean Out the Refrigerator

Begin at the top of the refrigerator and remove everything. Clean out each shelf as you proceed. If any of the drawers or shelves are removable, take each unit out, and use warm soapy water to clean it. You want to clean every surface, especially the ones on the door—inside and out.

Before placing your food back inside of the fridge, line the shelves with some parchment paper or plastic food wrap to make cleaning a breeze. If you have a small mess, just remove the layer of plastic, and it is clean!

Organize the Cabinets

If you are an avid cook, consider installing a retractable book stand. Your recipe will be at eye level as you mix all of your ingredients and perform magic. When you are done, you take your clean (flour-free) book and place it in the clean bookcase. The holder is moved under the cabinet out of your way and view until you need it again.

The extra spaces in the cabinets can store the small appliances that previously cluttered the countertops. Only place frequently used items on the counter, such as a coffee maker.

Do store the toaster, toaster oven, food processors, and blenders inside or under the cabinet. Keep all of the food products out of sight. You can also store the canisters under the counter or in a pantry.

Remember, if the counter is clear—it's easy to clean!

Revamp the Pantry

It makes no difference whether you have a pantry or not; just update the space where you store your food items. You will be surprised how many items are no longer fresh. Be sure to check the dates located on each product.

Toss any of the empty boxes or boxes that just have a small portion of the product left in the package. For example, if you have half a bag of rice, consider putting it into a covered container. This will also eliminate the chances of any bugs invading your space. You will also be able to find it the next time you need to use it.

Note: If your item needs directions; cut the directions from the package and tape it on the new container/jar.

It's important to check the dates on your spices because as seasoning makers including McCormick point out, the spices don't spoil, but the potency is lost with time. The intended flavor might not be what you expect if you use it in your recipe. It is a smarter choice to replace them regularly. This is a short list of how long some spices will last:

- Whole Black Peppercorns: 4 years
- Chili Powder: 3 to 4 years
- Dried Bay Leaves: 1 to 3 years
- Ground Ginger: 3 to 4 years
- Ground Cinnamon: 3 to 4 years
- Dried Oregano Leaves: 1 to 3 years
- Crushed Red Pepper: 2 to 3 years

Tip: Keep red spices such as chili powder, paprika, and other red peppers in the refrigerator to keep them fresh longer.

Beautify & Revamp the Pots & Pans
- Separate the pots from the pans.
- Store the tops separately.

If your décor is flexible; hang them on the wall as a decoration when not in use. When you begin to place your bakeware back into the cabinet, try using a storage divider, and stack the pan tops as well as the muffin tins.

Minimize the Utensils
- Take out each item and perform the process of keep-toss-donate-trash. You will probably find many duplicates and lots of bread ties.

Note: If your tongs no longer have a locking clasp; you can use the cardboard tube from an empty paper towel roll to keep the arms together!

- Everyday utensils can be stored in a wooden or plastic divider.
- Store all sharp knives separately to prevent injury.
- Trash any broken, stained, or extra unnecessary pieces.

Inventory the Dishes
Comb through the cabinets for any dishes which have become chipped or cracked.

Revitalize Tupperware & Similar Containers
- Match the tops and bottoms.
- Trash any stained containers.

Prepare an "In Doubt" Box
You have reached the middle ground of doubt! So many items that take a second thought could be the items that need to go out to the trash pile first. A good example is the electric French-fryer that has two-year-old grease caked on its surface. Let it go!

Oh, and the cute cake mold of the fifty states you baked (oh my) five years ago, and have not used since. Don't be sentimental now; let it go!
Suggestion: If you have a box of items which you aren't sure about, give yourself a test, stash the box of items for a month or so (just a small box). If you have not opened the box, you have answered your own question; donate the items.

The Kitchen Sink

It's time to tackle the kitchen sink. Just because you wash out the sink daily after you do a load of dishes, doesn't mean it is clean. Water spots, rust, soap scum, and food stains can build up if you don't stay ahead of them.

Porcelain Sinks: If you have a porcelain sink, you can make it gleam with this process:

1. Line the sink with paper towels.
2. Soak them with bleach.
3. Let them soak for 30 minutes, and discard them.
4. Rinse the sink with hot running water.

Note: Don't use bleach on colored porcelain because it will fade. Instead, use vinegar, baking soda, or a mild detergent (and a bit of elbow grease). Now that you have the sink clean, you can protect it from scratches and stains by installing a plastic mat on the bottom of the sink. The mat will protect the shiny sink from lingering acidic foods/liquids such as salad dressing, vinegar, and fruit.

CHAPTER 4
Declutter The Dining Area

There are more spaces to hide clutter than you can imagine in the confines of your dining space. If your home has a formal dining area as well as a breakfast nook, the dining room may not be used often for its purpose. It's a prime dumping ground for clutter.

Dining rooms tend to have storage pieces can include quite a collection of drawers and cabinets such as china cabinets or buffets. If you eat the majority of your meals at your kitchen island, you may have a tendency to store things there that you want to get out of sight.

Fancy serving pieces such as wedding gifts as well as other decorative items are easy to stash into the bottom of either cabinet, but you could be taking up valuable space you could be using to hold the items you actually use.

Gifts can be difficult to purge because of guilt but if you're not using the item, toss it. Donate it for someone who will use it, and be guilt-free. Just think how great you will feel when your dining room is tidy.

Put yourself to the test. Place a batch of questionable items into a storage box. If it hasn't opened in one or two months, it should be tossed. Set a reminder on your phone to check back in on it in two or three months. If you haven't missed it, it's probably safe to donate the item.

Make use of decorative baskets you already own to keep all items together or use a drawer organizer in our china cabinet drawer. Keep a few small storage boxes that make it easier to fold and store items such as your rectangular placemats.

The China Cabinet/Hutch/Buffet

Remove all items from the cabinet and clean it. Use a good wood cleaner to refresh the surface, naturally.

Take just five minutes to do a quick run in the china cabinet. You might be surprised what you end up with in your box of questionable items. Quickly, consider items you can easily part with and place them into a keep-toss-donate stack, so you are not tempted later to put the items back. Don't be tempted to put it in the attic!

It depends on how much silver you have, whether you clean it for now or wait until your 10-day tidy home plan is completed. Save the heirloom pieces and consider consigning, donating, or gifting the items.

When you enter your dining room, you want to see a clean table with a beautiful centerpiece. Imagine, the thought of it already put a smile on your face. When you walk into the dining room to a table full of clutter, you immediately feel stressed.

The 1-Touch Rule

Employ the 1-Touch rule in the dining area. As you're sorting through mail or coming into the house with a bunch of stuff, make it a goal to only touch the item one time before putting it in its proper space.

If it's unessential paperwork; just put it right in the trash or recycling bin. If it's groceries, just put them away right away.

By committing to only touching the item once, you are a lot less likely to have piles of stuff appearing all over the flat surfaces of our house! It can take a while to get into the habit of the 1-touch rule, but you may find the longer you aim to utilize it in the house, the more organized your home remains.

CHAPTER 5
Declutter & Organize The Bath Areas

Declutter/Organize the Bathrooms
Keep your goal in sight. You are attempting to maximize the bathroom space and make everything accessible and easily reached by all family members. Sometimes, it is not an easy task to find a one-plan-fits-all solution. However, these are some of the tips to help you with the process:

Group the Items
If you have a stockpile of products such as extra hair care products, group them together in an organized manner. If you have three partially used bottles of the same shampoo or conditioner, mix the similar products and toss/recycle the extra container. Be sure to check under the cabinet and in the shower stall.

Drawers: Remove all of the items from the bathroom drawers and place them in containers for sorting. If an item is obviously trash, throw it away immediately. At this point, don't linger on an item. Clean the drawer, so it can thoroughly dry overnight.

Countertops & Sinks: Use the same procedures as used in the kitchen space. It will depend on the material used on the sinks and countertops.

Medicine Cabinet Purge: You already have the medicine cabinet empty from giving it a thorough cleaning; now it's time to do the tedious job of checking the dates of the medicine from the cabinet. Throw away all expired prescriptions or over-the-counter medicines. If you have any ointments, also check for spoilage of them.

As crazy as it sounds, your medicine should not be stored in the bathroom because the vitamins and medicines can become damaged from the steam and heat from showers. Place them in the kitchen instead - just for safety purposes.

Store your antiseptics, bandages, gauze, or other first aid items in the medicine cabinet. You can use it to store extra swabs, nail clippers, or any smaller items. Consider placing your toothbrushes in the cabinet to keep them more sanitary.

Place a couple of hangers on the linen closet door for hanging blow dryers, curling irons, or extra towels. It all improves the appearance of the bathroom.

Regroup The Linen Closet: Go through the cabinet/linen closet and discard any torn or dingy towels or washcloths. You can reuse the damaged ones for cleaning rags. Remember Grandma's saying, 'Waste not; want not.' Store the extra toilet paper on the top shelf, out of the way of the regularly used items such as towels. You can also purchase a toilet paper stacker to save space.

Prepare an All-White Linen Closet
If your decluttering plan is part of the redecorating scheme; considering using all light color sheets, towels, and pillowcases. Designers believe it is more soothing to save the splashy colors for the throw pillows, blankets, and shower curtains; just a thought!
- **Hint:** If you have special linens and towels for guests; consider placing them in a plastic bin. Label them for easy access.

The Shower Curtain
It is beneficial to use a shower curtain liner made from cotton, hemp, synthetic, or vinyl. While you are deep cleaning, either replace the liner or machine wash it in hot water using a mild laundry detergent. Washing the liner weekly will help prevent the buildup of mold or mildew. If you prefer to hand-wash the liner, use ten parts of water to 1-part bleach.
Clean the outer shower curtain by following the manufacturer's instructions or in warm/hot water with a mild detergent.
Note: Leave the shower curtain closed when it is not being used so water cannot sit in the folds.

Limited Bathroom Space Solutions
If you are limited in space as many people are living in smaller homes, use an over the door shoe organizer. Purchase one that is clear, so you can place many items in the unit and know exactly where it is when it is needed.
Use a rule of thumb and corral any of the items that won't stack easily. Consider using small bins that can be stacked under the sink or in the drawers for makeup, and other small items that you can never find.
Place cotton swabs (Q-tips), cotton balls, and similar items in closed containers to keep them clean, organized, and out of the way.

Label the Shelves
If you have several shelves containing miscellaneous items, you can avoid a lot of digging/searching later. You can use masking tape or a label maker, to keep the children involved. Not only is it neater, but also a lot less time is spent with wondering where a certain item is when it is needed.

Refresh the Space
To finish off the bathroom space, add a box of baking soda in the corner of the closet to absorb any of the musty odors which can collect.

Corral the Children's Bath Toys
You can use several containers for the children's playtime adventures. You can use a milk crate or plastic laundry basket for the items. It will keep they neatly stored behind the shower curtain. If you want them hidden away in a closet, be sure they are completely dry to prevent mildew.

Under-the-Sink Storage
If you have limited space under the sink, it is probably best to remove everything first. Go through each article to decide if it's still needed; if not, toss it. Use a metal rack and store smaller things you may need in the lower section of the cabinet space. After you declutter, you can reorganize all the

stuff. Put away the items that do not belong there. Just remember, you will need to quickly remove the items if you have a plumbing emergency. That's why it's important not to have it packed to the max.

CHAPTER 6
Declutter The Living Room

It is unbelievable how disorganized a living room or den can become in such a short amount of time. Here are a few tips to be sure you cover all of the areas where clutter might be taking over your living space without you realizing the problem.

You will want to begin with the same boxes for keep-toss-donate-or trash. It is easier if you wipe each of the 'keep' items while you have it in your hands. If you have children, include them in on the action. You might not mean it but play a game/trick and inform him/her if their belongings aren't out of the collection boxes in fifteen minutes; they will be gone. It might not work, but you tried! The point is to remove everything from the space that doesn't belong.

Books & Magazines

Quickly, sort through the clutter of magazines and books that have accumulated and discard, recycle, or donate the ones you have already read. Place the books on the bookshelves after you have wiped down the covers.

The secret to magazines is learning when you have enough of them. If you have a huge stack, maybe you should reconsider rejecting the renewal except for your favorite ones (not all of them)!

Consider donating the discarded magazines and books to a nursing home facility or retirement home. Some of the books might be considered for donation to local schools, libraries, or even to correctional facilities. At any rate, you need them out of your house.

Sorting the Shelves

Comb through each shelf and decide how many knickknacks you really need on one shelf. The 'dust-collectors' are so cute on the shelf in the store but can make clutter quickly. Of course, it doesn't mean you need to toss Grandma's favorite teacup. Within reason, keep the cherished ones or consider passing them on down the generation line to achieve a clean and clear atmosphere in your space.

Browse through all of the movies and DVDs. Eliminate any empty cases that don't have a use anymore. You can recycle them or donate them along with the movies you won't be viewing again. Discard any damaged or scratched movies.

Sort through all of the end tables, and remove any garbage, loose papers, or unnecessary items. Use your keep-toss-donate boxes to stay organized. Remember; don't think about the item except momentarily.

Rearrange the Book Shelves

You can make a bookcase more presentable if you remove all of the covers that are tattered and torn and place them elsewhere. You want to place

focus on serenity, and you cannot do that if you are looking at the ragged edges of a book.
You can achieve an attractive backdrop by using a little bit of paint or adding some wallpaper to your space. Mix some round vases or pictures into the scenery next to a column of your nicely organized special books. Mix and match until you have a unique setting fit for a showroom.
Many organizers believe you should use one-third accessories, one-third books, and one-third empty spaces. Mix the shelves with 60% of the books placed vertically and 40% placed horizontally to create both spontaneity and balance. The point is not to make it too busy.
Take a picture in your mind or one on the phone to remind yourself of how good everything looks right now. Every three to six months, take the books down and dust the tops and spines. Flip through the pages and rotate the books to prevent any warping.
If you want to add some new dazzle to the area, consider adding some battery-operated candles to accent your newly arranged space.

Maintain the Kid's Toys
Children's toys will require some teamwork. Go back to the keep-toss-donate
boxes, and keep them handy. If your children are older, let them help with the process. If not, it might be easier to do the job—solo. Make a choice by deciding if they are toys or items the children use actively.
If they are for a younger age group, it's best to remove them from your space. Of course, you don't need to throw away the Three Bears book. However, you can place it into the bookcase instead of the toy box. (More on kids later.)

Walls - Stairs & Landings
The walls should be wiped down with warm soapy water. Don't forget to clean the baseboards. You can see dust bunnies across any room!
If you have any stairs or landings in your home, you will need to thoroughly clean each step with a whisk broom, a hand-held vacuum or a damp rag. If there are carpet sections, be sure to get along the edges thoroughly.
For all handrails and pickets; wipe each individual piece and around the bottom to remove any dirt that might have been captured.
For all spaces, use the crevice tool and brush attachment to remove the debris from the edges of the wall/baseboards.
Oil Stains on Carpet: If you have carpeted areas that have oil stains; you can use cat litter or baking soda on it to absorb the oil. Even professionals use this process.

Clean All Ceiling Fans
If you have ceiling fans, the living room is the best place to start. Since you are cleaning the house from top to bottom; it is best to pull out the vacuum cleaner hose and the broom to remove all of the cobwebs from the ceilings. Don't forget to check the fan since it will be circulating clean, fresh air. A

dusty fan can ruin all of your hard work. The process only takes about fifteen minutes.

To clean the blades, this is all you need to do:
- *Step 1:* Tape the fan's switch for safety, so it doesn't accidentally get turned on while you clean the blades.
- *Step 2:* Place some old sheets or a drop cloth on the floor and remove any furniture under the fan. The blanket/drop cloth should cover a radius of approximately two that of the blades of the fan.
- *Step 3:* Use a spray bottle filled with water and 2 Tablespoons of distilled white vinegar. Spray the inside of an old/damaged pillowcase and place it under each fan blade.
- *Step 4:* Cover your head with a baseball cap.
- *Step 5:* Stand on a ladder to place your head above the blades.
- *Step 6:* Slip the pillowcase over each blade to remove the bulk of the dust.
- *Step 7:* Use a clean cloth to dust the lingering dust and the light fixture.

Be sure to perform these steps before you vacuum the floors.

The Heating/AC Vents

Check the heating vents, and remove any buildup of dust in each space of the home. Change the filter.

As preventive maintenance, once each month:
- Vacuum the unit with the crevice tool.
- Remove the cover and soak it in soapy water.
- Scrub it with a soft brush.

Remember to have the ductwork cleaned out about every three to five years.

Clean the Couches & Chairs

If you aren't sure, the fabric of your couch the manufacturer should have a label somewhere indiscreetly sewn into the seam of the fabric. Check underneath the cushions or the base of the furniture. You should see a label with some of the following descriptions:
- *SW:* Water or Solvent cleaner is safe to use.
- *W:* Okay to use water for cleaning.
- *S:* Use only solvent-based cleaners.
- *X:* Use Only the Vacuum for cleaning.

Once you have decided how to proceed with the type of cleaner, use this process to clean the soiled couch or chair.
- *Step 1:* Use a brush or white cleaning rag to groom the entire space to help remove any dried-on spots of food or other debris.
- *Step 2:* Sprinkle a large amount of baking soda over the entire couch. The soda will help to absorb any nasty smells and helps break up any stains lingering in the fabric.

- Wait for 20 minutes to an hour before you use the brush attachment of your vacuum cleaner to sweep away the powder.
- *Step 3:* Clean the sofa with the below cleaner if needed.

Cleaning Tip: Be sure to test an unnoticeable spot before you spray the entire sofa.

CHAPTER 7
Revamp The Office & Your Budget

"Too many people spend money they haven't earned, to buy things they don't want, to impress people they don't like." —Will Rogers

The office is a space that seems to collect a lot of extra papers to look at 'later,' but sometimes, later doesn't happen. You need to become diligent and dive into the disaster one piece of paper at a time.

You might need to compile a box of questionable materials that might require a bit of concentration, such as the directions for the cable box. It isn't an item you need right away, but it's something that needs to be filed away. However, don't set it aside as part of the clutter/hoard to be discovered years later during another clean-up time. Look through the box while you are watching television, or between the commercials. Diligently, comb through all of the files and eliminate any unnecessary information. Any documents with your personal information should be immediately shredded if you don't need them, such as old identification cards or similar information.

Quickly, look over the receipts to see if they are over a year old—if so, toss them. If you are saving them for tax purposes, place them in a specific folder, and file them.

Bills over one-year-old should be thrown away. A paper shredder is excellent for destroying the documents to help prevent identity fraud.

Place everything back into the desk in an organized manner. If you don't have any desk organizers for the drawers, you can use some of the plastic containers from the kitchen that didn't have tops. You won't feel as wasteful. Later on, when you purchase an organizer, simply throw the containers away, or recycle them with no guilt!

Electronics & the Computer

Your computer keyboard and mouse, as well as your phone, are other excellent spaces that need to be cleaned regularly and thoroughly. Think of all of the spaces where bacteria can grow. Never use abrasive cleaners on any of the products. Always unplug the item before attempting to clean it to prevent electrical damage. Get in the habit of cleaning them weekly as part of your anti-clutter/cleaning adventure.

Organize the Office

Remove as much paperwork clutter as possible. If you have piles of mail building up on your counter or desktop, it may be time to eliminate the source. Shift your account statements to online service. The correspondence will slow down immensely.

Join the crowd and go paperless. There are many options with the use of the Internet. Forget digging for a bill and do what many families are now using. Use one website such as File this or Evernote for your convenience. You are taking up less space and removing the paper clutter.

No Space for an Office? While you are in organization mode; do you have your information stored in boxes because of a lack of space? Consider using a rolling microwave cart to store your necessary items. When you are ready to pay the bills; just grab the cart and carry it where you want to sit. The cart is always neat and uncluttered. Use some decorative boxes for a décor improvement.

Purge the Paperwork: At the top of the list of decluttering; it begins with your disorganized and outdated files just taking up space in your bookcase or filing system. Saving unneeded papers only clutters the cabinet with items you don't need and no place for the ones you do need.

Try to weed your files down to one file cabinet drawer. If you have a scanner, put them online and throw the junk away. Consider keeping your tax receipts in a safe spot for references next year. Place it in with other papers, including your insurance information, birth certificates, and other vital documents. IRS only requires files for seven years back.

While You're in the Office

- Cancel all subscriptions to store coupons or emails. You want to eliminate temptations when possible.
- Tip 10: Magazines: Magazine subscriptions are another item that can probably keep your budget-strapped down. Do you let them pile up like most people? If so, this is how the 'clutter' theory works. Purchase them singly if you want to catch up or better yet; use the Internet with its free Wi-Fi.
- Batch bill payments. It is an excellent habit to pay your bills monthly. You won't need to worry about due dates. The time saved will reduce stress, and you won't feel like you do nothing but pay bills. What a relief that can be if you have a busy lifestyle.
- Online Banking: Many bank accounts can be handled online without needing to visit a brick-and-mortar. Rates are usually lower because you don't have the additional personnel that you need to face in a regular bank. You do not have to choose a bank branch that is close to your home; it is as close as your computer.
- Depositing Your Check: You can easily hide your check (from your conscious mind) by using several methods. You can use a remote check deposit by snapping a photo of the check and submitting it to the bank without leaving your home. Thus, you are not as tempted to go shopping and get other cute trinkets.
- Clean Computer Files: The computer will clutter your mind with endless garbage unless you remove it.
- Reduce Social Media Contacts: Analyze the way you use the content on your wall. Does the feed provide you with inspiration or with ways to benefit your life? If yes, keep the contact. If the answer is no, remove the person or group. Negativity must go so minimalism can enter.

Regroup the Budget

If you are like many, you haven't got a clue where all your money has gone after the checks were deposited. Preparing a budget will allow you to spend as a minimalist and know where each hard-earned dollar has been spent. You must categorize by needs, wants, and likes or better known as luxuries. Identify your expenses using the past six months as a starting point. Be sure to include all family members when you make a list.

Needs: The lines become blurred with today's technological advances. The true basics are clean water, food, and a way to prepare it, shelter, warmth, and clothing. Unless an expense is required for your job, you don't actually need a cell phone, high-speed internet, or cable TV. Yes, that cable is a hard choice, but it really is a luxury. The lines are hard-drawn, but you have to be brutal when setting up a minimalist way of living.

Include all of the expenses such as food and water (to maintain your health), housing, transportation, and other essential needs, including healthcare and hygiene products. Consider clothing as a need, but only enough to remain appropriately dressed and comfortable.

According to the experts, a minimum repayment on a credit card is considered a need, and it could negatively affect your credit score (if minimum payments are not met). Needs are considered to be any payment if it can severely impact your life's quality, such as prescription medicines.

Wants: These are the items you desire to add to your budget plan but must be an item that is necessary to keep your other expenses at a minimum. It could include a new vehicle or an updated computer if needed for work (only if your computer is not working). A 'want' can also include back-to-school clothing.

Guidelines for a Spending Budget

As a minimalist, you will want to make room for happiness. Preparing a budget can eliminate the stress factor. Use these as a guideline to prepare your personal plan:

- Groceries – Essential items
- Grocery items beyond basic essentials
- Special Dining Out Events
- Bar fees
- Coffee
- Meals purchases at work or school
- Drinks and snacks purchased at school or work

Shelter Expenses

Utilities

- Water & Sewer
- Trash Pickup
- Electricity

- Gas for heating or Cooking
- Phone: Cell & Landline/Primary - residential phone
- Cable

Home Furnishings

- Remodeling or renovations
- Cell phone
- Satellite or cable TV
- High-speed Internet

Additional Savings – Emergency Funds

- Vehicle replacement fund
- Retirement
- Children's college fund
- Various financial goals

Personal Items

- Prescription medications
- Clothing & Clothing Maintenance
- Toiletries
- Salon Care: Haircuts, perms, color, massage

Gifting: Holiday, birthday, anniversary, wedding

Entertainment

- Video games
- Music Purchases
- Movie tickets
- Concerts
- DVD & movie rentals
- Books, newspaper and magazine subscriptions
- Vacations
- Health or other club memberships
- Parties: Birthday, holiday, social events

Pets

- Food
- Cat litter
- Veterinary care

Household Expenses

- Mortgage (1ˢᵗ or 2ⁿᵈ) and Rent
- Homeowners Insurance and Taxes or Renter's Insurance
- Homeowners Association Fees
- Repairs to the home
- Furniture
- House Cleaning Services
    - Domestic help: Babysitter, house cleaning help, pet sitters
    - Home maintenance: Exterminators, lawn care, painters

Family Expenses

- Children School and Activity Funds (if you have children)
- School Tuition and Books
- Day Care
- Child Support
- Alimony – Spousal support

Insurance Premiums

- Life
- Health
- Disability

Credit Payments – Minimum payments

- Card 1, 2, etc.
- Student Loans

Transportation

- Lease payment or automobile loan
- Vehicle usage and similar expenses for children
- Gasoline
- Automobile maintenance
- Tolls, public transportation, parking fees

Vehicle Expenses

- Car Payment
- Minimum fuel
- Vehicle Insurance
- Smog Check, License renewal, & taxes
- Repairs & Maintenance

Transportation/Miscellaneous

- Taxi service as needed
- Parking fees
- Tolls
- Bus/Subway fees

Once you have these expenses calculated; you have the totals of the items you 'want'. Then, subtract after-tax income. The total will exceed the surplus or shortfall of the money you will want to 'earmark' on your budget. If you don't have money for unexpected expenses, you may need to tighten up and discover new ways to increase your income levels. You may need to do a more diligent accounting of your 'needs' before you can receive a surplus for your wants.

Likes: This category is used for expenses of items that you wish to have but do not need them immediately. It can fall into a savings allotment, which will be discussed further in the following chapters.

Set Boundaries for Expenses Monthly

If you are on a fixed income, it is essential to designate where each dollar will be spent. Be sure to stick with it; meaning, don't decide mid-month to make a purchase not already noted in the budget's outline.

Teamwork is essential for the budget to be sufficient. You must also make your children stay within the guidelines. Of course, there may be times when you need to make purchases that are not planned for at the beginning of the month. In that case, you will need to extract money from another part of the budget, such as entertainment.

Learning how to make adjustments will take some 'give and take' from all family members. To begin, you will want to remain focused on the written budget on a daily basis. Once you have that mastered, check it weekly to be sure you are on the right path. When that is reached, the monthly plan will be easier to adjust.

By the second or third month, you should have a decent baseline of how you and your family are spending its money. Be consistent and pay your bills as they become due. You will enjoy the stress-free budgeting as you master how to live with your minimalist way of life.

Take five or ten minutes each week working with your budget. You will be surprised how quickly you can recognize the many ways you did not know you were overspending.

Once you have had a chance to monitor your expenses and income for a month or two, you'll be more aware of the areas you need to monitor more closely. Maybe your monthly expenses were way off, or maybe you did not account for veterinary bills or car repairs. Once you have worked out the kinks, it is essential to follow it to the letter.

By following these easy guidelines, you will soon discover there is one critical element of minimalism, and that is persistence. Merely beat down the expenses to a minimum, and make the adjustments to empower your cash flow. Remember, no budget is forever. Periodic checks will enable you to review and stay on the right course to a successful financial future.

Simplify Your Finances

You are probably wondering how many accounts you need to remain organized. These are a few suggestions to get you started on the right path:

Maintain one (1) primary checking account. Use this account for bill payments only.

Keep only one (1) credit card (maybe 2). The card can be used as a financial tool, but be careful not to overspend. Remember that you will be paying interest on the money when you make the purchases. Even if it is a sale item, the interest payments may exceed the sale price. Think twice! This is a vital step toward becoming debt-free. American Express is an excellent choice since its fee is due monthly.

Open one main savings account. Use this for emergency goals or shortages that occur within your budget for the month. Use it only when it is a 'must have' item or an emergency.

Automate: Direct deposit is excellent, and you know your check will be there with no bank holds and no time is wasted for a trip to the bank for deposit. Use this for your car payment, mortgage, or any other bills you encounter. You can also transfer money to your savings account using online features. Make paying bills simpler.

Batch bill payments. It is an excellent habit to pay your bills monthly. You won't need to worry about due dates. The time saved will reduce stress, and you won't feel like you do nothing but pay bills. What a relief that can be if you have a busy lifestyle.

Join the crowd and go paperless. There are many options with the use of the Internet. Forget digging for a bill and do what many families are now using. Use one website such as File This or Evernote for your convenience. You are taking up less space and removing the paper clutter.

Consider debt consolidation. It is best to have all of your accounts in one place. Don't use the high-interest companies. Search online to find one that features zero or low-interest rates and consolidate. Save the money of having multiple fees.

Downsize your car if possible. Do you really need a 4x4 when a compact model would serve your needs? Think of the money saved that could be applied to other essential items in your budget.

Cancel all subscriptions to store coupons or emails. You want to eliminate temptations when possible.

Magazines: Magazine subscriptions are another item that can probably keep your budget strapped. Do you let them pile up like most people? If so, this is how the 'clutter' theory works. Purchase them singly if you want to catch up or better yet; use the Internet with its free Wi-Fi.

Books: Purchasing books from the bookstore can be eliminated if you visit your local library. They are free. If you choose, you can also visit a thrift store or purchase them online for a minimal fee. Use the money from your entertainment fund, not the emergency fund.

Coffee, Tea, and Soda: If you are a gourmet coffee drinker and must have one for the office. Purchase an insulated mug and make your own at home. The same rings true if you believe that you must have to have a soda pop. Think of the savings if you work a full-time job.

Storage: If you have a storage unit, consider selling the items, unless they have sentimental value. Take a picture and add the money saved and proceeds of the sale to your emergency fund.

Most of all, you are eliminating stress and complications. You will be able to think of many other ways to get the ball rolling in the right direction to your savings potential. Clarity is the goal when you begin to use the minimalist budgeting techniques.

Reduce Your Utilities

You realize utilities such as gas or electric for heating purposes is going to be expensive. Sometimes, no matter how much you have in your budget, it doesn't seem to be enough. You can help remove some of the stress and discover new ways to live a minimalist lifestyle without breaking the bank and your nerves.

Heating Costs

Consider some of these ways to reduce your heating costs:

Free Solar Heating: Open those blinds and curtains. Let the sun keep your home warm during daylight hours. Just remember to close them up tight to hold in the trapped heat.

Reduce the Use of Fans: If you have a fan in the bathroom and kitchen; minimize its usage. It sends a lot of heat out with the undesirable odors. Run them a few minutes if needed, but turn them off.

Replace Filters Often: Whether you are renting or buying your home, it's important to keep the filters in your home clean. A dirty filter in your furnace or heat pump can make the numbers rise quickly on your power bill. Swipe or replace the filters in your fans once each month. You may also have a filter in your bathroom fan, but always check to make sure it is clean, so the air remains healthy.

Crank Up the Ceiling Fans & Lower the Thermostat: Always remember that hot air rises. If you have your fan running in reverse mode, the heat will return to the floor level. Bump the thermostat down a couple of degrees. The cooler air will make a significant difference in your monthly bill. You will also sleep better, and save money (no sacrifice there).

Clear the Vents: Make sure your vents are clean so they can deliver all of the heat you are paying for every month. Be sure all of the furniture is away from the vents to prevent damage and sent you the warm air.

Use the Fireplace: You can enjoy your fireplace as you save on your minimalistic budget. Enjoy the fire, but remember to close the damper when it is not being used.

Air Conditioning
Your air conditioner can run the bill up in no time. These are just a few things you can do to help keep the power company from ruining your minimalist budget:

The Dryer: Wait until it's dark outside to run the dryer, dishwasher, and any other heat-producing appliances. Line dry your clothes instead.

The Curtains: Keep the blinds and curtains closed during the hottest part of the day.

Insulate Ductwork: Whether you rent or own your home, it is important to fully insulate the crawl spaces, garages, attics, and any other areas where air conditioning is used.

The Thermostat: Install a programmable thermostat and set it to reset the temperature when you are not at home.

If you are still having issues with your utility bill, it may be time to call the company and ask for a checkup. Many times, the visit is free or a minimal fee. The report will show you how to put the pennies back into your savings, and not to the power company.

The Water Bill
Your budget can be greatly affected by your water usage unless you take a few precautions. Consider these ways:
1. Invest in low-flow showers and toilets. The initial cost would be something you could use your savings for that would be meeting your needs.
2. As the season's change, inspect all of your fixtures and pipes in and around your home. Even a minimal leak can raise your water bill and possibly cause damage to your home.

A dripping faucet and leaky pipes are necessary expenses.

Ways to Maintain a Budget as a Minimalist
Reset the Goals
Figure out your priorities and where you went wrong with the original plan. Look out for your short and long-term goals, including buying a car, purchasing a new home, retirement, emergency savings, and don't forget that big vacation you have not taken in several years. If you lose the original plan because you placed your ideas on a back burner, identify them, and get going to reach them. Start with these options:

Emergency Savings: Make this a priority. Consider saving up enough money to cover at least three months' worth of your expenses. No matter what the original goal was, be stricter this round. Be prepared if you have an emergency or lose your job.

Purchasing a Home or Vehicle: This goal may take a little longer. It could be four or five years away, but it is time to save the money, NOW, before your current car dies. Prepare for the unexpected as you begin your new round of minimalist living.

Remove the Debt: This is the hardest one, but it is important to become financially successful. You have to squash the debt.

Start over with a fresh budget and be sure to include these areas as a priority. Setting goals begins with a good budget.

Know How Much You 'Should Be Spending'

Live within your means! This is probably a statement you have heard many times, but it is imperative for you to achieve your goals. Once again, this cannot be stressed enough, understand where your money is going. This is the only way to keep your budget functional. There are no written rules on how to do this, but these guidelines will help you recreate and maintain a budget so you can easily reach your goals.

Break down the spending into these three main categories: financial goals, fixed costs, and flexible spending.

Fixed Costs: These are the bills that you pay monthly:
- Utilities
- Housing
- Insurance
- Cell Phone
- Legal Obligations – car payments, student loans, debt payments, etc.

Financial Goals: Whether you are saving for a home, car, or just paying off other debts, if you do not make these a part of the monthly bills, you will probably be lacking the money by the end of the month. You have to stay on top of your finances.

For example, if you have a card which carries a higher interest rate, that is a priority. If you have more than one card, pay them off according to those rates. Don't close the account, but move onto the next one and continue until they are all paid using their minimum balances (on the budget).

Flexible Spending: This category includes expenses that vary from month to month. You want to keep these in check, which includes entertainment, groceries, and dining out. Reduce the amount of money spent on food by eating at home or even inviting friends and family over for a nice dinner party.

Know What Money is Coming in and Going out

Once you know how much you *should* be spending on your budget, it is imperative that you know *where* it is all going. This basic guideline will help you identify which expenses need to be reduced.

Your Paycheck: The figure you will be looking at is your gross income/pay and is the total before any deductions, including your taxes. The net income is your take-home pay. These are the deductions that are taken:
- Social Security Taxes
- Medicare Taxes
- State Income Taxes (depending on your locality)
- Federal Income Taxes

You may also have these deductions taken from your check (so you don't have the extra paperwork):

Retirement Savings: This category is where your employer's 401(k) plan for retirement is deducted. When you sign up for the plan, you will choose a percentage to be contributed. If your employer pays into this account, try to match the amount. If you deduct 6% of your pre-taxed salary, your employer might match it with 3% (which is free money to you). At any rate, the money will add up quickly.

Insurance Payments: If you signed up with your employer for these benefits, the money would automatically come out of your check. This is just one more way to eliminate the headache of paying another bill on a scheduled date. This is a stress-free way to do this one, and you know the premium is paid promptly!

Flexible Spending (FSA) and Health Savings Accounts (HAS): These plans are used for various medical expenses (including prescriptions, co-payments, and other costs). These options are an option during open enrollment.

These are some of the ways to use these features:
- Acupuncture
- Contact lenses or prescription eyeglasses
- Laser eye surgery (LASIK)
- Chiropractic services
- Hearing Aids (repair and batteries included)
- Medications/drugs
- Insurance premiums not paid by your employer
- Smoking cessation programs
- Pregnancy test kits

These are expenses that would be difficult to pay if you don't have a plan in advance. Be sure to ask your employer for an itemized statement of your withdrawals, so you know what to expect in your paycheck. You should be able to get the information online.

Overhaul Your Spending Habits & Reward Yourself

The minimalist budget will enable you to live simple, but the process can seem endless. By calming the atmosphere and emotions, your desires will also dwindle. Try to remember, you cannot have it all, and more is less. Maintaining a minimalist budget is hard work. Therefore, recall the old saying, "All work and no play makes Jack a dull boy." As a child, you have probably heard it many times, and it's still true as an adult. You have worked hard to achieve your status. After all, acquiring the discipline and preparation for achieving your goals is difficult, to say the least.

When you meet a goal, have a special dinner at your favorite restaurant or have a salon or spa treatment. Plan ahead, so you have an extra incentive to reach - once your budgeting milestone has been achieved.
Move on and raise the bar, but always look forward to your accomplishments.
"You have succeeded in life when all you really want is only what you really need." —Vernon Howard

Chapter 8: Reorganize The Bedrooms

If you are like many people, your bedroom seems to be the storage space whenever it is clean-up time. If so, you already understand that you have your work cut out without a game plan. Get out the boxes and begin your routine.

The best plan includes removing all items from under the bed (dust bunnies included). Ideally, under the bed storage is good for those who are limited to space, but we tend to forget what is under the lurking space! Strip and clean the curtains to refresh the room. If you are considering a remodel, have a new pattern ready to hang with your nicely cleaned area. Choose a color scheme and stick with it. Your tidy home appearance will be beautiful.

The Bed

Strip the bed down to the mattress. It is essential to vacuum the mattress and bed springs to remove the dead skin (yuck), dust, and dust mites. Be sure to vacuum the perimeter of the bed, which is a haven for mites. Remove all of the bed linens and wash them. Pillowcases should be done weekly, and the bed protectors should be washed monthly. For blankets, decide whether it is washable or dry clean only. If it is clean, just fold and go. Most pillows are machine washable—and should be washed seasonally to remove any lingering odors, stains, mold, or bacteria.

Purchase an under-the-bed drawer for optimizing your spaces. Label the container so that you are always aware of its contents.

Prepare this aroma for the room:

Healthy Bedtime Spray for the Monsters

Even though this is not a spray you use on your body; it classifies a spot in the bedtime aroma section. Some customers have called it the 'Shoo the Monsters Away' spray remedy.

Try this blend using the specified amount of drops:
- Emulsifier - 30
- Orange - 8
- Lavender 12
- Roman Chamomile -2
- 8-ounce bottle of room spray base

How to Mix:
1. Mix the oils with the emulsifier and base. Shake well.

How to Use:
1. Simply spray the monsters away and freshen the room.
2. Spray a bit on the pillow for extra pleasure.

The Dresser

It is best to remove all distractions from the surfaces in the bedroom except for special items or items which require daily access. A few pictures and knick-knacks are acceptable as long as you don't have a resulting clutter zone. Many of the famous designers recommend a compartmentalized wooden box on top of the dresser. It will contain all of the daily items such as eyeglasses, remotes, phones, and similar objects. Everything is corralled into one neat space.

Bedside Tables

Your bedside table is another good hiding place for items when you don't want to do any chores. Take a box with you for the keep-trash-donate items. It is much simpler if you keep all of the items together, so later; you won't be tempted to rummage through the boxes (via packrat time).

Make a future plan for the drawers with drawer organizers. You can easily see what you want without destroying the room to locate the desired item.

The Book Clutter

If your bedside table ends up looking like a bookstore, it might be advisable to purchase a nightstand that has shelves. As you work, discard the books that you have already read. Only leave your current reading material or other essential items on the tabletop.

If you have a hobby such as needlepoint or knitting; use an under the bed storage container for the items. You can also place an attractive bench or cedar chest at the foot of the bed for hiding some items.

Ladies & Your Makeup

As with medicines you should not store your makeup in the bathroom. Find a spot somewhere in the bedroom to store your precious cosmetics and other similar products.

Check all of your products for expiration dates, such as sunscreen or lotion. If it is not the same consistency that it was when it was purchased and didn't have a date marked, it has probably lost its beneficial qualities. In other words, it's trash.

Go through hair products and personal care items. If the product has a unique smell, it is probably trash! These are some guidelines for your makeup:

- *Eyeliner Products:* Gel eyeliner lasts approximately six to eight months because of the double-dipping of a brush into a pot. However, a pencil is good for one year. According to sources at the *Huffington Post*, sharpening a pencil is not going to be a bacterial breeding ground, so don't worry.
- *Eye Shadow and Other Powder Cosmetics:* Powder products do last longer than wet formulas. Most products are good from one to two years. As with other products, it is smells, toss it!
- *Lipstick:* Expiration will be shown by texture, smell, or color changes. If you wipe/clean them off with a bit of alcohol, they will remain sanitized.
- *Foundation:* Packaged foundation in a pot usually lasts about six months, but a pump formula can last for one or two years.

- *Any Natural Products:* Consider keeping preservative-free/natural cosmetics in the refrigerator. The shelf life of many is approximately three to six months. However, check with the manufacturing company.

Jewelry

The jewelry is an area that may take a bit more time. Do that on your 'special' day set aside for special projects. You can do this action when you have some quality time to reflect and make the necessary decisions whether the item should be in the keep-toss-donate-or gift box. However, you can clean the outside of the box.

The Closet

The closet is another forbidden territory because you just know you don't want to throw any of your favorite items away. Look at the brighter side; if you haven't worn the item within the past year, it is time to bid the item a fond farewell.

Begin by letting go of the guilt of how many times you have left it hanging in the closet. If the garment or article has collected dust, it's definitely time to hit-the-road.

Maintain Dirty Laundry: Designate a spot in the closet or a hidden corner for dirty clothes until laundry day. Be sure all of the items are dry before you stow them away or you could have moldy clothing. Ideally, take them to the laundry room if space permits. Another option is to purchase an over-the-door hamper if you don't have the extra floor space.

Purchase Closet Rod Expanders: You can utilize your closet space by adding an extension rod to make the space efficient. You can create sections for hanging blouses and pants without the lost space between them and your shoes.

Use Shelf Dividers: It might seem a bit fussy, but shelf dividers are the answer to organizing any space. First, you need to count how many divided stacks you will need, whether it is for shirts, jeans, or sweaters. You can also use these dividers in the bathroom or any area that can benefit from them because they hook/slip over any solid shelf.

Measure the width and height between the shelf the ceiling or next highest shelf. You can choose from different styles such as white, wire, chrome, and many others. Tall solid dividers are excellent for storing handbags.

You can use a bookshelf with deep shelves for sweaters, tee-shirts, sweats, shorts, jogging pants, and similar clothing.

Roll the Clothes: Professional organizers have discovered you can get approximately 1/3 more shirts in a drawer using the fold-and-roll technique. This presents a huge advantage because you can see which shirt you are searching for because it is rolled and not folded flat.

Fold the shirt in approximately 4 inches from the bottom. Fold in one side of the shirt with the sleeve out, and repeat on the other side.

Roll the shirt from the collar downwards. You should be able to see the pattern on the shirt with this roll. This particular type of roll is similar to the military technique, but it is not as tightly gathered.

How to Hang Clothing:
- Similar colors together
- Hang the sweaters together
- Shirts together
- Pants and skirts together
- Dresses together

Purchase a batch of velvet hangers for the flimsy items that won't otherwise stay on the hangers. Remove the empty hangers to the laundry room. Don't leave a tangled mess on the floor or occupying precious hanging spaces. Besides, it looks messy.

Classify the Clothes:
With so many decisions, here is a way to categorize the items easily:
- **Keep Box:** Clothes you will wear for the next year, clothes that look good, and clothes that fit good
- **Cosign Box**: Clothes you no longer need which are in excellent condition
- **Donate Box**: All clothes in good condition
- **Trash**: Throw out the unusable (stained, torn, minus buttons) garments or reuse the material for another project.

Major Tip: Keep in mind; don't hoard it unless you have a plan, or you will end up with another messy disaster.

The Shoe Section

Place all of your shoes in a line and separate them into categories, for work or dress wear. Decide whether you wear them or if they need to be tossed or donated. If you haven't worn them in the last few months, get rid of them. However, don't throw away any seasonal items such as rain boots or winter gear.

You can purchase a sectional cubby that can be used as one unit to store your shoes and handbags. It will keep them off the floor and readily available when you are ready to use them.

The Scarves, Hats, and Purses

Scarves, belts, purses, and other accessories also need to go through the decision-making process. Purchase an accessory organization tool that will hold ten to twelve scarves on one hanger. They can also hang on a regular hanger in the closet.

If you have a lot of hats, you can purchase a hanger that used clips to store them. You can also roll the belts and ties and place them neatly in a dresser drawer.

Ways to Minimalize Your Clothing Between Seasons

Keeping your wardrobe appealing to the eye is all a part of minimalistic living. You can see your clothes and won't be concentrated on going shopping. The process involves creating what is called a clothing capsule. The process of getting dressed will be much easier when you know where to look. Use some of the suggestions and make your own capsule rules and guidelines. Just remember, keep it simple; if you don't absolutely love it; chuck it in the trash or donate box.

Benefits of a Clothing Capsule

You will be surprised how many benefits you will receive from taking the extra effort to prepare a clothing capsule. These are just a few:

- You will be enjoying the newly created closet space. It is so organized (making it easier to remain that way). You will be spending less money and time purchasing new clothes because you commit to owning fewer pieces you truly love.
- Your confidence will be boosted since you now realize every item in the space looks great on you in a flattering way!
- You can leisurely prepare for an outing or work. You know where all of your essential and fancier items are stored.
- The stress factor will be removed. You will no longer have that overwhelming feeling of fatigue of what to wear!
- You will feel and be grateful and content with what you have, instead of concentrating on your next shopping spree!

In a nutshell, you'll be spending less energy and time when you're getting dressed. You will discover the kept items make you look and feel great. You spend less energy and time getting dressed. Everything in your wardrobe feels and looks superb on you. Less time and energy is focused on your clothes, which means more time and energy are focused on you.

Begin Your Capsule

Make yourself set limitations on the number of items you add to the capsule. Don't stress out for a set 33 items you will read about in the next segment, but be reasonable and sort the items you will wear and see where it takes you. Include only items in the capsule that are worn daily.

What not to include in the capsule:

- Jewelry & Accessories: Earrings, necklaces, bracelets, scarves, etc.)
- Outerwear: Hats, Jackets, gloves, etc.
- Shoes: Casual, formal, and business
- Workout clothes: Sweatpants, leggings, etc.
- Undergarments: Socks, underwear, bras, and tank tops or camisoles
- Seasonal personal gear and swimwear
- Formal Clothing: Fancy skirts, business clothes, dresses, skirts, and similar items)

Decide on a Timeframe

Most people will switch the capsule every three months or at least when the seasons change. Store all of the capsule items in the closet of the items you are currently wearing. Store the off-season items in spare closets or dressers. Remember, simple, and clutter-free is the answer to serenity.

CHAPTER 9
For Kids Only — Minimalism

Children's clothing will require more persistence since he/she grows in spurts and go through more clothing. Use the same logic used in your closet.

Manage the Clothing

Make the sorting process much simpler by expanding your keep box; place the items being worn now in a box (or use the bed). Sort the clothes that are out-of-season in another section. After you finish sorting the articles, place them neatly into the dresser.

Remove the donate box outside of the room in case you need to make more space.

Project 333 Rules - How to Manage Children's Clothes

The 333 project is one of the most popular minimalist challenges that will invite you to dress your child with 33 items or less for three months. You can begin the process at any time, but it is sometimes a good idea to initiate the time during the months of October 1 until December 31 or another time of the year when your schedule is less busy.

- *Items to Keep*: The items you will use as the 33 items include outerwear, shoes, clothing, jewelry (if the child has any), and accessories.

- *Items Not Included*: You would not count underwear and pajamas.

- *Make a List*: About two months before you begin the purge, make an outline of the items you will keep. At the end of that time, box up the remainder of the items and place them in a box. Tape the box closed and put it out of sight. (Remember this later. If you have not needed the items, the professionals suggest donating the box without looking at the contents.)

- *Which Items to Remove:* Consider the items that will be most used. If you purchase new items for Project 333, use the one in and two out approach, but always stick to no more than the 33 items.

- *Sentimental Items:* Choose a drawer/shelf/container to hold on to sentimental things like the first outfit, first shoes, etc. Once again, be ruthless, and keep only a handful of pieces of clothing that your child really loved.

Ways to Make the Created Wardrobe Functional

Choose a cohesive style and color palette. You need to be able to mix and match your clothing, so you don't need enormous amounts of extra pieces to put an outfit together. Owning fewer items make getting ready for the day a much simpler task.

Decide when enough is enough. You can provide a seasonal capsule until each of the items it is totally functional. Once you have the items of clothing sorted with usable items that you must have, set the options in the same pod and close them for the year.

Bear in mind, to keep items that can be used for all times of the year in a space that is easily accessible. By reducing the clutter, you can quickly discover a jacket or swimsuit as the season permits without destroying the cleaned closet.

By making a capsule wardrobe, the collection of clothing will consist of items that are worn regularly and can be interchanged. Figure out exactly how many socks, bottoms, tops, and outerwear your child can go through weekly. If you are not sure what that amount will be, consider placing a laundry basket aside for nothing but his/her clothing.

For older children, you might consider this experiment a bit longer since they tend to be more fashion conscious. Add another three to five days of clothing for the calculations.

Be brutal with the choices and discard anything that is stained too small or big—or items that are not worn. Use the same keep, toss, and donate boxes as used with the toys. If you have more than one child, you need to consider not saving so many items for the next child. By the time the second child needs the item, it could be out of season or completely out of style. Don't use valuable space for storing questionable items.

By following these guidelines, you will discover there will not be any more digging for items that do not work well together. You will have clothing that can be coordinated with other items without worrying about whether they match. This learning process provides your child with a way of learning independence when he/she can choose what to wear.

About the Toys

Does your home seem like everywhere you look—you have an unending supply of toys? How many should you keep? What will you do with them? The answers are fairly simple, with a bit of practice.

Observe which toys they play with the most, keep the ones that can fit on the shelves, keep the ones that encourage creativity, and encourage them to donate ones they don't play with often to kids in need.

Keep in mind that toys can be educational and can play an essential role in his/her development. Those are the types of toys you will want to have in your home. Once you have these questions, it's time to proceed with how to eliminate the clutter.

Fads and Trendy Toys
Be firm and don't give in to all of the advertisements you see broadcasted. Companies will generate new toys every few months and plaster them over every television network that is available. Your child sees the toy as an item that must belong in his/her toy-box. Children are viewing these advertisements and do not understand why the room cannot be filled up with each of these new items. You have to draw the line and say no if the room is already at its maximum capacity.

Don't feel alone because every parent goes through this. The fad will pass, but maybe it is time for some commercial-free entertainment. So, just keep a realistic and healthy attitude toward the toy manufacturers and realize which ones will be educational and which ones are out there to make money for the businesses selling the 'trendy' products.

Limit Shopping Adventures
Have you ever been in a store and experience a temper tantrum because a child did not get a 'must have' toy? If it happens to you, you have to remain firm so your youngster won't believe throwing a fit will get him/her a new toy. By not giving in to the tantrum, you are teaching limitations. Don't worry about what others may think because you know your situation, and they don't!

Rent Toys & Save Space
Check in your area to locate a <u>toy library</u>. Consider borrowing toys instead of purchasing them. Check the extensive list to see if there is one in your area of the United States. Your children can enjoy the toy, but you can always return it instead of worrying about how to pay for it.

Beginning the Process
Plan ahead when it is a time of approaching events in the child's life, such as a birthday or holiday that will be adding more toys to the cleared space. Help your child understand you need to make room for additional toys. If you begin the process when the child is young, it will be a permanent thought pattern for the future.

Keeping the Organization
Some older children like to see the belongings on a higher closet shelf. Clear plastic containers are good for storing smaller pieces so you can quickly identify the contents. It will eliminate a lot of unnecessary searching and digging for a special something (we all do it).

Keep the clutter controlled by bargaining. Tell the child that he/she can have the Lego set once the trucks are securely parked in the correct spaces. *Make the items simpler to put away than they were to retrieve.* Think of the space from a child's perspective; the floor is his/her table. If you place the flip-file picture books upright in a plastic dishpan or similar container, your kid has to rummage through the stack to find the desired one. The unwanted ones will be on the floor but consider the alternative. Compare a normal/traditional bookcase where the tiny fingers can wipe out the entire shelf with one swipe. You should see the picture now!

Organize using the bottom to top method. The children's most used items should be located on the lower shelves and drawers or left on the floor. Designate the higher levels for the items which are seldom used. For example, the breakable bear collection is eight-feet off of the floor, whereas the favorite bear is awaiting company in the rocking chair.

Label Everything

If you have a toddler, use a computer printer to make some simple but graphic labels for the clothing articles. For example, use a picture of shirts, socks, dolls, trucks, or any other item that might remind your kid of where the item lives! Good luck with that one!

Put labels in the closets, inside of the drawers, on the edges of shelves, the plastic bins—everywhere. Make it a game and play 'match the label.' It can be a lot of fun, and the child is learning how to become organized.

CHAPTER 10
Declutter Laundry Spaces
Replace the Items in the Laundry Room

The Cabinets: Group all of the similar products, such as laundry detergent, bleach, and fabric sheets. Be sure you have some all-purpose cleaners available for quick cleanups.

Add some baskets or plastic containers to the tops of the washer and dryer for your convenience. Place one box for the clothes hangers or neatly hang them on a laundry rack if you have one.

Purchase some stackable plastic, wicker, or similar style decorative boxes for sorting the laundry. When you are in a time crunch, or any other time, you can use the smaller baskets for sorting the socks and undies that take so much time to pair and fold. Empty or full, the area is organized!

Sorted Laundry: If you have the extra space in the laundry room; place some sorter baskets in the area to keep dirty laundry organized. You can purchase the sorters reasonably priced, so as each piece of laundry can be added to its designated section as it becomes dirty, instead of the heaps of unsorted disasters that can happen. The canvas styles are very attractive and forgiving if you accidentally place a damp article in the hamper.

Note: Try to be sure all items are completely dry before you place them in the laundry hamper. The dampness could promote mildew on the clothing or other articles.

CHAPTER 11
Clean & Organize Spare Storage Areas

You have put off the least used rooms until last during your normal cleaning routines. It is time to tackle those junk collection havens to remove items you either don't need or don't use.

Real Simple Magazine once ran an article about a numbering system for miscellaneous articles. The plan is unique and can use your imagination in the process of design. It will work especially well for sewing or craft projects.

Choose some decorative boxes that are all the same sizes. Place fancy numbers on the outside end of each one and store them neatly on a shelf. Keep a catalog of what items are placed in the box. When you need something and have no clue where it's at; simply look at the catalog.

The Basement

The basement must also follow the keep-toss-donate-trash boxes. The basement in many homes is the graveyard for many 'you are going to fix it' items. As you begin the chore in the basement, think of how long the item has already been waiting. For example, you put that pair of shoes on the shelf; umm, no answer, huh? So many items are waiting for the trash pile. This is a molehill that has now become a mountain.

The Attic

The attic is another great spot for storing hidden treasures. If you store our seasonal items in the attic, you should sort through them the same way you did in the bedroom closet. Purchase a hanging caddy/rack for coats and similar items to conserve space. Be sure to have the keep-toss-donate-trash bins close at hand.

Seasonal Decorations: If you like to decorate with changes of the seasons, you need to figure out a way to keep them all separated. Use different colored/types of bins to distinguish what season the box is for, and label the outside of the container showing its contents clearly—no more digging. The Christmas decorations have a way of becoming disorganized. Purchase some plastic bins which are available to store everything from wrapping paper to your most fragile ornaments. Not only will you be thankful when you can locate the items, but you will also be saving spaces for other essential household items.

The Luggage: How many pieces of luggage does your family need? Be honest and keep the ones you use and donate the rest of the lot. Another useful tip, just in case you cannot part with the extra pieces, use them for storage—place off-season gear in them. Winter blankets can go in them during the summer months. The ideas are limitless, especially if you live in a crowded home. Make the extra pieces worth the space you are using.

The Garage

Broken furniture seems to collect in the garage. The items come along with explanations of; it only needs a screw, or I can cover that. Unfortunately, the items have started a party in the garage with chairs and tables on the guest list! What happened to the space you had for two cars? It is time to fix it or toss it.

Plan on going through all of the boxes to discover how many items can go to donate/toss stack, especially the ones already destined to be yard sale or thrift store material.

If you have cabinets and drawers, go through each of them. For small items such as screws, nuts, and bolts can be stored in baby food jars or other types of containers for storage organization. (You might need to choose day 11 after the plan).

After you finish sorting the boxes and other spaces, be sure to mark the boxes for its contents clearly. It is a good idea to date the box so that you will remember when it was last purged.

The Garage Refrigerator or Freezer: Remove everything from the refrigerator or freezer and thoroughly clean it, just as you did the one inside of the home. It is a good idea to check the contents of the unit, especially if you have stored a lot of meat or veggies in the freezer.

Note: If you are a hunter, consider donating or selling any leftover game meat to hunters in your area. Many of the clubs will use it to feed the dogs (even freezer burnt meat). It is better than throwing it into the garbage.

Sports Gear: Consolidate your gear into categories, making sure all of the camping gear is in one place, and the tennis or golf equipment is safely stored in another. Look over the equipment and discard any damaged items. Use your imagination and hang some of the items until the season changes and you need it again.

Hang the Tools: Consider putting pegboards on the wall so you can find the hammer or screwdriver the next time it is needed. Hang the yard or garden tools such as the hoe, shovel, or rake.

Use larger hooks to suspend large items such as bicycles to provide more walking space.

Plastic shelving is an excellent way to provide extra storage for smaller items. You can purchase the units that reach the ceiling for additional spaces for any items. Just be sure not to overload it. Check the weight limits when you make a purchase from a home improvement store, supercenter, or second-hand store.

Downsize your car if possible. Do you really need a 4x4 when a compact model would serve your needs? Think of the money saved that could be applied to other essential items in your budget.

Your Vehicle Needs a Cleaning Also: Make a new daily habit when you get home from work or other outings. Remove all of the trash and other items that don't live in the car.

CHAPTER 12
Methods Of Containment & Removal

"It is always the simple that produces the marvelous." —Amelia Barr

Set specific rules for kids clutter. Depending on the child's age, only allow toys in the bedroom. Designate the kitchen, dining room, and living spaces for household items only. For smaller children or toddlers, choose a space in the home, such as a corner where the toys can be neatly stored in containers, shelves, or bookcases.

Cubbies: A small plastic three-drawer organizer is an excellent choice for smaller items such as Legos, blocks, or stuffed animals. Remember to keep the most cherished ones.

Bins and Baskets: These are a safe and easy way to make clean up simpler. Label each of the bins if possible so that you and your child (age dependent) will know the correct location of each article. If your child has not reached the age to associate with reading yet, you can use some pictures for the label.

A Home for Similar Items: If possible, keep all of the stuffed animals, sports items, and other special items in the same container or space. Use the same logic with socks, underwear, pants, shirts, shorts, and other foldable items.

School Papers: It is essential to have a special location for school papers. Many schools use the phone system for relaying messages, which helps eliminate a lot of the paper clutter. However, there are many other papers that need to be filed. Use an inbox or folder system for incoming paperwork. Take advantage of the Google Calendar and enter the information on it as soon as you receive notification of any upcoming events.

Now that you have the items secured in special places, it's time to decide what to do with the items you have decided have cluttered your living space. The next step is to decide where the designated boxes you have to 'sell' and 'donate' will be placed. It's much easier than it sounds.

Removal of Clutter

Visit a local consignment store in your area. You can also sell items of value on Craigslist or eBay to make money from the items you've decided you don't need. Try local selling apps to make a quick and easy sale. All you need is a photo, a short description, and a price. Some of these apps will allow payments inside of the app.

1. *OfferUp:* You can take one to four photos and enter the title of the article you will be selling. Add the condition and set a price. You can also share your item to Facebook. You will receive a notification to let you know when someone wants your item. You get paid from the interested buyer once you choose a safe area to meet.
2. *5miles:* This tremendous local selling app requires at least one photo (add more if needed), and add it to the correct selling

category. You can also upload a video. Post your location, a description, and price for the item. Post it on Twitter or Facebook for additional advertising. The app goes beyond others and allows users to list local services, jobs, housing, and a list of yard sales. You can choose to be paid through the 5miles by using their credit or debit card or handle it by cash, the old-fashioned way.
3. *LetGo:* This is a favorite app since it can have your item up for sale in less than one minute. You can change your price and location or share the article you would like to sell and share it on Facebook. You will be contacted through the app for questions. You will have to handle the transaction made through the app, which is about the only downfall.
4. *Shpock*: This site offers an easy listing for your information. All you need to do is choose a category, provide a title, description, and price. Share on Facebook. The app is free, but premium membership is offered, which will remove the additional ads. You can add more photos and have the ability to move your listings to the top of the search result list.
5. *Trove:* As you are downsizing, consider using this site to sell your furniture. You can also purchase items! Choose a category, take a photo, and add the title with its details. The list is easy to list the condition, brand, width, depth, and height. You will need to sign into Facebook or Google to complete your listing.
6. *VarageSale:* Take a few minutes to add a title, category, price, and description of your item. To activate the account will require a Facebook login. The administration will verify your profile photo and real name before you are activated.
7. *Close5:* This app was created by eBay so you can sell your belongings in your locality. All you do is decide on a location, price, and description. Share your listing on Facebook. Set a 'Best Offer' for the item which allows the client to make the offer (less stressful for you). It is your emergency fund, so choose wisely.

Check These Resources

- *Staples and Office Depot*: These two companies will take your empty ink and toner cartridges. You can earn rewards which you can use in turn to purchase other essential items to suit your budget.

- *Best Buy*: You can receive a Best Buy gift card either online or in the store. All you need are old electronics such as computers, tablets, cell phones, GPS units, and many other items you may otherwise throw in the trash.

Purchase essential items in Bulk: Sam's Club is one of the most well-known choices, but check your area for other places. At any rate, if you have enough savings in your budget, it is worthwhile to purchase items when they are on sale.

Sell Jewelry: If you have jewelry that is collecting dust in your jewelry box, consider selling it online or at a pawn shop. You may be surprised how much extra money you can add to your budget with items you never wear. Each of these methods will allow you to recover some of the losses as you begin your minimalistic journey. It can also be a good starting point for your emergency funds. You will receive money for items you no longer need and still be formatting a baseline for your savings.

CHAPTER 13
Benefits Of A Minimalistic Home

"Truth is ever to be found in simplicity, and not in the multiplicity and confusion of things." —Isaac Newton

More Focus on Fun and Healthier Activities

Remove material possessions out of your life that can cause you extra work. Think of the time spent on a dune buggy that goes out only during the summer months. Take the extra time to go for a hike or to go fishing or hunting with friends. Do what you can to enjoy yourself anytime, whether it is playing with your kids or family members out in the yard picking a guitar. Have fun and enjoy life.

Once you have your budget in a workable manner, you will have more confidence and have time to enjoy life. You have removed the worry and stress, which can be linked to depression.

Focus Less on Material Belongings

Once you have gained the freedom from materialism, you will begin to think with a changed mindset. Once you have decluttered your living spaces, basement, and garage; you will discover how many things are just not needed in your life.

Think of the boat you have the garage that you only take out once or twice a year. You can - not only lower payments (unless it is paid for) - but think of the space where you could do other things. Have a party and celebrate the removal of unnecessary items. But, don't forget that the bulk of the sale should be added into your emergency fund account.

You Are Given the Freedom to Spend Your Money

You can ask anyone that has maintained a minimalist budget, and one out of ten will answer that the philosophy of freedom on the top of the list. Don't let that idea get too far ahead of the plan. When you begin to spend money on things that are important to you; you will start to minimize your spending. You will discover that buying it because it is on sale is not a good reason. Are you buying it because your neighbor has one? If the answer is yes; think about the pending purchase. Do you really need or want the item?

Appreciate Your Belongings

Once you have your budget plan in action and understand the differences between your wants and needs, the process will be much easier to accomplish. You will discover that you can fulfill your desires quicker than you realized. That is the turning point you are seeking in your minimalist budget.

There will always be something you 'want,' but as a minimalist, you will realize you cannot currently afford the item or service. The focus is clearer once your expenditures have been documented. Don't think of it as being deprived, because you really aren't. Think of the many ways you are blessed.

This is the viewpoint held by an individual who is a minimalist. You can decide what is important to you and your family. Now, go for it! It may take more time, but you will not be deeper in debt. That alone is worth the waiting time. You are empowered and capable – not deprived.

You'll Have Healthier Relationships

As a human being, everyone needs to connect with other humans. A minimalistic lifestyle and home will help you put a focus on people instead of the stuff they have. There's just more room and space and more energy for people in relationships to flourish. You cannot build a satisfying connection around possessions, not even shared possessions. Minimalism is making a conscious choice to use the things and people we love because the opposite will not bring you the connections for very long.

You Stress Less About Finances

The minimalist approach will free up your valuable resources of energy and time as well as money. When you become disengaged with being like all of your neighbors, everything else comes naturally. You have built your life on money, and so many times, you have found herself discontent. You need to tune out all of the commercials trying to say you can purchase at a special price, and devote your time to other things. Minimalism is a path to get out of debt. There isn't any need to spend money on items to impress people around you.

All you're doing is giving up items you don't need, so many of which would need maintenance as time passes.

Cleaning Is Easier

If you're like many people, you want to enjoy a clean house, but you hate doing housework. A minimalistic way of living will provide you with this incentive, so you're more likely to get it done and stay on top of the housework. For example, if you have to pick up, dust off, and deal with ten items on the countertop, it just takes too much effort after a long day! Multiply that by how many rooms you have cluttered. On the minimalist side of things, just move a few items, vacuum, and maybe pick up a couple of misplaced items. You are much more likely to get the vacuuming done.

Happiness Is Less Cleaning

Once you have fully cleaned and organized your spaces, you can simply do a quick clean/pick up of any misplaced items on the way to your bedroom before retiring for the evening. There's no reason or need to wake up in the morning to a cluttered mess. After you realize how easy it is to maintain a tidy and clean home, you will discover it is a great benefit to minimalism.

Minimalism Helps You Thrive as a Highly Sensitive Person

If you are in this category and also an introvert, minimalism is your friend. Because of this, having a calm and uncluttered home is important. Too much visual clutter or a chaotic environment can cause the feeling of being stressed and overwhelmed.

If you want your home to be your sanctuary, as a place where you can feel peaceful, calm, and recharged; minimalist living is for you. Learning how much an uncluttered, minimalist home and life would benefit you as a highly sensitive person is empowering and motivating.

You'll Cultivate Gratitude

<u>Harvard Medical School</u> defines gratitude as "a thankful appreciation for what an individual receives, whether tangible or intangible." Studies show that people who feel more gratitude tend to be happier, more optimistic, and feel better about their lives. You break the cycle of thinking if you just have the latest gadgets or the newest styles of clothes or the trendiest furniture; you will then finally be happy. You are choosing to feel grateful and happy for what you already have.

When you actively seek the good things in life, then appreciate the good things around you and feel grateful for them. When you come from a place of gratitude and contentment, you aren't searching for happiness in things you can buy. You look for happiness inside yourself. And in your fulfilling relationships, in the ways you spend your time that bring you joy, etc.

True happiness comes from within your heart when you notice and appreciate all the good things in your life; both tangible and intangible. True happiness comes when you actively look for a reason to *feel* happy and grateful—even in the times when that's hard to do.

Benefits of the Minimalist Budget Plan

Commit to your new way of life with your minimalist budget plan with the following benefits:

Priorities are redirected: You can see just what you and your family are spending. You have a blueprint each month to make the goals easier to obtain.

Waste is revealed. As you live day-to-day, life can become hectic. Unless you have a budget, you can get lost in all of the wasted time and money.

Stress is reduced. Many times, your financial standing is the leader of stress. You have a sense of control of your money - as it comes and goes out once you have a plan. You can feel more empowered with the ease of making your budget and sticking with the plan.

New habits are created. Once you realize that life is too short to stress over the old habits of spending money, you will have a minimalist budget. Once you have a clear picture of how to keep track of your income and expenses, you will be more conscious of spending your money unnecessarily.

Set the goals. Set those goal lines high, but not so high that you cannot do the climb. Once you have all of the facts noted using whatever method of organization you use, your life will be happier for you and your family. How much more can you ask of motivation?

Stay educated. You can view your money as a tool as you shift your mindset to focus on your future needs and your long-term goals. It is great to make those, but it is also essential to remain 'on task' and keep up with the times.
Improved motivation is evident. Creating and staying motivated with your new budget can be exhausting and mentally taxing until you have all of the figures in the right column. However, keep in mind that motivation is the first step, but you have to continue all the way through the process. Start one month at a time until you have it right. You will be glad when you can have a nice 'nest egg' for the 'rainy days' of your future.
You can be yourself. Always embrace your situation and don't think of your budget as a chore. It is the key to your financial success. Learning how to live on the minimalist budget may be contagious.
Make space in your life. Downsize your life, and you will be surprised how much money can be saved. Remember two things; follow the budget, and be frugal. You will begin to think about each purchase and how much it can or cannot fit in your simplified budget plan.
Change is good. Be ready to make huge changes in your life. Learning how to live with less is truly a blessing in disguise. You may be thinking that all you are doing is throwing away your stuff. In essence, you are doing much more than that. You are removing all of the waste that has taken over your life. By removing your paper clutter in the process, you are uncovering new ways to save money. By maintaining your budget regularly, you and your family are ensured that if an emergency should arise, you will be ready to face it.
You are not only growing financially, but you are learning how success really does feel! You sincerely have your minimalist mindset in gear. You are now preparing for your family's future and well-being.

CHAPTER 14
The Minimalist Mindset

"Purity and simplicity are the two wings with which man soars above the earth and all temporary nature." —Thomas Kempis

Minimalistic thinking allows you to become a gatekeeper about what's allowed in your home and in your life. You need to realize that happiness doesn't come from items. Consider the logic of why:

There's always a shiny new item right in front of you. New styles, models, features, and multiple new improvements are just around the corner. From kitchen gadgets to cars and unlimited technology, your world continues to move forward. Planned discontinuance will ensure your recent purchase will be out of use sooner; not later.

All new items will fade. By nature, all possessions are temporary. They look stunning in the store. However, think about it, as soon as the item is purchased, it will begin to age or spoil.

Possessions require maintenance. Your purchase will require focus, energy, and time for cleaning. The items can create more work since they will need to be cleaned and maintained. Many times they will become a distraction from the things that can truly bring you extended happiness.

Each purchase can add more stress to your life. For every extra physical item that you bring into your life, it will represent one more item to be scratched, stolen, or broken!

Shopping does not extinguish your oldest desire for contentment. Your overflowing closets and drawers stand as proof the purchases do not stop the drive. No matter how much you get; it's never enough.

Consider activities rather than shopping: Of course, the list can begin with decluttering a drawer or organizing your shoes, but that might not be ideal.
- Tackle a little bit of yard work and be too tired to consider the mall.
- Exercise with a friend and burn away a few pounds, besides making yourself feel great!
- Organize your photos and clean out your email files. Clear the junk out!
- Start a new novel and create a beautiful space. Create one of your own!

You will own less, not purging more: Shop more intentionally and thoughtfully. Stop buying things you do not need. Keep the standards high of all items you place in your wardrobe. If you add one, take one away, if not two to discard.

Value experiences over physical items: Millennials are prioritizing their vehicles and homes - less and less. They're enlisting more importance to personal experiences. One study found that 72% of millennials would rather spend more money on *experiences* than on material things.

Make better use of your time; become more intentional. You can start small but start now by letting just one item leave your space. You may not make a big step every day, but you're headed in the right direction. As you minimize your clutter, you are intentionally clearing objects that keep you from happiness.

Make gradual shifts in your attitude. Each decision you make will build your confidence and head you in the right direction. Your self-confidence will also get a boost as you clear your mind and space. With each decision, the process becomes quicker and easier. You are empowered to consume less and live more!

Realize, organizing is not the only answer. If you get stuck on one item or topic, just move onto something else and regroup your thinking pattern. There will always be situations or items you will need to add more thought to before a decision can be made. The process works in stages, so move on and keep the momentum going.

Make the commitment and play games to keep the process more fun. Make a challenge to yourself and set a goal of donating an article of clothing every day for one month. At that point, take the bag to a collection center. You will not only be helping others, but you are also learning the true meaning of a minimalist. You just removed items that did not bring your joy without realizing you reached one of your goals

Stop letting others have an effect on what stays in your home. The professionals stress the best way to achieve the benefits of minimalism is to start from within yourself. Make the example that others will desire to follow. Avoid making decisions on items you share with other family members or others living in shared situations. Cross that bridge only when absolutely necessary. Let the others be involved in the decisions of his or her belongings. By all means, stop comparing yourself to what you own as to what others have.

What Children Learn as a Minimalist

- You gladly share with others.
- You don't need to live life like everyone else.
- You don't need to buy things to be happy.
- You think carefully about our purchases.
- You live within your means.
- You love spending time with them.
- We are in control of our stuff.

If your children are still very small, adopting a minimalist lifestyle will be a lot easier than if they're older and have already accumulated a lot of stuff. However, don't let that put you off. It might not be easy, and you'll probably find yourself battling some resistance, but stick with it.

CHAPTER 15
The Minimalist Plan For Home Maintenance

"In order to seek one's own direction, one must simplify the mechanics of ordinary, everyday life." —Plato

You have reached a cornerstone and now have a clean house. Your next question is how to keep it clean. You won't be considered a clean freak because it is a minimalistic home for you to be proud to enjoy with your friends and family. This simplified approach is just what you need:

The Guiding Rule: Simplify! As you have learned, it's much simpler and less stressful once you realize less is more.

- Less furniture is much easier to clean.
- Fewer clothes will mean less clothing to wash, fold, and put away. You might have plenty of clothes, but you won't have them piled high in a corner lurking.
- Less kitchen clutter means you can clean the kitchen quickly after you prepare a meal. You won't need to shuffle the unessential items on the countertops!

Meditate While You Clean: You can remove a ton of stress if you put your mind in a peaceful place. Think of yourself as a monk sweeping the floors of a temple.

Wash While You Cook: On a similar note, wash as you cook. In any downtime, be cleaning up. I like to clean everything or at least rinse everything before I sit down to eat. I basically don't have to come back and clean up later. It takes me about two minutes after I'm done eating to clean up.

Don't Forget to Clean the Windows & Blinds: Pay extra attention to these two areas, especially if you have children or pets. The dust can accumulate quickly, making it unsightly and distracting as you continue your new minimalist behaviors. The natural light provides you with minimal portions of Vitamins C and D. So, bring in all the light!

Pair Your Cleaning Tasks

You probably already pair tasks without realizing you're doing it. But I like to intentionally pair tasks to make mundane chores a little bit more purposeful. There are three parts to pairing tasks.

Phase One: While you do a chore, do something fun while you're doing it, such as listening to an audiobook while you're dusting. Look forward and learn how to associate your tasks with your favorite show. Chores do not need to make you want to die.

Phase Two: Pair another chore alongside the one you're currently doing. If you're dusting, have your daily load of laundry in the washer. If you're folding laundry, you have the dishwasher going.

Part Three: Always pair the same tasks, so that you create a type of ritual you will start doing without thinking about it. If you always start a load of laundry before you start dusting, you'll naturally flow into that cleaning rhythm. It's one less thing to think about when you're cleaning.

Deep Clean the House Once a Week

Depending on the size of your space, you shouldn't need to spend much more than an hour a week on cleaning if you do the 10-minute maintenance run each day. Use this time for the deeper cleaning. Listen to a podcast and make this cleaning time a spiritual practice where you can zone out and get excited about your super clean space.

Make a New Weekly Cleaning Routine for Your Minimalistic Space

Perform A Mandatory Weekly Sweep: Continue picking up items throughout your home daily and place them in their appropriate spaces. The only task you should need to do is sweep and possibly an intermittent mopping if needed. Once a week, do a quick 30-minute cleaning. If you have roommates, get everyone involved. The floors should take less than ten minutes. If you have younger kids, let them dust the furniture.

Do A Thorough Dusting: You already know how quickly the dust can accumulate on surfaces. Just take the time to really dust your home with a special cleaner; not just a dry cloth or dusting wand.

Mop The Floors: Your floors will still require a thorough mopping weekly even if you have swept daily. The floors will look much nicer and be much cleaner. You will have less stress, especially if you're paddling around barefoot!

Make the Kitchen Sparkle

Consider these pointers for your kitchen:

1. *Clean-as-you-go:* Remove any messes, as they are made. Discipline yourself since it only takes about a minute or two to wash a few items. Get everyone in on the plan.
2. *Clear the Counters:* As with the floors, maintain your clutter and keep the counters clear except for essentials such as the coffeemaker and toaster. Wipe the surfaces once or twice each day.
3. *Weekly Spruce-up:* During your 30-minute cleaning session, not only do you sweep the floors, but also do a more thorough wipe-down of the rest of the kitchen. As a weekly cleaning, it won't take much effort to keep it clean.

Thoroughly Clean the Refrigerator: Inside & Out:

- Discard all of your leftovers the evening before your trash is scheduled for collection. Most leftovers are spoiled after three days.
- Wipe down all surfaces after the leftovers are extracted. Check for expiration dates of all leftover items to ensure it's all still healthy to consume.

Sort & Organize the Dishes
- In case you aren't aware, it's cheaper to run your dishwasher during the night time. The electricity is at a cheaper rate since it isn't prime time (5pm-9pm).
- Load your dishwasher before bed and set it to run at a later time. *(Many dishwashers have a 4-hour delay option.* Put the items in the cabinets the morning or after sorting your mail when you get home after work.

Laundry Extras
Several options work well for this task:
You should wash a minimum of one load of laundry each day. It will depend on the size of your family.
1. *Weekly or bi-weekly*: You can choose to take your oversized loads to the laundromat and get it all done in about 1.5 hours. It could save tons of time. Just bring them home to hang and put away.
2. *Wash All of the Bedding: Your* bedding should be washed at least weekly.
3. *Wash the Blankets & Throw Pillows:* You can clean pillows by tossing them in the washing machine or by vacuuming. Be sure to read instructions on the label before cleaning. Most blankets can be cleaned in the washing machine.

Tidy the Bathrooms
The bathroom can get pretty gross if you don't remain diligent. Try this process:
1. *Bi-weekly Cleaning:* If you keep things clean in the bathroom on a daily basis, all you need to do is a quick once-over every other week or so.
2. *Clean-As-You-Go:* It just takes a minute to wipe up a dirty bathroom sink or to give your toilet a quick swish-and-flush with the toilet brush. Scrub the shower just before you shower. Just do this when you see dirt.

Observe Kids' Toys
It's impossible to keep things perfectly clean when you have kids. Just use your minimalist approach:
1. *Use Baskets:* It's important to have plenty of baskets and other such containers. When it's time to clean up, just toss the stuff in.
2. *Quick Clean-Ups:* Throughout the day, messes are made, and we ask them to do a quick clean-up. It'll be messy again in 10 minutes, but at least it's a manageable mess. At the end of the day, the last clean-up lets us have some quiet time with a clean house.

Tidy the Office
Make a habit to daily sort any paperwork or mail or paperwork. You won't dread piles of paperwork accumulating which could take hours to sort. It

only takes a minute of your time and helps keep countertops as well as your mind clear of clutter.

Yard Work Challenges

If you have a huge yard, it's nice for the kids to play in, but a hassle to maintain.

You do have a few choices:

If you just don't have the time or energy to keep the yard up by yourself, consider hiring someone for the task. You can still do some of the hobby-type work with minimal effort. Consider your budget, but it would surely clear your mind.

In essence, you should own just a few plants and only ones that can maintain themselves and no junk. The less you have in your yard, the better. Try a Zen-like rock or gravel garden instead of grass. Be a naturalist and let the grass go wild (just kidding).

Your Monthly Minimalist Cleaning Routine

Clean the Carpeting: If you can't wash your carpet, just sprinkle (using equal parts) with some borax and baking soda over your carpet and let sit for two to three hours. Vacuum it up and enjoy!

Wash or Spruce-Up The Curtains: They accumulate dust the same way your blinds do. Just be careful and read the directions before you clean them. Some can be tossed in the washing machine and dryer, while others may just need to be wiped with a damp cloth.

CHAPTER 16
Natural Cleaning Supplies

You have the opportunity to clean your house top to bottom using professional tips, why not have special cleaning supplies for the task? Your question is answered in this segment. You will have the supplies to clean and a few suggestions using natural oils to deliver a tantalizing aroma to your minimalist home.

You want to be sure your minimalist home can be enjoyed to its fullest if all surfaces are clean and shiny. As previously mentioned, the term minimalist means different things to different people. It is much better on your budget if you make your own products and know how to use them. You have the peace of mind, knowing you and your family are in a safe environment.

Cleaning Containers for Homemade Supplies

Before you get started, it's essential to store all of your cleaning products securely. Choose a space such as the top of a closet or consider putting a safety lock on the cabinet in case you have a youngster who likes to explore. These are just a few of the items you will need:

Buckets: If you need to do more than a spot clean, you will need a bucket or two. If you use a mop, a mop bucket would be needed. Otherwise, a smaller bucket will come in handy for cleaning other areas such as baseboards. You must be diligent with a toddler lurking. If you have a toddler, chances are you would like to remain within your spending range for household cleaners.

Spray bottle or two (glass is preferred): You will be mixing many chemicals that may need different types of containers. It is best to purchase high-quality containers, but if you're on a budget, Dollar General will have one or two to choose from in stock.

Plastic Containers with Lids: Ziploc-type containers are an excellent choice with its secure lid. Just make the chosen cleaner mixture is clearly marked for future use. Some products will have a shelf life.

Shaker Containers: Choose a container with a tight-fitting lid when possible. Save a parmesan cheese container or make your own using another option of choice.

Caddies or Tool Containers: You will need to corral your tools and cleaners in a caddy that will easily fit in a closet or pantry that is out of reach of children. Store them in spaces where the most clean-up is needed.

Natural Cleaning Products

Baking Soda: Toss the Comet and Ajax aside by using a portion of baking soda. It is good from scrubbing the toilet, to the sparkling carpet, and everything in between. It is also a great deodorizer and natural air freshener.

Distilled White Vinegar: You will achieve a natural disinfectant which is safely mixed using a one-to-one ratio with water. Use it to clean the cabinets, countertops, and floors as a great grease cutter. It's awesome for cleaning stainless fixtures. Spray the mixture onto your rugs or carpets. If you don't like the smell of it, just open the windows for the air to clear. Instead of purchasing an expensive product for the dishwasher such as Jet Dry, add a little vinegar into the cycle. Consider adding it to your laundry cycle in the place of regular fabric softener.

Vinegar Clean-Up in a Bottle: If you prefer a spray bottle; all you need is a solution of three parts of water to one part of vinegar. Use it for any cleaning job from shining windows to the garbage disposal.

Cleaning Tip Warning: Don't use vinegar on colored fixtures or brass; it might cause discoloration.

Vinegar for Limescale: The white spots in your sink are lime deposits from mineral-rich hard water. Try this formula to clean the surfaces:
1. Soak a paper towel with vinegar.
2. Wrap the towel around the spotted area.
3. Wait for ten minutes.
4. Buff dry with a paper towel.

Hydrogen Peroxide: Add a sprayer nozzle to a bottle of peroxide since the elements can break down when exposed to sunlight. Use a one-to-one ratio of water and peroxide if you want it diluted further. Spray down all of the countertops in the bath and kitchen areas to kill germs. You can also use hydrogen peroxide to remove stains including juice, blueberries or other berries, and blood.

Rubbing Alcohol: Ethanol or isopropyl alcohol is a common ingredient used in rubbing alcohol. The fumes are powerful, so be sure to use in a well-ventilated space. The fumes are also flammable, but it is excellent as a disinfectant and works as a great solvent for dissolving oil and dirt.

Stainless-Steel Cleaner: Use a soft cloth to wipe any surfaces going with the grain to remove fingerprints.

A Super Disinfectant: Combine one part each of water and rubbing alcohol into a spray bottle. Clean any germ-ridden spaces as well as your personal items, including thermometers and your earring posts.
1. *Sponge & Cloth Refresher*: Saturate the cloth with alcohol in a bowl to stand for about ten minutes. Rinse it, and you're done—no more stressing over the bacteria traveling.
2. *Sinks & Chrome Cleaner:* After you're done with the sink for the day; just spray a bit on the surface to clean, disinfect, and shine. Buff the basin and fixtures with a dry cloth. It can also be used on brass
3. *Sofa Stains*: The alcohol won't penetrate the fabric, and it will also evaporate quickly. Spray over the stained area and wipe with a clean sponge. Let it dry. If it feels matted, brush the spot using a soft bristle brush using a circular motion.
4. *Disinfect Your Keyboard, Mouse, phones, and remotes.* The degreaser and disinfectant elements will dry - almost instantly.

Borax: Borax is made of Boron, which is an essential mineral the body actually needs to function correctly but, just like with most things, in excess, it can be harmful. Is it safe? You <u>can</u> decide.

Liquid Castile Soap: If you find vinegar offensive, use this soap as a great multipurpose cleaner. Use it as a personal care product and cleaning. Add a bit of water and tea tree oil for another multipurpose cleaner.

Microfiber Cloths: Purchase one of these cleaning cloths to clean your entire house (not the toilet). All you need is water to clean the surface. Choose a different color for each of your areas, so you don't cross contaminate.

Microfiber Cloth Mops: You can also purchase a chemical-free version of microfiber for a cleaning option using just water.

Squeegee: A squeegee will change the way you look at window cleaning. All you need to do is spray the chosen window cleaner on the window and away goes the grime. You can also purchase one that has a sponge attached if your outside windows are particularly dirty. Just dip the sponge in the cleaner bucket, scrub the window, and squeegee away the grime. You will need a couple of towels in the workspace to avoid spills or drips.

Sponges: You probably already have a stash of odor-free sponges that will work great with your new natural-cleaning products. You will also benefit with a Magic Eraser, a melamine sponge. It is best used by adding water first. If that doesn't remove the stubborn mark or dirt, just dip it in a little soapy water. You can also use your all-purpose cleaner with a little peppermint or lemon oil on a sponge mixed with warm water. Be sure to test a space before using the Magic Eraser to ensure it is safe.

Scrub Brushes: It's important to designate separate scrub brushes for particular jobs to avoid any cross-contamination. You can use a small toothbrush for small spaces such as around spigots (of course, a new one).

Broom & Mop: You will need the old-fashioned team, but just for quick clean-ups or spills. You can choose different types of mops, including a twistable mob, sponge mop—or my favorite, a refillable mop with microfiber pads. Just throw the pads in the washer for a sanitary clean the next time it's needed.

Dusting Wands: The best dusting wand to choose is one with a removable, washable duster. It should be capable of reaching the tall ceilings and corners with ease.

Vacuum Cleaner with Attachments: Select a high-quality vacuum that is within your budget. Be sure it has a good warranty. All you need to do is empty and clean the canister, or replace the bag often for the best results. Lastly, if your budget allows, a <u>wet/dry</u> vacuum could save you a ton of stress.

You will also use many other items, including:
- Lemons
- Natural salt
- Oven cleaner (see recipe)

- Bleach
- Wood polish (see recipe)
- Glass Cleaner (see recipe)
- An all-purpose cleaner (see recipe)
- Kitchen cleaner or wipes
- Rubber gloves
- Paper towels and cleaning cloths
- Toilet Brush
- Funnel

Special Cleaners
All-Purpose Cleaner
1. Fill a 32-ounce spray bottle up to an inch or two below the fill line. Leave room to add the soap and essential oil.
2. Add approximately 2 tablespoons of castile soap (peppermint, citrus or any scent you like or even unscented).
3. Add 10 to 20 drops of tea tree oil.
4. Shake gently to combine.
5. This cleaner can be used anywhere you would use a vinegar cleaner or any other conventional multipurpose cleaner around your house.

Glass Cleaner
This fabulous cleaner is great to have around for all those cute little fingerprints!

Items Needed:
- Water (2 cups - filtered or distilled)
- Essential Oil of choice (10 drops)
- Vinegar (2 tbsp.
- Spray bottle (glass is preferred)
- Microfiber cloth

How to Use:
1. Combine each of the fixings into the spray bottle.
2. Spray on your windows or any other glass surface using the fragrance of your choice; many use lemon-scented ones.

Lemon Household Cleaner
Items Needed:

- Water (8 oz.)
- Distilled white vinegar (4 oz.)
- Tea Tree Oil (15 drops)
- Lemon essential oil (15 drops)
- Glass - cleaning spray bottle

How to Use:
1. Fill the bottle with all ingredients and mix.
2. Shake the contents before each cleaning job.

Tip: It is advisable to use a glass container when possible. The citrus essential oils are highly concentrated and have acidic properties. Sometimes, it is best to store the products in glass for this reason.

Lemon Dishwasher Powder - Detergent

You want to be sure the food you serve your youngster is served on clean and sanitized dishes. You will get that with these amazing non-toxic chemicals.

Yields: 24 loads @ 1 heaping tbsp. per load
Items Needed:
- Baking soda (1 cup)
- Arm & Hammer Super Washing Soda (1 cup)
- Borax (1 cup)
- Lemon essential oil (20 drops)

Variations of Items Needed:
- *Unscented Product*: Leave out the essential oil
- *For Hard Water*: Add a ½ cup portion of Epsom salts.
- *Citrus Aroma*: Add 10 drops each of lemon and orange essential oils.
- *Peppermint & Lemon*: Use 10 drops of each oil.

How to Prepare:
1. Combine the components in a large mixing bowl.
2. *To Use:* Put one heaping tablespoon per load in the dish detergent compartment. Run as usual.
3. *To Store:* Pour mixture into a glass bottle or other container with a lid. Dress it up with an antique colored canning jar. It will keep the mixture dry until it's needed.

Lemon & Clove Liquid Dish Soap

Lemon and clove are fresh scents to include in your kitchen tools. The combination will make your dishes streak-free and sparkling clean.

Items Needed:
- Lemon essential oil (10-15 drops)
- Citrus castile soap/unscented castile soap (8 oz.)

- Clove essential oil (5 drops)

Variations of What You Need:
- *Citrus:* Substitute lime, orange, or grapefruit for the clove.
- *Grease Fighter:* Add a splash of white vinegar to the warm dishwater.

How to Prepare:
1. Pour the soap and oils into a storage container and shake well.
2. *To Use:* Add 1-2 squirts to the dishwater and scrub away.
3. *To Store:* Store on the counter or safely away from your toddler's reach.

Lemon Juice for Stubborn Stains

If you have a stubborn sink stain; try this remedy:

Items Needed:
- Powdered Borax (½ Cup)
- Lemon Juice (juiced - ½ of 1)

How to Clean:
1. Use a sponge to dab the mixture, rub, and rinse with hot water.
2. The method works well on stainless steel, porcelain, enamel, and many others.

Soft Abrasive Cleaners

If you prefer using a product such as Soft Scrub to clean your porcelain sinks or similar spaces, you can use a natural source without using bleach.

How to Clean:
1. Get the sink wet.
2. Sprinkle a portion of baking soda on the surfaces.
3. Use a cleaning rag to clean the surface until the sink or other surface is sparkling.

Scouring Powder

Items Needed:
- Salt - not iodized (.5 cup)
- Washing <u>soda</u> (.5 cup) Ex. Arm & Hammer
- Baking soda (1 cup)
- Optional: Lemon essential oil (5 drops)

How to Clean:
1. Pour the components into a bowl or jar.
2. Mix well and store in a shaker.
3. If you do not have a shaker, use a jelly jar and punch holes in the top.

4. Clean it using the concoction whenever you have a stubborn stain.

Tip: For tougher surfaces, apply undiluted white vinegar and water to the surface. Sprinkle the powder on the surface to sit for about five minutes. Scrub with a sturdy brush and rinse with vinegar and water.

Natural Toilet Bowl Scrubber - Deep-Clean
Items Needed:
- Vinegar (1 cup)
- Borax (.75 cup)
- Tea Tree essential oil (.5 tsp.)
- Lemon essential oil (5 drops)

How to Use:
1. Combine all of the ingredients in a medium glass container.
2. Measure the portions (¼-½ cup) in the toilet bowl. Let it sit for several minutes.
3. Use a brush to remove the stains.

For a Spray: You can also make it a bit thinner to use as a spray.
For a Scrub: Add a ¼ cup portion of baking soda to the mix and use gloves to scrub the toilet.

Natural Homemade Drain Cleaner
You don't need to purchase a bunch of fancy cleaning products for maintaining a clean and clear drain. Use one of these simple solutions:

Product 1: Clear The Drain
Items Needed:
- Baking Soda (.75 cup to 1 cup)
- Vinegar (.5 cup)

How to Clean:
1. Pour the baking soda in the drain.
2. Pour the vinegar into the drain and immediately cover the drain.
3. Leave everything to sit and work for about 30 minutes, but don't use the sink during this time.
4. After 30 min., run hot water through the pipes for about 2 to 3 min.
5. For really tough clogs you may need to repeat, but if you do this on a regular basis (about once a month) it keeps my drains clear and fresh without any problems.

Product 2: Simple Drain Freshener
Items Needed:
- Baking Soda (1 cup)
- Cream of Tartar (¼ cup)
- Salt (1 cup)

How to Clean:
1. Make a habit of pouring one-half cup of the mixture down the drain.
2. Pour a quart of boiling water in after you have added the mixture.
3. Do this every few weeks.

Homemade Natural Disinfectant Wipes
Items Needed:
- Wide-Mouth mason jar (1-quart size or 4-6 cup capacity & tight-fitting lid)
- Cleaning cloths - 10x10 squares (15-20)
- Filtered water (.75 cup)
- White distilled vinegar (.75 cup)
- Lemon essential oil (15 drops)
- Lavender essential oil (8 drops)
- Bergamot essential oil (4 drops)

How to Prepare:
1. Combine all of the fixings in a mason jar or other type of glass storage container. Note; the essential oils could have an adverse effect on plastic.
2. Swirl the components to combine.
3. Push the rags into the solution to soak. Securely close the lid and rotate the jar as needed to keep the rags moist.
4. Use any time for a quick clean up, so your toddler has a clean place for his/her precious cargo.

Natural Wood Cleaner
You don't want to take any chances with your table when cleaning it. This sounds almost good enough to eat:
1. Squeeze juice of one lemon into a small jar.
2. Pour in 1 tablespoon of olive oil.
3. Measure and pour in 1 tablespoon of water.
4. Thoroughly shake until it emulsifies.
5. Pour a small amount on a soft cloth and clean all of the wood furniture. This is also excellent if you have wood paneled rooms.

Dusting Spray for Cleaning Furniture
This is a fabulous choice to bring the luster back to your furniture. However, this mixture shouldn't be used on glass, walls, granite, or stainless steel since it contains oil. Avoid using it on fine antiques or unfinished wood.

Items Needed:
- Vinegar (.5 cup)
- Water (1 cup)

- Oil of choice (2 tbsp.) ex. grapeseed, sunflower, or olive
- Cedarwood essential oil (5 drops)
- Lemon essential oil (10 drops)
- Brown amber bottle

How to Clean:
1. Pour the vinegar and water into a spray bottle.
2. Add in your oils and shake.
3. Cover the bottle and store.
4. Tip: A brown bottle is suggested since the essential oils are potent and could damage a plastic bottle over long periods of time.

Special Cleaner for Fabric Couches & Chairs
Items Needed:
- White Vinegar (1 tablespoon)
- Dish Washing Liquid (1 teaspoon)
- Warm Water (1 cup)
- Baking Soda (1 teaspoon)

How to Clean:
1. Baking soda is the base, and vinegar is the acid that creates carbon dioxide. The results are lots of cleaning bubbles.
2. Add the dish liquid into a spray bottle with the vinegar.
3. Pour in the warm water.
4. Combine the mixture over the sink. Add the baking soda, and quickly screw on the top of the sprayer.
5. Use the mixture to clean the entire surface of the couch.
6. Be sure it is thoroughly dry before you place any items directly on its surface.

Natural Air Freshener Spray
What You Need:

- Filtered water (6 tbsp.)
- Vodka (1 tbsp.)
- Essential oil (10 to 40 drops)
  (Citrus, Peppermint, Jasmine, & Lavender)

How to Use:
1. Place the alcohol and oils in a small spray bottle.
2. Shake well and add the water.
3. Shake before you spritz whenever you want to be energized.

Here are a few more versions using another method for sprays. Each is three ounces:

Fresh Floral:
- 4 drops Frankincense oil
- 8 drops Juniper oil
- 6 drops each:
- Jasmine oil
- Rosemary oil

Energy Boost:
- 20 drops Lemon EO
- 8 drops Eucalyptus EO
- 2 drops each:
- Cinnamon EO
- Peppermint EO

Sweet Citrus:
- 10 drops Lavender EO
- 8 drops Sweet Orange EO
- 4 drops each:
- Bergamot EO
- Vanilla EO

Lavender Linen (2 Ounce Size)
- 1 tsp. Witch Hazel
- 15 to 20 drops Lavender
- Almost 2 ounces distilled water
- 2-ounce dark spray bottle

How to Use:
1. Add the lavender, witch hazel, and distilled water.
2. Spray your linens and pillows for a tantalizing effect.

Gel Air Fresheners

You will be amazed when you see how simple this really is to make. Lemon and lavender are good for serenity.

What You Need:
- 1 packet Knox Gelatin
- ¼ cup Vodka
- 1 to 2 d. food coloring
- A ¾ cup of water
- 15 d. essential oil (Grade oils are okay for this process.)

How to Prepare:

1. Bring the water to boil in a small pan and add the gelatin pack.
2. Stir until it is dissolved. Allow it to cool at room temperature.
3. Pour into a small jar. Add the oil, vodka, coloring, and any decorative items.
4. Stir and place in the refrigerator until it is set.
5. You can have fun with this one by adding decorations in the gel. You can also add a wick to the bottom of the glass and make a gel candle.
6. *Note:* As the aroma fades—add a few more drops.

CHAPTER 17
Super-Clean — Specific Spaces
Super-Clean the Countertops & Backsplash:
If you have white countertops, a cleaner with bleach included or soft-scrub (see the recipe) can be used for stubborn stains. Be sure to follow the manufacturer's instructions, so you don't damage the surfaces. These are the basics for four common countertops:

Butcher-Block Countertops
Items Needed:

1. Warm, soapy water
2. A mild bleach solution
3. A non-abrasive kitchen cleaner

How to Clean:

1. Use a toothbrush along the edging to remove any debris.
2. If the surface feels tacky, use a baking soda and water paste.
3. Then, rinse thoroughly.

Marble Countertops
Cleaning marble countertops is a bit different. It should be cleaned regularly with a soft, damp cloth (microfiber works well) to prevent streaks. Rinse it thoroughly to remove any residue. Wipe it dry because air drying can create water spots.

If acidic foods stain the surface such as wine, orange juice, or tomatoes; you may need to have the professionals clean the spot.

Ceramic Tile Countertops

You can use soap and water to clean ceramic tiles, but you need to be sure to rinse them thoroughly because soap can leave a filmy residue behind. Add some vinegar to the water to alleviate this issue. Never use an abrasive pad or cleaner.

Note: Even though the tile doesn't stain easily—the grout will—with bacterial buildup as a result. Use a mild bleach solution and a toothbrush to clean the grout.

Concrete Countertops
Clean the surface with warm and soapy water. Rinse it thoroughly. You can use a mild bleach solution, but never use a scouring pad or abrasive cleaner on the surfaces.

For stubborn stains, make a paste of baking soda and water. You may also use talc mixed with a mixture of bleach, ammonia, or hydrogen peroxide.

Apply the paste to the stained area, and use a soft brush to scrub the stain gently. Rinse thoroughly.

Super-Clean the Garbage Disposal

If you smell something that seems rancid, it could be the garbage disposal needs some cleaning also. Simply, grind a few lemons in the unit to make it fresh and clean. Repeat the process every few weeks. You can also sprinkle baking soda in the drain for several hours before running the disposal. For a deeper clean, use this method for the garbage disposal drain:

Items Needed:
- White Vinegar (1 Cup)
- Baking Soda (.5 cup)

How to Clean:
1. The mixture will fizz (remember pop rocks candy from the 1970s) with a popping noise.
2. Wait a few minutes.
3. Pour boiling water down the drain.
4. Fill the drain with 2 cups of ice.
5. Pour one cup of salt in the drain over the ice cubes (rock salt or sea salt is a good choice if you have it).
6. Turn the cold water faucet to the on position.
7. Turn on the disposal unit.
8. Run the disposal until the ice is gone.
9. The grime and debris should be loosened. Cut a lime or lemon in half and let the disposal chew them up for a deodorized drain.

Clean the Dingy Copper Pots

Copper pots hanging in a kitchen makes it have a charming, homey effect. Not only that, but it also saves a lot of space. However, you want to keep the surfaces shiny. Try one of these natural remedies that might surprise you:

- **Catsup:** Give catsup a whirl; it will look really gross, but the acid will help cut through the tarnished surface.
- **Apple Cider Vinegar:** Pour some AC vinegar into a paper plate and let it soak. Rinse the pan and dry it completely.
- **Lemons & Salt:** Cut the lemon into wedges; dip a wedge into the salt, and rub the pan until it's clean. Rinse the pan quickly and thoroughly in cold water, and wipe it dry.
- **Beer:** Put some beer on the pot. Let it sit for a couple of minutes. Rinse and wipe it until dry and shiny.
- **Cottage Cheese:** This is a cure that works without any scrubbing. Leave a layer of cottage cheese on the bottom for approximately five minutes. Rinse it completely and dry.

Don't Trash Your Favorite Mug
If you have stained coffee mugs, try this solution:
- Use sea salt or coarse salt mixed with a little lemon juice and scrub.
- Also, try baking soda and water made into a paste.
- This also works well on stained tea cups or coffee mugs, and even the cutting board.

Tackle the Oven Naturally
Use natural products to clean the oven manually. You can choose from several techniques for general cleaning of your oven.

Natural Oven Cleaner: Option 1: Simply apply a layer of baking soda and spray it with a vinegar solution. It should form a paste. Leave the mixture on the surface of the oven for five minutes. Wipe the oven with a damp rag or sponge.

Natural Oven Cleaner: Option 2: First, take a look at one of the general natural cleaning option using baking soda:

Items Needed:

- Baking soda
- Water
- Spray bottle

How to Clean:

1. Begin by spraying the oven with water until it's damp.
2. Sprinkle a ¼-inch layer of the soda, making sure you cover the entire surface.
3. If you see a dry spot, respray it with the water.
4. Let the mixture rest for at least three to four hours with the oven *OFF*.
5. Wipe the paste with an old towel to remove the grime.
6. It could take several applications, but thank goodness, it is natural.

Natural Oven Cleaner: Option 3: If you're in a hurry, this will help remove the stuck on grease and food.

Items Needed:

- Baking soda (3 tbsp.)
- Warm water (1 cup)
- Castile soap (1 tbsp.)

Variations:

- Lemon & Clove: Add 5 drops each.

- Lemon: Add 10 drops essential oil
- Lemon & Rosemary: Add 5 drops of each oil.

How to Clean:

1. Add all of the ingredients into a spray bottle. Shake well to mix.
2. *To Use*: Spray the oven liberally and let it sit for about 15 minutes.
3. Wipe it clean with a cloth or sponge. Rinse and let it air dry.
4. *To Store*: Store the leftovers for up to two weeks. Shake to combine before using.

Pamper the Bath Space

Many professionals recommend using disposable disinfecting wipes for the faucet and handle to reduce bacteria buildup greatly. Several studies provided facts indicating the bacteria found on the toilet set are some of the same germs tested in the kitchen sink.

What a terrible thought, but cross contamination can happen. If you use a cloth cleaning rag in the bathroom, be sure it doesn't get washed with the same towels used in your kitchen. Think of the vicious circle of bacteria, from the kitchen to the bathroom before you wash your hands!

Use toothpaste as a scouring agent or multipurpose cleaner. It will shine the faucet, remove crayons from the wall, and serve many other purposes. Think of that when you start getting to the bottom of the tube. Why not try it and be frugal? You might use it from then on!

The Ventilation Fan

The bathroom vent fan can sometimes be overlooked, and it's a huge mistake because it could be circulating a lot of dust and possible mold spores from the bathroom.

Step 1: The safest thing to do first is to trip the circuit breaker. Use a tool to remove the protective cover. Prepare a container of hot water with dishwashing soap and let the cover soak.

Step 2: Use the nozzle attachment on the vacuum cleaner to remove the gunk from the fan blades and other nooks and crannies. Use a clean paintbrush to remove the debris from the motor.

Step 3: Wash and rinse the cover.

Step 4: Replace the cover.

Super-Scrub for the Toilets

- Pour ¼ Cup Chlorine Bleach
  OR
- Pour ½ Cup White Vinegar into the bowl.

Don't use either product at the same time. Let the product used sit for about an hour. Brush the entire interior with the brush and flush.

Cleaner for Limescale: Sometimes, Coca-Cola will remedy the issue of limescale buildups. The cola's natural acids will breakdown the lime

deposits. Pour the end of a glass of cola into the toilet, swish it around with the toilet brush, and see if it helps. The stains might be too deep, but many have reported the Coca-Cola does work!
However, at any rate, you can begin the cleaning process of the toilet by pouring a cup of baking soda into the toilet bowl. Let the soda soak for a few minutes. Use a stiff bristle brush and scrub the toilet as needed. Flush. If you still have some difficult spots, you probably need to use a damp pumice stone. It is abrasive but gentle enough not to damage the surface. The toilet brush should also be thoroughly cleaned after each use to prevent from spreading the bacterial germs. After you have cleaned the bowl, secure the handle of the brush between the bowl and the seat. Pour some bleach over the bristles and let it soak for a few minutes. Rinse it with a bucket of water.
It's essential to keep a clean toilet at all times. Imagine how the bowl releases particles/bacteria into the air each time it is flushed. It is similar to a fireworks display. If the bacteria linger, you could get sick from salmonella or E. coli as it flies around or lands on the handle and seat. It is best to close the lid before you flush. It is also best to store contact lenses and toothbrushes in the cabinet. Think about it; it's a risky health practice that has been performed for years. It's about time to change.

Super-Clean the Tub & Shower
Some heavy-duty products may be necessary to remove mildew stains and soap scum build-ups. If you have a shower caddy—it could be time for a replacement—or you can remove it and wash it. You can use a toothbrush for cleaning any small spaces such as the tub jets.
For the shower walls and sides of the tubs, use a mild abrasive and a sponge or cloth. Don't use a brush inside the tub because it can scratch the surface.
Tile Grout: Mix 1-part water and 3-part baking soda mixed into a paste. Apply to grout and let sit. Spray the area with a vinegar and water solution. Scrub with a toothbrush. After the cleaner finishes foaming; rinse with plain water.
For Deeper Stains: The nasty grout can be tackled with a mixture of 1-part bleach, 10-parts water, and a soft bristled brush.
Clean The Shower Head: Use an old toothbrush and bathroom cleaner (such as the new version of Soft-Scrub) to clean the shower head. If you have mineral deposits blocking the holes, you can soak the showerhead using a rubber band, a plastic bag, and white vinegar.

This method works well with heads made from stainless steel, chrome, or other protected metal surfaces.
1. Slip the rubber band over the top of the showerhead (loop the band around the arm at least twice so the bag will remain in place.
2. Wait for one hour.
3. Remove the bag and rinse with water.
4. Polish with a soft rag.

If the vinegar solution isn't sufficient, you will need to remove the showerhead for more extensive cleaning. Use the following process to make the job a little simpler:

Disconnect the Showerhead:

- Cushion your tool with a cloth as you work, so the surface finish is protected.
- Use a screwdriver to remove the nut at the shower arm.
- Rinse the showerhead under a faucet (upside down) to remove any loosened debris.
- Dismantle and clean the shower head. If you still see buildups; use a toothbrush, safety pin, or toothpick to poke out any leftover deposits.
- Soak the parts in vinegar overnight.
- Thoroughly rinse the showerhead in the morning.
- Reassemble and install the showerhead.
- Wrap new plumbing tape around the threads of the shower arm for a good seal.
- Reattach the head to the shower arm with a wrench.
- Use a soft towel or rag to prevent damage.

Towel Racks & the Hand Towels

Always use the sanitize setting on your washing machine or bleach the towels. Replace them every three or four days. Think of this as you are stripping the bathroom for its deep cleaning. Why not rewash all of the towels for a clean start?

Thoroughly clean the towel bar. If possible, don't install the towel rack near the toilet. Think of the germs, especially with a moist towel. In the future, be sure to use a towel bar so the towel can thoroughly dry. With a crumpled towel, the moisture can create bacteria.

Quick & Easy Ways to Refresh the Space

To finish off the bathroom space, choose a corner of the closet, and add a container of baking soda to help absorb any of the musty odors which can collect. Avoid using products, including Lysol or Febreze, because they do have a host of chemicals that could be harmful to you.

Essential Oils: (Optional) These are a few of the most popular scents to add to your cleaning products. Essential oils provide many benefits, but for now, the focus is on disinfecting and cleaning qualities. Be sure you purchase essential oils - not fragrance oils. However, the list is unlimited:

- Tea Tree Oil: Antifungal, antibacterial, antiviral, antiseptic & antimicrobial
- Eucalyptus: Deodorizer & anti-infective

- Lemon: Antiviral, anti-infective, antiseptic & antifungal
- Lime: Air Freshener
- Grapefruit: antiseptic & air freshener
- Clove: Air freshener
- Orange: Air freshener
- Lavender: Antifungal, anti-infective & antiseptic
- Peppermint: Antiviral, antiseptic, antifungal & Antibacterial
- Rosemary: Antiviral, antiseptic, antimicrobial, antifungal & antibacterial

Super-Clean the Carpeted Spaces

Use preventive maintenance to eliminate part of the dirt that can enter your home and become embedded into your carpet. Begin by arranging doormats in front of each of your home's entrances. Vacuum your carpeting at least twice each week to ensure your youngster cannot pick up any undesirable morsels. You also help control dust, dust mites, and other irritants. Invest in a strong vacuum with a HEPA filter.

Choose Nontoxic Alternatives

If you have small children, you will want to use a non-toxic, non-irritating alternative to chemical cleaners. Be sure to clean up spills using a cloth immediately. Don't rub; blot the spot. Try one of these solutions:

- Sprinkle baking soda, cornstarch or cornmeal over greasy stains.
- If you have a red wine stain, try a rag with plain club soda to help remove the spot.
- Help remove any sticky 'stuff' using a piece of ice. Scrape off hard substances with using a butter knife. Then, mix one cup of water with 1/2 teaspoon liquid dish detergent together or mix 1/3 cup white vinegar with 2/3 cup warm water. Spray with the mixture to clean the spot.
- Steam clean using plain water. For extra tough stains mix 1.5 cups of white vinegar with 2.5 gallons of water.

Steer clear of the cleaned carpet for at least six hours. Carpets that don't dry efficiently are prone to mildew, mold, and fungal growth. Open the windows for fresh air circulation and thoroughly vacuum the spot. For extra deodorizing, use a shaking of baking soda.

Avoid wet-washing the carpet on humid days. Use fans, pointing them directly them over damp carpeting. Choose products you know will be safe for your toddler, such as the ones described in this cleaning book of guidelines. After the carpet dries, just sprinkle with baking soda and wait a few minutes for it to absorb the odors. Vacuum as usual.

Carpet Freshener

Items Needed:

- Cinnamon Leaf essential oil (30 drops)

- Clove Bud essential oil (10 drops)
- Lemongrass essential oil (30 drops)
- Eucalyptus essential oil (30 drops)
- Bicarbonate soda/Baking soda (.5 cup)

How to Prepare & Use:

1. Simply blend all of the ingredients in a wide mouth jar.
2. Close the lid for 24 hours.
3. Add a sprinkle when the carpet needs refreshing, and leave it there for 10 to 15 minutes before you vacuum away the residue.

Super-Clean the Laundry Space
The Washer
Items Needed:

- White Vinegar (for a natural source) or Bleach
- Baking Soda
- Microfiber Cloth
- Tooth Brush

Step 1: Select the hottest water setting and fill the washer to the highest load size and the longest wash cycle.

Step 2: As the washer is filling, add one cup of bleach and one quart of white vinegar.

Step 3: Add one cup of baking soda. Close the washer's lid, and agitate for approximately one minute.

Step 4: Let the water, vinegar, and baking soda (or bleach) soak in the tub for about an hour. It is easy just to leave the top open.

Step 5: While the tub is soaking, remove any removable parts for a soak. Don't forget the bleach and fabric softener cups if they are removable. After they are rinsed and dried, you can replace them.

Step 6: Use a small brush such as a toothbrush to clean the topmost part of the agitator and other difficult spaces to reach spots.

Step 7: Make sure to clean the sides and the top of the machine lid.

Step 8: After one hour of soaking, close the lid, and let the cycle run its course.

Step 9: You can clean around all of the dials with a vinegar solution.

Step 10: Repeat one more hot wash with another quart of vinegar to clear away any loosened residue left from the first wash/rinse cycle.

Step 11: After the washer completes its cycle, wipe the bottom and sides of the washing tub with a vinegar mixture to remove any lingering residue.

Tip: Leave the lid open to allow a thorough drying out to prevent mildew.

Clean the Dryer
The first step is to remove the lint filter and give it a thorough cleaning. Use a duster in the filter well to retrieve the lint out of the trap. You can also use the vacuum cleaner's narrow wand/crevice tool for speedier cleanup time. Wipe all surfaces with a white vinegar solution.

Check the duct work behind the dryer. Use a vacuum to remove all of the lint and dust. Check the outside of the vent to be sure the flap can move freely. If not, the lint will block the vent and be a possible fire hazard.

Wash the exterior of the dryer with warm, sudsy water. Rinse the soap residue away by using a clean damp rag. Use a dry one to shine the surface.

Refresh the Clothes Washer and Dryer
Add one or two drops of oil into the washer (lemon and lavender are fresh aromas). Pour a bit of your chosen oil on a cloth and toss it in the dryer. It will make your clothes and the house have a wonderful smell.

Last but Not Least: Pamper Yourself
Homemade Liquid Hand Soap
It is best to purchase the items needed and make your own healthy formula to pamper your hands. After all, saving money with a high-quality product is what a minimalist home is all about.

Check these two options:

Option #1: Baby Mild Hand Soap
Items Needed:
- Pure castile soap (2- 5-ounce bars) ex. Baby Mild
- Distilled or filtered water (1 gallon)
- *Optional*: Vanilla extract or essential oils
- *Also Needed*: Large Pot

How It's Made:
1. Grate the soap bars until you have a large pile of shredded soap.
2. Warm up your water in a very large pot. Let it boil if you aren't using distilled water. Lower the setting and let it cool (hot, not boiling).
3. Stir in the soap chunks. Keep stirring until all the little flakes are dissolved.
4. Remove the mixture from the heat. Let it sit for 12 to 24 hours. The mixture will thicken during this time. Stir occasionally throughout the day.
5. Stir in your essential oils or vanilla extract, if using. Start small and put in enough until you get the right amount of aroma for you.
6. Pour the mixture into containers. This will make quite a bit. I was able to fill three soap dispensers and five other fairly large storage containers.
7. Enjoy your toxic-free, frugal, and easy homemade liquid hand soap.

Option #2: Simple Liquid Hand Soap
What You Need:
- Liquid castile soap - Your favorite

- Filtered or Distilled water
- Optional: Foaming Soap dispenser

How to Prepare:
1. Combine the fixings.
2. Fill a soap dispenser with a small amount of liquid castile soap; roughly 1 tablespoon.
3. Adjust the amounts depending on how thick you like your soap.

Minimalistic Bugs No More

Nothing is more worrisome than to be bothered by a mosquito. You can keep them away naturally without commercial chemical products. Forget those pricey products that don't work.

Healthy Bug Repellent Lotion Bar

This is what you need:

- Organic Coconut Oil (.25 cup)
- Castor Oil (.125 cup)
- 10 drops each of:
    - Eucalyptus Oil
    - Citronella Oil
    - Clove Bud Essential Oil
- .33 cup each of:
    - Raw Cocoa Butter
    - Beeswax pellets

How to Prepare:

1. Put the pellets, castor oil, cocoa butter, and coconut oil in a heavy-duty saucepan using the medium heat setting.
2. Once all of the oil, butter, and wax are melted; remove from the burner to cool (3 to 4 minutes).
3. Blend in the essential oils.
4. Empty it into a preferred mold, tin or jar

Suggestion: A basic soap mold will do the trick. Be sure the container can handle the hot product. Cut the bars into chunks and place in a decorative container.

Directions for Use:

1. Rub the bar between your hands to help the solution melt enough to rub gently over your exposed skin.
2. You will receive a pleasing smell which is so mild; it's safe for your children.

Bug Spray: Option 1

What You Need:

- Boiled or distilled water
- Natural witch hazel
- Choose from Clove, Lemongrass, Tea Tree, Citronella, Cajuput, Cedar, Eucalyptus, Catnip, Mint, or Lavender.
- *Optional*: Vegetable glycerin

How to Prepare:

1. Fill an 8-ounce bottle half full of water.
2. Add the witch hazel and ½ tsp. of vegetable glycerin (if used).
3. Add 30 to 50 drops of the chosen scent.
4. *Note*: Remember when the oils are increased, you are also increasing the aroma.

Bug Spray: Option 2

What You Need:

- Emulsifier (1 tsp.)
- Vinegar (4 oz.)
- Eucalyptus (50 drops)

- 25 drops each of:
  - Spearmint
  - Lemon

How to Prepare & Use:

1. Blend the essential oils in a spray bottle with the emulsifier, and the vinegar.
2. Shake well to mix.
3. Spray around the baseboards to keep the bugs away.

Bug Repellent: Option #3 for a Cold Air Diffuser

What You Need & Instructions:

1. 1 drop of each essential oil: Lemongrass |thyme |basil |eucalyptus
2. Add about 70 ml of water.
3. Combine each of the ingredients.
4. Use as desired.

"The secret of happiness, you see, is not found in seeking more, but in developing the capacity to enjoy less." —Socrates

CONCLUSION
Maintain A Minimalistic Viewpoint

"Simplicity is the glory of expression." —Walt Whitman

The process of decluttering enables you to remove 10% of your items but also remove 10% of the budget. Live frugally. Once again, be honest—will you miss that small number of belongings? However, you must realize that clutter is present in many forms. You find it on daily 'to-do' lists, on your email account, and the Internet with mindless scrolling. You are cluttering your mind as well—good or bad—it distracts you from your personal goals. Keep only one (1) credit card—or maybe two. The card can be used as a financial tool, but be careful not to overspend. Remember that you will be paying interest on the money when you make the purchases. Even if it is a sale item, the interest payments may exceed the sale price. Think twice! This is a vital step toward becoming debt-free.

Appreciate what you have, and get organized. According to the National Association of Professional Organizers, in your lifetime, you will spend approximately one year looking for items—just one more reason to live with fewer items to clutter your home and your mind.

Clean up as you go, and only touch it once! Both of these make everything much easier. Cleaning up as you cook makes cleaning up after eating much quicker, especially if the dishwasher is empty. The dishes won't be piling up in the sink—but rather be put in the dishwasher ready to be cleaned.

Find a supportive group of people who understand your challenges as you prepare your home using the minimalist approach. By having an intentional community to provide you with encouragement and support during your journey will surely increase your success rate.

It is a learning process, and you will make mistakes. Practice the guidelines and stay in touch with your personal style. Carefully and intentionally are the best advice you can receive when it comes to shopping. It is difficult to stop the old habits of impulsive purchasing items, but with practice, you can improve. You will soon discover—living with less is much less stressful! While it may seem that reducing clutter in your life is an impossible task, you absolutely can do it! Just take baby steps—start right now by addressing your own belongings. Find a support group and challenge each other!

Try it now—visualize what your life could be at the end of your journey. Imagine how your home can look with fewer items cluttering all of its surfaces. Think of the ways you could spend the time if you don't have a stack of dirty laundry or a pile of discarded toys laying around your space. Stay motivated and remove those unhappy visions. It will help you get through the tough times.

Finally, if you found this book useful in any way, a review on Amazon is always appreciated!

DESCRIPTION

Don't be confused because *Minimalist Home* includes all family members—no question about that! Simplifying family life should be a quest for the entire family. These are the topics you will learn more about minimalistic behavior:

- Minimalism Mindsets & Habits
- What Minimalism Is & Isn't
- Making a Plan
- Declutter & Organize the Kitchen
- Declutter the Dining Area
- Declutter & Organize the Bath Area
- Declutter the Living Room
- Revamp the Office
- Reorganize the Bedrooms
- For Kids Only: Minimalism
- Declutter Laundry Spaces
- Clean & Organize Spare Storage Areas
- Methods of Containment & Removal
- Benefits of a Minimalistic Home
- The Minimalist Mindset
- The Minimalist Plan for Home Maintenance

Each of these topics are fully explained, so you will soon understand the theories involved with minimalist behavior and how to maintain your home.

"It is always the simple that produces the marvelous." —Amelia Barr

MINIMALIST MINDSET

Minimalism Habits & Mindsets to Declutter Your Life, Retake Your Personal and Financial Discipline, and Make Your Passions A Priority to Achieve A Better Life!

By
Jenifer Scott

© Copyright 2019 by Jenifer Scott - All rights reserved.

This book is provided with the sole purpose of providing relevant information on a specific topic for which every reasonable effort has been made to ensure that it is both accurate and reasonable. Nevertheless, by purchasing this book you consent to the fact that the author, as well as the publisher, are in no way experts on the topics contained herein, regardless of any claims as such that may be made within. As such, any suggestions or recommendations that are made within are done so purely for entertainment value. It is recommended that you always consult a professional prior to undertaking any of the advice or techniques discussed within.

This is a legally binding declaration that is considered both valid and fair by both the Committee of Publishers Association and the American Bar Association and should be considered as legally binding within the United States.

The reproduction, transmission, and duplication of any of the content found herein, including any specific or extended information will be done as an illegal act regardless of the end form the information ultimately takes. This includes copied versions of the work both physical, digital and audio unless express consent of the Publisher is provided beforehand. Any additional rights reserved.

Furthermore, the information that can be found within the pages described forthwith shall be considered both accurate and truthful when it comes to freely available information and general consent. As such, any use, correct or incorrect, of the provided information will render the Publisher free of responsibility as to the actions taken outside of their direct purview. Regardless, there are zero scenarios where the original author or the Publisher can be deemed liable in any fashion for any damages or hardships that may result from any of the information discussed within.

Finally, any of the content found within is ultimately intended for entertainment purposes and should be thought of and acted on as such. Due to its inherently ephemeral nature nothing discussed within should be taken as an assurance of quality, even when the words and deeds described herein indicated otherwise. Trademarks and copyrights mentioned within are done for informational purposes in line with fair use and should not be seen as an endorsement from the copyright or trademark holder.

INTRODUCTION

Congratulations on purchasing this book and thank you for doing so.

There's only one thing that's needed to live a life that is simple, yet perfectly filled with contentment and happiness. Get rid of everything that is unnecessary. It may be the integral step that is needed, but you'd be surprised at just how difficult many people find this step to be.

Sifting through your belongings, deciding what stays and what goes can be a bittersweet experience, maybe even stressful for some. Going through each item that you own and asking yourself the one fundamental question all minimalists do - do I really need this? - Is going to be more time consuming than you anticipated if you don't have a plan, let alone know where to begin. Before you begin yanking stuff off your shelves and out of your closets, you need to understand what you're getting yourself into by familiarizing yourself with what minimalism is going to entail. Minimalism is about being intentional with what you allow into your life and what you surround yourself with. It is a tool which is about teaching you how to live your life with purpose and intention, focusing on what you value most in your life by removing the material objects which are distracting your focus.

Minimalism is going to free you from the chains of the modern "clutter culture" that we live in by reminding you that true happiness lies not with your belongings, but in the relationships and experiences that you have. It reminds you that happiness isn't waiting for you at the department stores, but at home where your family and your friends are.

For far too long we have subjected ourselves to rushing from one task to another, putting in longer hours at work at the expense of spending time with our loved ones or pursuing our passion, struggling to stay on top of all our bill payments yet somehow falling deeper into a debt cycle we find it hard to get out of. Minimalism is about to change all of that, and the following chapters are going to show you just how to do it.

There are plenty of books on this subject on the market, thanks again for choosing this one! Every effort was made to ensure it is full of as much useful information as possible, please enjoy!

CHAPTER 1
Minimalism And Happiness

Looking around your home, all you see are piles of stuff around you. You find yourself spending far too much time searching for things around your house, even though you were sure you knew right where you left it. Searching among piles your stuff, you occasionally get frustrated because it takes far too long to find what you're looking for. Sometimes during the search, you come across items you don't even remember you had. Does this sound all too familiar?

If you answered yes, then you've got far too much stuff. Having a mess around the home is one thing, but far too much clutter could be drowning you. Every home tends to get messy every now and then, but when you've got clutter, its constant presence could be stressing you out more than you realize.

Why Too Much Clutter Could Be Drowning You

Most people are drowning in their own clutter and they don't even know it, piles of letters, mail, and magazines in one corner. Papers, documents, and stacks of books in another, expired food in the fridge. Closets bursting full of clothes, some of which you may not have worn in over a year or even forgotten about. Old shoes, furniture that needs repairing but you haven't quite had time for, so they are stashed away in the corner of your garage. Souvenirs and mementos you've had since your childhood, gifts you've received over the years but never used.

Chances are that there is at least one area (if not more) around your home that is just piled with far too much stuff. When you look at that pile, you don't even know how the mess accumulated to that extent. Why does it seem so hard to constantly try and stay on top of the material possessions that we own? And yet, we keep buying even more stuff to add to the growing mess. For many, having clutter around the home comes down to the simple process of too much stuff coming in, not enough going out.

There could be several reasons why you're drowning in your own clutter, the first being that you simply don't put things away where they belong. How many times have you walked in through the front door and tossed whatever it was you were holding at the nearest available spot? Did you stop to ask yourself where the item truly belongs? Getting into the habit of haphazardly chucking things in random places around your home and then forgetting about them is how clutter keeps accumulating. We have limited space around our homes, and it can be difficult to place items away when there really is "no proper home" for them to go. Every item around your home should have a designated "home", which can be difficult if all your free space is being taken up by items you don't even need or use anymore.

Cleaning is not exactly an activity to look forward to, and when you procrastinate and keep putting off cleaning the mess around your home, that's how clutter starts to build. The bigger the mess, the longer it is going to take you to clean. A 5-minute cleanup is now going to take 2-3 hours to get done when the mess has grown far too big.

Your home is like a boat on the ocean, and the clutter is the water that keeps filling up that boat until you eventually sink to the bottom under the weight of it all. You are responsible for the clutter that is in your life, especially when you keep buying stuff that you don't necessarily need. Every time that you add even more stuff to your home, you're filling your boat a little more. Not enough clutter going out and far too much clutter coming in will eventually sink you right down to the bottom. You don't want to wait until that point before actively doing something about it.

The problem is that most people don't realize just how negatively impacted they are by the chaos and disorganized mess that is going on in their lives. It's only when you start getting rid of all the unnecessary things that you begin to see and feel what a difference it makes. If you feel that your life is surrounded by far too much clutter, how many of these negative impacts are you already experiencing?

- **You've Lost Your Motivation** - Just thinking about cleaning the mess in your home leaves you feel overwhelmed that you lose your motivation entirely, and that lack of motivation is now starting to affect the other areas of your life.
- **You Find It Hard to Get Anything Done** - Productivity can be low when you're distracted by all the mess that is surrounding you. Not just at home, but at work too. A messy cubicle and work desk can make it hard to get anything done, even more so if you spend far too much time looking for items because you can't find them among the mess.
- **You Feel Lethargic and Tired All the Time** - Being constantly stressed out tends to do that to you. You may think you're not stressed or bothered too much by the piles of clutter you see around you, but subconsciously you are. Some people just look at clutter and automatically feel tired at the very thought of having to work through the mess and clear it up.
- **You Hold Onto the Past** - Holding onto clutter is the same as holding onto the past. You find it hard to let go of some items, even when you know you should, because of the sentimental value and memories which are attached to it. Sometimes you don't even want to get rid of it because it was a gift and you're worried about hurting the other person's feelings. You know you're never going to use it, but you hold onto it anyway. Holding onto items that are no longer of any use to you is only going to keep you from moving forward because you can't look ahead when you're constantly looking back.
- **You've Lost Your Sense of Purpose** - Clutter has a way of affecting you mentally and physically without you even knowing it. Being surrounded by disorganization makes it hard for anyone to

concentrate. When it becomes impossible to have clarity in your life, you begin to question and wonder what you're doing with your life.
- **You Procrastinate More Than You Should** - Clutter encourages procrastination. When you're constantly putting off clearing and cleaning up until "tomorrow", that kind of thinking is going to develop into an unhealthy behavior pattern which is going to extend into other areas of your life, and procrastination is never a good habit to have.
- **You seem to Experience More Disharmonies** - Clutter has been known to be the cause of many arguments and squabbles amongst family, friends, roommates, and coworkers. If you are the one who is responsible for the clutter, being nagged or pressured into clearing it up is going to aggravate you and that will spark an argument. If you are the one who is having to live or deal with a messy individual, on the other hand, you will be the one constantly chasing after them to clean up after themselves, which is still going to aggravate you anyway and spark an argument.
- **You Feel Depressed Looking At Your Mess** - When all you see is mess surrounding your life, you can't help but sometimes feel hopeless, wondering how it came to this. These feelings will be amplified over time if nothing is done about the clutter, and as it grows, so too do your feelings of misery and despair.
- **You've Forgotten What's Important in Life** - Clutter and mess are nothing but a distraction, taking your attention away from what you should be focusing on in your life. The time and the hours that you spend cleaning up could be put to better use doing something productive, something that is going to bring you one step closer to your goals. Clutter distracts you from what's important in life, taking up more of your attention and time.

For all of these reasons and more, a change for the better is needed. That change is minimalism.

What Is Minimalism?

It is an approach which is going to help you reclaim your freedom. If you're yearning to be free from the feeling of being overwhelmed all the time, free from the feelings of guilt, stress and worry, free from feeling like you're constantly trapped in a cycle that you can't get out of, minimalism is the tool that is going to open that new pathway towards a better, lighter, freer and happier you.

There is nothing wrong with having material possessions. We all need to have some items to live a comfortable life. It only becomes a problem when we start to attach far too much meaning to our belongings that we forget about the truly important things in our life, the things that money can't buy. The relationships you have with your family and friends, your good health, gratitude for the many blessings that you have, your passion, your goals, and your dreams, the desire to grow and become all that you can be. Those are the things that matter the most, and when we become far too caught up in materialism, these other aspects are often forsaken.

Owning a couple of material possessions that bring you true happiness is perfectly okay. Minimalism is just the tool that is going to help you be more conscious, more deliberate about the things that you do bring into your life. It is about clearing away all the other unnecessary, non-essential items in your life so you can make room and space for the items that bring you true joy. It is about freeing yourself from the burden of being weighed down by the unnecessary mess to make way for a life filled with more meaning and organization. It doesn't just involve clearing the physical clutter, but the emotional and mental clutter too. Minimalism is about clearing away the distractions to focus on what's important.

Your home would look a lot different without all the unused items which are taking up space. Imagine living in an environment that is simple, clean and with lots of free space and surfaces. Imagine opening your closet doors and being greeted with a view that is simple and stress-free, where clothes are not being cramped and squished together and piled haphazardly on shelves. Doesn't that image seem a lot more pleasant? What about a schedule that is less cluttered and filled with only the very important tasks and appointments instead, which leaves you more free time to focus on doing something for yourself? Doesn't that sound a lot better?

Minimalism is a concept which extends to almost every aspect of your life. It's not just limited to cleaning out your home or your work station. Minimalism even extends to relationships, where you only maintain and keep meaningful and important ones. It even extends to your daily schedule, where you focus on doing less and having a schedule that is not as cluttered as it normally would. Doing less, but everything that is on your schedule is going to be something that is both productive and important.

Minimalists live their lives a lot more efficiently simply because they save a lot of time by having less to deal with. Less clutter means less time spent organizing and cleaning up. Fewer possessions mean less time being distracted. A lot of people are hesitant at first to take up this approach because the very thought of having to part with your belongings - sometimes A LOT of belongings - can be terrifying. The idea of living with less is not something a lot of us are accustomed to. What if this lifestyle isn't what you thought it would be? What if you need to get rid of items that you are not using, but love far too much you couldn't bear the thought of giving them away?

It is okay to have those fears. You're about to begin a new lifestyle change, some concerns are bound to happen. The beauty of minimalism which you will come to realize is that there are not fixed rules which determine the way that you live, none at all. There is not one way or one approach that you absolutely must abide by. The way you live your life as a minimalist is going to be entirely up to you and what works best for you. You can be a minimalist and still have an expensive car. You can be a minimalist and still own a Mac, a house and an iPad. If you need all those items to live and survive comfortably, there is absolutely nothing wrong with owning them. You can still have all those things and call yourself a minimalist. Find what works for you.

Minimalism doesn't mean tossing out almost everything that you own before you can call yourself a minimalist. Minimalism simply means living only on the necessities. It means having one car instead of two. If one car is more than enough for you to survive comfortably, it means owning one iPad instead of two if one is all you need. It's about owning 10 items of clothing which you love and use all the time and getting rid of the old, barely used ones that don't even fit you properly anymore. That's minimalism. Downsizing and simplifying instead of overcomplicating and cluttering.

As you prepare to begin, it is important to note one thing. Reducing the material belongings that you have does result in minimalism, but it is not minimalism itself. Donating and getting rid of a lot of things that you don't need any more doesn't automatically make you a minimalist. It is just one aspect of minimalism, not the entire thing. To truly begin embracing this mindset and this approach to life, minimalism calls for reassessing what your priorities are. Your priorities are what are going to help you get rid of the excess and anything else that doesn't bring value into your life, including relationships. Minimalism is about getting in touch with what's important to you so you can invest more time and effort into it for greater happiness. This mindset is meant to show you that physical and material possessions don't bring you nearly as much joy as you thought it did initially.

Minimalism is going to encourage you to take a deep-dive into reassessing what your passions, your dreams, and your goals are. It is going to encourage you to shift your focus and invest your energies into your passion and the things that matter. Getting rid of the material possessions is just one part of the journey, and the more important part of the process is making the transition towards focusing on your priorities and coming to the realization that life could change for the better when you're not focused on the wrong aspects.

The transition to minimalism is going to be a difficult journey for many. We are all attached to at least some of our possessions, and getting rid of them is going to be a hard task. If you find yourself struggling with this part of the process, take some time to process and figure out what items are worth keeping and which are okay letting go of. The amount of possessions you have at the end of your decluttering process is not what matters, as long as the ones which are left behind are enough to let you lead a happy life. Some people are happy owning less than 100 items, while others may need 150 items to keep them happy.

Before you begin to declutter, it is important that you remember not to get rid of stuff simply because you can, or because you're beginning this new process. Going overboard and clearing out everything that you can without stopping to think about whether it is worth getting rid off could lead you to throw out something that you might actually need or love. When you get rid of something and then realize later on that you actually needed it, you're going to have to go out and spend more money buying a replacement. Money - which you could have saved instead because buying a new item was unnecessary if you still had the old one. Decluttering can be a very emotional phase of the journey, and you should take your time working through the process instead of rushing for the sake of getting it over with.

A good approach to begin easing yourself into minimalism is to test the waters first before launching yourself completely into the process. If you cleared out your bookshelf and kept only a few essential books which are needed or make you happy, don't get rid of the cleared books immediately, but rather store them away somewhere for several weeks. If at the end of several weeks you find that you were perfectly happy living without those books, then you know that you can live without them. If you can live without them and still be happy, then it's okay to either donate them or toss them. This way, you give yourself time to adjust and if you find that there's still something in the pile that you cleared away which you need, there's still time to salvage the situation.

One of the most liberating benefits that come with being a minimalist is how these now freed-up resources can be then applied to the other areas of your life. Owning less stuff means saving more money since you're not spending as much, which then leaves you with more money to spend when there is something which you genuinely need. You wouldn't need to scramble to find the resources anymore because you already have them on hand.

Why Become a Minimalist?

Because you don't want to spend the rest of your life being controlled by a life of excess consumerism, clutter, distractions and just far too much going on. Money and belongings will never be able to buy or bring you the kind of lasting happiness that you seek, and if you continue to chase after the wrong things in life, all the good things in life may just pass you by before you have a chance to grab onto it. You could own everything your heart desires and still feel like something is missing, or that life is incomplete.

That feeling is not going to go away, not until you learn how to focus on the meaningful aspects of your life which have nothing to do with how much you own. Minimalism is appealing to you right now for a reason, and that reason is that you seek something more.

In fact, have you ever thought that you might already be a minimalist without even knowing it? You could already be displaying tendencies towards minimalism if you do any of the following:

- You have empty sections or rooms in your home that are clear and unused.
- You don't have a lot of debt because you don't spend more than you make.
- You don't feel the urge to buy something every time you're in a department store.

- You've been spring cleaning, donating and getting rid of items for a while now and you're perfectly comfortable doing it.
- You don't hold onto unnecessary items, even if they were gifts from friends or family.
- You can't stand the sight of clutter because it drives you crazy.
- You are inspired by stories of travelers who can spend months on vacation with nothing more than a backpack.
- You've been curious about the concept of minimalism ever since you heard about it.

The Incredible Benefits Which Minimalism Brings

For almost every action and decision we make, we hope to get some benefit out of it. If you decided you wanted to change the way that you live, you're doing it because you want to reap the benefits that come with this change. That's why they call it a change for the better, and one of the greatest benefits that come with living life as a minimalist is the lasting happiness that this mindset is going to bring. At the end of the day, there is nothing that we want for ourselves more than happiness. All the material possessions in the world are not going to mean much if happiness still seems to elude you.

Minimalists are happy because they base their happiness on the number of things that they own. Their happiness comes not from belongings, but from life itself, and it is entirely up to them to determine what's important and what's going to make them happy. Minimalists have found that this lifestyle has helped them eliminate discontent by focusing on what matters most, reclaim their time and taught them to live in the moment. This approach has helped them pursue their passions and reconnect with their goals in life once again because they're not distracted by buying the latest car or the latest iPhone model which has just been released. They know that those aren't their goals anymore and thus, they are focused on creating a more meaningful life experience instead.

Other benefits that come with being a minimalist include:
- Helping you get out of debt by consuming less and saving more.
- Connecting you with work that you love by focusing on your priorities and keeping materialistic distractions at bay.
- More time for yourself to do something meaningful instead of spending that time cleaning or running from one task to another by focusing on the tasks that matter instead.
- Less mess, less stress.
- Cleaning becomes quicker and easier.
- You can always find what you're looking for around your home.
- Efficiency and productivity levels increase.
- Greater peace of mind when you learn how to focus on what matters most.
- An increase in self-confidence which comes from relying on yourself instead of being reliant on your belongings.

- Less fear of failure when you're not constantly worried about losing your material possessions because you no longer associate happiness with items.

If you know anyone who has embraced minimalism, they will be able to tell that the benefits you stand to gain will go far beyond anything that you could read about or hear about. It is one of those experiences that you need to live to see first-hand what a difference it is going to make.

CHAPTER 2
Living Life By Principles

Minimalism offers a unique perspective for those who follow this approach to living, teaching with a message that a life that is spent pursuing meaningful experience is a life that is far better than one spent chasing material possessions. This is a completely different approach than the one we have become so accustomed to, a life where we have grown up constantly surrounded by advertising messages which remind us we will never be enough without the latest product or gadget.

Buy this watch and you will be happy. Buy this car and all your dreams will come true. You are not complete unless you have this or that. It is never-ending, and the social media society which we are living in today is doing nothing to help the situation. Advertisements like this constantly push perfectionism through possessions, delivering subliminal messages that we need to constantly keep buying, buying and buying in order to fill our lives with happiness. In a world like this, we have completely lost sight of the simpler things in life that bring even more joy than any gadget or car ever could. In a world like this, we need minimalism now more than we ever have before.

Unlike what those advertisements want us to believe, we don't need a lot of things to be happy. True minimalism finds happiness in having less in order to be able to give more. Minimalism is here to remind us that we are good enough just the way that we are, despite what those advertisements say. We are perfectly capable of being happy even without the latest of everything. A life where far too much time is spent checking your notifications, checking your emails, picking out your clothes or spending even more than you should on something you don't need is not a life where you will find the happiness that is going to last a lifetime.

The very word "minimalism" may imply "less", but this approach to living offers you more than you realize. More clothes, more shoes, more watches, more cars, more collectibles aren't going to make you happy. More freedom, more time, more room for what's important, better health, less worry, more time with loved ones, more time spent pursuing your passion. That's where lasting happiness resides.

The Principles of Minimalism

Minimalists don't live their life by a set of rigid rules, but they do have a set of principles which provide them with guidance on how to make the most out of this concept. Among the basic principles which all minimalists abide by are:

- **Omit Needless Items** - This is going to be the primary principle and the constant theme which keeps resurfacing as you make your way through the rest of this book. Omit needless items, not every item that you own.

- **Identifying Essentials** - Minimalists are clear about which items are essential for them to live a happy and comfortable life. They select their items based on what's important to them, what makes them happy and which of their belongings is going to have the biggest impact on their lives and their careers. If the item serves a purpose and a benefit in your life, then don't get rid of it just yet. Minimize the number of times you check your emails in a day so you have more time for yourself. Arrange fewer meetings and more meaningful quality time with friends and family instead.
- **Everything Counts for Something** - Everything that a minimalist chooses to keep around in their life counts for something. Every item that they choose to maintain is one that is worth holding onto, and you must be clear about what those reasons are.
- **Be Filled with Joy** - As minimalists work hard to declutter their life from the unnecessary, they work just as hard to fill their lives with something which brings them meaning and joy. Spend time with your children, reconnect with old friends, take that vacation you've been wanting to for so many years, take up a new hobby, discover a new interest, anything that puts a smile on your face, fills you with excitement and brings you joy is worth spending a little bit more time on.
- **It's Not the End** - There is no end to minimalism, and when the decluttering process is over, it doesn't mean it's over. Minimalism is an ongoing process, and you're going to constantly be revisiting and observing your life, determining what else can be done to improve.
- **Everyday Is a Mindful Day** - Practicing mindfulness and awareness of their surroundings is how minimalists stay focused and grateful, finding joy in the little things in life. A simple get together with an old friend is something to be grateful for when you are mindful about how happy it makes you feel. Finding some unstructured time for yourself at the end of a busy week is something to feel happy about when you are mindful of how much this is helping you relax and unwind. Decluttering your calendar is something to be grateful for when you are mindful that it is freeing up more time for you to focus on your passions instead. Minimalists find a lot of reasons to be grateful and happy throughout the day, and it begins with practicing mindfulness.

How a Minimalist Approaches Life
There is an old Zen proverb which goes something like this:
"There was a horse galloping down the road, and it seemed like the man on the horse had somewhere important he needed to be. Another man standing alongside the road asked "Where are you going?", to which the man on the horse replied "I don't know. Ask the horse!"
Reflect upon that proverb for a minute. Does it resonate with you on some level? That feeling that life is somehow controlling you, and you have lost

control of the direction in which you are headed. You always seem to be in a hurry, rushing from one appointment or task to the next, but you have no real sense of purpose about what you're doing or where you're going. A life where you have lost control is one you cannot find contentment and happiness.

A minimalist approaches with the realization that if we only have so much space to spare, why would we let that limited space be occupied by the things that don't matter? This helps to put a lot of things in perspective, and the secret to how they find happiness in owning so little. Minimalists approach life by reminding themselves:

- **It Doesn't Need to Cost Money to Be Happy** - When you no longer attach meaning to the things that you own, the pursuit of happiness no longer lies with objects which are going to end up costing you money. It doesn't cost anything to spend time with your family. It doesn't cost you anything to spend time laughing and catching up with friends over good food and a few drinks. It doesn't cost you anything to meditate and unwind after a long day. It doesn't cost anything to be surrounded by people that you love and who love you in return. And all of these things will add more value to your life than anything you could ever buy in this lifetime.
- **They Are Not Static, They Are Dynamic** - You grow, you adapt and you change. You don't remain static for the rest of your life, and neither does minimalism. The lifestyle is going to adapt, change and grow right along with you. The way your life looks right now as a minimalist is not going to be exactly the same 10 years later, it is a process that is dynamic and constantly changing, never static.
- **To Pursue, But Don't Forget** - One of the main themes of minimalism is focusing on and pursuing your passion and the things that bring you joy. However, life does go on and there are still things that need to get done daily for survival. Minimalists go about their day like everyone else, waking up each morning, managing their families, heading off to work, coming home and then repeating the process. These other aspects of life need to be pursued for survival, but minimalists don't allow themselves to forget to pursue what matters too.
- **It Is the Intentional Purchases That Matter** - Minimalists know that it is their intentional decisions and choices that matter at the end of the day. Even with the purchases that you make. It is not about restricting yourself to what you can or cannot buy, but rather making intentional and mindful decisions about why you're making your decisions and how it is benefitting you to do it.
- **It Is About Making Life Simpler, Not Easier** - Don't fall into the trap of thinking minimalism is going to magically take away all of life's troubles and make it easier because it isn't. Minimalism is about living a simpler life, which may make the difficult parts easier to

handle. It is about creating simplicity to be able to handle the bigger challenges when you're not distracted by the unnecessary in your life. Minimalists make room in their life by removing the clutter so they can contribute more meaningfully.

What You're Going to Require to Begin Living like a Minimalist

With simplicity being a key theme of minimalism, being content with everything that you already have is a good requirement to start with. You can declutter and strip yourself down to the bare essentials and necessities, but you will never truly be able to rid yourself of the clutter in your life for good if you don't first learn to be content with what you have.

A lack of contentment will lead to the habit of constantly buying more things each time you feel dissatisfied, which is not what minimalism is about. The root cause of your need to purchase is because you are discontent with what you have right now. That's why you found yourself continuously buying things that you don't need, and the more you have, the more you just seemed to want. You constantly want more fun, more excitement, something greater, something better, something cooler. Nothing will ever be enough, and there will always be reasons to remain unhappy if you're not content with what you have, even though it is more than enough to keep you happy.

Which is why the very first requirement of minimalism is contentment, think about what it is that you genuinely need right now. Food, water, a roof over your head, clothes to keep you warm. A family, friends who care about you, a stable job helps pay the bills, a phone that works to keep in contact, a computer that works to help you get your job done. If you've got all that - you already have a lot to be grateful for. The latest gadgets and technology, the most stylish clothes, new pairs of shoes, a fancy car that you can show off, a bigger house that boasts your success, those are not essentials, nor are they necessities. You don't need those to be happy.

To begin living like a minimalist is also going to require that you put a stop to buying anything that is considered a non-necessity. Understandably, this is going to be a challenge if you have never done it before, and a great approach to help you through this process is to create a 30-day list for yourself, and it works wonderfully well at curbing impulsive spending and buying. From this moment on, each time you want to buy something that is considered a non-necessity, put it down on your list. Write down the date next to it so you know how to keep track once those 30-days are up. Keep that item on the list for the next 30-days, and if by the end of that you still have a strong desire for it and you've got the funds to spare, go ahead and make that purchase if it is going to make you happy. This is an effective approach to take because you many times you will find that your urge to purchase dissipates by the time those 30-days are over, which means you never really needed it to be happy anyway.

Minimalists have made it a requirement for themselves to learn how to be happy by doing instead of owning. It is absolutely possible to be happy living with only the necessities once you learn how to be content and realize you already have all that you need. When you focus and turn your attention instead to doing things which you know are going to make you happy instead of buying things which you think are going to make you happy, the need for stuff is going to fade away over time. Once you reach a certain point, there will be nothing left to buy anyway.

Minimalism is going to be a big change in your life, and good change like this isn't going to just happen overnight. You're not going to decide today that you want to embrace minimalism, wake up the next morning and find that everything has fallen perfectly into place. Like all good change, this is going to take time, and the consciousness of it all is the key to making the biggest difference. Being conscious of the needs vs. wants, the more vs. enough is going to be what helps shift your consciousness towards contentedness, which therein lies the foundation of what minimalism is all about. Socrates once said, "the secret to happiness is found not in seeking more, but by developing to enjoy less".

When you put your necessities into perspective, eliminating the non-necessities becomes an easier process. When you start to realize that you don't really need a ton of clothing when you don't wear half of it, it's easier to get rid of it. When you realize that the gadgets you have now are more than enough to get the job done and keep you happy, you don't need to go out and get more. A lot of the things which we think are necessary are not necessities. One of the problems that we are faced with is that we tend to categories our belongings as necessities, and that's because we are so used to having them around that we never thought we could live without them.

Like your car for example. We often see cars as necessities because they make our lives more convenient, but are they really a necessity? Surprisingly, they aren't, especially when there are lots of people out there who are surviving just fine without them. If you live in a location where decent public transport is easily available, that makes surviving without a car much easier. Public transport, not to mention rideshare options are abundantly available in most cities, and if you feel like getting in some exercise, you could always consider riding a bike instead of owning a car.

Something else that we think of as a necessity is having a closet full of garments. But do you need a closet that is bursting to the brim? You don't need to own lots of clothes, and if you are one of those people who only rotates between a few pieces of clothing which you feel most comfortable in, you'll quickly realize how true this is. It is possible to own just half the clothing that you have in your closet right now as still be perfectly happy. Why? Because everything that is going to be left in your closet is items which make you the happiest. Having a few, pieces of quality clothing which are going to last you several years is more than good enough to keep you happy. Minimalism requires that you simplify your life and the things that you do. Eliminating the physical clutter from your life is a good place to start, but simplifying the things that you do extends to your social life, work schedule and all the other daily tasks which you usually find yourself occupied with. Take a look at your daily task list and ask yourself, is everything that is on this list right now important or urgent? How is completing this task going to benefit or impact me? If there is no significant benefit to be had, then perhaps the task is not as urgent as you think it might be. Simplify the clutter that is in your schedule by listing your commitments down, and then picking a few of the most important ones to get done in a day. Avoid over-cluttering and scheduling and scheduling commitments to yourself back to back, you need some breathing space and time for yourself in between for - that's right - the important things.

Simplifying your schedule is probably going to be as challenging as decluttering the physical items around your home. Many people find it hard to say "no" or to have to refuse an appointment or a social event for fear of disappointing others. Learning to say no is one of the hardest things to do, but it is important to remember that you cannot please everyone at the expense of forgoing your own happiness. If an appointment or a task is not important, and it is going to take up too much time away from what you should be focusing on, it's time to learn how to say no.

Cut back on your to-do list, because you don't need to do every single thing on the list. You only have a set number of hours in a day, and you don't want to spend all that time filling it with meaningless tasks which don't bring you happiness. A to-do list is going to be never-ending, and the only way it is going to be simplified is if you do something about it. Another common misconception that many walks around with is the notion that we need to be "busy" all the time. Being busy and being effective are two completely different things. Minimalists could have 5 items on their to-do list, but every single item is important and will produce the highest impact on their lives. Those 5 items meaningful items are going to be a lot more effective than having 10 items which produce little to no impact. Get the important stuff done first. Everything else can wait.

Minimalism's Little Rules

Okay, so there may not be any hard and fast rules when it comes to living your life as a minimalist, but there are some rules that minimalists could go to if they need a little guidance when it comes to decluttering.

- **The 20/20 Rule** - The first rule is going to eliminate the need for you to hold onto things under the "just in case I might need them" train of thought. How many times have you found it hard to get rid of old items in the past just because you were worried you might need them someday? The idea that you might need to hold onto your stuff in case there is ever a need in the far-off, hypothetical future where you may need it is how you end up with too much clutter. When you do hold onto those items, have you ever needed them up to this point? Be honest with yourself. Rarely do we end up using our "just in case" items and they end up doing nothing more than taking up space in your home. It's time to do away with these items, and the 20/20 rule is where you begin. Start by getting rid of all the "just in case" items which are under $20 dollars that you could easily replace in under 20 minutes. That way, if you ever find yourself in a predicament where you need one of these "just in case" items, you can easily replace them for under $20 dollars in under $20 minutes. Odds are that you won't miss or ever need all the "just in case" items you have been holding onto, and you won't need to replace them at all. Plus, your home is decluttered as an added benefit.

- **The 90/90 Rule** - Rules may be restrictive, but there are certain occasions where they may come in handy. The 90/90 rule is one of them. When attempting to simplify your life, you may sometimes find yourself stuck even before you've had a chance to properly start, particularly when you're being faced with a whole pile of your belongings which you need to start sorting through. When we find ourselves face to face with all your possessions, suddenly determining which items are valuable and which are not becomes almost impossible. Letting go then, becomes a nearly impossible task, because how do you decide what you should get rid of and what you should keep? Enter the 90/90 rule. Take a good look at everything that you own, and then pick something. Anything will do, doesn't matter what it is, as long as you pick something. Once you have your item, ask yourself if you have used this anytime within the last 90 days. If the answer is no, then ask yourself if you are going to use it within the next 90 days. If the answer is still no, then it's time to let it go. The 90/90 day rule is just there to serve as a guideline, and you don't necessarily have to follow those numbers if they don't work for you. It could be a 60/60 day rule, maybe even a 120/120 day rule. Pick a number that works best for you.

- **The 10/10 Rule** - Think about everything that you own right now and ask yourself one very important question. How important is this stuff to you? Those material possessions which you worked so hard for, spent your hard earned money on, scrimped and saved to finally purchase, how much value does it really add to your life? Would you be surprised to find out that it matters less than you think? You might be with the 10/10 materialism rule. Here's how it works, take a pen and paper and write down the 10 most expensive items that you own within the last decade (10 years). This could be your car, laptop, mobile phone, any jewelry that was purchased, maybe even your home. List the 10 most expensive big-ticket purchases you made in the last 10 years. Grab another piece of paper and make a new list, this time with the 10 things which add the most value and meaning into your life. This list could include experiences like spending time with your loved ones on a vacation, or watching your kid's dance recital, maybe even having a lovely meal and catch up session with your parents. When you compare your list, it is likely that these two lists are going to have absolutely nothing in common. Now, ask yourself, which list brings you the greatest amount of happiness? You may just be surprised by your answer.

CHAPTER 3
Reality Check

As aesthetically pleasing as minimalism can be, especially around the home, the concept goes far beyond that. Being visual creatures, we tend to focus on what is in front of us since our perception is primarily rooted based on sight. What we consistently see in front set influences our state of emotions, it only stands to reason that the less mess and clutter you are surrounded with, the less stress you're likely to feel.

It is what helps to shape, condition and develop our mindset. It isn't just about learning to live with less so you can tell people that you are a minimalist. By embracing this approach, you are standing up against consumerism and rejecting the notion that our happiness is rooted only in material things. It is about learning how to be grateful, remain grounded, and learning how to be content and appreciative of everything that you have. It is only when you fully embrace minimalism that it dawns on you that you really don't need more stuff in your life at all. That the messages we have been exposed to all along have been wrong. We don't need one more thing to be happy, and there's no such thing as when I buy this then I will be happy because it doesn't exist because no matter how many things you buy it will never be enough. The only thing that is a guarantee is how stressed out you are going to be when you observed all the clutter of unnecessary and barely touched items around your home, wondering why you bought them in the first place.

Managing Your Expectations

You're ready to be done with your messy home, and you're ready to jump into minimalism, excited for the changes that it is about to bring into your life. Before you do though, there is something called the expectation gap that must be managed. This gap is what separates you from where you are right now, to where you would like to be in the future.

Let's say for example that you aim to be thriving as a minimalist within the next 3-months. Having high ambitions and goals is great, but the expectations that come with achieving that target will be accompanied by feelings of stress and anxiety from the pressure of wanting to achieve your target as soon as possible. Being focused far too much on the outcome will cause you to lose sight of being focused on the journey instead. Instead of having enjoyed the process of your journey towards becoming a minimalist, you're not having fun and all, and somewhere along the way, you'll begin to question why you wanted to initiate this change in the first place because this is not what you expected.

Expectations can act as a shackle that makes life more difficult than it should, or needs to be. There's nothing wrong with having standards and expectations, not at all. In fact, they give you something to work towards and to strive for. However, there is a very critical difference between standards and expectations. By its very definition, expectations are the beliefs we hold that certain events or outcomes are going to happen, and these expectations are based on strong assumptions that we hold about what the future might look like.

Imagine this scenario for a minute. Your husband or wife has had a long day at work. You want to do something nice for them to brighten up their day, and you decide to prepare a wonderful surprise dinner for them. You've done the grocery shopping, cooked their favorite foods, set the table and everything is primed and ready for their return. When your spouse returns, however, they will immediately walk into the house and say how they've had a horrible day and they're not feeling very hungry so they're going to go take a bath to try and relax. Your immediate reaction might be to feel anger or disappointment. After all that effort you put into it, they're not even appreciative, happy or excited the way that you expected them to be. But it isn't your spouse's fault that they failed to live up to your expectations, because these were your expectations, and no one, not even your spouse, is obligated to fulfill any of them.

That example illustrates why there is a need for us to manage our expectations. If possible, these expectations should be avoided altogether, as it can cause a great deal of grief if they are not met. You are bound to have had similar experiences in the past, where you've been let down and disappointed because things didn't go the way you thought it would, not realizing that expectations were the reason behind the emotions that you felt. Before you begin your new venture into minimalism, you need to manage your expectations to avoid being disappointed if you find it wasn't all that you expected it to be. An expectation, when you get right down to it, is nothing more than your "best guess" about a possible outcome which you think might happen. These best guesses are made up of nothing more than your opinions and your hope. Once you realize that, you can begin working on keeping those unrealistic expectations at bay by:

- **Never Making Assumptions** - If you don't know a definitive answer to something, always ask and never assume. Assumptions are merely another way of "guessing" what's going to happen, and you will save yourself a lot of time, energy and disappointed by forgoing it.
- **Taking It One Day At a Time** - You never know what the day is going to bring. You could plan out your schedule to the minute, but unexpected situations will happen every now and then and these are beyond your control. Learning how to take it one day at a time is how you prevent yourself from feeling disappointed if things don't go according to plan.
- **Know the Difference Between Goals and Expectations** - Your goals are concrete and fact-based, whereas expectations are based upon your opinions and hopes. A goal is something tangible that you can work towards.

- **Be Realistic About the Outcome** - Expecting something to be easy is where the trouble begins. If you begin your journey towards minimalism expecting things to be as simple as clearing out the excess stuff in your home and you're done, you're going to find yourself challenged every step of the way when you start realizing that it is not that simple and there's a lot more involved in the process.
- **Preparing for Possible Problems** - There are bound to be challenges along the way, even more so when something involves a major life change like switching to minimalism. Anticipating the possible problems along the way which might come up is how you prepare yourself and save yourself from feeling discouraged or disappointed.
- **Being Adaptable** - It is easy to feel emotional when things don't go the way you planned, but that's what reality is. Things will change, and situations will shift all the time, sometimes in the moments when you least expect it. Sometimes they're good changes, and sometimes they aren't, but the more adaptable and open you are to these changes, the better you'll be able to manage what comes your way. Challenges never last forever, and just because of the unexpected happened, it doesn't mean you failed at achieving your goal.

Keep your expectations low, but let your standards remain high. Having high standards is not about achieving perfectionism, but rather it is the determination and commitment you are making to yourself not to take shortcuts or to cut corners. High standards it the commitment that you make to yourself to always put your best effort into everything that you do.

The Myths and Misconceptions

Possibly the reason for a lot of the confusion and misconception is that minimalism is such a unique concept that is unlike anything we have become accustomed to growing up. It is an extremely personal journey, and since everyone is different, it stands to reason that it is always going to be approached and practiced differently based on the preferences of the individual. What one person may view as valuable, another might not, which is why you'll never find two minimalists with the exact same setup in their homes.

Minimalism is a concept as diverse as the people who practice it. People of all ages, races, genders, religions, and nationalities are practitioners of this movement which just continues to grow as more people are becoming aware that true happiness and freedom lies in letting go of their attachment to their worldly possessions. Yet, this concept continues to be misunderstood by a large percentage of people, surrounded by myths and misconceptions that cause confusion and hesitation.

Myth: Success Is Defined By How Much We Earn

Zig Ziglar said it best when he said: "money will not make you happy, but this is something everyone wants to discover for themselves". Changing the mindset that has been around for a long time is not going to happen overnight, but minimalists are slowly working towards making that change in their lives, and that's a good place to start.

Myth: Being a Minimalist Is Only About Reducing How Much Stuff You Own

It is also about your expectations, and as we have learned, keeping your expectations low is how you remain focused on the journey, not the destination. Minimalism is not just about how much stuff you own, it is the pathway to a life of content in every aspect that extends far beyond materialism.

Myth: My Home Is Going to Be All Stark, Boring, and Barren

Only if you want it to be. Your home is your own, and what stays or goes is entirely up to you. Minimalism simply encourages you to keep the meaningful things around while discarding everything else that is unnecessary and no longer serves a purpose in your life. A minimalist home can still have decoratives and bright colorful patterns that brighten up space if you want it to. A minimalist home can still have beautiful paintings or pictures of your family and friends on the wall if you want them. Actually, the only real difference between the home of a minimalist and everyone else is the absence of clutter and junk. Minimalists still decorate their homes, but they do it with simplicity. They still have several pieces of furniture around, but only what they need to live comfortably and nothing more. Your home is your own, and you can keep or discard anything you like as long as you're happy about it.

Myth: Being a Minimalist Means No More Fun

Again, only if you decide on it, minimalism isn't restrictive in any way, and what you do or don't do is entirely up to you. In fact, minimalism could actually help you carve out more time for fun and excitement in your life by helping you declutter your schedule and only keep the tasks which are important. All the other mundane tasks which take up too much of your time with no real benefit are the ones which are robbing you of the fun you could be having while doing something that you loved instead.

Myth: Being a Minimalist Means I Can't Own Nice Things

Would it surprise you to learn that you could own even nicer things than what you had before by being a minimalist? When you no longer spend on the unnecessary, you're left with a lot more room in your budget to spend on quality necessities instead. Owning fewer things doesn't mean you don't anything nice, and many minimalists are doing quite the opposite. Investing in quality items when there is a need for them means minimalists actually own much nicer things when they're not focused on only purchasing cheaper products while compromising on quality.

Myth: You Are Only Allowed Once of Each Item

Having fewer possessions doesn't necessarily mean you only have one of each item. The whole having only one of each approach is only going to work for the items which make sense. Having just one bookshelf or one television makes sense, but having just one spoon, fork or plate is not going to make sense, especially if you have other people living in your home. It is safe to say that this one is an absolute myth and completely untrue. Minimalism has no rules or limits, and you should have multiples of some items if it is the sensible and logical thing to do.

Myth: Minimalism Means You Can't Live In A Big Home

Living in a smaller home doesn't make you any more of a minimalist if your home is still full of clutter. The size of your home is not what matters at the end of the day, it is what your home is filled with. If you have a family of four or five, it wouldn't make sense for you to squeeze everyone into a one bedroom unit just so you could call yourself a minimalist. Being unhappy and uncomfortable is not what this concept is about, not at all. You can live in a big house that is suitable for the size of your family and still be just as much of a minimalist as someone who is living in a considerably smaller abode.

Myth: Minimalism Is Just Material

The material aspect of it all is what most people tend to focus on because that's the immediate thing which springs to mind when you mention the word "minimalism". Say the word to someone who is unfamiliar with the concept and they're likely to think "it means I have to get rid of all my stuff". Those who practice minimalism, however, knows that the main takeaway lesson here is about reducing the chaos and clutter in your life, and this can come from anywhere. It could be your busy, packed schedule that is causing you chaos and is in need of minimalism. It could be your emotional or spiritual side which you have lost touch with because of all the distractions that your life is filled with. Perhaps that is in need of some minimalism. Or it could be any one of the relationships in your life that are weighing you down which might benefit from some minimalism. The material aspect of it all is just one, the small portion that makes up the overall concept of what minimalism is all about.

Myth: Everything in Your Home Needs To Be White

Only if white happens to be your favorite color. Sure, the pictures we see of minimalists homes do look rather impressive with their one-tone color scheme, but if it doesn't work for you, there's no reason you need to follow along. Fill your home with as many colors as you like if it makes you happy to do it. Your home is your sanctuary, your happy place, and it should be filled with any color scheme you like.

Myth: You Need to Either Be Only a Minimalist, Or Have Kids, But You Can't Do Both

Why not do both? True, maintaining a clean and clutter-free environment may seem like an almost impossible task with kids around, but that doesn't mean that minimalists refrain from having kids altogether. Or that they have to choose only one approach to go with. You can be a minimalist and be a parent at the same time, and in fact, this could provide a wonderful learning opportunity to teach your kids about the valuable things in life from a young age. Kids don't need dozens of toys or electronics to be happy when they can get that same amount of happiness or more by spending quality time together as a family building experiences and memories instead.

Misconception: Minimalists Are Lazy People

Minimalism is unique to the individual who practices it. There are some who may be lazy it is true, but that doesn't mean that all minimalists are like that. Living a simpler life doesn't mean you're automatically lazy. The notion that we have to be "busy" all the time to be considered productive is one of the biggest misconceptions around. There are hardworking people and there are lazy people, but minimalism is not a determining factor. If someone is lazy from the start, that is simply who they are and it has nothing to do with minimalism.

Misconception: Minimalists Are Extreme When It Comes To The Environment

Minimalism cares about the environment, but that doesn't mean you have to go to extreme lengths for it. Minimalists simply do their part for the environment by making a conscious effort to consume and discard fewer resources, but again, this would entirely depend on the individual. Different people will have a different approach to the way that they live their lives, and not everyone who embraces the life of a minimalist is going to go to extreme measures just to feel satisfied knowing that they have done their part.

Misconception: Minimalists Need to Be Vegans or Vegetarians

You don't have to be, but if you want to for your own reasons, you could be. Not all minimalists are vegans or vegetarians. Once again, a completely personal choice that is entirely up to you.

Misconception: Minimalists Are People Who Are Young, Single and Free

You can embrace minimalism at any stage of your life. Young, single, old or married, it doesn't matter since there are no age restrictions with this approach to living. A lot of minimalists actually embraced this lifestyle at an older age when they want a clean slate or to start over because they may not necessarily be happy with the direction their life has taken. No matter what your reasons may be or why you decided to get started, minimalism has no age limit and you can do this at any stage in your life. Even kids can do it if you show them how to.

Misconception: Minimalists Don't Keep Books Around

It's not that they avoid keeping or holding onto books entire, but rather they make a selective choice about the books that they keep around. It's all about keeping it simple and only keeping what's important. The Kindle has also made it less necessary to keep physical copies of books around the home when you can easily store everything you need on one digital device, saving you tons of space in the process.

Misconception: Minimalists Are Constantly Counting and Keeping Track of Their Possessions

Some minimalists may do it, others may not. Minimalism is all about preference and personal choice. What one minimalist does, another might not. There's no rule that says everyone has to live in the exact same way. If it makes someone happy to count their possessions and limit the number of things they allow themselves to own, they are free to do just that. There is no magic number, only a number that works for you. If it makes you happy to only own 50 items, go ahead and do it. If it makes you happy to own 100 items, why not?

Misconception: Minimalists Aren't Sentimental People

You don't need to keep boxes upon boxes of sentimental items to be considered someone who is sentimental. Minimalists are sentimental too, they just do it a little differently by finding value and only holding onto the things which they consider to be the truly important pieces of significance to them. You'd be surprised to know that a lot of minimalists actually choose to display their most sentimental items somewhere around their now clutter-free home because they have the space for it. Instead of being tucked away in a box gathering dust and being forgotten, displaying them around the home serves as a reminder for them about what they value the most.

Misconception: Minimalists Can Be Rather Pompous and Condescending

Some people just naturally have that kind of personality, but it is in no way a reflection of how other minimalists are. Everyone is a unique individual in their own right. There could be some minimalists who love the way that they live and want to share that with everyone that they know but is perhaps going about it in the wrong way which is why they come off as pompous and condescending. That might not be their intention at all, having some individuals like that doesn't make all minimalists automatically pompous or condescending.

Misconception: Minimalists Avoid Spending Money

Only because this makes sense, why would you continuously waste money on unnecessary items that you don't need and most like will not end up using at all? Those funds could be directed towards better use, such as saving for retirement, putting it into your kids' college fund, or saving for a rainy day. It's not that minimalists avoid spending money altogether, but rather they exercise precaution over the things that they do spend on. Minimalism doesn't restrict or stop you from spending money, it simply reminds you to stop and think before you part with your hard-earned cash by asking yourself if you really need it. Minimalists are also wiser with their spending, choosing quality over quantity. Plus, they have come to understand that spending money doesn't equate to happiness.

Misconception: Minimalists Cant' Have Any Collections

If your collections make you happy and add meaning to your life, you're more than welcome to hold onto them. Keep the collections that hold valuable meaning for you, and balance that out by getting rid of the items that don't hold quite as much value and wouldn't be missed. Some collections are worth holding onto, and it is up to you to decide what stays and what goes. Having a passion which involves collectibles doesn't mean you're not a minimalist.

CHAPTER 4
Getting Started

Alright, so we have come to the part where it's finally time to get started on becoming a minimalist. All those pictures of beautiful, clutter-free, visually appealing homes you've been enviously eyeing on the Internet, that's about to be what your home now looks like. Not exactly the same of course, but close enough.

People still tend to underestimate how distracting clutter can be. It is a form of visual distraction, and just because it doesn't seem like you're thinking much about it, somewhere in your brain it still bothers you. Every visual thing that we encounter tugs on our attention, even if it is just a little. Have you ever wondered why a minimalist home seems to have that calming effect whenever you look at it? Or even when you walk into one? That's because there's not a lot going on there that is distracting you.

Not to mention how easy it is going to be from now on to clean your home when you don't have a whole bunch of stuff that you constantly need to dust, or piles of stuff on the floor making it hard for you to sweep and vacuum. The more you have, the more time you spend cleaning, it really is that simple, and you're going to now save yourself so much time that you're going to wonder why you didn't start adopting this approach years ago.

Minimalists work hard to keep their home neat and free of clutter because they don't want anything in their home that is weighing them down, stressing them out or wasting their time. A minimalist is content with the things that they already have because they have managed to make the shift in their mindset from I need to acquire to I already have more than enough. The clutter in your home is a reflection on who you are. For example, you're holding onto things longer than you should, even when it no longer serves a purpose because you're afraid to let go of the past. You constantly keep buying because you may be operating based on the fear mentality, and you would rather than unnecessary items stored away just in case rather because you believe it is better to be with them than without them. Maybe the clutter that is piling up in your home which you never seem to have time to clean is a reflection of your too-busy schedule.

What Can I Expect My Minimalist Home to Look Like?

That depends on course on the kind of home you have, what your personal decorative tastes are and just how extreme you plan to go with the decluttering process. The pictures you see on the Internet are some examples of what your home could look like, but that doesn't necessarily mean that's how your home should look like. Think of them as inspirations instead to give you an idea of where to begin. However, there are some basic characteristics which are standard in the home of a minimalist:

- **The Furniture** - Your furniture is going to be cut down to only the very few essential pieces that you are going to need and nothing more. The furniture would depend on the room it's in. The bedroom, for instance, might only require a simple bed, a dresser, and a nightstand as the few basic staple pieces of furniture. Depending on your tastes, space, and needs, you could choose to have a rug, perhaps a bookshelf or even a small couch by the window if that is where you like to sit and relax. The room should only have what is needed, nothing more.
- **The Surfaces** - The thing you will immediately notice about minimalist homes is how much free space is available when it's not being littered or cluttered with piles of stuff. Most minimalists will aim to keep the flat surfaces of their home neat, clean and free, save for a few pieces of decorative items here and there. There will definitely be no stacks of papers piling up, or piles of books and papers, or things thrown about in a haphazard manner.
- **The Decorations** - Minimalists choose accent decorations which care carefully chosen and selectively placed around their home, and it is usually done to spice up the place a little. Instead of having a completely empty coffee table surface, there might be a simple vase with some flowers placed as an accent decoration. Minimalists like being clutter free, but they're not that extreme.
- **Clearing the Kitchen** - The best place to start in the kitchen would be by clearing the sink of any dirty dishes before tackling the other parts. Spend a good 10-15 minutes clearing and scrubbing the dishes, and cleaning the sink area and the surrounding areas. Once you're done, step back and take a few minutes to admire how clean it now looks, then take that motivation and bring it with you as you begin scrubbing and clearing away the other parts of your kitchen. Anything that is expired in the fridge and pantry needs to go immediately.
- **Separating Into Piles** - This one works especially well for clothing. Separate your items into piles of either Keep, Maybe and Toss or into piles based on how often you use these items, which could be Frequently, Occasionally and Never. Put everything that you're unsure of in a separate pile that you can come back later and revisit, so you don't spend too much time sorting through your items. Although it is important to think carefully about each item, you don't want to spend too long making a decision because you need to keep the process moving. Otherwise decluttering would take forever.

Beginning the Decluttering Process

This is going to be a massive project. Deciding what to get rid of would be the first part of your decluttering challenge. The second is the actual decluttering process. Looking around at everything you have to do, you might start to feel overwhelmed at the immense workload that's waiting for you (depending on the size of your home and how much stuff you have). Where do you even begin and how long is this going to take? Try and relax, take a breath and use the following guide to help you work through the process one step at a time:

- **Working in Sections** - You don't need to do your entire home all at once, this is going to be almost impossible to do unless you're living alone, without much belongings and in a very small place of your own. There's no need to rush through the process, so don't put any pressure on yourself trying to finish everything in a day. Take your time working through each room, focusing on the task of decluttering and carefully considering which items should stay and which should go. You might end up getting rid of something you didn't mean to if you were to hurry through everything, take your time, and do it one room at a time.
- **Checking Out the Furniture** - The furniture is usually going to be the biggest items that you own, taking up the most space in your room. Start the simplifying process by checking out your furniture and determining which items can be donated or relocated to a different part of the house where they might be more beneficial. Remember to only keep what you need, and the fewer pieces of furniture you have, the better, but keep it within reason of course. Eliminate your furniture without sacrificing your comfort and happiness.
- **Start With the Flat Surfaces** - Once you've finished sorting out the furniture, look at all the other flat surfaces around your home and start working on clearing those one surface at a time. Pick a countertop, a table, perhaps even a part some shelves that need clearing away. Once you've finished with one flat surface, move onto the next. Again, this doesn't have to be done all at once, take as much time as you need and work methodically through the process.
- **Clearing the Floors** - Except for furniture, there is nothing else which should be touching the ground and blocking your pathway. The floor should be completely clear of everything except furniture, no piles, no boxes, and no stacks of items. Once you have removed most of the furniture except the essentials, clear everything else that may be lying on the floor. Either find a different home of it, donate it or toss it in the trash if it can't be donated.
- **Out of Sight** - Everything in the home of a minimalist as a "home" of its own. The books have a home (bookshelf). The stationary has a home (desk drawers). The artwork has a home (hanging on the walls). The clothes have a home (closet). Nothing is cluttering and left out in the open because everything has been neatly stored away out of sight until it is needed. A minimalist always knows just where to find everything that they need in their home because it is organized and kept where it should be.

With every stage of the decluttering process, you need to look at each item you're about to remove carefully and ask yourself if this is essential.

Furniture, clothing, books, even stationary and decorative items. Everything. If you can live without it, then you can get rid of it. The main goal now is to just strip each room in your home down to the bare essentials which you need for survival. Everything else may be added later on if it becomes a necessity.

Decluttering Your Workspace

An uncluttered workspace is a beautiful thing to look at. Those beautiful pictures online just inspire you to sit down and work for hours because of how peaceful it looks, with the bright sunlight streaming through the windows and nothing but a laptop and a coffee mug on your desk. Which makes you reflect on what your current workspace looks like right now.

Much like your home, the workspace of a minimalist is going to be different based on the individual. Some people might like the more extreme approach where the only thing that sits on their desk is a laptop and nothing else. Others might like to have one or two accented decorative items on the desk, along with the computer to help add more of an aesthetic appeal that they like to look at.

When you think about decluttering your workspace, whether at home or at the office, think about the items which are most essential to you - the items that you used throughout the day. The workspace that you set up for yourself should have all the minimum requirements that you need to function effectively and productively. If what you need to function productively on top of your desk is a laptop, a notepad and a pen to scribble ideas, have only those items on top of your desk and tuck everything else away.

As for organizing the rest of your items, you want to think about simplifying and streamlining the workflow process to make it as efficient as possible for yourself. If your desk comes with drawers, the first drawer should be arranged according to what you need to function most effectively, the second drawer with what you don't need as frequently and so on. In short, arrange your drawers by order of importance. Anything else that is not essential to your workflow can be removed.

Even your laptop or computer can be decluttered and kept simple. Some minimalists even have just a desktop with no folders on it at all. Again, the setup that you choose for yourself needs to be based on what you need to work. Here are a couple of tips to help you declutter and streamline your productivity:

- **Downsizing Your Inbox -** Do you have multiple emails that you use? Streamline that by downsizing to just one email and one inbox for all your needs. That one inbox rule extends to beyond your computer too, if having papers is unavoidable in your line of work. Limit it to just one inbox tray for all your papers, including the sticky post-it notes and reminders. This is useful at work, and if you have colleagues who are in the habit of dropping documents on your desk when you're not around, have a conversation with them and ask if they would be so kind as to put the papers on the inbox tray on your desk instead. Make it a point to clear your inbox regularly, both your emails and the inbox tray on your desk. Create folders in your emails to sort them so there's nothing on your main page except for the new emails that come in each day. If you no longer need the email, delete it. As for the inbox tray on your desk, clear it as often as possible, either weekly or daily if you can manage it. Anything that you don't need to hold onto to can be trashed.

- **Clear Flat Surface** - The same rules apply to your work desk as they do to the other flat surfaces in your home. Keep it neat, clean and clutter free except for one of two items. Unless you're actively working on some papers or documents, there should be none of these on your desk at any time. Post-it notes should be tucked away in your drawers until you need them, along with any pens, stapler or other basic stationary which you use regularly. Clear away as much as you can and leave nothing on your desk but a laptop and maybe one or two accented decorations again. No, knick-knacks, not trinkets, not even little souvenirs from colleagues should be displayed on your desk. Anything that is unnecessary and not contributing to your work routine needs to go.
- **Nothing On the Walls** - Is your home office wall cluttered with all kinds of stuff posted on it? Well, the walls are going to have to be stripped bare too. Like the rest of your home, there should be nothing on the walls except for one or two pieces of decorative artwork for ambiance. At work, clear your cubicle walls of any visual clutter that should not be there. Everything should be stripped bare so there's no distraction happening. Since you don't have four walls to work with here, if you need to have a motivational image or two for inspiration, downsize the image according to your cubicle measurements so it doesn't take up too much space.
- **A Simple Filing System Is All Your Need** - Is there even a need to keep physical paper copies anymore when everything is easily stored online in the cloud? If you simply must have a hard copy of certain documents, simplify your filing process by only limiting it to one copy per document. You don't need multiple copies of each anymore, and if you're worried about losing the digital copies of these documents which you might be keeping on your computer, back them up online and have a copy in the digital space instead of the physical one. At least there's no visual clutter to look at, and it's a much better approach than filing where you still run the risk of losing the documents should you misplace the file.

I'm Afraid to Let Things Go

That's perfectly understandable. You have probably spent most of your entire life up to this point being surrounded by belongings that you don't know any other way or how you would survive without them. The inability to let things go is the fear mentality, and you worry about parting with your items because of all the questions that raise fear within you at the very thought of it. What if I need it again? This has an emotional connection to me, how can I let it go? What if I'm giving away something that I might later regret? What if I need it next time and I can't buy it anymore?

You may think it is wasteful to get rid of your things, especially when they're still in good condition, but so is holding onto them when they are going to serve you no purpose. If you don't love them anyway, why hold onto them when you know you might never use them? It is wasting valuable space in your home. It is wasting your time when you have to spend several extra minutes tidying up or keeping them clean. It is a waste of resources to hold onto them when you could donate them to someone who might need it more than you do.

If something holds a sentimental value to you, but you know it's never going to be used, take a picture of these items for you to keep before you donate them. The reason you have an emotional attachment to them is not because of what they can do for you or how they can be used, it's because of the memories they might hold. Taking a picture of them is a way for you to find balance, where you still get to hold onto these items in a way, while still donating them to someone with a greater need. You still have the memories with you, but they now take up no space in your home.

For the items that you genuinely can't bring yourself to give away because it would upset you far too much, start a separate storage box for them. This way there aren't just strewn about the home randomly and neatly organized instead.

What To Do With the Stuff You Don't Need?

If you're wondering what to do with all of the items that are tossed in the trash, there are several options which you could consider:
- Having a yard sale where interested neighbors can come and pick out which items of yours they would like.
- Donating them to charity organizations like Goodwill.
- Selling your items on eBay.
- Donating them to friends or family who might be interested or have a use for them.
- Sell your used books online or consider donating them to the library if they are still in excellent condition.
- Recycling your stuff.
- If there are unused items which are brand new and recently bought but you've changed your mind about them, consider giving them away as gifts instead.

Setting Goals and Making Plans

New habits can be a challenge to form and keep. Even harder when you don't have a goal which gives you something to work towards. Yes, minimalism is a habit that must be formed. You're about to completely change the way that you live as you know it, and as excited as you are to begin this journey, it is still going to take some time to get used to it. All change comes with its own challenges. Have you ever tried to form a new habit without having a proper goal set out for yourself? You're excited and pumped up, ready to get going, but along the way, you lose that motivational spark that got you started, and you end up giving up midway through the process. It happens more often than you think.

It is easy to try and implement a new habit in the beginning during the first few weeks, only to have that initial excite wane as you progress over the next few days or weeks. It's sometimes hard to make a new habit stick, even with the best intentions. Busy schedules, hectic lives, tiredness, temptation, and even emotions tend to get in the away and side sweep us. This is why diet fads never last long, and weight loss intentions come and go. We lose interest in the initial novelty of it all and despite what we hope for, we find ourselves slipping back into our old routine and way of life before we know it.

Since we don't want that to happen with your intention to become a minimalist, it is important to set goals and make plans for yourself to help you stick to this routine until it becomes a lifelong habit. As you begin this process, lay out all the goals that you have for yourself. Write them down, and then look again at the list you have just written. If you've got more than two or three goals written on there, you need to break it down and work on it in stages. Just like decluttering your home.

Trying to do too much too soon is a common downfall of many good intentions. Just like clearing out your home, if you try to tackle everything all at once, you're only going to end up feeling overwhelmed and stressed out by the whole process. It is okay to take your time working through your goals too. Slow and steady wins the race at the end of the day. Pick out one goal to start with if that is easier for you to manage, but have no more than three goals at a time which you're working on. Pick out one goal and tell yourself that you're going to spend the next 30-days committing to making this goal a reality.

That's all you need to do. One goal, 30-days. If you manage to accomplish that goal before the end of that 30-days, move onto the next goal. No fuss, no frills, no stress, just one goal at a time. By simply making this one tweak alone to the process, you're relieving yourself of an immense amount of pressure you might otherwise feel when you're rushing to keep up with your goals. Always remind yourself that there is no urgency, and whenever you find yourself feeling pressed, stop and ask yourself what's the rush? Having only one goal to work on at a time allows yourself to devote your full attention, focus and commit to what you're doing. It also allows you time to enjoy the process rather than simply going through the motions for the sake of doing so. When you mindfully focus on what you're doing, you're aware why you're doing it and how it is benefitting you, which keeps you motivated to move forward.

CHAPTER 5
Financial Freedom Through Minimalism

It's been established by now that minimalism isn't just about clearing out the stuff in your home. It involves several other areas of your life too, like your finances for example. Minimalists still spend money, they just spend their money differently. How have they managed to do that? By not making money or material possessions the primary focus of their life anymore.

Now that you have decluttered most of your home and your closet, it's time to tackle the nation material objects, starting with your finances. You're going to be amazed by how much clarity being smart with your money and having a minimalist budget is going to be. There is one caveat that needs to be mentioned, however, and that is simplifying your finances doesn't necessarily mean you'll be spending significantly less money. Minimalism teaches you to focus on quality over quantity, and quality items don't always come with an affordable price tag. You'll be spending less frequently, but not necessarily on less expensive items, and therein lies the difference between minimalism and living frugally.

Minimalism vs. Frugal Living

Yes, minimalism and frugality are two very different concepts. One is focused on owning fewer items, while the latter is focused on spending less on items. Living frugally teaches its followers to get on getting the most out of their money by being thrifty. Using coupons at the supermarket, scouring the internet or catalogs for the best sales and deals. Trying to find the cheapest possible option, that's what being frugal is. Frugal people can still own a significant amount of possessions because they're not focused on decluttering, they're focused on stretching their dollars to the limit. A frugal person will take $50 and get three new pairs of shoes which are of average quality but cheap, while a minimalist will take that same $50 and just get one pair of quality shoes that will last a long time. Since they're not focused on owning fewer times, living frugally can lead to the accumulation of clutter over time.

A frugal person will:
- Never purchase items at full price
- Do most of their shopping at thrift or discount stores
- Look for the best deals they can get before spending their money
- Live below their means to save money
- Use coupons if it means even greater savings
- Be willing to buy second-hand, depending on the item and the quality
- Do their buying in bulk from wholesale stores for even bigger savings

A minimalist will:
- Get rid of all the unused items in their home
- Donate the clothes that they have not worn in over a year
- Say no to buying the things that they know they don't need
- Be willing to spend money on experiences instead of items

- Have no emotional attachment to the items they own
- Work on simplifying every area of their life
- Set goals and priorities which help them live intentionally
- Focus on prioritizing quality over quantity

Minimalism and frugality are different, but they're not exclusive. If you're wondering whether it's possible to be both a minimalist and be frugal, the answer is yes. In fact, being both makes you a powerhouse. As a frugal person, you want to spend less on what you intend to buy, and at the same time as a minimalist, you're only planning to buy what you need. Being both means you still care about quality, but you're not willing to overpay for it because you care about how your hard earned dollars are being spent.

How Minimalism Is Going to Transform Your Finances

It is amazing what simplifying your financial life can do for you. Taking responsibility and taking control of your spending is bringing you one step closer to financial freedom. Instead of constantly struggling every month to stay on top of your spending and your bills, you are not going to take back control by being mindful about where your money is going.

Financial minimalism teaches you how to stop feeling overwhelmed and guilty about how and where you're spending your money by taking the first step towards owning your finances. To be accountable for your spending habits, a responsibility which will lead to making more informed choices about the decisions that you make in regards to your spending. There's going to be less of the "I don't know where my money went!", and more of the "I know EXACTLY where my money went."

Minimalism is going to help you transform your finances by:
- **Encouraging You to Prioritize** - Learning how to embrace and focus on only the things which matter to you is going to now be carried over into your spending habits. When you shift your focus to experiences rather than material possessions, it can be easier to determine what you want to buy and what you don't. If you know your priority is to save for a vacation with your family, you're not going to want to spend on getting a new t-shirt which you don't need, even if it is on sale. If you know your priority is to take your parents out to a nice dinner for their anniversary, you're going to redirect your resources towards that instead of spending on another pair of shoes you don't need.
- **Budgeting Based on Priorities** - Once you've got your priorities sorted out, the next step is to plan a workable budget based on those priorities. This too becomes much easier when you know what's important to you, and setting a budget based on those priorities will set a clear direction as to how and where your money should be spent. Having a budget will also help you put your spending into perspective. Take a look at where your money is going right now. If those areas of spending are not in line with your new priorities as a

minimalist, cut them out and redirect those funds towards your savings or paying off debt.
- **Increasing Your Savings** - All that money which was previously spent buying frivolous and unnecessary items can now be channeled and put to good use by saving it instead. Increasing your savings and putting more money aside than you could before will leave you with enough to put a little aside for a rainy day and pay off any debts you've got. Less shopping, more savings and debt paying, and one step closer to financial freedom when you're no longer weighed down by debt.
- **Fuelling Your Motivation** - When you start seeing how quickly your debt is reducing as pay it off with the money you now have leftover from not buying unnecessary stuff, you'll be motivated to keep going as the finish line to becoming debt free draws one step closer with each payment that you make. Getting rid of debt is one of the most liberating financial experiences because, without that burden, more doors and possibilities start to open. You can take that vacation with your family you've been wanting to for so long, or pursue your passion with the funds you now have to spare not having to pay off any debt. With no additional monthly payments and more money left over from unnecessary spending, you now have the freedom to explore the things that you love the most.
- **Starting An Emergency Fund** - Everyone should have an emergency fund just in case. These funds should be easily accessible (but not too easy to avoid temptation) and only to be used in an absolute emergency when you've exhausted all other options. As you free yourself from all the clutter that's taking up space in your life, see which items can be sold so that money can be used to help you give your finances the boost that it should have had years ago.

Financial Freedom Begins with Simplifying Your Finances

Cutting down and simplifying your finances begins with cutting out all the unnecessary expenditure. Common expenses that the average person would have every month include:
- Rent or mortgage payments
- Homeowner's insurance
- Utilities
- Car payments
- Gas bill
- Cable TV bill
- Internet bill
- Mobile bill
- Grocery shopping
- Miscellaneous shopping (new clothes, shoes, books, etc)
- Credit card (or cards depending on how many you have)

- Student loans
- Miscellaneous debt
- Gym membership
- Health insurance
- Medical expenses

Once you've got a list of your monthly expenses, assess which items can be eliminated so that list becomes simplified? Some expenses can't be helped of course, but for the ones which can be removed, ask yourself, "Do I really need this to make me happy?" Your priorities are going to help you cut back on a lot from the list above, and here's what a minimalist monthly expense might look like instead:

- Rent or mortgage payments
- Homeowners insurance
- Utilities
- ~~Car payment~~ (sell the car if not needed)
- ~~Gas bill~~ (no longer needed without a car)
- ~~Cable TV bill~~ (canceled subscription because you barely watch cable anyway, and Netflix has made it easier to enjoy your favorite shows online so all you need is the internet)
- Internet bill
- Mobile bill
- Grocery shopping
- ~~Miscellaneous shopping (new clothes, shoes, books, etc)~~ (don't need this anymore now that you're focused on accumulating less)
- ~~Credit card (or cards depending on how many you have)~~ (paid off from the money saved by spending less)
- ~~Student loans~~ (paid off from the money saved by spending less)
- ~~Miscellaneous debt~~ (paid off from the money saved by spending less)
- ~~Gym membership~~ (don't need this, exercising outdoors is just as good and free)
- Health insurance
- Medical expenses

That list has now become significantly shorter without all the unnecessary spending incurred:

- Rent or mortgage payments
- Homeowners insurance
- Utilities
- Internet bill
- Mobile bill
- Grocery shopping
- Health insurance
- Medical expenses

Of course, everyone's monthly expenses are going to look different based on lifestyle and needs, this example is just to illustrate how much you could be saving by simply cutting back on the things that you don't need. As you get more adjusted to living like a minimalist, you'll be able to reassess your budget and expenditure as you go along and make even more adjustments when you feel there are other areas which you no longer need. Minimalists find happiness in being content with what they have, and when you've already got everything that you need to be happy, you stop looking for more ways to spend your money.

The bottom line with debt is that to get out of it, you need to spend less than what you're making. Everyone can find ways to keep things simple, regardless of how much money you're making or what your monthly spending patterns are like. There is always some area that you can cut back on. Logically, it should be a simple enough concept to follow. Spend less, save more, yet many Americans are still knee deep in debt and relying on multiple credit cards just to get by. If your spending continues to exceed what you make each month, the only thing that is going to grow (besides your clutter) is your debt. Simplifying your finances means to take a realistic look at what you actually need to survive comfortably each month, versus what you think you need to be happy.

How to Get Started With Your Own Minimalist Budget

Tackling your finances can be just as overwhelming and stressful as decluttering the physical items in your home, but that doesn't mean it should be used as an excuse to hold you back. It will only hold you back if you allow it to.

Unlike what you might think, getting started with a minimalist budget actually begins with a change in your mindset, before you start jumping in right away into your finances. You can't begin your budget anew if you're still carrying around old habits and ways of thinking about money. Change your mindset first and foremost about borrowing or owing money, whether this is to a financial institution or someone that you know. It is common to hear many people talk about how they bought a new car because they got a really great deal or it, or because the monthly payments were really low and it was simply too good a deal to pass up. These people are trying to stretch out their finances as much as they possibly can by trying to secure the lowest monthly payments. They do it because they believe that this is going to make them happy living beyond their means in a lifestyle which - if they're being honest - can't really afford, but feel entitled to.

Becoming a minimalist is going to require you to flip this kind of thinking on its head. Minimalists need to think along the lines of ownership, instead of what the lowest monthly payments are. Don't ask how much it is going to cost you every month, ask instead - what is the outright cost of buying the item? This isn't just limited to new car purchases, but any big-ticket items that you're going to pay for in installments (owing money). When you limit your available payment options, like your credit cards, it will make you stop and consider if you really can afford this item you're about to spend money on, more importantly, whether you need it.

To change your mindset, you need to establish a very clear set of financial values to help you out. Examples of these values could include living a life that is debt free, or saving at least 20% of your monthly income, or even to have at least a 30% buffer separating your income and your expenses. Having a clear set of financial values will help you then work on your priorities and finally, set your financial goals, which will help get you from where you are right now to where you want to be.

Examples of what your financial priorities might look like based upon the values you set above include making it a priority to pay off as much of your debt within the next 2 to 3 years and then using that money to channel it towards increasing that 20% savings you initially targeted. Or it could be to increase your income by another 20% so there's an even greater buffer percentage between your income and your expenses. From there, your goals could be to have at least $10,000 in your savings account by the end of the year or to have at least one credit card paid off and canceled by the end of the year.

These are just some examples of course, and there's a lot of ways which you can go about this based on what your values and priorities may be. If you're really struggling with this and you don't know what your priorities are just yet, don't worry, there is always a solution to work around it. If you need some guidance until you've found your footing and you've got a better idea of what your financial values and priorities are, you could begin your minimalist budget using the 50/20/30 system.

With the 50/20/30 system, you're going to allocate 50% of your income towards meeting your monthly needs. 20% of your income is then going to go towards your savings and paying off your debt, while the remaining 30% of your income is going to be allocated towards your wants. When your "wants" is significantly reduced the deeper you go into minimalism, the percentage allocation of that column can be slowly channeled towards growing that 20% savings to an even bigger number. Minimalism is great because it shows us that the key to happiness is not in satisfying our "wants" at all, and to prioritize your experiences over materialism. That is the foundation upon which minimalism is built. This works out great for your finances since the less you spend the more you get to save.

Learning to eliminate the wants becomes easier when you learn to ask yourself do I value this and does this serve my financial priorities and values? If the answer is no, then you know what to do. Let's say for example you're currently looking at spending about $150 to $200 on your monthly hair treatments at the salon because you want to. Once you've decided to embrace minimalism and your values have shifted, you begin to question whether this expenditure is then serving your purpose. How is spending almost $200 a month serving your financial priorities? More importantly, is this contributing to moving closer to the financial future that you want? The answer is going to depend again, on what your priorities and your values are. Some people may say yes, others may say no. if you find that this expense is not fitting in with your new lifestyle as a minimalist, then it is time to scale back and cut it out from your budget.

You are setting your minimalist budget for a reason, and it is important that you stick to this budget no matter what. No matter how tempted you may be, remind yourself why you established this budget in the first place, especially during the first several weeks or months when you're only just beginning to transition into minimalist and adjusting to the new lifestyle.

After you have tackled simplifying your monthly expenses with the help of your values, priorities, and goals, it is now time to work on simplifying your accounts and credit cards. How many credit cards do you currently own? One? Two? Four perhaps? What about a savings account? How many accounts do you own? A simple minimalist budget might look towards having just one savings account and only one checking account, and perhaps one credit card for any possible emergency situations where you might need one. Everything else needs to be removed.

You only need one checking account to handle all your monthly expenses and one saving account where you build your financial nest egg. Having only one of each makes it easier for you to focus on where your money is going and it simplifies your banking process too. Similarly, you should only aim to have just one credit card, perhaps even no credit cards at all if you can manage that. It is going to make it much easier for you to track your spending and stay organized on top of your finances when you don't have so many things to focus on at once. It might come as a surprise to know that the reality is, you only need one of each to survive, but think about it. Is there a genuine need to have several checking or savings accounts? Why separate your savings into several different accounts (vacation, emergency, etc)? Having multiple things to organize can turn out to be a very messy system, and if you're one of those people who is constantly borrowing from one account to help you fund another account, keeping track of your expenses becomes more complicated than it needs to be. A jack of all trades becomes a master of none, and diversifying your savings into several different savings accounts leaves you with barely anything in the multiple accounts you hold.

Consider starting your minimalist budget with just one account each for checking, savings, and retirement. It keeps your finances extremely simple, makes saving money much easier, and makes it easier to organize your budget when your finances aren't spread out all over the place.

Another great approach which minimalists take to simplify their budget and spending is to automate as many of their payments as possible. Anything that can be automated, do it! Automate your savings to be directly deposited into your savings and retirement accounts, automate your debt payments and your bill payments. This is going to make it much easier for you to stay on top of all your payments so you avoid those pesky late payment charges.

Creating a minimalist budget is also going to require that you look back at all your past spending habits and purchases, which will then allow you to question any future purchases you are going to make from this point forward. It is important to do an honest evaluation of just what your spending was so you could determine a pattern or spending habits. Getting to know your spending habits better will lead you to identify when you might be lapsing back into your old ways. It is just as important to question all your future purchases by asking the question you already know is coming - is this necessary for me? It took you a long time to earn the money that you are now thinking about spending, so every purchase you make needs to count and be worth that time and effort spent earning those dollars.

After successfully establishing a budget for yourself, there is one final part of the process that needs to be taken care of, setting up a regular financial meeting with yourself so you can review your progress. Getting organized, simplifying your finances and setting a successful budget is one thing, but maintaining and implementing it effectively over time is another. There will be changes in your life along the way, which means there is never going to be a perfect plan or a budget that you create just once and you're set for life. A constant and regular review of your budget is essential to keeping up with your finances, making sure that this budget still works for you. Regular reviews also give you the opportunity to make any changes or needed tweaks to your budget to make it work better. Start by committing to at least one day out of the week where you revisit your budget and expenses for the week. Observe how well you have managed to stick to what you committed to, and how much progress you've made so far.

CHAPTER 6
DECLUTTERING THE DIGITAL

Who would have thought that minimalism would extend to decluttering your computer and other digital aspects of your life too? It is amazing how much of our lives can actually be simplified if we think about it. You may be asking yourself why there is a need for digital decluttering. Why would you need, for example, to declutter your computer when it seems to be working just fine right now? Computers need to be decluttered just as much as the rest of our lives because having too many things stored on it is only going to slow it down gradually. Not to mention how too much clutter is going to leave you with very little space to store your files if you don't clean out your system every now and then.

Having a digital cleanup routine can be just as beneficial as having a physical cleanup routine. Just because the clutter on your digital devices may not be as evident or visible as the ones directly in your environment, that doesn't mean it doesn't exist. The clutter will still be there, building up file after file, document after document, and we don't even realize it until we start to wonder one day why our devices don't seem to be performing as optimally as they should.

Digitally decluttering is not just about saving space and making your devices work faster though, it is also about enhancing your productivity. We give very little thought to the fact that the clutter we see every day on our phones and our computers is actually an invisible killer that squashes your productivity levels. The way your desktop is set up right now has an invisible impact on you mentally. Too much going on causes you to be easily distracted, and instead of jumping onto an urgent task right away as soon as your computer starts up, you idle and linger for several minutes looking at all the other stuff that's going on before getting started on the task you should have begun 10-minutes ago. How often has this happened to you?

Do You Put As Much Effort Into Digital Decluttering?

How much time and effort do you spend digitally decluttering? Once in a while? Frequently? Almost never? If you do conduct the occasional cleanup, do you think you're putting in the same amount of effort on this digital cleanup as you do for the physical decluttering process? Digital clutter may not be as problematic as physical clutter, but it is troublesome nonetheless, and the thing is, you will never be able to eliminate it entirely the way that you can with physical clutter because of how much our lives are now tied to the digital space. Whether we like it or not, technology isn't going anywhere anytime soon, and in fact, we seem to be getting more dependant on it now more than ever. Since it isn't possible to completely eliminate this kind of clutter, the best thing you could do for yourself is to learn how to simplify it so navigation becomes easier.

Digitally Decluttering Leads to Better Productivity

Modern man relies so heavily on their digital devices. From the moment we wake up to the time we lay our heads down on the pillow at night, our lives are intertwined throughout the day with the digital space. Computers, laptops, mobile phones, tablets, even smartwatches are supposedly here to simplify our lives and make things easier so we spend less time on our workload, but it has become quite the opposite. That's because if the lifestyle that we lead is already naturally cluttered, to begin with, this tends to carry over onto our digital lives too. All the extra "hours" you supposedly would have gained from quicker and faster internet processes have now been lost wading through mountains of emails that need to be sorted out, searching for documents online, and of course, countless hours spent aimlessly browsing through social media apps.

Leonardo Da Vinci once said that simplicity is the ultimate sophistication, and he was right. Clutter is nothing but a distraction, not to mention how unappealing it looks visually. Here's what the computer of a minimalist might look like (this is going to be different for everyone based on your needs). Think of a desktop which is clean, clutter-free and perhaps even emptied folders. All you see when you log in is the image that you have chosen as your desktop wallpaper. A simple, minimalist approach which helps them to immediately focus on what needs to get done for the day without the distraction of unnecessary folders vying for their attention. A completely empty desktop with no icons is simplicity at its finest. Every minimalist might have a different approach to it which works for them of course, but this is just an example of-of what their computer might look like. Minimalists choose to purposely not have a cluttered desktop, despite the fact that it may seem easier to have your most frequently used apps or documents on it so you can quickly access them with a simple double-click. It may be easier, but there's a reason why minimalists choose not to do this. It's because having too much going on and let it be the first thing that you see when you sign onto your computer causes visual distraction and stress. Imagine logging onto your laptop and seeing nothing on the screen but a simple, calming picture that you've chosen as your desktop wallpaper. Now, imagine logging on and seeing about 20 different folders and documents all at once on your screen, just screaming reminders at you about how much work needs to get sorted through. Which is going to be the one that causes you the most stress? A simple tweak, but one that makes a big impact on your mental and emotional state of being.

Minimalists instead choose to organize all the icons on their desktop into a folder. All the documents and folders that currently sit on your desktop right now as the very first step, and you can sort through them later. Once you've cleaned that up, you can begin working on creating separate folders according to your document needs, labeling each folder "Work", "Pictures", "Contracts", and anything else you might need. Every document should have a "home", which is a folder, of its own. Transfer all of these documents onto your computer's hard drive and store them there instead of the desktop.

Once you've done that, it is time to pick your desktop wallpaper. It is important to stick to the theme of minimalism, even when choosing your wallpaper. Keep it simple, clean, serene, calm and peaceful. A quick search on Google will reveal plenty of minimalist wallpaper options to choose from. Plain colors or perhaps a nice, serene nature scene might work. As long as your wallpaper doesn't have too much going on that it becomes distracting. It is entirely possible to streamline the digital aspects of your life, and you can accomplish this by going through the following steps:

- **Decluttering Your Social Media** - The number one distraction and productivity killer these days are social media. Facebook, Instagram, Twitter, SnapChat, Pinterest and more take up far too much of our time as we spend scrolling and searching without any real purpose or intention. You tell yourself you're only going to check these social media apps for a couple of minutes, but the next thing you know half an hour has gone by and you've fallen behind on a task you should have started. Decluttering begins with your social media apps, and it's time to work through them one by one. You don't need to delete your accounts, but you do need to start thinking about downsizing in terms of your connections and who you follow. Facebook friends that you barely know or haven't had a real conversation with in years don't need to be on your list, delete them. This one action alone makes a tremendous impact on your newsfeed and the less material you have to scroll through, the less time you're going to spend online. Do the same thing across all your other social media platforms. Your social media connections should only be limited to the few important people in your life to keep it meaningful. Remove everyone whom you rarely have a connection with to streamline your experience.

- **Downsizing Email Time** - It was mentioned in Chapter 3 about how you should consider downsizing to only have one email account. Or perhaps two, if you want to keep your office email address and personal email separate. How many email accounts do you currently own besides the one you need to use at the office? You don't need to have Gmail, Yahoo Mail or Hotmail simultaneously; there is no real need for multiple email accounts. Pick just one email account to work with and eliminate the rest. Once you have done that, it is time to assess your email content and streamline your inbox. Unsubscribe to emails which you no longer have any interest in. Emails which are not relevant, beneficial or impacting your life in any major way does not need to stick around. All those subscription emails reminding you about the latest promotions and sales are unnecessary distractions and they make your inbox look messy. Hit the unsubscribe button. Next, work on your email content and delete anything that is no longer relevant to you. For the emails that you do need to keep, create separate folders to organize these emails according to content. Your main email home page should only contain new emails which come in daily and nothing more. By streamlining and eliminating the unnecessary, you will then be able to work on minimizing the amount of time spent on emails. For personal emails, make it a point to only check it twice a day at most, once in the morning and once at night. Aim to spend no more than an hour responding and catching up on emails. Work emails should be kept during work hours only, and anything else that takes place after hours can be left until tomorrow unless extremely and absolutely of utter importance. We're talking urgency like your career is on the line. If it isn't then emails are not a priority and they can wait.

- **Purging Your Mobile Phone** - If you managed to successfully declutter your computer, tackling your mobile phone next should be a walk in the park. Of course, some might still find this challenging, having to delete the apps on their phone, and it might seem odd at first to have your phone screen looking surprisingly empty and vacant. Once you get used to the simplicity of it all though, you'll wonder why you didn't get on this sooner because of how much easier it has made going through your mobile phone. Begin by going through your current apps and removing anything that you no longer need, want to use. Your home screen should only contain the apps which are of utmost importance to you, and the ones that you frequently use every single day. Would it amaze you to find out that having just one page for all your apps is completely possible? Consider purging your contact list too, deleting any numbers that you no longer have any use for. The most important numbers are going to be those of your family and friends anyway and really, that's all you need when you get right down to it. That, and a couple of important contact numbers and details from work. That is all your contact list should contain. Repeat the same steps for your other digital devices.

You never know just how easy and hassle-free your life can be until you begin to streamline and organize it, and that's why minimalists love this concept so much. Suddenly, they have more free time on their hands to do the things they love and to spend it with the people they love when they're no longer bogged down by all the unnecessary. Reducing your screen time may seem like an impossible thought, but once you make a conscious effort to do so, you're going to see a big difference. Far too many of us are too caught up with technology, allowing it to run our lives and rob us of precious quality time.

Other Strategies to Help You Digitally Declutter

Other helpful strategies and approaches which you could take to digitally declutter include:
- Avoid using your desktop as the default "save" location for all your items. Remember how every item in your home has a "home" of its

own? Create "homes" for your important documents by sorting them into folders.
- Set reminders to prompt you when it's time to clean things up.
- Don't download unnecessary apps that you don't need. Remember the minimalist way; everything must have a purpose, an impact, and a benefit. If it doesn't, then you don't need it.
- Streamline your push notifications by turning off the unnecessary ones and only keeping the important notifications turned on. You don't need notifications from your social media apps, they're only distracting you. Notifications should only come from text messages and important reminders.
- Turn off your personal email notifications; you don't need them to be turned on all day. Controlling how many emails you receive in a day will significantly cut down your screen time.
- Track down the documents which are wasting space on all your digital devices right now and consider either getting rid of them or storing them digitally in the cloud instead. These documents could sneakily be taking up space on your computer, and if you haven't used them for so long you even have forgotten that you have them, then it's a safe bet that you could probably remove them for good.
- It is time to unplug and deactivate all those online accounts you no longer use. You've probably signed up for dozens of services and accounts online, some which you have long forgotten about but still keep receiving emails from. If you can't even remember your login details and passwords to those accounts, why still keep them around? Streamline your online life by ridding yourself of anything and everything that is unnecessary.
- Unfollow groups and pages on Facebook that you are no longer interested in, especially if it's not relevant to you anymore. Remember, social media should be kept for only keeping in touch with people, and perhaps some companies or groups that you genuinely have an interest in or care about.
- If you don't know someone on social media immediately, consider rejecting their friend request. You don't need to have 500 people on your friend's list if those people are not people who matter to you. Quality over quantity is something which can be extended towards your social circle too. Having only 10 quality contacts on your social media is much better than having 100 that are of little significance to you.
- If Facebook is reminding you that it is someone's birthday today but you don't feel any inclination to reach out and send them a quick birthday message, that's a good sign that it could be time to remove them as a friend. If they were someone important, or someone who mattered a great deal to you, you will always want to reach out on special occasions.

Going Paperless

Going paperless is something that is going to be another big adjustment for many. Particularly, if you have been so used to relying on paper documents and hard copies to get you by all this time. But that old fashioned system of having files and drawers crammed full of paper is nothing but clutter. With the busy and hectic lives that most of us live these days, having to sort through all these documents and files is going to be a very time-consuming process, and we simply don't have that kind of time to waste, especially for minimalists. Simplify and declutter your filing process by not filing your documents. That's right, stop the filing process. Everything can be stored online on digital drives these days, and there is really no longer any need for having paper hard copies these days. Even contracts and important documents are now being sent electronically.

G-Drive, DropBox and even iCloud have made it so easy, quick and efficient to drag and drop your files, uploading them to the cloud in a matter of minutes. The best part is how they don't occupy any physical space in your environment at all. Clutter-free! Even better is that you can access these files when they're stored online from anywhere you may be, as long as you have a strong internet connection and a digital device to log into your account. No more having to travel back and forth lugging heavy important documents which you might misplace or lose anyway, which makes the cloud option the safer choice. The files will be there forever, and you don't have to worry about losing them the way that you would with physical copies of these documents. If you want even more protection and peace of mind (because you happen to be one of those people that constantly worry about losing your files if your digital devices happen to crash), you could always back up your documents on an external hard drive as a safety measure too. Filing all your documents online is the simplest approach that makes the most sense. You can quickly and easily sort and locate any document that you need within a matter of minutes, thanks to the search function that these online storage systems provide. The search feature is even available on your laptop, and this beats spending unnecessary time having to sort through physical copies of documents trying to find what you're looking for any day of the week.

Even your pictures can be stored online quickly and conveniently, eliminating the need for physical photo albums which only take up space in your home. All the pictures that we take are done through our mobile phones these days anyway, so why not take it a step further and store them online too? Save your pictures in the cloud and like the documents, you will be able to quickly and easily access them anytime, anywhere.

We all live in a digital world these days, so really we need to start asking ourselves why is there still a need for so much paperwork in our lives? Especially in our offices, some people may still be reluctant to make the change, simply because they're so accustomed to having physical hard copies that they can hold in their hands. It gives them a sense of security, being able to hold these physical copies for themselves, and the push to go digital is going to take a bit of time for them to get used to the idea. Transferring all your paperwork to the digital space is going to take some time to sort through, but then so was decluttering your home. That probably took you a long time to work through but look at how beneficial it turned out to be now that you did it. Well worth the effort, wouldn't you say? The same thing goes for your digital documents.

Think of how much lighter and freer you would feel in your home office and your work office without all that paper cluttering and taking up space on your desk and shelves. Going paperless is not as challenging as you might initially think, and to begin, you simply need to begin questioning your existing documents. For every note, form, and paper, ask yourself if this document is something that you are going to need long term and if it is, can it be made digital. The answer is going to be yes or no, of course, depending on the type of document you have. A post-it note reminding you about to pick up some bread and milk afterward, for example, does not need to be made digital because you're not going to need it again. An important document like your employment contract, for example, is something that can be made digital (if it isn't already) because this is an important document which you're going to need to hold onto for some time.

Another way of going paperless is to simply stop printing everything out. Read them on your computer, tablet or mobile phone. If you're only going to print them out to read and then toss in the recycling bin when you're done, that's a waste of valuable resources (minimalists care about the environment, remember?). Other ways to cut down on your paper trail include:

- Avoid sending faxes, because they are outdated anyway since everything can easily be emailed or shared across the cloud.
- Avoid sending letters and memos, emails are the more sensible approach, and you don't waste any resources doing it.
- If you rely on the use of forms at work, consider transferring these forms online and getting people to fill them out there instead.
- Send digital invoices instead of paper invoices. There is plenty of software available that allows you to quickly create digital invoices in mere minutes.
- Switch to using contracts online instead of printing out physical copies and manually mailing it to the receiving party. It is easy to sign contracts digitally these days.
- Checks are an outdated system of payment, everything is done online these days anyway.
- Cut back on your paper magazine subscriptions and switch to online subscriptions instead. Almost all newspapers and magazines are available digitally these days.

CHAPTER 7
LIVING WITH A NON-MINIMALIST

Living with people can sometimes be a challenge on its own, but doing it whilst also being a minimalist? That's probably going to be twice or three times the challenge. Your journey towards minimalism is going to come with a series of challenges, one of which is going to be skepticism and doubt you're going to receive from others. They could be your family, your friends, children, roommates, even your colleagues at work who have noticed you furiously cleaning out your cubicle in a decluttering spree and wonder what on earth you were doing. Even harder when the doubt and hesitation usually come from the person who would normally be your biggest supporter, which in this case would be your spouse. The one you're living with.

Suddenly your biggest and most dedicated supporter is going to be the one who becomes the greatest challenge, especially when they find it hard to see why you've chosen to go down this road and completely change everything the two of you have become so comfortable with as you built your life together. It can be hard when the person that you love the most doesn't seem to grasp the benefits and see things from your point of view, and it could take a long time and a lot of convincing before you can successfully get them on their side. You might even have to brace yourself for the fact that they might never fully embrace minimalism because it simply isn't something that they want. That could be a very tough pill for you to swallow if you're so used to doing everything together. To make matters even more difficult, the two of you are living together, sharing one space, and all the stuff that comes with that space.

Whether it is your roommate, friends or your spouse, living with someone is not always going to be smooth sailing all the way. When you decide to make a life change for yourself, you have to brace for the fact that they might not always be on board or supportive of what you're planning to do. You may think that you are making the best decision in the world, while they might see it as you're doing something totally insane trying to give away more than half of your belongings. The transition to minimalism is going to involve a lot of change, and when there are other people in the mix who are not going down the same path that you are, adjustments need to be made.

The Survival Guide to Living With Loved Ones Who Are Not Minimalists

You may not always see eye-to-eye with your family (if you're living with more than just your spouse in your household), but there are several things you could do to help make the transition into minimalism easier not just for them, but for yourself too.

- **Respecting Decisions** - It is important to respect everyone's decision in this scenario, even if their decision may not be something you agree with or what you hoped for. Trying to force everyone to go along with your lifestyle when they are not prepared for it (or want to

do it) is going to create a lot of tension and arguments in the relationship. If your spouse, children or roommates are not ready to be on board with your decision to be a minimalist, respect their decision and let them be.
- **Seeing Is Believing** - Sometimes, the most effective approach that you can take would be to let others see for themselves just how beneficial becoming a minimalist can be. Since they are living with you, they are bound to notice the positive changes which are taking place in your life, especially when you're happier than you were before. Not only are they going to see it, but this new, happier, positive energy is going to rub off on them too, and they'll eventually start to see that you might be onto something with this whole minimalist living approach. Who knows, they might even like it enough and want to reap the same benefits they see you experiencing and try it out for themselves too.
- **Avoid Being Defensive** - It can be frustrating when you're trying to convince others to see things from your point of view and they're not being supportive. Sometimes they might even be critical and naturally, you feel like you want to defend your decisions and your choices. You're going to have to make some hard decisions as a minimalist when it comes to your belongings in particular, and your spouse, family or kids might even question you constantly about the choices you're making. Don't let that get you bent out of shape, and instead of being defensive, try to calmly explain your decisions and provide them with as much information as possible. Remember that they don't understand why you're doing this, and their questioning it to find some answers to help them make sense of it all. It is not a direct attack on you in any way.
- **Regular Discussions** - It is important to have regular discussions with your spouse and family about the decision that you make as a minimalist. This helps everyone find common ground and compromise, which is a huge part of ensuring that everyone is happy at the end of the day. It is important to learn how to work together for the long term, because this is going to be a lifelong journey, and you don't want your family to be unhappy along the way.
- **Talking About Your Progress** - As you progress, talk to your family about each step that you take so they know what's happening every step of the way. At each stage of the decluttering process when it comes to common and shared spaces, you may need to explain why and where you are in the minimalist process. Talk to them about what you intend to do before you clear space, whether their belongings are involved or not, and once they understand and agree, go ahead with your progress.
- **Creating Organized Spaces** - If you happen to live with someone who's a collector, a good compromise would be to help them create

an organized space in the home where they can store these items. When you declutter, you're not going to be able to get rid of their collectible items if they're not ready to let these things go. That's just going to cause an argument between the two of you. You're not going to be able to stand the items being strewn about in a disorganized manner either since this is not going to be aligned with your new minimalists' values. Compromise and find common ground to work it by talking things through and helping them create an organized space they would be happy with displaying their items, and you get to be happy not having "clutter" around your home.

- **Avoid Assumptions** - Don't assume that your spouse, family members or roommates are going to automatically know what's going on or what you're up to. You may know what you're doing and what's required as part of your journey towards minimalism, but that doesn't necessarily mean that they understand it. You know why you're decluttering the bookshelf, but that doesn't mean they do. Assumptions may lead to misunderstandings and arguments, and you want to avoid that by reminding yourself that your family may not always understand the decisions behind your actions. Avoid assuming and always seek to clarify instead.
- **Explain the Benefits** - The benefits of minimalism may have got you all excited and eager to begin, but for your family who has no idea what this concept entails, let alone how beneficial it can be, they're not going to understand why you decided to do a complete 180-degree change. To them, there is nothing wrong with the way they're currently living, and they're not going to see a need for anything to change. It is up to you to explain the benefits of this new approach you have decided to go with, and to let them know how you believe it is going to help you. If you believe minimalism is going to make you feel calmer, let them know. If you believe minimalism is going to be beneficial for your finances, let them know. If you believe it is going to help you reconnect with what's important in your life, let them know.
- **See Their Side of Things** - As much as you want them to see things from your perspective and why you believe minimalism is something you should embark on, it is equally important that you see things from their perspective too. It may be hard for you to understand why nobody seems to be seeing the benefits the same way that you do, but likewise, they will have a hard time understanding why you don't see how upset these changes may cause them to feel. You're about to change everything they have become so accustomed to, and getting rid of a lot of things in the home which they may have formed attachments to. Imagine if someone in your family suddenly decided that they want to get rid of stuff around the home, a lot of which may be your stuff which you like. That's not going to be something you're

automatically okay with. Empathize with them and put yourself in their shoes and it will make the process much less stressful on yourself and them.
- **Set an Example** - You can't force someone to go along with what you want, but you can set an example for them to follow. When someone is having a tremendously positive effect on your life, the changes are going to be hard to miss. Your family is bound to notice eventually, and slowly they'll start warming up to the idea, possibly even consider jumping on board the minimalist concept with you. Being a good example is especially important if you have young children in your home. They observe, notice and copy everything that you do, even the things you think they may not be paying attention to. It is through the example that you set where they are going to learn true happiness doesn't come from material possessions. Be the best example that you can be, and they will eventually come around.
- **Don't Force Change On Them** - You can't force someone to change if they're not ready for it. The desire to change needs to come from within, and it is never going to work if they feel like they are being forced into doing something they don't want to. You may think that you're doing them a huge favor by helping them declutter their home, but that is not how they are going to feel. You would feel angry if someone just tossed out your stuff without talking to you about it first, and it is only natural that they would feel the same way. If they're not ready for it, don't force them into it.
- **Don't Let Stuff Come In Between** - At the end of the day, they are just stuff, and the last thing you want is for it to let it come in between your relationship. Don't forget that minimalism is about holding onto and focusing on what matters the most, and the relationships that you have with the people you love will always win over any amount of stuff, any day. If you're frustrated that your spouse or family is getting in the way of your decluttering process because they want to hold onto something that you want to get rid of, allow yourself to feel frustrated, but don't hold it against them. Learn to let go of those feelings quickly by reminding yourself you can work on finding a compromise later and move on.
- **Start With Your Own Stuff First** - Since minimalism was your idea to begin with, it is only fair that you work on clearing your own stuff first before moving onto theirs. True, the outcome may not be as effective as you would have hoped, seeing as how you might only have been able to clear away a portion of what you would have liked to, but it's better than nothing. You need to start somewhere, so start by working on purging your own stuff first. Perhaps when they see how much better the house looks without as much clutter around, they'll want to get in on the decluttering process too. True, it is easier to notice someone else's mess first before you even notice your own,

but that's what you're going to need to do if you want to make this arrangement work.
- **Don't Be Discouraged If They Don't Like It** - Not everyone is always going to like or want to do the same things as you. That can be disappointing, but don't let that discourage you if they don't like minimalism as much as you wanted them to. You chose to be a minimalist because you believed it would benefit you and make you a better person for it, and that's the motivation that you need to remind yourself of whenever you feel yourself losing heart.
- **Ask them to Help** - They may not be on board with becoming 100% minimalist just yet, but you can still ask for their help to keep the home neat and tidy after you have decluttered what you could. Sit them down for a chat and tell them you worked very hard to get the home neat and clean again, and you would appreciate it if they could support you by helping to put things away in their proper place to keep the home clutter-free. Young children might need a little bit more explanation and guidance with this one, but again lead by example and they will eventually copy what you do. Let them know that you have given every item in the home a "home" of its own, and if they could help you out by returning these items to their "homes" whenever they can, that would make you very happy.

It may not always be easy living with someone who isn't a minimalist or on board with what you're doing, but there are certain things that you can do to help make the living arrangements easier. The most important thing to remember is to constantly communicate every step of the way so neither party gets caught off guard by what is happening. If someone is unhappy with something, talk about it and try to find a workable solution you will both be happy with.

Above all else, be patient with them. They are still your family at the end of the day, and nothing is worth compromising on that relationship. One day of decluttering the bookshelf, living room or closet is not going to immediately inspire them to start picking up minimalism right away. Be patient and keep doing what you're doing, they'll eventually come around and be supportive of your efforts when they see how much better and happier you are.

How to Now Deal With Your Other Loved Ones Who Are Not Minimalists Either

Deciding to become a minimalist and live a simpler, happier and more meaningful life can be a very exciting prospect. For the people who decided that this is what they want to do. Everyone else is going to simply look at you with confusion and wonder why on earth you would suddenly decide to give away half your stuff and think that you could be happier without them. You can't blame them for feeling this way, and after all, you might even have felt that way for a long time. This is what most have us have grown up with all our lives, being surrounded by the consumerist lifestyle, and many people don't know any other way of life.

Undergoing this change is very exciting for you because you have now seen the light, but all your other loved ones might have it difficult to understand your decision and how this is going to affect them. You are about to embark on a new life-changing journey that is supposed to strengthen your relationships and bring you closer to the people you love, but when you're going through changes that they don't always understand, it can be hard to feel the close connection with them during the difficult transition. Here's what you can do to make it a little bit easier on yourself.

- **Know That You Might Have to Explain Yourself** - You might not like having to do it, but in this case, you probably have to consider making an exception. Other family members, friends, and even colleagues (since you'll be decluttering your office too) are going to have some comments. Maybe even a lot of comments. Some of these comments and remarks might rub you the wrong way, even if they did not intend for it to be. What you're doing is going to be something that they're not used to, perhaps never even heard of, and they're going to have a lot of questions, comments and perhaps even suggestions about it. Why are you doing this? What are you going to do with all your stuff? Why do you need to give it away? Is this going to change who you are? Some of your loved ones and friends might even have concerns about whether this is going to impact the relationship that they have with you, and the best thing you could do to assuage all those fears is to take the time to explain what you're doing and why. Explain all the ways in which minimalism is going to benefit you. Explain what the process involves. Explain what you're going to do with all your stuff. Explain how this is going to improve your relationship when you're no longer distracted.
- **Thank Those Who Are Being Supportive** - Some family and friends will immediately be supportive and have your back no matter what. These people are the true stars because they never judge the decisions that you make and instead do their best to support you in any way that you might need. They will still be curious about what you're doing, but to those who love and care about you the most, your happiness is all that they need to get them on your side. They serve as reminders of why you're choosing to do this, so you can now turn your focus towards these precious relationships because they bring you more happiness than buying a new jacket or a new pair of shoes ever could. They respect your choices and they don't belittle you for them, even if those choices are not something they would have chosen for themselves. Take a moment to truly thank them for their support and let them know how much it means to you on this journey.
- **Be Honest** - Hiding bits and pieces of information or trying to do things under wraps has never panned out long-term. Besides, you're not going to be happy if you have to hide parts of who you are from your loved ones because you think they might not understand what

you're doing. Honesty will always be far and away, the best approach to take, even more so in times like this when you're about to make a big change in your life. Answer any questions that come your way with complete honesty. It is okay if not everyone is going to agree with you.

- **Highlight the Positive Sides** - The biggest question that most people are going to ask is - why you're doing it, and when they do - highlight the positives more than the challenges. It's not about trying to convince them by only talking about the good things, but it's because challenges are not going to last forever, whereas the benefits that you are going to get out of this experience will last you a lifetime. So why dwell on something that is only a small bump in the road in the grand scheme of things? Talk about the positives to help others see where you're coming from, like how minimalism has made you happier because you now have more time to spend with the people you love and pursue the things that you love.
- **Avoid Sounding Preachy** - Phrases like "you should" or "you must" are going to make you sound preachy, and make it seem as though you're trying to push your new lifestyle onto the rest of your family. Rubbing your loved ones the wrong way by trying to be too pushy is only going to turn them off to the idea of minimalism instead of helping them to understand and embrace the choice that you have made.
- **Learn to Adopt a Sense of Humor** - You might get a few jokes thrown your way, and some of your friends might resort to teasing you about what you're doing. Adopting a sense of humor approach is going to help you learn to take it in stride instead of taking it personally. They usually don't mean any harm by it, and family and friends always tease each other at a comfortable level anyway. If you're feeling sensitive about the comments because you're still working through these changes yourself, learn to see the funny side of things and smile or laugh along with them.
- **Avoid Taking Things Negatively** - Not every comment that is being said is done out of spite or with a negative intention behind it. True, your loved ones and friends may not be on the same wavelength as you about this subject right now, but avoid assuming that everything they are saying or doing is associated with negativity. They could just be making a general comment or observation with no malicious intent behind it. If you're not sure, it doesn't hurt to clarify things with them instead of jumping to your own conclusions and getting mad at them.

Change is always going to be difficult, even if it is for the best. Explaining the change is possibly even harder when you're trying to convince someone else to see where you're coming from. The best thing you could do for yourself is to give them some time to adjust, they'll get used to it eventually, just like how you need some time to get used to your new life too.

CHAPTER 8
TRAVELING LIGHT

You got your suitcase ready for your vacation and you're ready to start packing. As your suitcase starts filling up, you begin to wonder if it's going to be enough. Perhaps you need another for all the stuff you can't quite fit into this one? But then is one more going to be enough? Maybe you should pack a dressier piece of clothing in case you might need it. Or maybe a couple more pairs of shoes so you've got some options to work with. Do you need a raincoat or a lightweight jacket? Maybe both? Suddenly one suitcase becomes two or three pieces of luggage that you're carting around with you and to the airport. Does this sound just a little too familiar?

Packing light seems to be a struggle for many. How do those backpackers and travelers on YouTube seem to fit everything that they need for three weeks or more into just a backpack? That almost seems like magic when you're struggling to fit even one week's vacation worth of items into a medium-sized suitcase. You end up with all sorts of items you never initially planned on bringing with you but decided to at the "last minute" just in case you might need them. The "just in case" scenario often never happens, and you're carrying a heavier load than you should for nothing.

Minimalism isn't just sweeping into people's homes and their lives anymore, it is taking the travel world by storm too, as more travelers find even more ways to whittle down the items that they carry to the bare minimum that is needed for them to survive comfortably on their trip. Most backpackers and travel bloggers especially have become experts at carrying just one piece of luggage with them, a miraculous feat which leaves the rest of us speechless and wondering is that all they packed?

A quick search online will lead you to several videos and posts where minimalist travelers talk about how liberating it is to be able to travel quickly and efficiently without anything weighing or slowing them down. With everything that they need all in just one backpack or suitcase, moving around at the airport and in between cities has never been easier. Nothing feels unnecessary or superfluous, and they feel much happier traveling because none of the stress which is associated with over packing or lugging around heavy baggage is a problem they have to deal with.

Minimalist Travel Explained

By now, you would already be familiar with the resonating theme in minimalism, which is to only have what you need and nothing more. This concept is now going to carry over towards your travel habits, whereas a minimalist traveler, you're going to pack only the absolute necessities, and not a scrap of clothing or item more. When you can fit your entire life into a mere backpack or suitcase, then you know you're doing something right.

By right, traveling as a minimalist should enable you to travel the world for a year and still be able to survive with just one bag alone. By limiting yourself to just one piece of luggage, it is going to discourage you from the urge to buy souvenirs and knick-knacks that you're never going to use for long, just for the sake of being able to tell people where you got them. When someone gives you a souvenir, do you really put it to good use? They're probably doing the same thing to the souvenirs that you bring them too. There's really not much you can do with a decorative piece of item with just the name of the destination printed on it.

Minimalist travel encourages you to seek out simplicity over the need for luxury, to put more emphasis on the experiences that you gain rather than the hotel you're staying in or how much you could buy and bring home with you. Minimalism is encouraging you to be efficient in every aspect of your life, even travel.

The society that we live in today places far too much emphasis on material possessions. The homes that we live in are a reflection of us, and many people dream of owning a big, luxurious home because they believe it is a reflection upon the success they have achieved. We buy expensive cars we can't afford because we want to show the rest of the world that we can have them. We seem to desire things rather than personal needs, focusing on what we can buy next instead of focusing on our health, relationships or passion. To put it plainly, the things that we own matter more to us than they really should. Our homes may be filled, but our hearts continue to remain empty - the only thing that can fix that emptiness, is minimalism.

Once you start adopting minimalism in your home, it won't be long before it spills over into the rest of your life. You start actively seeking out other areas of your life where you can rid yourself of excess "baggage", quite literally when it comes to travel.

To become a minimalist traveler, you're going to have to learn how to differentiate between what you want and what you need. For example, you may want to pack your hair straightener and bring it with you on your holiday, but it may not be something that you need if you can survive a week without having to straighten your hair. You may want to pack a pair of heels because you're so used to wearing them in your daily life, but you don't need to pack them because there is rarely going to be an occasion during your travels where you're going to need your heels. Leaving how to separate the "need" from "want" is going to cut down a lot of your travel items just by switching your mindset alone.

Your Guide to Travelling Like a Minimalist

Here's how you get started learning to travel like a minimalist:

Where to Begin

- **Downsizing Your Bag** - In keeping with the spirit of simplicity and downsizing, the first place to start would be to downsize the size of your bag. Instead of a medium or large suitcase, you're now going to get into the habit of only packing a cabin sized bag or even a backpack. You're going to fit one or two weeks worth of items into just a backpack or a cabin sized bag because you decided to do it. How many times have you fallen victim to the "oh I still have space in my bag, I guess I can fit in a couple more items". Not anymore. Becoming a minimalist traveler begins with the intentional choice to choose a smaller bag for your travels and nothing more.

Bonus tip: Consider investing in a lightweight backpack to save your weight limit at the airport.

What's Next?

- **Analyzing Your List** - It's time to downsize your list, and you're going to now analyze every item on your list and ask yourself do you really need this? Which items from your last trip did you bring but ended up not using at all? What non-essential daily habits do you think you could cut from your routine for the next week or two while you're on vacation? Are there smaller or more versatile versions of these items that you plan to bring? Did travel size toiletries for example? Packing is a personal thing, and downsizing your list is going to depend on what you absolutely need to bring with you on this trip and what you can temporarily do without.
- **Your Clothing Color Palette** - With only a few clothing options to your name now that you're a minimalist, getting into the habit of buying items of clothing with a color palette that allows you to easily mix and match your items is going to transform your packing habits like never before. Instead of needing 10 items of clothing to create a week's worth of outfits, you can shave it down to 5 items of clothing and still get a weeks' worth of outfits by mixing and matching your items.
- **Packing Cubes Are Your Friend** - Minimalists are all about keeping things neat, tidy and organized. Not just in their homes, but in their suitcase too. Packing cubes are going to keep your items neatly stored away and easy to find, which makes living out of a suitcase that much easier. Don't you just love the simplicity of minimalism?

Make your life easier by packing clothes which are not only comfortable but don't wrinkle as easily. You might like the idea of creating what's known as a capsule wardrobe, which is where you only choose a few, selected pieces of clothing which you can wear for any occasion and it matches everything that you own. You are always going to have access to shopping places no matter where you go, so if an emergency pops up (which is very rare), you could always quickly run out and get what you need.

Packing and Knowing Your Essentials

You're only going to bring with you what is absolutely needed and necessary while you're on the road. Among the essentials that you absolutely cannot leave home without, for example, include:

- Your passport and travel documents
- Your cash
- Emergency credit card
- Mobile phone and phone charger

These items are at the top of your priority list because you should never leave for a holiday without them.

The second tier of priority items would include the following:
- A lightweight sweater or a jacket
- Toothbrush
- Comfortable shoes
- Only one spare outfit for emergencies
- A water bottle

As long as you've always packed these essentials with you, you could go anywhere and still be okay. Everything else that you need can easily be purchased at your destination.

Minimizing Your Toiletries and Makeup

We've become so accustomed to packing our toiletries for the trips that we take and we have come to think of them as essential items. However, you're not going to need all the toiletries that you think you do. A minimalist would be able to survive with just the following items:
- Soap
- Toothbrush
- Toothpaste
- Deodorant

Lotions, shampoos, and conditioners are optional items because they can easily be picked up at your destination. If you only have a specific preference of shampoo and conditioner and you're not comfortable relying on unknown shampoo brands which might be available where you go, pack travel sized bottles of both to bring with you. Seek all-in-one or multi-purpose items to make traveling even easier if you can just bring one item but use it for several different functions.

Minimizing Your Clothing

Whether you're traveling to a destination with a warmer or colder climate, a minimalist packer can get by with these few staple pieces of clothing:
- One pair of pants (black so it can match all your items of clothing).
- Either one skirt or one pair of yoga pants, depending on your preference for comfort (NOT both).
- 4-5 T-shirts (depending on the length of your travel)
- A lightweight sweater or a jacket (pack both of you're going somewhere where the temperatures can get very chilly)
- 2-4 pairs of underwear (you can wash and wear)
- One sports bra as an additional versatile item
- 1-2 pairs of socks
- An extra pair of shoes
- Bathing suit (depending on your destination)

That's what a basic list of a minimalist traveler might look like. It is going to vary, of course, depending on where you're going, and to help you get the most out of your clothing items, here's what you should keep in mind:

- Always make comfort a priority and pack the most comfortable clothes you have.
- Get used to washing your clothes on your travels, because this is going to remove a lot of clothing items off your list.
- Go with a consistent color palette to easily mix and match your items.
- Only pack shoes you can walk in for hours without breaking a sweat because they'll be your most comfortable pair.

A great tip to remember when it comes to curbing your urge to pack more clothes than you should is to remind yourself of the fact that you're going there for a holiday, not a fashion show. No one is going to be paying attention to the fancy clothes that you wear, and no one is going to notice that you repeat your outfits because guess what? You're not going to be seeing the same people every day. Be as fashionable as you want at home, but keep your holidays simple, free and easy.

Minimizing Your Travel Gadgets

We can't leave home without our tech, but besides your mobile phone and charger (which are technically the only essentials) what else could you shave off your travel list when it comes to electronics? The minimalist traveler can usually only be seen traveling with their:

- Mobile phones
- Phone chargers
- Headphones

And that's it! Since our phones are able to do almost anything our tablets and computers can do these days, there's no need for anything else other than your phone. Some minimalists will choose to bring an extra DSLR camera with them if they're avid photographers who love capturing moments during their travels.

Life Is More Meaningful Beyond the Bag

A minimalist traveler is perfectly happy with a simple backpack and a few pieces of items because they know that it is the experiences they are going to get at their destination which is what really matters. Being a minimalist traveler is going to keep your spending modest too because buying souvenirs and knick-knacks are no longer going to become your priority.

All a minimalist needs to be happy is one piece of light luggage, their plane ticket and travel itinerary, and the excitement of exploring a new destination. Here are some other great tips to keep in mind that make minimalist travel an even more enjoyable experience:

- If you do happen to make several purchases during your travels (assuming they are absolutely necessary), consider mailing them home if you're still going to be on the road for some time.
- Nothing should be in your pockets except your wallet and your passport. This makes moving through airport security a much quicker process.

- Instead of bringing the entire guide book with you, consider photocopying only the sections that you need to lighten your load. Alternatively, you could just look up the information on your phone.
- Make copies of your important documents, which would be your passport, ID and credit cards or any other valuable documents you may have with you (if you're traveling for business perhaps). Alternatively, you could consider scanning and emailing these documents to yourself so you always have a copy which is easily accessible on your phone.
- It is a good idea to save some emergency contact numbers on your phone and your itinerary where you can easily access it quickly if needed.
- High-tech, quick-drying fabrics are going to be your best friend if you're doing a lot of wash and wear on your journey.
- Avoid over planning your trip, your itinerary should be kept simplified too. Rushing about too much from one place to the next will keep you from enjoying the experience the way that you should.
- Focus on a few meaningful experiences instead of trying to see everything on your trip, which may not always be possible. Quality over quantity at the end of the day, right?
- When traveling to the airport, arriving earlier than you think is necessary will keep you from feeling stressed rushing around hoping that you don't miss your flight.

The Benefits of Travelling Like a Minimalist

Many people would think of minimalist travel as a compromise, when in fact nothing could be further from the truth. When it comes right down to it, it's not about compromise, but efficiency. Plus, aside from having light luggage and only one bag to worry about on your travels, there are several other benefits which come from traveling like a minimalist that will make you wonder why you waited so long to get started:

- **Everything Become Faster** - Going through airport checks and security becomes faster. If you don't have to check in your luggage, the process becomes even faster when you're not wasting time standing in the queues and you can rely on those automated check-in machines and save yourself a lot of time in the process.
- **No More Baggage Claim** - Sail in and out of airports with ease when you no longer have to waste precious minutes waiting at the baggage claim area like everyone else. While all the other travelers are waiting for their bags to emerge, you're already at the airport exit hailing your cab to your hotel. Plus, you avoid dealing with the stress of having your luggage being misplaced or lost in transit.
- **No Worries About Losing Your Bag** - Losing your bag at the airport can be an absolute nightmare. You've arrived at your destination but your bag has not, and there's no telling how soon airport personnel is going to be able to help you sort that out. There's

nothing worse than arriving and having to spend extra money and time shopping for all your essentials again. This never has to be an issue again when you learn to travel with just a cabin sized bag or backpack.

- **You're Always First in Line** - Or among the first few people in line at customs and immigration anyway. This is usually where a lot of people get trapped in the bottleneck queues waiting for their turn. By skipping the baggage claim routine, you can ensure that you beat everyone else to the punch, making your airport transitions smooth and as hassle-free as possible.
- **Saving Money on Baggage Fees** - With no checked baggage, you'll save yourself some extra cash, along with the hassle of having to check your bag at the airport. Minimizing your travel gear significantly cuts the expense that comes with overweight baggage. Every airport would have its own requirements and restrictions, and baggage fees are just another added expense which is unnecessary and can easily be removed.
- **Saving Money on Storage** - Let's say you arrive at your destination in the wee hours of the morning and you can't check in just yet because the hotels only have a certain check-in time. With just one bag to contend with, you save yourself some cash not having to pay for bag storage somewhere while you explore the city waiting for your check-in time.
- **Finding Things Is Significantly Easier** - When you've only got the bare minimum with you, you're always able to find exactly what you're looking for within a matter of seconds. Open up your bag and everything you need is right there when you travel like a minimalist. No more wasting time digging around, having to pull out several items to and make a mess rummaging around trying to find what you're looking for.
- **Less Ironing to Contend With** - Especially if you make it a point to pack clothing items which don't wrinkle as easily. Simply wear, wash, dry and wear again. A simple change in your routine which can relieve you of a lot of the travel stress.
- **Your Items Always Match** - You can't go wrong when you've only packed a specific color palette that goes with almost everything and can easily be mixed and matched. No more being caught off guard and suddenly finding yourself with nothing to wear because the items that you have don't go well together and the rest of your clothes are still drying from the wash.
- **You're Always Comfortable** - How could you not be, when you've made it a point to specifically only pack comfortable clothing items? There's nothing that kills a holiday faster than feeling uncomfortable in your clothing, it distracts from the experience when all you want to do is get back to your hotel room and out of your clothes.

- **You're Less Annoyed Overall** - A lot of people tend to underestimate what a stressful experience traveling can be. The long queues, the endless waiting in lines, rushing about from one place to the next, moving through hoards of people trying to get from point A to point B as quickly as possible is not always an easy thing to deal with. By minimizing the complications that you face during your travels, you eliminate a lot of the stress that goes with it too.
- **Packing and Unpacking Can Be Done in Mere Minutes** - The less you pack, the faster you unpack (and pack again when it's time to leave). Some minimalists who have been doing this for a long time can easily be packed and ready to go in 10 to 15 minutes because they have so few items to deal with. Not only does this save a lot of time, but it also gives you peace of mind when you know exactly what items you came with and what you should be left with. When you're not rushing about, you're less likely to leave your stuff behind.
- **Run When You Need To** - Sometimes, no matter how much you plan and prepare, there may be an occasional moment where you might have to sprint through the airport to make it on time. With no wheelie bags or heavy suitcases to contend with, when you need to run, you'll be able to run as you mean it. The lighter your luggage, the faster you move.
- **No Matter Where You Are, You're Set** - Having all the essentials that you need to survive comfortably means that no matter where in the world you go, you're always able to get by because you have all that you need.

CONCLUSION

Thank for making it through to the end of this book, let's hope it was informative and able to provide you with all of the tools you need to achieve your goals whatever they may be.

Minimalism is a simple concept, yet one that can invoke profound change in the lives of those who choose to adopt this approach to living. Less stress, more balance in our lives, a healthier and happier mind, body and soul, all the things that we have struggled to hold onto have been right in front of us all along. We've just been far too distracted by the clutter in our lives to truly appreciate it. Buying new things may make you happy when you do, but that happiness will always be short-lived, and none of it can even come close to the kind of long-lasting happiness that minimalism can bring.

The world we live in may be moving at a rapid pace, but minimalism shows us that we can intentionally slow things down for ourselves by choosing simplicity over clutter in every facet of our lives. Our homes, jobs, relationships, travel, even our devices can be simplified if we wanted. We may not have intentionally chosen the consumerist life we lived before, but we now have a choice to choose something better for ourselves. Because a better life, a simpler, happier life rooted in all the things we value the most is a life worth decluttering for.

Finally, if you found this book useful in any way, a review on Amazon is always appreciated!

DESCRIPTION

Here's to new beginnings.....

A fresh start. A brand new beginning. A change for the better.

Those are all the things so many of us yearn for, but very few fail to accomplish. Why? Because we simply don't know how to go about it in the right way. We have spent most of our lives up to this point believing that our happiness lies in how much we earn, what we own and the things we can buy. We believed that the more we bought, the happier we will be. Yet, how many times have you found yourself returning to those feelings of dissatisfaction, unhappiness, and discontent even after you've bought something you were so sure would make you happy?

On average, almost all of us own more things that we really need to survive. Do you really need to own more than one car if you live somewhere public transport is easily available? Do you really need to own 10 jackets when they all serve the same purpose? Multiple pairs of shoes, some of which you haven't worn in months or even forgotten about? Why do we need to own multiples of the same item when they all serve the same purpose?

Not only is this clutter taking up space in your home, but it is also adding to your stress and you don't even realize it until you wake up to the fact that you could be drowning in your own clutter. It's the time that things started to change for the better, and that change begins with minimalism.

Minimalist Mindset is going to walk you through:
- What minimalism is and why you should do it
- How drowning in too much clutter could be holding you back
- The principles that minimalists live by
- Managing your expectations
- Debunking the myths and misconceptions about minimalism
- Getting started on the decluttering process
- How to achieve financial freedom through minimalism
- What it's like to live with a non-minimalist
- How to travel light and travel free

This is the answer to a better way of living you have been searching for all along. This is the key to holding onto that long-lasting happiness which has eluded you for so long. This is your new beginning.

MINIMALIST BUDGET

Save Money, Avoid Compulsive Spending, Learn Practical and Simple Budgeting Strategies, Money Management Skills, and Declutter Your Financial Life Using Minimalism Tools & Essentials

By
Jenifer Scott

© Copyright 2019 by Jenifer Scott - All rights reserved.
No part of this book may be reproduced or transmitted in any form or by any means, electronic or mechanical, including photocopying, recording or by any information storage and retrieval system without written permission of the publisher, except for the inclusion of brief quotations in a review.
The following book is reproduced below with the goal of providing information that is as accurate and reliable as possible. Regardless, purchasing this book can be seen as consent to the fact that both the publisher and the author of this book are in no way experts on the topics discussed within and that any recommendations or suggestions that are made herein are for entertainment purposes only. Professionals should be consulted as needed prior to undertaking any of the action endorsed herein. This declaration is deemed fair and valid by both the American Bar Association and the Committee of Publishers Association and is legally binding throughout the United States.
Furthermore, the transmission, duplication or reproduction of any of the following work including specific information will be considered an illegal act irrespective of if it is done electronically or in print. This extends to creating a secondary or tertiary copy of the work or a recorded copy and is only allowed with express written consent from the Publisher. All additional right reserved.
The information in the following pages is broadly considered to be a truthful and accurate account of facts and as such any inattention, use or misuse of the information in question by the reader will render any resulting actions solely under their purview. There are no scenarios in which the publisher or the original author of this work can be in any fashion deemed liable for any hardship or damages that may befall them after undertaking information described herein.
Additionally, the information in the following pages is intended only for informational purposes and should thus be thought of as universal. As befitting its nature, it is presented without assurance regarding its prolonged validity or interim quality. Trademarks that are mentioned are done without written consent and can in no way be considered an endorsement from the trademark holder.

INTRODUCTION

At first glance, a minimalist budget sounds like it's all about less: spending less, doing less – less fun, less life?!

This book will show you that a minimalist budget is really about more – putting more simplicity into your finances, becoming more efficient at managing your spending, saving more money, getting more of what you want out of life.

Imagine your financial journey as a trip through an unfamiliar land. Do you have your sights set on a destination in the distance, and you are just not sure exactly how to get there? Or do you feel aimless and lost, walking in circles and returning to the same place over and over again? A minimalist budget provides a map to guide you on your financial voyage, helps to keep you on track in the most efficient way possible, and gives you guidance on how to avoid dangerous pitfalls and wasteful dead-ends.

Using a minimalist budget allows you to take the complexity out of your financial life, see the big picture of where your money is going, and take control of what your money is doing for you.

There are many reasons you may be looking at this book. Perhaps you have always been conscious about spending and saving your money, and want to read about the methodology of doing it efficiently. Or perhaps you have had trouble with managing your spending, and want to get your financial life back on track. Maybe you make a six-figure income but just can't figure out where all your money is going every month.

No matter what your financial background and existing spending habits are, this book will show you what minimalist budgeting is and how to apply it to your goals and spending wants and needs. It will show you how to be persistent in your budgeting approach, even if you encounter setbacks and life changes.

With a minimalist budget, you can still have things that bring you convenience, comfort, and happiness. But the key to the minimalist budget approach is intentionality in how and when you buy things. By applying the concepts described in this book and being honest with yourself, you can take control of your possessions and spending. You can direct your resources meaningfully and with intent, helping you achieve your financial goals.

CHAPTER 1
Minimalist Budget Essentials: Entering The Minimalist Mindset

What a Minimalist Budget is and What it's Not

To many people, a minimalist budget sounds like an extreme form of being frugal. They imagine someone eating canned foods and sleeping on a mattress on the floor, spending their days clipping coupons. In fact, a minimalist budget is a very different concept from being frugal.

A minimalist budget is about streamlining your finances, prioritizing your financial goals, and having a good knowledge and control of your income and expenses. It's about being able to direct money toward the things that are most important to you. It's about reducing clutter in how you approach your finances and your possessions.

It's important to keep in mind that a minimalist budget does not necessarily imply spending less money. You can still choose to have expensive things, even luxury items, as long as they have a purpose and meaning in your life. However, a minimalist budget is likely to encourage you to spend less. Once you carefully account for your spending and prioritize your goals, you will be more efficient at using your money toward what you really want in life, instead of wasting your resources on trivial things.

A minimalist budget will help you to shift your priorities away from acquiring things just because they are a good deal, and toward getting things and experiences that you really value in life. What you value may not necessarily be less expensive, but you will not clutter your life with things that are not important. For example, instead of owning twenty pairs of shoes, all of which you got on sale for a really good deal, you might have just a few high-quality pairs that you really like, and which fulfill specific purposes in your life.

Living on a minimalist budget is about being efficient with your money and focusing on just the essentials in your financial approach. This differentiates it from being thrifty or frugal. A thrifty person looks for the best deals, uses coupons, accumulates points and rewards on their credit cards. Trying to get the best deal is commendable, but without a minimalist budget mindset, it's still easy to waste money by buying things just because they are on sale. This is where a minimalist budget will help you. You can prioritize your goals, avoid impulse purchases, and make the most out of your time and money.

How a Minimalist Budget Can Improve Your Life

Simply put, a minimalist budget can help you get freedom and simplicity into your life. By using intentionality to direct what your money is being spent on, you can stop wasting money on things that don't matter. You can direct your cash flow toward the things you really want in life, in the short term, and in the long term.

A lot of people are stuck in a cycle of earning money and spending it. If they work hard and earn more money, they just end up spending more money, because they start wanting more expensive things. They never actually feel content with what they already have, and it's hard for them to "get ahead" in life because they are hardly aware of where their money is being spent. Our society is very focused on acquisition as the source of happiness, and it's very easy to fall into this pattern.

A minimalist budget can stop the acquisition cycle and make you content and in control of your finances (and your life). At the core, we still have a hunter-gatherer mindset – we like to look for things! In modern life, this often materializes into shopping, (sometimes without a particular objective, just to see what's on sale or to find a good deal), browsing Craigslist or eBay to see if there is anything we might like to buy, looking at shopping catalogs, and doing other activities that involve just looking for something to buy.

A minimalist budget can free you from the cycle of searching for something to buy, getting that something, briefly experiencing either fulfillment or regret, and then moving on to looking for something else to buy. This cycle does not actually make you happy – it's a waste of your time and money. Inside, you know this, because while you feel excited looking for something to buy or anticipating a purchase, after you actually acquire that something, you do not feel that happy. Even if it's something you have wanted for a long time, you feel a slight sense of being let down, a little disappointed (and in some cases, full-on regret!) The only thing you can think of doing to make yourself feel better is to look for something else to buy next – perhaps accessories for your recent purchase, or just the next acquisition.

On the other hand, living on a minimalist budget can stop this wasteful purchasing cycle. It will show you ways to feel content and fulfilled by guiding you to your goals and letting you bring things into your life that actually have meaning and significance. By using a minimalist budget, you can streamline your purchasing process, focus on getting only the things you really need, and work on the financial goals that really matter in your life.

Another important benefit that a minimalist budget offers is less stress. For many people, worrying about paying their bills or other obligations can be a constant struggle. Ironically, this can be the same people who frequently make impulse purchases. Many relationships are strongly affected by money management or lack of it. Money is one of the leading reasons for arguments for couples. Relationships between parents and kids (of all ages) can be put under stress from differences in purchasing and entitlement viewpoints.

This is where a minimalist budget can help you. If you do not start controlling your money, your money ends up controlling you and negatively affecting your relationships with others. Using your minimalist budget, you can take control of your financial life. You can stop unnecessary spending so that your bills are lower to start with, and then you can get rid of your debt. You can plan a future that focuses on mindful spending and adding value to your life and your relationships.

Your Mindset and Attitude are at the Core of Minimalist Budget **Success**

Before focusing on the budgeting and planning aspects of minimalism, you have to get into the minimalist mindset. If you are not in the right mindset, you will find yourself trying to cheat yourself: see if you can slide that fancy latte in under the grocery expenses, borrowing money from your emergency fund for that shirt that's on sale because it's such a good deal and you can't miss it! (Even though you have dozens of other shirts).

If you are not really focusing on your financial goals and priorities, a minimalist budget will feel like it's working against you, preventing you from enjoying life and getting the things you want. Eventually, you will just decide that the minimalist budget is not for you and give up. You will miss out on the great opportunities that the minimalist budget approach offers: to make you fulfilled, efficient with your spending, and goal-oriented.

If you have the appropriate mindset, you will understand that your minimalist budget is helping you to be more efficient, moving you toward your goals, the important things in life, making you happier.

Much like yoga or other mindful activities, getting into and being in a minimalist mindset is a "practice" – a continuous process rather than something you achieve and set aside. If you are used to spending money on trivial things, the initial minimalist practice will feel challenging – like stretching or trying to do physical activity after you have been sedentary for a long time. But the more you practice being in the minimalist mindset, the more second nature it becomes, and the more you will enjoy actually putting your minimalist budget thoughts and ideas into reality. Eventually, your old habits of mindless spending will seem very wasteful to you. The "thrill" of looking for something to buy will be replaced with contentment, and knowing that you are doing something that's useful for your life.

The good news is since you are reading this book, you are already well on your way to incorporating the minimalist mindset into your life. Chances are, you have already begun to understand that spending money is not making you happy. Conversely, it's probably making your life worse! Perhaps you have recognized the cycle of looking for something to buy and the lack of lasting fulfillment that follows the purchase, and want to end it. Or you have allowed your spending to create financial issues in your life, and you would like to get back on the right track.

As a part of your minimalist mindset practice, direct your thoughts toward the reason you are considering living on a minimalist budget. Think about the buying cycle you have been in, and where it got you, both from a financial perspective and from the perspective of how it has made you feel in the long-term. As you are faced with temptations and opportunities to purchase things, return your thoughts to this and ask yourself to make a new decision this time, a decision that will get you out of the mindless spending cycle.

An important part of your minimalist approach is letting go of comparing yourself to others. Many of our purchases, both impulse ones and planned ones, are caused by us comparing our possessions to those of our friends, relatives, co-workers, and neighbors. We often give little thought to whether a particular object will really bring value or happiness into our lives. Instead, we focus on how we measure up to others – with our gadgets, vacations, cars, and many other things. We want to feel normal, to fit in, or to be better than others.

Wanting to fit in is normal, but keep your own happiness in mind the next time you consider a purchase that's based on keeping up with others. Ask yourself if you are acquiring something that will add value to your life, make things easier for you, or make you happy. There will always be someone in your life who can spend more money than you – that's a competition you cannot win, and you don't need to, to be happy.

It's also important to let go of entitlement. Many advertisements focus on convincing you that you "deserve" their product. Do you not deserve a new car, the latest phone, an island vacation? The marketing strategy works, because most people feel like they deserve nice things – they are not bad people, and perhaps they have been through a hardship that makes them feel more "deserving." However, this is not a helpful mindset to have, as you can always say you deserve more, and you can never have enough with the *"do I deserve this?"* approach. A more helpful strategy is to ask yourself *"do I need this?" "will it make me happier?" "how does it fit into my budget compared to other things I value?"*

Money is a resource, and you have to make active decisions about using this resource. If your impulse purchasing is frequently fueled by the thought that you deserve something, make that *"do I deserve it?"* into *"can I afford it?"* and think about the things you are making tradeoffs with by making that purchase.

Living on a minimalist budget is as much about the journey as the destination. It's not just about getting to the goal you set for yourself – it's about living a life where you feel good about your financial behavior and efficiency. You won't miss your wasteful spending, because you just won't feel like you need to spend money to be happy.

As you practice living with a minimalist mindset, return your thoughts to these concepts frequently – letting go of entitlement and comparisons, seeking contentment and long-term fulfillment in life, and not just a spending distraction. The following chapters will discuss in more detail how you can use this mindset to create a minimalist budget and use it to improve your life.

End of Chapter Exercise

Select one of the following quotes related to minimalism:
- *"Simplicity is the ultimate sophistication."* —Leonardo da Vinci

- *"The secret of happiness, you see, is not found in seeking more, but in developing the capacity to enjoy less."* —Socrates
- *"Too many people spend money they haven't earned, to buy things they don't want, to impress people they don't like."* —Will Rogers
- *"You have succeeded in life when all you really want is only what you really need."* —Vernon Howard
- *"There are two ways to be rich: One is by acquiring much, and the other is by desiring little."* – Jackie French Koller
- *"Nothing is enough for the man to whom enough is too little."* – Epicurus

Recall the quote the next time you go shopping.

CHAPTER 2
Defining Goals And Priorities

This chapter will show you how to set priorities that are in line with a minimalist budget mindset. We will take a look at how a minimalist budget can be used to achieve specific goals, such as eliminating debt or building up savings.

Set Your Priorities

Your minimalist budget should support what is important to you, so it's critical to examine and understand your own goals and motivations. Your goals and motivations may change over time, and this is ok because your budget can change over time as well. Your priorities could be about paying off debt, saving money for a specific purchase, or by a specific timeframe or age, retiring at a certain age, giving money to your children or a charity.

Keep in mind that each dollar you spend on something else works against this goal. It does not mean you should not spend money – we all need basic things like food and shelter, and we want to live our life fully. However, examine each purchase decision while weighing it against your goals and priorities. Is the fancy coffee or the sweater on sale more important than your goals? Your answer in each case will depend on many factors, but being in the minimalist mindset will help you make the right decision.

If you are not sure how to set your goal, consider the following ideas. You may pick something directly from the list, or a combination of these items, or a modified version of these that fit your own circumstances:

- Pay off debt: This can be credit card debt, student loans, hospital bills, money you owe to friends or family, a car loan, etc. Debt can be very stressful to deal with.
- Do not spend more than what your income is: This goal can work in conjunction with paying off debt. If your spending habits continually exceed your income, you will always find yourself in debt in the future, even if you pay off all your current debt. This goal is a good step toward setting up for an even better one if you are not doing this yet.
- Put away money into savings (emergency funds, special expenses, retirement accounts)
- Regularly donate a portion of your income to a charity or organization that you are passionate about or that has a special significance in your life.
- Save up for a special gift or event, for yourself or someone you love (graduation, wedding, honeymoon, a vacation, a big purchase that means a lot to you).

These are just some of the financial priorities that may be important to you.

Considerations for Setting Your Financial Priorities

In setting your financial priorities, you have to consider what your own life circumstances are, what feels right to you. You will be more successful at sticking to your minimalist budget if your goal is something that really calls to you, something you've wanted for a long time, or is passionate about. If you are working toward the financial goal that really matters to you, every day using your minimalist budget will make you feel good about yourself. Every trivial purchase you forgo will actually make you feel happy because you are trading off this purchase with something much more valuable to you. It's important to be realistic about the goal or goals that you set for yourself. If you are used to a lifestyle where you allow yourself to have anything on a whim, making a drastic change can make you feel demotivated. Pick goals that you can honestly commit yourself to and try living on a budget that supports these goals.

Another aspect to consider during the process of setting your financial priorities is the topic of ownership. Concentrate on owning, not borrowing, when acquiring things. Avoid stretching your budget by seeing what cars or toys you can lease, or what you can afford as payments. Be realistic about the lifestyle you can really afford.

Also, consider the difference between buying things and experiences. Things, by themselves, do not actually make us happy. Experiences are really what we remember, even if they are enabled by things that we bought. Reflect on your goals and what experiences are important to you. Can they happen without the same level of spending? For example, instead of getting a pool for "family time," are there other experiences that will bond you as a family and still be a fun and memorable time without the expense? If you like a certain sport, do you have to have the latest and most expensive equipment to enjoy the sport itself? Or can you spend less on the equipment and go on a vacation involving this sport instead? Examine your priorities and determine where, instead of buying things, you can focus your money and effort on experiences.

As you work on defining your goals and priorities, limit yourself to only one or two goals to work on at a time. Tracking progress toward many goals at the same time can get complex. There is also the matter of how to store money toward many goals, while at the same time keeping your financial life simple. Selecting many goals will split your savings contribution to each goal to a small amount, and you may get discouraged because little progress will be made toward any one goal. Remember that a minimalist budget should make your life less complex and your goals easier to attain. Your goals should be selected in the spirit of that notion.

Finding Motivation

Your motivation for living on a minimalist budget may be very straightforward – you have a large amount of debt, and you want to pay it off, or a future expense you want to save up for, or perhaps you just want to simplify your life. But sometimes the financial goal by itself may not be enough to prevent you from an impulse purchase and make you stick to your budget. It's important to identify a long-term motivation that you can think about when tempted to spend money, something that will motivate you even after your debt is paid off.

Here is a thought-starting list of motivations you can use. See if any of these apply to you and motivate you to spend less on trivial things. Can you come up with other motivations that really move you, something that really matters to you?

- Retire early
- Quit your current job and get another one that may pay less, but involves something you really want to do
- Being able to help your parents or your children with their finances
- Travel the world
- Help others in need

As you can see, these motivations are goals in a way, but they are less specific and involve long timeframes – years, decades, or even your lifetime. Your motivations can be just one thing, or many things, as long as you focus on something specific that you really care about accomplishing. Your motivations are in the background of your financial goals and priorities. These are the things that will inspire you to stick to your budget, to avoid that compulsive purchase, to keep trying to accomplish your financial goals even if you have a setback.

The process for incorporating your financial priorities into your minimalist budget will be explained in the next chapter.

End of Chapter Exercise

Select a goal that you have not achieved yet.

- ☐ Paid off all credit card debt, student loan debt, car loan, and current bills
- ☐ Saved up one month's worth of living expenses
- ☐ Saved up six months' worth of living expenses
- ☐ Started to put away money for retirement
- ☐ Saved up enough money to retire comfortably

Now, set your sights on your goal!

CHAPTER 3
Budgeting And Money Management Strategies

This chapter discusses the approach to creating and managing a minimalist budget. The methods and concepts in this chapter demonstrate how minimalism is applied to budgeting in a practical way. We will also take a look at behaviors and practices that facilitate minimalist budgeting.

For the purpose of creating your own minimalist budget using these guidelines, it is easiest to consider your income and expenses on a monthly basis, as many bills and other obligations occur at a monthly frequency. The examples in this book typically show how budgeting strategies apply to a month's worth of income and expenses. However, the same techniques and concepts can be applied over a span of days, weeks, months, and years.

Analyze Your Income

Your minimalist budget starts with knowing how much money you have coming in.

If you have a regular income (a job or another source of money that pays a relatively constant amount at regular intervals), use the net monthly amount you get as the input to your budget. "Net" means the actual sum of money you can deposit into a bank after all applicable tax and social security deductions.

If you work seasonally or have work where the income varies predictably over the course of the year (the tourism industry or fishing enterprises are good examples of this), your monthly income for budgeting purposes should be the average over the year. To get the monthly average, divide your net annual (yearly) income by 12 months.

If the money you have coming in is not consistent, and it's hard to predict how it may vary in the future (for example, if your pay is based on commissions), utilize the "worst-case" amount you may get – for example, the lowest monthly pay you have received over the past year.

Do not count on any money you may or may not get in the future – raises, bonuses, promotions, inheritances, winning the lottery – all these can be incorporated into your minimalist budget if and when they materialize, but not before then.

Of course, if your income does change significantly (up or down), your minimalist budget needs to be adjusted to comprehend the change.

In the medium and long-term, you can also consider what else can be done to increase your income:

- In your current job, focus on what actually makes you money. If you are a commissioned, hourly, or self-employed worker, this means making the most of your available working hours and earning opportunities. If you are a salaried employee, reflect on what earns you raises and bonuses and put your energy into activities that are tied to getting you that additional money. Don't get caught up in

spending your days on tasks that your employer does not care about, or you can delegate those tasks to others.
- You can also acquire a side job or applying for a higher-paying position. Ask yourself if you are making good use of your free time now and if this time can be directed toward earning money. There are many online resources (Craigslist jobs and gigs, indeed.com) where you can look for part-time jobs that fit your skill set and availability.
- One source of money that is very well aligned with the minimalist strategy is to review your possessions and sell things that are cluttering your life. Think of what you own and how often you use these things, and how much happiness they bring you. Can you turn them into cash so that they can be used toward your goals and things that actually matter in your life? Online resources such as Craigslist or eBay can be good ways to make some money on the things you don't have use for.

Analyze Your Current Spending and Estimate Future Expenses

Understanding where your money is going to is a critical input into your minimalist budget. Make a list of what you have spent for the past several months and group purchases and expenses into categories. If you use a credit card, credit card statements often organize your purchases into categories for you, or you can use the following list when organizing what you have spent.

Some of your expenses will be fixed – that is, they don't change month to month. Examples of fixed expenses are:
- Rent
- Mortgage
- Car loan
- Insurance premium payment

Other expenses are variable – that is, they can vary month to month, either depending on external factors or choices that you make:
- Utilities (these may vary with your usage and outside temperature)
- Cable/phone bill/internet bill/other service subscriptions
- Groceries
- Transportation
- Clothes and personal care
- Medical expenses
- Entertainment
- Travel
- Gifts
- Other categories that apply to you (kids' activities, pets, hobbies, fitness, etc.)

After listing and organizing your expenses, do a quality check. Do your last month's expenses and savings contributions actually add up to your income?

If you used a credit or debit card to pay, it's easy to account for all the expenses (or at least, the places where you spend the money). If you used cash, not only do you have to keep track of your bank or ATM cash withdrawals, but you also have to keep a diligent record on how this cash was spent.

As you evaluate your expenses, many of them should not surprise you – if you have a mortgage, this is the amount you have signed up for. Most of your expenses for groceries, transportation, and service subscriptions will probably be more or less constant every month.

However, watch out for spending amounts and categories that surprise you: were you aware of how much you were spending on eating out or new clothes every month? Is this level of spending in line with your long-term goals and priorities? Establishing awareness of your financial behavior and weighing it against what you really want to accomplish with your money is critical to creating and following a minimalist budget approach.

Now, you have to estimate your future expenses in each category. Estimating your fixed expenses is easy – this is the same amount you have spent in the past. If you anticipate a change (for example, if you know your rent payment will increase next month), then use the new amount.

Estimating variable expenses will take some judgment and decision-making on your part. If the expense varies more or less randomly, or due to events that you can't reliably predict, you can calculate an average monthly spending amount for each category for future planning purposes. Calculating an average is easy: you add up the amounts spent in each month that you tracked in the past and divide by the number of months. For example, if in the last 3 months you have spent $400, $600, and $500 on groceries, the average per month is ($400 + $600 + $500) divided by 3 months, or $1500 / 3 = $500 on average for groceries per month.

Some variable expenses may vary predictably. For example, if you live somewhere where the weather is really hot in the summer, your utility bill may be higher in the summer months due to using the air conditioner more. You can estimate the expenses that vary predictably by examining what you have spent in the past and projecting that pattern into the future.

After completing your expense analysis, you should have a list of expense categories and an estimated expense amount for each category. The next section will show you how to use this information to make a budget. For the purpose of deciding how much to allocate to variable expenses, start out by making a budget for the next month. Once you can do this, you can repeat the process for future months, where your variable expenses may be different. Later in the chapter, you will also learn how to incorporate expenses that don't happen monthly, and how to review and maintain your budget so that it is up to date.

Create Your Minimalist Budget

Now it's time to create an efficient and streamlined spending plan – a minimalist budget. You will use your financial priorities from Chapter 2, together with your income and spending list from earlier in this chapter.

The process for making a budget involves creating a monthly expense list that you commit yourself to. This plan has to work with your obligations and life priorities.

We will go through the process using an example, and you can follow through with your own inputs.

First, list your monthly net income:

Income	$2000

Next, list the monthly expenses you are obligated to right now. This list will vary person to person, but typically this is what you must pay no matter what (at least in the short term, without selling your house or making drastic changes in your life). Things like your mortgage or rent, utilities, and car payments are in this category. Many of these expenses will typically be fixed, but some – utilities, for example – may be variable:

Income	$2000	Rent	$400
		Utilities	$100
		Car Payment	$200

Now, take your net monthly income and subtract these must-have monthly expenses. How much do you have left? This is the amount that your budget will use toward achieving your financial goals, and also toward your discretionary spending.

In the example above, the remaining amount is $2000 - $400 - $100 - $200 = $1300.

Now, this is where the financial goals you have defined earlier come into play and become specific amounts of money. If your goal is to pay off debt or save a specific amount of money every month, decide what this monthly amount needs to be and make this money an entry into your expenses list.

This amount will depend on several factors, such as your minimum debt payment, how much you owe or want to save in total, and over how much time. Chapter 4 contains a lot of detailed guidance for determining your savings and debt repayment amounts. As a good starting point or general guideline, allocate 20% of your net income to your financial goal.

In our example, 20% of $2000 is $400:

Income	$2000	Rent	$400
		Utilities	$100
		Car Payment	$200
		Savings	$400

Keep in mind that accomplishing some financial goals may take time, and you have to plan how your budget will be affected by them over the years. If you are planning a career or job change, or anticipate life changes that may affect your ability to contribute to your financial goal (having a child, for example), your plan needs to comprehend this. For example, you may want to set a more aggressive savings rate for now, if in the future, you will have other expenses.

Next, you create a budget plan for everything else on your list. It helps to arrange the list by priority, specific to your needs and preferences. This way, if you have to make tradeoffs and make decisions on where to decrease from your current level of spending, you can focus on areas that are lower in priority. The prioritization list will really be about your own values and circumstances in life. For example, different people will put different priorities on things like having a nice meal at a restaurant, having a gym membership, sending their kids to private school, drinking high-quality coffee, etc. None of these are life necessities, but they are things that may be valuable to some people and not to others.

A lot of the expenses in your budget will be variable – that is, you did not spend the same exact amount of money on them in the past, and you have to estimate how much to allocate to them in the future. Review the previous section in this chapter if you are not sure how much to allocate to each category.

Now calculate your total expenses. This is just the sum of all the expense categories on your list, including your savings goal. The total expenses will be either greater than your income, less than your income, or equal to your income.

Review the resulting budget:
- If your total expenses are greater than your income: Where are you willing to make some compromises and reduce your variable expenses? You have to ask yourself whether your past spending in each category is in line with your goals and values. Did your past purchases in each category result in things in your life that were valuable and useful to you? Remember that you cannot change your fixed expenses. Your savings goal should not be changed either. As long as you have made a realistic target, you need to be committed to it. Your strategy is to reduce your variable expenses, especially the areas where you can exercise discretion in how you spend the money.
- If your total expenses are less than your income – you have some breathing room in your budget! Allocate this extra money toward your savings.
- If your total expenses are equal to your income, then you have made a budget!

Here is how we continue our example:

Income	$2000	Rent	$400
		Utilities	$100
		Car Payment	$200
		Savings	$400
		Phone / Internet	$100
		Groceries	$300

			Clothes	$200
			Entertainment	$200
			Travel	$200
			Total Expenses	$2100

Uh-oh, did you notice that our planned spending exceeds our income? Through this process, keep in mind that this is a minimalist budget – while you may value or like some things, can you live without them or find alternatives that do not cost as much? Many things that we do every day only clutter our lives with activities and spending but do not really provide anything lasting or meaningful. For each expense category you have on your list, ask yourself whether this item is really helping you to live a meaningful life that is in line with your values and long-term goals.

In our example, you can decide that you don't need $200 worth of new clothes every month and can do with $100. Or perhaps you can reduce your entertainment and travel budgets. In the end, you should have a plan where your savings goal is still intact, and your monthly spending plan does not exceed your income:

Income	$2000	Rent	$400
		Utilities	$100
		Car Payment	$200
		Savings	$400
		Phone / Internet	$100
		Groceries	$300
		Clothes	$100
		Entertainment	$200
		Travel	$200
		Total Expenses	$2000

The bonus chapter at the end of this book will give you ideas for how to make your money go further in various categories of spending.

How to Approach Expenses That Do Not Happen Monthly

Your budget is a plan for your monthly income and expenses, but it also has to comprehend items that happen less regularly, or only during certain times of the year but not every month. Examples of this are property taxes, holiday gift expenses, vacations, etc. Keep in mind that these are expenses that you plan - this does not include unexpected expenses and financial setbacks, which are discussed in chapter 5.

One of the most straightforward ways to comprehend irregularly occurring expenses into your monthly budget is to calculate the total you need for the expense, and then divide by the number of months from now when you will need this sum of money. For example, if you are anticipating that your property taxes are $1000 and they are due in 5 months, then you need to save $200 each month from now on for this expense. As you are planning farther ahead, you can start calculating the total that you will need over the course of the year, and then just divide by 12 months, similar to how the concept of a variable income was handled.

Planning expenses that do not happen monthly, or happen at irregular intervals, are critical to your minimalist budget. Forecasting how much these expenses will cost will prevent you from continuously trying to compensate for these items and falling behind on your monthly savings and debt repayment plan. At a very minimum, your minimalist budget needs to prevent you from spending more than what you make. Failing to account for incidental expenses is a big pitfall that can wreak havoc on your spending and make you feel like you are not in control of your money.

As you incorporate planned special expenses, like vacations and big-ticket purchases into your budget, you can also see more clearly how they affect your monthly spending and tradeoffs with other usages of your money. Keeping these expenses in mind for budget planning may make you re-evaluate the necessity of these purchases.

There are several items to keep in mind with irregularly-occurring planned expenses:

One consideration is how to "store" the amount that you save monthly for these expenses.

This will depend on personal preference:

- With a cash based approach, you can withdraw the money each month as cash. Of course, there are possible downsides to this as concerning the secure storage of this money and potentially missing out on earned interest, but this is an option that may fit some situations.
- With online banking, you can store the monthly allocation to a savings account. Regularly check your math to make sure the amount in the account corresponds with the total you should have for all the irregular expenses. It is best not to leave the money allocated toward your irregular expenses mixed inside the account you use toward your monthly expenses.

In addition to making a plan for saving for irregular expenses, carefully consider the overall necessity of each expense in this category with your minimalist mindset. Property tax amounts are a given, as long as you are living in the same house. However, items such as vacations, gifts, and other optional expenses should be given a lot of thought.

The primary consideration is not necessarily "How little can I spend?" but rather, "How can I direct my money more effectively with what I am trying to accomplish?" Consider the last few trips and vacations and gift-giving sessions. Was your previous approach a good use of your money, did it make you and those around you happy? Is there a more financially effective approach that will also make you happy? The answer to this is highly personal and will depend on many individual factors.

We are all familiar with the concept that simple gifts that were made or acquired with a lot of thoughts are the memorable ones. Or that sometimes you can have just as much fun on a "staycation" (that's a vacation where you stay at home) as on a real vacation, as long as you are doing what you enjoy. These concepts may or may not apply to your personal situation, or perhaps you already have some of your own ideas about how you can make expenses like these more financially efficient and meaningful. Your minimalist mindset practice will guide you to how best to make your overall financial goals compatible with these expenses.

Simplify Your Financial Life

A very important part of living on a minimalist budget is decluttering your financial life. As you recall, minimalism is not about spending as little as possible and using a jumble of cashback incentives and rewards. Instead, reducing the number of credit cards and bank accounts, you have will help you track your expenses and simplify your life.

The minimalist budget accounts are consist of:
- One debit or credit card for purchases
- One checking account, where your income gets deposited and where the money for your monthly expenses are stored
- One savings account, where you have your emergency savings and money for non-monthly expenses
- Retirement accounts (401k, IRAs, etc.) will depend on your particular job and life situation, but in general, a simplicity in the management of retirement accounts is also helpful in tracking your money. Some people are hesitant to invest in a retirement account simply because they don't want to deal with picking investment options, rebalancing their portfolio, and other money management things that may sound complex or intimidating. Fortunately, retirement investing has some very straightforward options:
    - For a really simple approach, choose a target year fund. These funds automatically allocate your contributions toward different types of investments to be appropriate for when you are going to need the money. The allocation is typically more aggressive and growth-oriented if you have a long time before you need the money, and more conservative and income-oriented if you are retiring soon (and/or are expecting to make withdrawals soon).
    To pick a target year fund, just select your approximate retirement year, or the year when you think you will need to start withdrawing the funds. Because there is some work associated with the automatic rebalancing of investment allocations, target year funds typically have somewhat higher management fees than index funds (more on those next), but considering how hands-off this option is, the fees are quite reasonable at most investment firms.
    - Another very simple investment approach is to invest in index funds. Index funds are designed to track a specific subset

(index) of stocks, funds, and other investments – for example, the S&P 500. Index funds simplify your investment choices and tax returns over picking individual stocks, or even individual non-index funds. They typically have low management fees, as they just track the average performance of other investments. You can just pick a handful of index funds to have an allocation among stocks and bonds that is appropriate for your age (search for "age appropriate investment allocation" online for more on this aspect).
- o If you have multiple 401k and other retirement account plans accumulated from changing jobs, consolidate them into a single self-directed IRA account. This will give you the benefit of being able to see how your money is invested all from just one portal, which facilitates adjusting the overall distribution in your portfolio.

In addition to simplifying your accounts, it is also important to simplify how you access your statements and other financial information. Whenever possible, sign up for e-statements – they are easy to access and store. You can dispose of your paper statements and other documentation – it will physically declutter your life. Be sure to exercise appropriate precautions in how you dispose of confidential and sensitive information (something that contains your account numbers or social security numbers), and how you choose and store passwords for your electronic logins.

When you get an e-statement or a bill, pay it right away – this will avoid you accidentally forgetting to pay it, which usually incurs penalties and fees. If you are waiting for a paycheck before you can pay a bill, for most credit cards, you can schedule a payment to occur in the future, before the due date.

Combining some or all of your recurring debt obligations into one loan can be a great way to simplify the way you perceive and manage your debt. Getting multiple bills throughout the month can be a stressful thing in itself, not to mention the complexity of managing the various due dates, amounts, and agencies to pay the money to. In addition, if you are currently paying a high-interest rate, you can save money by consolidating the loans under a lower rate. You can check on consolidated loan interest rates at your own bank, check rates from other banks online, or investigate if you can transfer the debt to one of your existing loans that have a favorable interest rate.

Regularly Review Your Minimalist Budget versus Reality

With a minimalist budget approach, it is critical to be very aware of your income, your spending, your savings, and your progress toward your goals. Schedule a regular weekly time, where you review your financial performance. If you have a partner with whom you share your financial goals, include them in this review as well. The weekly cadence is important, as it gives you enough time to identify if you are off course and still meet your monthly goals.

At each review, ask yourself the following items:
- Is my monthly income what I expected, or have there been unexpected changes? If something has changed, is this a one-time occurrence or do I need to adjust my monthly budget permanently?
- How am I doing with setting aside or paying money toward my long-term financial goal? Are there unexpected factors that are preventing me from following my plan, and how can I incorporate them into my monthly plan for the future?
- Am I staying on track with my monthly expenses for this month?
- How was my performance versus my budget last month, did I stay on track?
- Very importantly, look for additional ways to cut out unnecessary spending in your life. This should be a continuous process, but as you review your actual performance versus your budget, you may see some areas where you can direct your focus.

At first, the review process may seem boring or difficult, especially if you are not a numbers person. However, you will be amazed at how satisfying it is to look at the evidence that you are following your plan and making your goals into reality. Regular budget performance reviews will also allow you to see how factors that are outside of your control (a tax hike, fuel prices) are affecting your expenses and adjust your plans to take these changes into account.

It is also important to regularly review your accounts online – that includes things like credit card activity, bank deposits, and withdrawals. With online banking, this can easily be done in minutes. Do a quick check on your accounts every few days, which will flag any unexpected activity for you and prevent surprises in the future.

As you document expenses and plan future spending, it's important to be as exact as possible with your numbers. Don't "guesstimate" what you might have spent on groceries or your night out. Check your credit card statement or your receipts and write down the specific amount of money involved. Remember that estimating is likely what got you to seek using a minimalist budget in the first place – you want to have better control and understanding of your finances.

End of Chapter Exercise

Select the amount of money that most closely approximates what you have spent on eating out at restaurants last month (including fast food):
- ☐ $0
- ☐ $50
- ☐ $100
- ☐ $200
- ☐ $300

- ☐ $400
- ☐ $500
- ☐ $1000+

Did know the answer off the top of your head or did you have to look it up?

CHAPTER 4
Minimalist Budget Tools

In the previous chapter, we examined the overall minimalist budgeting methodology, as well as the methods to implement and execute your minimalist budget. Now, we will take a look at some specific tools and techniques associated with minimalist budgeting, and how you can stay organized and focused on your goals. We will also look at some specific budgeting strategies in more detail so that you can choose an approach that makes the most sense to you.

Payment Automation

Automating payments for your loans and savings deposits can greatly simplify your financial life, and simplicity is at the core of using a minimalist budget. Most financial institutions will allow you (in fact, they prefer you too!) to make regular automatic payments and deposits. If you have trouble to get yourself to put away money every month toward savings and end up spending it, payment automation is a trick you can use to "hide" money from yourself, so it's not even there for you to spend it.

For debt payments, make sure to automate at least the minimum required payment and more if you can afford it (see the next section for more on how to make decisions in this area, and how this should balance with allocating your savings).

For your credit card, make sure to pay the full statement balance every month, not just the minimum, to avoid high-interest rates.

For mortgage, rent, and lease payments, and everything else that has a set amount due every month, the simple strategy is to just set the automated payment to the amount due (unless you are also trying to prepay your mortgage).

Automating payments gives you several advantages:
- It prevents you from accidentally forgetting to pay your debt or credit card balance, which in most cases triggers fees and/or high-interest rates.
- It also makes it easier for your mind to think of the payments as a given, not something that's optional so that you don't even contemplate using that money and adjust your spending plan as if the pre-allocated money was not even there. If you automate a reasonable amount to go to your savings every month, pretty soon you will not even miss the money, as you will be used to living without it. The savings will accumulate in your bank account all on their own. We will discuss strategies for determining how much to put into savings later in this chapter.

Reverse Budgeting

Payment automation is closely tied to the reverse budgeting method. With reverse budgeting, you set aside money for specific purposes as your top priority, and spend what's left as you wish. Instead of deciding in advance what you will spend on each category of expenses, which can be tedious and can discourage people from doing any budgeting at all, you focus on just your goals on obligations.

For example, if you have $2000 as your net income every month, with a reverse budgeting strategy you can decide that you want to put away 20% of your income ($400) toward savings. You automate this payment and use the money you have remaining ($1600) toward everything else in your life.

Reverse budgeting is a great way to build savings, especially when combined with automatic contributions to a designated account. As you may have noticed, the budget-building strategy used in Chapter 3 is also tied to reverse budgeting – we figured out our net income, designated money to basic living expenses, and then allocated a specific amount of money to our financial goal.

In addition to a savings goal, you can also incorporate your basic living expenses and your minimum debt obligations into your reverse budgeting allocation. Set this amount aside, and you don't have to plan or budget how you spend the rest of the money.

With reverse budgeting, you need to have a reliable system of separating the money you set aside for your savings from your discretionary money. This means the money you are setting aside needs to go into a separate savings account, while your discretionary money stays in your checking account. As an alternative, you can withdraw your discretionary money as cash every month, while keeping your savings in the bank.

The downside of reverse budgeting is that you can still engage in making impulsive purchases and overspend in some categories because you are not examining closely where your discretionary money is going. If you have some extra money coming in, you are likely to spend it on something discretionary instead of putting the money toward repaying your debt faster, or toward your long-term financial goals. As with any budgeting method, your intention of being a responsible spender and saver is critical to your financial success.

The Zero-Based Budget

This budgeting approach has a somewhat technical-sounding name, but the concept itself is very simple: your income minus your expenses should equal to zero. It does sound very simple, but many people fail to properly account for this concept and end up in debt.

Making a zero-based budget uses the same overall strategy as what we have discussed in the previous chapter. First, you write down your income, obligations, savings target, and various categories of expenses. Then, you make a plan where resources, goals, and priorities come together – which usually involves some tradeoffs.

While the reserve budgeting approach gave you some discretionary money for which you did not need to have any specific plans, with a zero-based budget, you are accounting where every dollar from your income goes to. It is a more rigid system, where you have to stay organized in how you track your spending. However, it gives you the advantage of deciding where each dollar would be most useful – making extra payments on debt obligations, saving up for a vacation – as opposed to just letting you spend any extra money. The reverse budgeting method is very much in line with the minimalist mindset because it requires you to plan and spend purposefully.

The 50/20/30 Budget

The 50/20/30 budget (also known as the 50/20/30 rule) guides your budgeting strategy by giving you the relative proportions of spending and saving that you can follow. This rule can help to keep your budget balanced and your financial goals on track. To follow the 50/20/30 rule, make the following spending and saving allocations when creating your minimalist budget:

- 50% of your net income is allocated to the absolute necessities that you cannot avoid paying. This is typically your rent or mortgage payment, utility bills, and the absolute minimum you can spend on food, transportation, and other must-have items. This category is your highest priority. Be very critical of your spending habits when including items into this category! Just because you are used to buying something, it does not mean you cannot live without it.

  If you find that your absolute minimum necessities consistently exceed 50% of your income, then you need to make a lifestyle change. This may include downsizing your house, getting rid of a car payment, or moving to a less expensive area. Examine what your necessary expenses consist of, and ask yourself how you can reduce them. There are a few ideas on this in the bonus chapter at the end of this book.

- 20% of your net income is allocated toward savings. If you have debt obligations, the money is allocated toward debt repayment – and as much savings as you have left over. After repaying debt, the money goes toward retirement savings, emergency funds, saving for near-term and long-term expenses, and other money allocation toward the future. This category is your second-highest priority after paying for the absolute necessities in life.

  If you have debt obligations, little or no emergency funds, and little or no retirement savings, you have to make some choices about the relative distribution of your money toward these savings types. Here are some ideas about how to approach this:

  Debt: Of course, you have to make minimum debt payments. Depending on the interest rate, you may want to pay back more than the minimum payment so you can pay back the loan quicker and focus on contributing to your savings. If the interest rate is sufficiently high, you may never be able to pay back the debt without making higher than minimum payments. Using information from your loan provider (or you can search for a "debt repayment calculator" online), determine how long it will take you to pay back the loan at your current rate of repayment and how much interest you will end up paying. If you have extra money in the 20% savings category, consider paying more toward your debt to shorten the repayment duration and reduce the amount of interest you will pay.

Emergency savings: As a general rule, you should have 6 months' worth of living expenses saved for emergencies. This includes the absolute necessities category, plus minimum obligations on debts. Build up your emergency savings to this amount as soon as you can, while making at least minimum debt payments.

Retirement savings: The importance of saving for retirement early cannot be overemphasized. You can find many articles and examples that illustrate what a great advantage an early start of retirement savings gives you (search for "saving for retirement early vs. later" online). Even as you are repaying debt and contributing to your emergency funds, consider putting away at least a little toward long-term and retirement accounts. This is especially important if your employer matches some of your contributions – make sure to contribute at least the amount to take full advantage of the matching – it's free money.

- 30% of your net income is allocated to discretionary expenses. Discretionary means that the expense is optional, and you can decide how you want to spend this money. This includes categories such as entertainment, vacations, and any other purchases that are not essential to your survival. This category has the lowest priority. If you have an unexpected expense or a financial setback that impacts your ability to contribute to the absolute essentials or savings and debt repayment, the extra money can come out of this category.

In some cases, the line between necessities and optional expenses can be blurred. For example, most of us have a smartphone and can't imagine effectively functioning without it (though, we actually can, unless you need your phone to perform your job). Or it can be as silly as saying to yourself, "I can't survive without those new shoes or that fancy cup of coffee." Be mindful of the instances where you convince yourself that something is a necessity.

The good news is that using the 50/20/30 approach automatically makes you decide on the tradeoffs among your optional expenses. As long as you are honest with yourself that you can possibly live without a given expense, you can list all the things you would like to spend money on and choose among them. You can even change the allocation over time for some variety – for example, spend more on eating out and entertainment one month, and buy yourself some new clothes or gadget next month. The choice is yours, as long as you keep it within the 30% allocation.

For example:

Income	$2000	Necessities (50%)	$1000
		Savings (20%)	$400
		Discretional (30%)	$600

Since the 50/20/30 rule is based on percentages of your income, you can apply it no matter whether you live on a big salary and have a lot of expenses, or you do not have that much money coming in, and you live frugally. The important thing to keep in mind is that it's up to you to decide what you consider a necessity in life and what is optional and allocate your budget accordingly. Do not underestimate the importance of the 30% savings category, and do not "borrow" from it or buy things telling yourself that they are "an investment." Your future self will thank you for being diligent and properly contributing to that 30% savings category, as this is the budget allocation that lets you get ahead in life.

Here are some downsides to the 50/20/30 budget:

- First, sometimes it can be hard to separate wants from needs: which expense goes into the necessities category, and which goes to the discretionary category. You need to eat food, but do you need a steak and a salad for dinner, or would anything more expensive than ramen noodles be an indulgence?
- Another downside is that the allocation can cause you to be wasteful. If you have extra money left over from your 30% discretionary category, you will feel tempted to just spend it instead of saving it, because you have technically met all your savings and debt repayment obligations for the month.

The 50/20/30 budget can be a very useful guideline, but it does require you to closely track the allocation of your purchases into the necessity and the discretionary spending categories.

The 80/20 Budget

The 80/20 budget is a simpler alternative to the 50/20/30 budget. The concepts are similar, but with the 80/20 budget, you do not have to track necessities separately from your discretionary spending. You simply put away 20% of your income into savings, and the remaining 80% is yours to spend on everything that you want and need.

As with the 50/20/30 approach, automatic withdrawals into a savings account is critical for the 80/20 approach, so you are not tempted to spend that 20% and learn to live without it.

You also have to be mindful of how you spend that 80% of your income. This amount still needs to cover basic necessities and obligations. You don't have to budget for various spending categories, but you need to be disciplined enough to prioritize where spending your money is essential (for example, your rent payment) and which expenses are not as important.

The 60/40 Budget

The 60/40 budget (also known as the 60% budget) is another very simple method you can use to keep your expense allocation on track. The 60/40

approach puts an emphasis on expenses that you have commitments to, whether they are wants or needs. It also gives you a good structure for allocating your savings into different categories. Here is how it works:
- 60% of your income is allocated to existing commitments: mortgage or rent, service subscriptions. Your basic living expenses for food and transportation go into this category as well. If you find that the sum of your expenses in this category exceeds 60% of your income, then you have made too many commitments. For ideas of how to deal with this issue, review the minimalist budget ideas for recurring expenses in the bonus chapter at the end of this book.
- 40% of your income is allocated to savings and discretionary spending. The breakdown is as follows:
  - 10% is for short-term savings. This includes money for unexpected expenses, vacation savings, gifts, and other expenses for the near future. This money should be easily accessible, though not combined into the same account as your monthly expenses.
  - 10% is for long-term savings. This includes big purchases like cars or down payment on a house and money for big medical bills and emergencies. This money is typically invested, but still accessible.
  - 10% is for retirement savings. This money goes into your 401k or IRA account, within applicable contribution limits.
  - 10% is completely discretionary – you can spend it on anything you want.

The 60/40 budget is a great way to guide your savings allocations while at the same time, ensuring that your basic living expenses are covered.

If you have a lot of debt (outside of a mortgage obligation), you can temporarily use contributions, 10% for long-term savings and 10% for retirement savings to pay down the debt. The following sections explore the various approaches to debt repayment.

Paying Off Debt with the "Snowball" Method

Debt obligations can be very stressful. Especially if you have multiple loans, it's easy to start feeling like you are drowning in bills, statements, and due dates, and not making any real progress toward repaying any of it.

The snowball method is all about building momentum in your progress toward repaying your debt obligations. Just like with building a snowball, you start out small and work toward big results.

The overall idea behind the method is to pay off your smallest debts first, build encouragement and momentum, and go on to tackle the big debts. It's a mental technique to show yourself that you can take control of your financial life. Here is how the snowball method works, step by step:
- First, review your budget to make sure you have enough money to cover the minimum payment for every one of your debt obligations.

- Arrange the debt obligations by size, from smallest to largest. Disregard the interest rate on each debt with this method.
- Allocate an additional amount of money, on top of your minimum obligations, that you will use for debt repayment.
- Every month, use the additional debt payment amount toward your smallest debt obligation. Only pay the minimum payment on the other debts.
- Once you pay off your smallest debt, use the money you paid on it (the minimum plus the extra allocation) toward the next smallest debt.

For example, let's say you have four debts, with the following minimum payments:

Debt	Total Owed	Minimum Payment
Hospital bill	$300	$50
Credit card	$1000	$100
Car loan	$5000	$150
Student loan	$10000	$200

You have allocated the money needed to make the minimum payments ($500), and in addition, you are able to contribute an extra $100 per month toward debt repayment.

Using the snowball method, you would make the minimum payments on each loan, plus put the extra $100 toward the hospital bill ($150 total toward the hospital bill per month). In a few months, the hospital bill is paid off, and you put that money you paid toward the hospital bill ($150 per month) as an extra payment toward your credit card ($100 minimum payment + $150 extra = $250 per month toward the credit card). Continue this until all the debts are paid off.

The advantage of the snowball method is that it lets you demonstrate to yourself that you can make tangible advancements in paying off your debt. It's the most effective way to quickly reduce the number of bills coming in, so you stop feeling overwhelmed and start feeling like you are making real progress toward debt management.

The downside of the snowball method, as you may have guessed, is that it does not take into account the interest rate on the loans so you may be paying a higher rate for a longer period of time. This is a valid argument, but remember that the snowball method is about building motivation and encouragement. If you prioritize paying for the loans with the highest interest rate, you may be saving some money on interest, but the progress you are making may seem less tangible. Without seeing real progress, you may lose motivation and stop contributing the extra money toward debt repayment, thus negating any savings related to interest rates.

Paying Off Debt with the "Avalanche" Method

Unlike the snowball method of repaying debt, the avalanche method does not necessarily give you small victories or encouragements up front. Instead, it focuses on making debt repayment as efficient as possible by having you pay off debt with the highest interest rate first.

If you have read about the snowball method and just can't imagine yourself not putting your money toward the debt with the highest interest rate, then use the avalanche method instead. You have to be patient and methodical, sticking to your extra payment strategy even if a year later you are still paying on all of your loans.

Taking our earlier example, we arrange the debt by interest rate this time:

Debt	Total Owed	Minimum Payment	Interest Rate
Credit card	$1000	$100	10%
Car loan	$5000	$150	6%
Hospital bill	$300	$50	5%
Student loan	$10000	$200	3%

In this example, you also have $100 extra to spend toward debt repayment each month. With the avalanche method, you would pay the minimum on all the loans, plus an extra $100 on the credit card bill each month. It would take you longer than with the snowball method to pay off a debt completely, but you will save money on the interest you are paying for this debt.

The avalanche method takes discipline and may not bring you a sense of accomplishment as fast as the snowball method. However, it's rooted in solid financial logic and can save you money if you commit yourself to it.

Paying Off Debt with the "Snowflake" Method

The snowflake method utilizes small amounts of savings or extra cash you find yourself with to chip away at your debt. You still pay the minimum obligations on all your debts, and in addition look for opportunities, no matter how small, to save money and contribute it to debt repayment.

The advantage of the snowflake method is that it does not require rigid planning for allocating extra money in your budget toward debt repayment. You only allocate the minimum payment amounts in your planning phase. After this, you have to be diligent throughout the month to find additional money to contribute toward debt repayment. This can be little things, like not buying your usual latte on the way to work, having a garage sale, or selling something on Craigslist.

Although each contribution may be small, a consistent and diligent approach to looking for little bits of extra money in your daily life can add up to respectable chunks of cash over the course of the month.

In choosing which debt to contribute the extra money to, you can combine the snowflake method with either the snowball or avalanche methods.

Pay with Cash

In today's world, purchases are greatly simplified with debit and credit cards, not to mention the ability to pay through an app on your phone or smartwatch. Impulse purchases are all too easy, as you only see the transactions on your statements and probably don't feel any less poor right after completing the purchase.

On the other hand, getting and using cash can be a bother, as you physically have to go to an ATM or a bank, and then store the cash and carry it around. Make the difficulty of dealing with cash work to your advantage, and use the cash for all in-person purchases. Even the trouble of having to take out the cash from your account can help to prevent the purchase. And as you hand over the cash, physically parting with money can lead you to be more prudent in future purchasing decisions because you feel the impact immediately.

You can use cash for most every day, in-person purchases. For larger purchases that may require buyer protection or a refund, use a credit card.

The Envelope System

The envelope system can work hand in hand with the cash approach described above. The approach is simple: each month, leave enough money in your checking account to pay for your current bills, debt obligations, and savings target, and take out the rest as cash. Next, list the categories of your monthly expenses and allocate an amount to each category, as shown in Chapter 3. Assign an envelope to each category, and put the cash amount that you have allocated to that category in each envelope. Each month, you can only spend the amount in the envelope for each category. You can refill the envelopes either once a month, or after each paycheck.

As a variation on the envelope system, you can also use clips (with some labels), which may be easier to manage in your wallet or purse than envelopes. As another variation, you can also use a small accordion folder and assign a pocket in the folder for each category.

For online purchases, you can use a "virtual envelope." Write down your total allowed spending amount for the category on an envelope (or a piece of paper). When you make a purchase online, subtract the amount you just spent from your allowed amount. When you get to zero, you are not allowed to buy online anymore.

If you make several shopping trips per month (let's say, for groceries), only take the amount of cash you intend to spend on the individual trip, not the whole month. That way, you don't talk yourself into splurging on something on the first trip, while finding yourself with insufficient cash to buy even the basics at the end of the month. If you get to the checkout and you don't have enough cash to pay for everything, put some items back – that's prioritizing in real time!

The envelope system requires discipline and the ability to be honest with yourself. No borrowing from other envelopes! If you are really craving some fast food but you don't have your "restaurants/fun" envelope with you, then you cannot spend on fast food because you did not plan for it. If you are making a purchase that involves multiple categories (let's say, if you are buying some fuel and a beverage at a gas station), you have to be diligent and take the cash out of the appropriate envelopes. Admittedly, this can get logistically challenging, especially considering you also have to put the correct change back into the correct envelope, but the logistics become easier to handle with practice.

The envelope system approach really encourages you to plan ahead and to be frugal with your spending. Once your grocery envelope runs out of money, you're done buying groceries for the month – knowing this can prevent you from wasting food or buying unnecessary items at the store. Once your fuel envelope runs out of money – well, you better plan ahead and walk or carpool when you can, and don't make unnecessary trips.

If you are sharing your budget and the envelope system with your significant other, you can either split the allocations or have your own set of envelopes, or in some cases; one partner may control the envelopes for specific categories. It is very important to agree on a plan ahead of time and to stick to this plan. If something unexpected comes up (you ran out of money for a category), you will need to discuss and agree upon a strategy with your partner.

If you have some money left over in an envelope at the end of the month, this is great news. You can reward yourself (put it into your fun/entertainment category), or keep it in the same category and save it toward the next month. You can also take the extra money and apply it to paying down debt, or toward your savings goal. If there is a category where you never find yourself overspending and always have money left over, consider "graduating" that category to being eligible for credit card usage or combine the category with another one.

The envelope system makes it impossible to overspend if you are diligent at using it and are being honest with yourself. The approach is great for habitual overspenders and impulsive buyers — you physically cannot spend more than you what planned on! The system also lets you easily identify areas where you may be consistently budgeting too little or too much money. It's important to review your monthly performance versus your envelope system and make adjustments to your plan or your lifestyle as needed. The good news is, while it's easy to review credit card purchases once a month when you get your statement and spend frivolously until then, the envelope system makes you evaluate your spending decisions in real time.

The "One In, One Out" Rule

The One In, One Out rule can help you to control your spending and curb your acquisition of "stuff." This rule can be applied to non-consumable goods, such as clothes, shoes, cars, etc. The concept is that when you buy something, you have to get rid of something that you own in that category. If you buy a new pair of shoes, get rid of a pair you already have. For compulsive shoppers, this can be a great tool in questioning the necessity of the purchase.

Another way to use the rule is that you have to use up or wear out the item before getting a new one. This ensures that you have made maximum use of your current possessions before moving on and getting something new.

The No Spending Day

The no spending day approach can be a great tool for trying out living without your daily spending "needs," without committing to quitting them outright.

Schedule a regular "no spending day" once a week.

For example, you can forgo that cup of fancy latte, bring leftovers for lunch instead of buying a meal, or walk when you would have normally called a ride-sharing service. Chances are, you will see how easy it is to give up a regular expense in your life, and make new habits that do not involve spending.

You can take the "no spending day" further and make it into a "no spending week," or "no spending month," where you do not allow yourself to make any discretionary purchases just for that time period. It can be a very empowering experiment – and lets you save a little (or a lot of) money once in a while.

Budget Tracking Methods

There are several ways to approach your budget planning and tracking. If you are not a math or spreadsheet person – don't worry, the key to minimalist budgeting is simplicity.

- The "classic" paper and pen approach. This method may be a little "old-fashioned," but some people may prefer the simple and concrete way this system lets them record and access their budgeting information, rather than having the numbers in a computer or online. Sometimes a piece of paper with numbers on it just feels more "real" than digits on an electronic screen. If you do go with this approach, make sure to have an organized system for recording and storing your information. You can use a journal or notepad (get one with lines, as opposed to just blank pages), or have a folder with pockets where you file your records.
- You can also do your financial tracking electronically, which makes it easy to quickly find and update information, make copies of it, and store it in a place where you can easily assess it on the go – on your phone or laptop (By contrast, paper versions can get lost or damaged, and they are not as convenient to make copies of).

    There are several excellent online tools that let you plan and track your budget. Simply search for "budget tracking tool" or "budget tracking app" online and check out the selection to see which one

might best suit your preferences. Some apps are more or less online spreadsheets, where you can enter your income, planned versus actual expenses, savings, and debt payments. Others (for example, mint.com) offer the ability to consolidate viewing all your financial accounts into one app and send you alerts about upcoming bills and unusual account activity.
- You can also track your budget with a simple spreadsheet on your computer, using Excel or a similar program. The examples shown in this book can be done quickly and easily using a spreadsheet program, or even just a Word or Notepad type of application.

The most important attributes of your budgeting method should involve being easy to access, read, and update. Your budgeting method has to work for you. If just the thought of getting out your budget and reviewing it gives you a headache, try a simpler approach. Fancy expensive budgeting software won't help you if you tend to avoid using it because of its complexity.

In this chapter, we have looked at a number of tools and methods to help you organize your minimalist budget, pay down debt, and facilitate your finance management. In the next chapter, we'll take a look at how to address issues when working with a minimalist budget.

End of Chapter Exercise

Imagine you can sell back anything you have purchased (and still own) for its original purchase price. The only catch is that you have to deposit your refund into an emergency fund so you can't just replace the things you sell back with a newer version.

Look around to see what you are willing to sell back (don't forget to check the closets). Pick the amount that most closely resembles the maximum total "refund" that you can get for your emergency fund:

- ☐ $0 (not willing to return anything)
- ☐ $100
- ☐ $500
- ☐ $1000
- ☐ $5000
- ☐ $10,000+

How does this amount compare to your real-life emergency fund?

CHAPTER 5
Dealing With Compulsive Spending, Setbacks, And Unexpected Expenses

Budget-related setbacks generally fall into one of two categories: those we absolutely have no control over, like natural disasters, and those we failed to control. There is also a gray area in between, based on considerations of how much control we actually have over ourselves.

This chapter will help you to analyze your setbacks, adjust your budget and your mindset, and plan for the future so that you can control the setbacks you cause yourself, and the setbacks that you cannot control do not affect you as negatively.

Expect the Unexpected

Some financial setbacks are certainly not anything you can prevent or control – accidents happen, things break, our friends and family ask us for help. Sometimes, all these things happen at the same time, and your rainy day becomes a perfect storm! However, you can do some "preventative maintenance" in life to help lessen the impact of the unexpected expenses:

- Examine your "unexpected" expenses for patterns: Just because you have not planned for an expense, it does not mean that it was not predictable. Doctor and dentist visits, home and car maintenance, and property taxes are items that are likely to happen sooner or later, and you should include planning for those into your regular budget allocation. Chapter 3 explains how to approach expenses that do not happen monthly, and Chapter 4 shows you the various approaches you can take to incorporate that allocation into your budget.
- Have an emergency fund: Even if you already have many financial obligations, putting away just a small amount every month can be extremely helpful. Review Chapter 4 for how you can allocate an amount toward this goal. It's important to remember that this is not your "I ran out of money, and I feel like buying something" fund. While the emergency fund should be easy to access, it should only be used for extreme cases such as medical emergencies or natural disasters.
- Do some preventative maintenance: This applies to your home, your car, and your own body. Repairing a faucet is a lot less expensive than repairing water damage that a broken faucet can cause. Leading a healthy lifestyle is a lot less expensive than dealing with the illnesses associated with things like overeating, smoking, not exercising, and not washing your hands. There is a reason that cars come with maintenance schedules – things are likely to go wrong if you don't follow them.
- Get insured: Car insurance, health insurance, homeowners insurance, even pet health insurances are tools you can use to

mitigate the financial impact when disaster strikes. The coverage should be appropriate for shielding you from the costs that you can't pay for yourself. You can also "self-insure" yourself for some expenses by putting away money into an emergency fund as if you were paying an insurance premium.
- Look for alternatives: Some expenses can be significantly lowered or delayed until you can pay for them. If you have an unexpected medical bill (this applies to veterinary bills too), you can negotiate with the hospital to pay a lower amount or to pay in installments. If you have to make a trip, you can check into using frequent flyer miles or drive instead of flying. If you have to make car or house repairs, you can consider doing the work yourself if you have the necessary skill set, or you can ask someone you know to do it in exchange for help with something you can do.

The Psychology of Overspending

We may not be able to control natural disasters, but studies show that 40-80% of purchases are impulse buys. For spending decisions, we do have some control over, it's important to examine what causes us to make the decision to buy. The reasons can be very personal, and they may be rooted deeply in our experiences and natural tendencies. However, we can group the reasons into general categories that can help you understand the background for your own overspending:
- Influence from others and social pressure: Humans are social creatures, and much of our behavior is tied to interacting with others. Our purchases can be caused by us comparing ourselves to others, the fear of missing out on the fun or the good deals that other people are enjoying and getting involved in herd mentality about the necessity of certain purchases. There is also what we consider social obligations: gift reciprocity and gift-giving occasions (where some competition can occur as well).
- Shopping momentum: Once you have purchased what you intended, your mindset tends to remain open to making acquisitions. It felt good to set a buying goal and accomplishing it, so naturally, we want to do it again. This is where budgeting and being deliberate with deciding what you acquire is very critical.
- Stress and external factors affecting our disposition: Stress can make us avoid purchasing decisions, so we end up buying more than we intended. Stress can also make us feel like we deserve a treat or something extra because we are under pressure, so we go shopping and buy ourselves something to improve our mood. Positive moods can affect us too, as we can be overly optimistic about our finances. It's important to recognize when you are susceptible to make poor buying decisions. Avoid going shopping when you are stressed out, make good plans, and stick to them.

- Living in the present: Normally, the concept of living in the present is a good thing, but when making purchasing decisions, we tend to put a lot of emphasis on how we feel at the moment as opposed to planning for the future. Making a purchase has the ability to give us instant gratification, and we may fail to consider how our actions will affect us in the future.
- Unrealistic expectations: Sometimes, we fail to be realistic about the amount of money we allocate to the various categories in our budget. We make a budget that's very restrictive compared to the lifestyle we are accustomed to, and we get discouraged when trying to adhere to our own plans. It's important that your minimalist budget is sufficient to cover the basic necessities and also allows you to stay inspired and motivated by your plans.
- Money abstraction: The way we earn, store, and spend money today allows us the option never actually to see or handle cash. Modern payment methods such as credit cards, electronic payment transfers, and the ability to pay with your watch or phone make life convenient. However, they also make money less "real" – money becomes just some numbers; you don't have to part with anything when you make a purchase. The repercussions for overspending are delayed, and there is nothing to discourage you from overspending at the time of the actual purchase.

While this information may help you understand why you are spending more money than you intend to, the following sections contain suggestions for taking control of your spending. Remember that living with a minimalist budget is largely about mindfulness, about doing things in a purposeful way. While you may not be able to change your natural tendencies and impulses, understanding yourself is critical to modifying your behavior.

Embrace Money and Embrace Yourself

No one is perfect. Even with the best of plans, we tend to forget, procrastinate, lose our focus, and get demotivated once in a while. This is normal.

Keeping in mind that our hunter-gatherer mindset is what drives us to look for things to purchase, the habit of spending money on unnecessary things can be hard to break. In addition, once in a while, all of us experience financial setbacks that are out of our control.

It's important to examine how you view money and your relationship with it. Avoid negative thoughts about money – it seems to be attracted to people who like it, and it tends to run away from people who don't like it. Money in itself is not "evil," as some people think, but it can cause financial problems if not handled properly. Money is an opportunity.

As they say, "money can't buy happiness" (or love), but it can certainly enable us to do the things that make us happy. To make your money work for you, you have to realize that managing money is about tradeoffs. You can choose how to direct the money you have to accomplish the most happiness. You can also choose to make additional money, so you have additional options.

When you make mistakes with money, remember that people can change. If you have certain habits, it's not necessarily who you are. With the right mindset, you can change your habits and behave differently, more in line with what you value and who you want to be.

If you find yourself unable to avoid impulse purchases, do not get discouraged. When faced with the next challenge, remind yourself about the feeling of regret in your past purchasing experience. Use this as a motivation to avoid making the purchase, and thus not feel this regret again.

It's helpful to write down the reasons that have caused you to make an impulsive purchase, not pay your bills on time, or fail to allocate your planned amount toward savings. Once you have your reasons on paper, review the list for patterns. Are there factors that keep happening over and over that cause the problem, and how can you minimize or avoid the influence of those factors? Even if the reasons are random or seemingly out of your control, think of ways you might account for their unpredictability in the future. Can you put away a little money toward the unexpected every month, or avoid situations that might lead to fate wreaking havoc on your financial plans?

Distinguish Between Needs and Wants

Be very questioning about every purchase. Ask yourself if what you already have is enough to keep you happy. Can you possibly do without the item that you are considering? Getting more is not necessarily better; it just fills your life with meaningless things. Some things can be enjoyable, even useful, but still not qualify as a necessity.

Focus on Simplicity and Function

With that said, a minimalist budget is not meant to make your life difficult – quite the opposite, you should focus your money on things that make your life simpler. If you forgo buying a microwave and a dishwasher because you can live without them, going without those things (for some) actually may make life more complex. You may spend more time cooking and cleaning, and when you don't feel like dealing with that, you will just go out to eat and spend more money, negating the savings of not buying the appliances.

Your possessions should be a balance of meeting your essential needs, simplicity, and bringing enjoyment and satisfaction into your life.

Avoid Temptations and Plan Your Purchases

Some of the time, our urge to buy something is triggered by a specific situation – driving or walking by a store where you like to shop, getting a catalog in the mail, or receiving an email about a sale. There is a reason grocery stores often put candy in the checkout lane – no one really needs candy, but seeing it can trigger the urge to buy it, for a lot of people.

- Examine what triggers your urge to buy unnecessary things and remove these temptations from your life.

- Unsubscribe from sale notifications, catalogs, store emails, and other things people send you to get you to buy things.
- Avoid shopping malls and other places where you will be tempted to make unplanned purchases. Do not go to the store "just to see what's on sale." You will end up buying something you do not need.
- Unfollow items on social media that focus on reviewing and promoting things to buy.
- As much as feasible, limit your exposure to advertisements and other media information that is trying to get you to buy or invest in something. As we watch TV or even drive by billboards, we are bombarded by all kinds of suggestions about how you should spend your money (and what a good deal it is). Ignore these distractions and focus on your goals and priorities.

Always plan your purchases in advance. To avoid impulse buying, walk away as soon as you give yourself any of the following reasons to buy something:
- It's on sale, for a limited time
- I might need it in the future
- I deserve to have one of these
- Someone else I know has this

None of these are good reasons to acquire something – it is a waste of your money. Follow these steps once you decide that a purchase is truly necessary:
- Research the specific item you want to buy. Look at the product reviews and specifications to make sure it fits your needs.
- Consider alternatives – something you already own or can purchase. Are there other items or variations of this product that can fulfill your needs and be more cost-effective? Ask yourself if you like everything about this item. Do you really love it, or can you wait until you can find a better variant?
- Consider ownership cost (will this item make you buy more things, like accessories or require maintenance or other additional expenses?)
- Consider additional aspects of owning this product, other than cost. How often will you really use it? Where will you keep it so it will not clutter your life? Do you have to get rid of something else first before you have room for this new item?
- Research how much the item costs. Is it possible to acquire it online at a lower cost? Is getting this item in used condition an option? Are there windows of time when buying this item may be less expensive than usual? (Seasonal sales are a good example of this).
- Determine the price you can acquire the item for and allocate the cost into your budget. In some cases, the allocation may be a savings amount over months or even years, and in other cases, this can be a one-time expense in your monthly budget.
- Give yourself some time to think it over. This is the key to avoiding an impulse purchase. Wait at least a day from the time you have

decided to make a purchase before going ahead and proceeding with the transaction. If you find yourself in a situation where you say to yourself "*Well, I'm here now, so I might as well buy it,*" this is a sign that you have not planned this purchase in advance and likely don't actually need this item. The longer you can wait before purchasing, the better. You will be surprised how many times you will reconsider the purchase after walking away from the store, or after living without it for a few days or weeks and realizing that you don't actually need it in your life. You will actually feel a sense of relief that you did not buy it!

- After completing the proper considerations, make an informed and purposeful purchase!

By using this process, you are making sure that the things you acquire are really what you want, that they will have room in your life and won't clutter it, that they are useful and have good value. This is shopping like a minimalist.

Form New Habits

At first, making a decision not to make an impulse purchase will be difficult. Your mind has made well-worn "tracks" in your decision-making landscape, and its tendency is to direct you to buy things! However, as you make new decisions not to purchase something, your mind will become more used to this line of thinking – making new "tracks," in a way. This will not happen overnight, or just by you reading this book – change takes time, and behavior changes take a mindful effort.

After some time practicing the minimalist mindset, you will notice that you actually feel more content and satisfied if you decide not to buy something. The decision not to make an impulse purchase will become easier, until it is second nature, and you are actively seeking out other ways to make your financial life, or your life in general, more efficient and less wasteful.

Forming and breaking habits can take time, but the more you do something, the easier it is to get yourself to do it next time. Practice making the right decisions for your budget, and you will become better at it.

There is a nice bonus in getting used to living with less: you become more appreciative of what you do have in your life. If you are used to quickly giving in to your own whims and wishes, your frequent acquisitions mean less and less to you. On the other hand, giving up something and only having it occasionally makes it into something worth appreciating! Do this with something you are used to giving yourself "as a treat" frequently: this could be a fancy latte on the way to work, a glass of wine with dinner, buying new outfits, or electronics. Rather than depriving yourself of the treat entirely, reduce the frequency - if you have a fancy latte every day on the way to work, only allow yourself to buy it once a week. You will notice that something which you used to take for granted is now really special and fun! As part of human nature, we are equipped to really appreciate good things if we receive them in moderation, not all the time. Take advantage of this, and maximize your enjoyment of things through the minimalist approach.

Distract Yourself and Keep an Open Mind

As a strategy, distract yourself with an activity that does not involve spending money. Go for a walk or schedule some quality time with friends and family. There are many things you can do for free, or very inexpensively, that can bring joy into your life. Keep in mind that spending money does not directly lead to happiness.

Of course, what is fun to one person may not be that much fun to another. In order to expand your own options of simple and inexpensive ways to enjoy your life, spend a week writing down at least one thing per day which you would enjoy doing, and which costs very little or no money (including transportation). This activity also should not involve looking for things to buy. Here are some ideas for the list:

- Go for a hike on a nearby trail.
- Look at books at a local library, or check out what books you already own.
- Check for free books on Amazon (many classic books are free, and the reason they are "classic" is that many people have liked them through the ages)
- Volunteer for a cause that you care about.
- Schedule some family time – play some games.
- See a local high school sports game.

There are many distractions and fun things to do that do not involve spending much money. See the "Entertainment" section of the bonus chapter in this book for additional ideas on this topic.

You can also distract yourself by thinking of achieving your financial motivation (from Chapter 1). Won't it be nice once you are finally able to put your dreams and aspirations into action? Imagine yourself in the act of enjoying what you have planned – traveling, helping others, retiring in comfort.

Learn from Experience and Adjust to Life Changes

Remember to regularly review and adjust your minimalist budget to comprehend any life changes. Check how frequently you have expenses that you think of as unexpected or covered by special circumstances. Can you anticipate these expenses better in the future, and either find a way to prevent them or incorporate them into your financial planning?

If you anticipate a future expense that either temporarily or permanently will affect your budget (for example, the birth of a child or the need for a new car), review its impact on your finances in advance. Can you start putting away money into savings now to avoid a larger adjustment later? Identify some areas where your spending is discretionary and which can be easily adjusted when needed.

Learn from your experience as you utilize your minimalist budget in real life. If you make an impulsive purchase, think back to the sequence of events that led you to buy it. Did you go shopping for one thing and ended up buying something else? Try to avoid similar situations in the future – when you go shopping, make a very specific list of the things you want to buy and the amount of money you want to spend on them. Also think carefully about how the impulse purchase has made you feel immediately after, as well as how it's making you feel now. Did it make your life better? Are there other things you would have rather had instead of having made that purchase? Return to the reflection on your post-purchase feelings the next time you are faced with buying something. Chances are, if you have not planned on buying it before, then you do not need it.

Your attitude toward money and your confidence in yourself are important for getting you back on track when you experience financial setbacks. Learning to live on a minimalist budget will take time and adjustment. The reward of living a simple and empowered financial life is worth the work.

Impulse Buying Prevention Tricks

So you have made a budget, organized your wants and needs and planned out your purchases, but when you actually go to the store, you still end up buying things you have not planned on. You know that you want to declutter your life and live simply, but you just can't pass up a good deal, and those purchases are wreaking havoc on your budget.

Here are some additional tricks and techniques to try to curb your unplanned purchases:

- Set a minimum for every purchase that's not in your budget. For example, for purchases over $20, you have to wait 24 hours before you can buy it. For purchases over $100, you have to wait a week. For purchases over $1000, you have to wait a month. You can adjust the amounts to fit your budget.
- Make a deal with someone so that every time you make an impulse purchase, you will give them the amount of money you have spent on the purchase. All of a sudden, good deals stop being so good because you have to pay double!
- When going to a store, bring only enough cash with you to buy what you have planned on. Don't take any debit or credit cards along.
- Calculate how many hours of your work the item is worth. Even if you work for a salary, on commissions, or are self-employed, chances are you know roughly how much you make per hour while working. Convert the cost of the item you are considering to hours of your work and see if you still feel that it's worth that much of your effort.
- Invoke the "one in, one out rule." Think of an item you already own that's similar to what you are considering purchasing and commit to getting rid of this item.

- Even if you are looking at the item in person, pull up online reviews of it (you can use Google or Amazon for this). Go right to the negative reviews and ask yourself if you still like the item as much.

End of Chapter Exercise

Imagine that due to industry downsizing, you have just learned that your net income will be reduced by 10% starting next month. Calculate how much less money for you this amounts to.

What would you have to change in your life to avoid taking on any additional debt obligations? Name some categories where you can likely cut down on some expenses based on your current spending habits:

- ☐ Entertainment
- ☐ Groceries
- ☐ Restaurants
- ☐ Transportation
- ☐ Vacations
- ☐ Can you think of any other areas?

Now, can you apply your strategy to your real-life spending for a month and put away that 10% toward your savings? Can you keep it up for two months?

CHAPTER 6
The Interaction Of Your Minimalist Budget With Your Family And Friends

This chapter addresses the potential positive and negative aspects of the role your partner, kids, and friends can play in your minimalist budget approach. It's important to keep in mind that the lifestyle changes driven by your minimalist budget are likely to impact other people. This can be either a positive or negative effect. While you should not care what strangers think about your budget strategies, the people who are significant in your life can be important factors for your minimalist budget.

Partner / Spouse / Significant Other

Combining personal finances can be a challenge in a relationship. There are a lot of choices to make about how each person will contribute financially, and what the spending priorities and goals are.

If you have a jointly-owned budget with your significant other, it's critical that you have mutual understanding and support in your budgeting strategy. Shared goals and shared financial information are important to achieving your financial goals.

If you have not already, start with discussing your financial goals and come to a general consensus on your priorities. Some of the topics to cover in your discussion are:

- Where do you both see yourself financially in five, ten, twenty years?
- What kind of lifestyle do you envision now, and in the future, for your life together? Does one of you want to retire early, and the other would like to work longer but wants to go on some vacations?
- If you are just starting out with sharing your financial goals, how do you want to handle personal debt, credit card balances, student loans, and other obligations? Do they need to be comprehended into your combined spending and saving plan?
- Do you prefer to assign each partner to specific categories within the budget (i.e., one person would be responsible for living expenses, and the other one would focus on debt repayment and savings), or how would the responsibilities be shared?
- If your incomes are very different, does this have an impact on how you approach your banking and do you need a plan for properly recognizing each person's financial contributions? These can be very personal choices.

Your discussion should make it clear to both of you which aspect of your finances you are combining, and which ones you will keep separated. For example, you can allocate shared financial responsibility to some expenses, while retaining some money for discretionary spending. If you are living together but are not married, your shared budget should include at least your household expenses. It's not typical to share credit cards and bank accounts before being married, and even after getting married, this can be a highly personal choice.

When you create your minimalist budget together, the overall process is the same as what is involved in creating a personal budget: you need to define your income, basic living expenses, and financial goals, and then create a spending allocation that is consistent with your priorities and resources. For shared budgets, the areas that will be most impacted by differences in opinions will be savings allocation and discretionary spending. However, keep in mind that lifestyle choices will also impact your basic, non-negotiable expenses – for example, deciding on the size of the house you want to live in will impact your housing expenses.

Of course, consensus on everything is nice but hardly realistic. When there is a difference between yours and your partner's opinions (and there will be), it comes back to one of the basic concepts of a relationship: compromise. There is no formula for this, but in general, both of you will have to make tradeoffs.

A shared minimalist budget has to meet your individual needs and preferences. Perhaps you can alternate months on how to allocate your discretionary spending. You can also agree to temporarily or permanently reduce some expenses in favor of the others: if one of you likes to eat at nice restaurants, and the other one wants a vacation, cutting back on restaurant spending will be required, but you can both enjoy the vacation together.

You will also have to make choices that are personal, and there are no right answers. If your incomes are unequal (and chances are, that's the case), you can assign financial obligations and discretionary spending amounts that are proportional to each person's income. For example, each person would contribute 10% of their income to savings, and 10% of their income would be completely up to them how to spend. You can also assign specific categories of expenses to each person – for example; the grocery budget goes to the person who is most frequently buying the groceries.

The weekly budget reviews discussed in Chapter 3 are a great tool for measuring and communicating your financial performance when you are sharing a budget with someone else. This is the time to jointly plan and review your financial standings, discuss trade offs, and agree on compromises. Ensure that any issues are communicated clearly and calmly and that you both are in agreement on the issue remediation strategy. The budget reviews are not a complaining or blaming session – rather, you both need to determine what factors you can control and what each of you can contribute to achieving common goals.

In addition to regular budget reviews, another useful tool for organizing a shared financial life is using a budgeting app that you can both access on your phones. Such an app will allow you to quickly review your actual spending versus targets in various categories and track the status of your bill payments and other obligations. If both of you are diligent about updating and reviewing the info in your budgeting app, it can be a great communication and visualization tool for your financial accomplishments, as well as areas where you had to compromise.

An important aspect to keep in mind that the goal in compromising for your minimalist budget is not to keep everything even: this for that, "*I deserve to buy a new watch if you get to have a new phone.*" Instead, it's about agreeing on what really brings fulfillment into your shared life, what makes you happy, together, in the most financially-effective way possible. Sometimes, accumulating things or looking for things to buy is a distraction in a relationship. Once you stop chasing after "stuff," you and your partner may find that the simpler, goal-oriented life brings you closer together.

However, if you find that you frequently cannot come to an agreement on your budgeting strategy and its implementation, you may need to address underlying relationship issues. This may involve discussing your basic goals and motivations in further detail or seeking professional counseling. On the other hand, if you can generally come to an agreement on goals and priorities, but struggle with the complexities of actually making a combined budget, you can seek help from a financial planner or get advice from an objective third party.

When you live on a minimalist budget, make a distinction between spending consciously and conscious spending. You and your spouse may be very aware of your own and each other's spending – that's spending consciously. Spending consciously may make you and your spouse feel guilty about your purchases. It can even create conflict, as it may induce feelings of being judged or being compared to one another. Spending consciously may not necessarily reduce your spending, but conscious spending can. Conscious spending implies being purposeful about how you allocate your money, which is the underlying notion of minimalist budgeting. Your strategy should not involve making each other feel bad about spending money – quite the opposite, minimalist budgeting is about finding happiness and meaning in putting your money toward accomplishing your goals.

Discussing financial goals and spending motivations can become a powerful tool in getting to know more about your partner and achieving a new closeness. There is a reason why we value certain things, plan (or fail to plan) our spending and saving – perhaps it's the values we were raised with or something we have learned from our parents through their mistakes or life experiences that have shaped our financial habits. Getting to know your partner's motivations and coming to a consensus on goals and strategies can help you with strengthening both your financial position and your relationship.

Kids

Sharing your expenses and budgeting with your significant other can add complexity to your strategy. Sharing a budget with a family that includes kids can be even more challenging! But as we have learned, the concept of minimalism is about making things simpler and putting your time and resources toward the things you really want in life. A minimalist budget can help your family spend more time together in a rewarding way, and not focus so much on acquiring things.

While walking back to my car at a rest area one time, I saw an unusual scene. A couple and their four young kids were on the grassy part of the rest area, and the father was leading them on an exercise of doing jumping jacks. It looked like a very happy scene, with both the kids and adults smiling and laughing and little ones trying their best to imitate the older ones in the exercise. It was such a simple and amazing idea, to do something together with your kids, which is fun, free, does not require any special equipment, and is a good way to stretch out on a long road trip. All this, while kids in nearby cars were busy looking at their electronics, with the kids and parents mostly ignoring each other.

In a way, that scene symbolizes the minimalist budget approach – it shows that you do not have to spend money to enjoy life and have a great time with those who matter in your life. You can take a simple activity and substitute it in place of the clutter of electronics, snacks, and searching for the next thing to buy, which often consumes not just our lives, but our kids' lives too.

You can be doing your child a great favor by demonstrating that less can be more, that getting more stuff is not necessarily the key to happiness. There are several ways you can expose your kids in your minimalist budget approach and help them participate in it. Of course, some children are just too young to understand the concept of money, or that there is a finite amount of it you can have (even some adults struggle with the latter!). Utilize the following strategies:

- Set an example: Your kids are good at observing you and getting a sense of your values in life. Are you purposeful in how you acquire things and about the possessions you have inside the house? How strongly are you attached to the things you own and your spending habits? Your priorities in this matter can be a strong influence on your kids' behavior in acquiring new toys and just wanting to buy things when you go somewhere.
- Communicate with your children: The details of the information you give your kids will depend on their age, of course, but even in very simple terms, you can explain the benefits of minimalist budgeting and your reason behind using it. As much as is feasible, discuss some of your spending options with your children. Try to make them understand that there are choices associated with getting things and doing activities. Older children may jump to far-reaching conclusions – that you are getting rid of all your possessions and discontinuing using money. Be clear and consistent about the ways your minimalist budget approach will affect your kids. As with most changes, it will take time and practice.
- Also as much as practical, make them actively participate in making choices about optional spending – while providing for their necessities, of course. See if would they rather have this toy or that

one, go to an amusement park, or have a new game. Being an active participant in decisions allows your kids to understand early on that life is about choices. It also helps them to realize why you can't always agree to get them that latest gadget, or game, or candy at the checkout lane.

- Lower your kids' expectations for instant gratification: Just like adults, kids are exposed to a lot of advertisements that tell them what they should want next. Instead of enjoying the toys they already have, they are conditioned to want the next cool thing, which results in a lot of wanting, complaining, and even whining. Practice moderate giving in to the wanting of new things. It will take consistency, and it may take time, but your child will be happier in the long term by learning to want less.
- Simplify toys: Especially for really young children, toys do not have to be overly complicated. Instead of modern electronic toys, which are easily broken and require battery replacements, consider classic, old-fashioned toys. In addition to being more practical (and fun and educational), these are likely to be more cost-effective as well. Simple toys encourage children to use their creativity and imagination and to play cooperatively with their siblings or other children to put together a story or a game.
- Monitor and regulate exposure to advertisements: By simply watching TV with commercials, your children get conditioned to wanting more and more things, no matter what they already own. You can set limits on the amount of TV they watch or even eliminate TV altogether and substitute content without advertisements – for example, shows from Amazon Video or Netflix.
- Many kids' rooms are simply overflowing with toys and clothes. There is no available storage space, and it's hard to determine what's actually being made use of. Having too many toys is not necessarily a good thing – children cannot process having too many options to choose from, and an overabundance of play choices can cause anxiety and stress. In addition, the clutter of too many toys and clothes makes it difficult to clean and organize. Review what your kids already own and simplify.
- The decluttering process can be adjusted to the child's age and personality. Older kids, in particular, will not want you to decide for them what they need and don't need. Depending on your child's age, you can involve them in deciding what they would like to keep and what can be donated or discarded. You can also look for things that haven't been used in a long time (have they been stored in the shed or the basement for months or even years?), or things that are broken, or clothing items that the child outgrew.
- Your child may be reluctant to let go of things, even if they are not being used. To make the process easier, you can declutter in stages –

perhaps get rid of one toy per week, or designate a clean-up time once per month when a certain number of toys or clothing items have to be disposed of. Make sure to communicate the reasons for cleaning up and decluttering. Children can be very motivated to let go of their possessions if they know that their toy is going to be donated to a child in need.
- Point out the benefits of having implemented a simpler and decluttered lifestyle: Your children may not notice it on their own, but you can make some observations for them to note – for example, that their room is easier to clear and things are easier to find. A minimalist budget may also allow you to shift your resources toward something you can enjoy as a family – for example, a vacation that you could not afford before.
- It's hard to demonstrate decluttering your life if your children receive a lot of gifts from others. Discuss your minimalist strategy with friends and family members who give your child gifts and set rules in place about what is an appropriate amount. If someone wants to contribute more than the gifting limits you have set, you can suggest that they make a donation to your child's 529 (college savings) plan.
- Stick to your rules: If you have set a limit of gifts or implemented the One In, One Out rule (discussed in Chapter 4), make sure to follow up and stay consistent in how you enforce these rules.
- Be ok with saying "no": Kids are not known to be long-term thinkers. Many of their wants and (expressed) needs will end up being things they don't use. In addition to guiding their choices, you often have to limit their choices or stop the acquisition process altogether by just saying "no." The ability to say "no" also goes a long way with well-meaning adults in your life who want to give your kids hand-me-downs and gifts. Be able to decline, when needed, gracefully.
- Instead of toys, give the gift of your time: Cherished memories are not made with things – they are made by spending time together and enjoying each other's company. Instead of focusing on how much to spend on your child's toys, focus on how you can have a great time together, as a family. In your child's point of view, your love and attention are much better than any toy you can give them. The gift of a great experience is also something you can encourage others to give to your children instead of toys.

Here are some ideas on how to meaningfully contribute to your child's experiences and development, while taking away the focus on acquiring more things:
- Spend time outdoors: You can go hiking, fishing, mountain biking – find an activity that suits your child's preferences and interests.
- Build or repair something together: Whether you are handy with tools or not, having a project to which you can both contribute can be a great way to make memories together. This can be a car or bike

- repair and maintenance, a treehouse project, or repairing a broken toy.
- Take a class: This can be music, a sport (swimming or karate, for example), or a cooking class for kids. You can find a class you can take together with your child, or this can be a class where your children can spend time with their siblings and friends, or make new friends.
- Learn something new together (even without taking a class): You can try a new hobby – painting, sewing, or a new sport.
- Do arts and crafts: You can work on the same project as a team, or set a theme and show off your art skills to each other.
- Go to a venue: A movie, a play, a concert for kids, the zoo are all great places to enjoy the moment and build memories together.
- Make a meal or creative snacks: Use your imagination and have fun in the kitchen.

Children don't need you to fulfill their every wish to be happy. They need you to provide for their basic needs, and they need your love and attention. A minimalist budget household will take out the clutter out of your kids' lives, encourage them to use their imagination in play, and will curb the cycle of wanting more things. This way, you can focus on what really matters in life.

Friends and Acquaintances

Even if they don't directly impact your household income and spending, your friends and acquaintances can still play a very large role in either supporting or undermining your minimalist budget approach. Friends can be a great positive influence on your motivation, and they can become role models for your goals and budgeting strategy (as well as showing us what to avoid by setting a negative example!). On the other hand, friends and other people in your life can also encourage you to focus on spending and demotivate you in other ways, both intentionally and unintentionally.

There are a number of strategies for preventing overspending due to the influence of other people in your life:

- Use minimalist budgeting to prioritize your goals: If spending time with friends is important to you (and your activities together involve spending money), make an allocation in your budget for this. You will need to evaluate other spending areas and make compromises as needed, but this is what minimalist budgeting is about.
- Communicate: Let friends know if an activity they are suggesting is not within your budget. You can also discuss your spending goals and priorities, and explain your reasoning for implementing conscious spending in your life. Your friends should know that your behavior is not just about having insufficient funds to spend, and they should not interpret it as you not wanting to spend time with them.
- Be honest with yourself: If you are facing an impulse purchase while shopping with someone else, question your own motivations. Do you really like this item, or are you trying to make an impression, or are

you just avoiding the awkwardness of putting the item back? Finding the real reason behind wanting to buy something can also help you to find the motivation to avoid the purchase.
- Look for alternatives: If you have a social pattern that frequently makes you spend money on going out, entertainment, or shopping for fun, try to focus on the aspect that really matters to you: spending time with friends. Think of how to focus on the experience aspect, and not on the buying aspect of enjoying time with others. You can suggest alternatives to your friends or brainstorm ideas together. The bonus chapter of this book contains some ideas for how to reduce entertainment-related costs.
- Remember your minimalist budget tools: If you are worried about overspending when going out with your friends, don't forget the option of bringing only cash with you to limit how much you can spend.
- Have an accountability partner: If you have trouble staying within your budget on your own, recruit a friend who will hold you accountable for your spending, and discourage you from impulsive purchases. You can use this as a strategy for shopping trips or while on vacation with a friend, or you can even have regular budget reviews together, which can serve as a motivation to stay on track.
- Participate only in activities that you can pay for and have an exit strategy: Social situations can get complicated when it comes to paying. First, plan ahead and participate in activities you can afford and can pay your fair share for. It is also helpful to have an exit strategy if you want to leave a social situation gracefully without spending too much: make backup plans, or ask a friend or family member to text you so you have a reason to leave.
- Limit comparisons: As discussed in Chapter 1, our spending habits can be fueled by considerations of what someone else already has. Focus on your own happiness and buying priorities. Sometimes it's easy to justify an expense because someone you know has the same thing. In addition to questioning whether you need to make that purchase in the first place, also try to look at expenses as a fraction of your income, before you compare what you spend to other people's spending.

Don't be quick to envy people. Everyone makes compromises in how they spend their time and money. The neighbor who just got a new car may be able to afford it by working long days and not spending any time with his family. The friend who just went on a fun island vacation may be drowning in debt. Remember that you are doing what's right for you and your finances and other people have different life circumstances.
- Curb your assumptions and expectations: Remember that everyone's priorities are different. Once you decide how you want to allocate your money, even if it's a very purposeful and efficient spending plan,

your friends may have different priorities. Don't judge how others are choosing to spend their money. If you are deciding on a trip or activity together, make a plan that works for everyone's budget (or make a choice of whether you can participate or not).
- Be ok with saying "no": Even with the best of intentions, our friends and family can cause us to acquire things we don't need. Sometimes this involves a friend asking us to go on a spontaneous shopping trip or egging us on to make an unplanned purchase. At other times, it is friends and relatives offering us free items when they move or clean out their house. Keep your own goals in mind and know how to decline offers that are not aligned with your own priorities.
- Become a role model yourself: By using a minimalist budget to simplify your life and work on accomplishing your goals, you can demonstrate the benefits of this approach to others. You may even set someone else onto the path of financial simplicity and mindfulness that a minimalist budget brings you.

End of Chapter Exercise

Think of what proportion of your discretionary purchases are directly or indirectly influenced by people you know:
- ☐ None or very few
- ☐ Some (less than 50%)
- ☐ A considerable amount (50% or more)
- ☐ Almost all

Are you investing both time and money into your relationships?

BONUS CHAPTER
Minimalist Budget Meets Frugality

As we discussed in Chapter 1, living on a minimalist budget is not the same thing as being frugal. However, there is an overlap between the two aspects. The same person may seek simplicity and purposefulness in their budget, at the same time as aiming to save money and make their dollar go further.

Many of us work very hard at finding the best deal for big purchases, but daily waste money on small items. Often, the small things are the ones that end up cluttering our lives and prevent us from being able to put away money toward achieving our goals. It's important to be consistent and use your minimalist mindset approach for all your purchases.

Examine your expenses and ask yourself whether each one is an efficient use of your money. The exact ways to organize and streamline your savings will depend on the specifics of everyone's personal situation. Consider the following ideas and ask yourself if you can come up with even better approaches for making the best use of your money.

Housing and Utilities

Most of us have a commitment to a rental agreement or a mortgage, so it's understandable that housing-related changes cannot be done lightly or quickly.

Here is what you can do in the short-term to make your spending on housing and utilities more efficient:

- Be mindful of your energy usage that can lead to higher utility bills. Heating and cooling the house is likely a major part of your utility expenses. A programmable thermostat can go a long way to simplifying how you control the temperature and avoid unnecessarily heating the house while you are not in it. As a free substitute for a programmable thermostat, you can also set reminders on your phone for changing the temperature before going to work or going to sleep.
- To further reduce your utility bills, consider energy-saving steps, such as using energy-efficient lightbulbs, making sure your window panes are properly insulated, turning down the water heater temperature, and unplugging electronics you are not using frequently. Energy-efficient fans can also be a great money-saving alternative to air conditioning.
- House maintenance items, such as changing your air conditioning filters and cleaning your vents can go a long way to extending the life of your air conditioning unit and saving you money in the long run.
- If you own your appliances and you have to replace one, pick an energy-efficient model that will save you money over time.
- If you own your home, regular home maintenance will help you avoid big repairs down the road. Critical maintenance items include properly servicing your water heater and septic tank, regularly

cleaning your refrigerator coils, cleaning your AC unit and humidifier, and clearing the gutters. There are also many great resources online to help you reduce your utility costs and perform home maintenance.
- Investing in maintaining your home is a good thing, but be mindful of what home improvement projects you take on. The effort and money you put in needs to add value to your life. For example, if you are remodeling a room you barely use, ask yourself if you are getting the most value out of this spending, and does it make your life better.
- If you own your home, refinancing your mortgage to a lower rate can also save you money.
- If you have extra living space in your home, consider renting it out.
- If you are renting your home and your lease is coming up for renewal, negotiate a lower rental rate with your landlord. As part of your negotiation, you can offer to sign a longer lease term in exchange for a lower rate. You can also offer to do small maintenance tasks or give referrals to your landlord's other properties.

In the medium and long-term:

Consider whether the reason you live where you live still applies. Can you make your life simpler by moving to a different house/apartment or a different area altogether? For some people, house and lawn maintenance is something that brings joy to their life. For others, it's time- and money-consuming work, and moving to a housing arrangement where the association takes care of maintenance may greatly simplify their life.

Here are some options to consider and research. See if they may fit your minimalist budget better than your current housing choice:
- Downsize your house: If you are not using all the rooms in your house, they become a source of extra cleaning work and higher utility bills. Consider moving to a smaller house or apartment where you can fully utilize the available living space.
- Move to a less expensive area: If you live in the city, consider moving to the suburbs, where the cost of living is usually lower. You can also find an area with lower housing costs and lower property taxes. This can involve moving to a different neighborhood close to where you currently live, or if your job and personal situation allows you to, you can look at moving to a different region, state, or even to a different country.
- Consider other housing options: If you live in a house, investigate moving to an apartment or condo where the association fees cover the lawn service and some of the maintenance. For some people, moving to a mobile home community has worked out as a great way to save money.
- In some situations, a great option for lowering housing costs is to move in to live with someone else and share living expenses. This can involve moving in with your parents, a friend, or a roommate.

Of course, these ideas may not fit all lifestyles and situations, but it's important that the place where you live (and into which, likely, a significant amount of your budget is going to) represents your minimalist budget mindset.

Cable/Phone Bill/Internet Bill/Other Service Subscriptions

Review the following items to ensure you are getting the most value from spending money on various service subscriptions:

- If you have a subscription to a streaming service, such as Netflix, Hulu, Amazon Video, Pandora, etc., review how much you actually use these services. Can you live without some of them? Are you willing to give it a try for a few months? Keep in mind; you can often get a month for free from a lot of these services, so canceling for a few months and then re-subscribing (if needed) will at least save you some money in the short-term. And you may find that you don't miss it that much after all.
- If you have subscribed to a service for a specific purpose that no longer applies (for example, to watch a specific show via a streaming service), cancel the subscription as soon as it has fulfilled its purpose.
- Keep track of your subscriptions. Making a list of each service that you have subscribed to and its respective cost can make you realize that you have a lot of savings opportunities in this area. In addition, review your subscription bills carefully. Especially when it comes to phone, internet, and cable bills, providers often add charges that they don't advertise with their initial offers. Make sure you know what you are paying for, and how much.
- Some subscription services, specifically those that physically deliver food or other items to your house, will allow you to skip a delivery. Utilize this option when you are out of town or just don't need the item during a specific week.
- Some subscriptions will give you discounts for referring other people to the service or for adding more users to the account. Make sure to take advantage of these savings opportunities.
- If you have a cell phone, this is likely one of your most expensive subscriptions. And higher data usage rates usually mean that you pay a higher subscription fee. Check your actual data usage – do you really need an unlimited data plan? Review the phone subscription packages your provider offers and check if your actual usage allows you to switch to a less expensive package.
- To reduce your data usage, utilize Wi-Fi as much as possible. You can also check for and limit the apps that are running in the background using up your data and your battery.

- Many cell phone carriers will give you a discount if you sign up for automatic payments or paperless billing – take advantage of this money-saving option.
- Depending on the terms of your contract, it may be useful to shop around and switch to a less expensive package with another provider. After you check competitor rates, you can also negotiate with your current provider to match the lower price.
- Don't be in a rush to get the latest phone. Keeping your current phone longer and buying an older model when you do have to replace it can save you a lot of money. In addition, you can avoid contract fees by not buying your phone from your service carrier – purchase a new or used no-contact phone. If you have friends who have to have the latest model, ask if you can buy their current phone when they upgrade.
- When it comes to saving money on your cable and internet subscriptions, shopping around for better deals and negotiating with your service provider can save you a lot of money. As a possible negotiation tactic, you can even cancel your service until you get a better offer from the service provider. Living without a cable or internet subscription for a month may sound impossible, but it's easier than you think with many businesses offering free Wi-Fi.
- You can also save on the cost of renting your internet router/modem. If you are being charged this fee, simply check what model router you have and purchase one – they are not very expensive. Once you return the equipment you were renting to the service provider, make sure that the rental cost is no longer on your bill.
- Cable is expensive, and there are many alternatives that can save you money. Depending on what you usually watch, you can look into substituting cable with streaming services, such as Netflix or Hulu, or a single-channel subscription, such as HBO. With services like YouTube TV, you can still watch network television, and many networks make their content available for viewing via free apps, as well. With an inexpensive antenna, you can watch your local TV and HDTV for free. Don't forget that getting movies for free at the local library is an option, and the selection there can be better than on many cable channels!
- With all your subscriptions, be aware of what contracts and early termination fees you are signing up for. Sometimes paying an early termination fee makes sense to save money on the subscription itself, but this factor should be taken into account both when considering a new subscription, and when looking at unsubscribing from a service. In addition, be aware of any applicable data limits and other conditions that can cost you a lot more money than what you thought you were going to pay.

- Most importantly, ask yourself if your subscriptions are really adding value to your life and making you happy. Can you find alternatives that are free or do not cost as much?

Groceries

- For grocery shopping, make a plan, and buy only what you need. Most of us throw out a surprisingly large proportion of the food we buy (or it's still in an expired state in your refrigerator, and you are just not throwing it out). Follow this process when going shopping for food:
    - Before going to the store, decide how many days you are buying food for (how many meals are you making?).
    - Make a list of the perishable things you need for this many days. Note that this does not have to be specific things – you can list categories of items such as "main dish meat," "salad ingredients," "sides," and purchase them depending on what is on sale or looks freshest. Less perishable items like olive oil should make it to the list when you are running low on those.
    - Stick to this list when you are shopping – no impulse purchases!
    - Toward the end of the number of days you have shopped for, check how useful your list was – did you run out of anything too early, or end up with too much of something? Adjust your next shopping list accordingly.
- Check your refrigerator, freezer, and pantry for items you already have, before going grocery shopping. Can you use some of what you already have as part of your ingredients? Challenge yourself and your family to make a meal plan that will use up your existing food items before they expire – you can be creative or look up recipes online by searching for ones with specific ingredients.
- While shopping for groceries, it helps to track your total, either using your phone's calculator or rounding up the price and making tally marks on a piece of paper. This way, you avoid bad surprises at the checkout, and knowing the total helps you to make purchasing decisions as you go. If you often end up with a grocery total that's higher than what you budgeted, use the "cash only" strategy – leave your credit card at home and bring what you intend to spend in cash. You may have to decide which items to put back, but being on a budget requires compromises.
- Don't buy more groceries than you need, especially when it comes to perishable food. Sale offers often induce us to buy a higher quantity (for example, via "buy one, get one free" or 5 for $10 deals). Keep in mind that in most stores, the same discounted price applies even if you buy just one item. At warehouse clubs such as Sam's Club or Costco, buying in bulk can save you money, but only if you actually use all of what you purchase.

- On the other hand, if there are less perishable items you buy consistently, stock up when these items are on sale.
- Buy ingredients you can re-use across multiple meals, and avoid items that can only be used for a specific dish. To save time and money, buy enough items to make a big meal, and use what's left over for lunch or other meals later in the week.
- Also, to save both time and money, consider the option of shopping online and picking up your order at the grocery store. This helps you to avoid impulse purchases, and you can easily review the available deals to select the items you want to buy.
- Check for deals at other grocery stores. You may have picked where you shop based on the store's location, quality, selection, or prices, but don't overlook what other stores can offer you, even if you have to drive a little farther.
- Simplify your meals. A delicious dinner does not have to have a lot of ingredients or require a long time to prepare. Look up quick and simple recipes – you will spend less time on grocery shopping and cooking and have more time to enjoy other things.
- Try generic brands or brands owned by the grocery store. These often use the same ingredients as brand names but are less expensive because they are more cost-effective for the grocery store.
- Buy fruits and vegetables that are in season. They are less expensive, fresher, and taste better than out of season produce that has been shipped in from a long distance away. You can also check the country of origin of the produce to get an idea of how far it had to travel to get to your store.
- Be selective about who you go to the grocery store with. Our friends or spouse can influence us to make impulse purchases or buy more than how much we actually need. If you go grocery shopping with kids, set strict rules about the items you intend to purchase and stick with the limits you set.
- Don't go shopping for groceries when you are hungry (and, from the advice above, don't bring people who are hungry with you). You will end up buying more than you planned on because your wants start to feel more like your needs when you are hungry.

Restaurants

Restaurant expenses can be high, compared to grocery shopping. For some, eating out simplifies their life or adds value to their life by being a reason to spend time with friends and family, and that's just fine. For others, eating out is a device to compensate for ineffective grocery trip planning.

As part of your minimalist budget planning, it's important to consider the amounts you spend on groceries and eating out, as well as how they compare to each other. Ask yourself if more effective grocery planning would reduce the need for eating out at restaurants. If your reason for eating out at restaurants is mostly to spend time with friends and family, consider whether simpler alternatives would also fulfill the same purpose – for example, making a meal together at home, meeting up at a bookstore, going for a walk together. If you do decide to go out to a restaurant, consider these tips for saving money:

- Look for special offers. A lot of restaurants have rotating deals, such as free appetizers when you buy a meal, or a "kids eat free" day. There are many restaurants that will treat you to a free meal, drink, or dessert for your birthday. You can also take advantage of coupons and offers in the local paper, ads that come to your house, or discounts on websites such as Groupon.
- Get discounted gift cards for restaurants. Individual restaurants sometimes sell discounted gift cards on their websites. In addition, you can get discounts on websites, such as restaurants.com and in warehouse clubs.
- Going to a restaurant can give you an opportunity to have a unique meal that you would not necessarily want to, or be able to cook at home. Take advantage of this and try items that you would not cook yourself – otherwise, you could have saved money by making the same meal at home.
- Be aware of how much you spend on beverages and consider drinking water instead. Beverages at restaurants are usually overpriced compared to enjoying the same carbonated drinks or beer at home after buying it from a grocery store. Limit your beverage purchases at restaurants to what actually enhances the meal – such as a wine that pairs with a certain dish. Otherwise, drink water – it will also enable you to enjoy the flavor of your food better.
- Same as with beverages, desserts at restaurants are often overpriced. Skip the dessert at the restaurant, and if you still want something sweet when you get home, have ice cream or another frozen dessert option available for this purpose. Frozen desserts can usually be kept for a long time, so they are more practical than buying pastries for this purpose.
- Getting your meal to go can be a great money-saving option, as you can save on the tip and prepare your own salad or other add-ons.
- Order only an appetizer or split an entrée with another person. Restaurants often give us a lot more food than we can eat, and taking leftovers with you is not always the convenient or practical option. Try ordering just an appetizer and see if you still feel hungry after eating it. You can also order one meal to share between two people, or one meal and one appetizer. You will often find that this is quite enough food.
- If you do get a meal that's too much for you to eat, stop eating as soon as you are starting to feel full and ask for a container to take it to go.

- Going out to a restaurant for lunch instead of dinner is also a good option: lunch prices are typically lower, and portions are smaller, so it's easier on your wallet and your stomach.
- Don't assume that a "special" is a good deal. Specials are often experimental recipes or dishes made with an item that the restaurant has too much of. Check what the "special" price is and make a comparison against your other options.
- Eating at a restaurant should not be your "go-to" option for getting food. Restaurants are both more expensive than making meals at home, and they often offer poor nutritional value compared to what you would choose if cooking. Limit your restaurant meals to special occasions, and look for more practical alternatives if you eat at restaurants to socialize.
- Impulse snack and beverage purchases can cut into your budget plans. When you review your spending, make sure that you are aware of the amount you spend on this category — question whether you could have spent the same money in a better way. You can either incorporate these purchases into your planned budget (and stick to your decision) or make a conscious decision to plan your meals in a more effective way.
- Keep in mind that cheap food is not necessarily better for your budget in the long term if it lacks nutrition and ends up causing health issues. At the same time, a very expensive meal at a restaurant may not be great for your health, either. Be purposeful about choosing the food you eat and how you purchase it.

Transportation

Simplifying your transportation costs depends largely on your life situation — what your lifestyle and family needs are, whether you live in an urban, suburban, or rural area. Some changes may be easy to implement, while others will require time and lifestyle adjustments. Here are some of the ways you can reduce your transportation-related costs:

- Consider what vehicles you own and why you own them. Similar to housing, changing your car or downsizing from several cars to one for the household can be an important decision with lasting consequences. Review your vehicle usage (how often do you actually use it, do you need the size, towing capacity, luxury accessories, etc.). Also, review your financial obligations for the vehicles you own (the amount and duration of lease payments or loan payments). Take into account items that may be costing you money unnecessarily or complicating your life: maintenance and repair costs, car insurance, fuel cost, parking fees. Decide if you can make your life simpler and more financially practical, by either changing the kind of car you have or eliminating a vehicle you own from your life altogether.
- Perform regular maintenance on your vehicle. This will save you money by reducing the number of breakdowns and other unexpected

expenses, which could be much more costly than maintenance. Even a simple thing like maintaining the proper pressure in your tires can save you money on fuel costs (not to mention increasing your driving safety). Using only the recommended grade of octane is also important, as this is the fuel your car was designed to work with.

- Instead of owning two or more vehicles in your household, consider downsizing to just one and make an arrangement where one of you is the "chauffeur," or you and your spouse can take turns giving each other rides to work.
- Don't speed and obey driving laws. Speeding and parking tickets can be expensive. In addition to costing you money, speeding and other driving violations can also endanger people's lives. Driving sensibly (not speeding and not driving aggressively) will also improve your fuel economy and save you money on fuel costs.
- Other ways to reduce your fuel costs include getting a credit card that gives you cash back on gasoline purchases or buying fuel from a store chain that offers discounted fuel prices to members.
- Make smart purchasing decisions and shop around. When you are looking to buy a new vehicle, parts, or car insurance, make sure to do your research, so you are getting good value for your money. When buying a vehicle, in addition to considering the price of the car itself, also make sure to evaluate maintenance, insurance, fuel consumption, and other costs of ownership.
- If you are financing a car, compare rates from multiple financial organizations. Unless you are receiving a 0% interest rate, put down the largest down payment you can afford, to reduce the amount of interest you will pay.
- When buying car insurance, review what coverage you actually need and don't select coverage options just because they are offered. If you are a good driver, it may also make sense to choose coverage with a high deductible – it will save you money on monthly premiums, although it will cost you more if you have an accident. In addition, check the discounts offered by the insurance provider. You can get a discount by being a part of an affinity group, taking a defensive driving course, having a good driving record, or combining your insurance coverages (home, life, and auto) into one provider.
- Go eco-friendly. Walk or use a bicycle when you can. This is good for your wallet, your health, and for the environment. If you drive somewhere that involves multiple destinations, consider parking your car somewhere that allows you to access more than one destination on foot.
- When possible, use public transportation. This will allow you to save money on fuel, parking fees, and to reduce the wear and tear on the vehicles you own. If you have sufficient public transportation

- options, you can even avoid owning a vehicle altogether, allowing you to save further on vehicle insurance and maintenance.
- If you need a vehicle infrequently, consider renting one when you need it, or signing up for a car share network. Same as with public transportation, this will let you avoid the cost of vehicle ownership.
- To save money on public transportation, taxis, and ride-sharing services, examine how much you spend per month on this type of expense. Decide if you can make your life simpler by walking, riding a bike, or sharing rides with others.
- To save on transportation while traveling, consider multiple options of how to get to your destination. For example, buses can save you money compared to air travel, and they can get you to remote destinations that commercial airlines don't service. When you do fly, consider various route options, as flying through an airline hub city or taking connecting flights can save you money.

A final note to simplifying your transportation budget: analyze not only how you can reduce or simplify the transportation expense itself, but also the reason for why you are making the trips in the first place. For a week or so, write down the places you are going to and then review the overall picture of your travels. Are there any trips you can combine, and are all the trips done for something that brings value and purpose to your life? Are there other activities you can do that involve shorter or fewer trips but still fulfill the purpose?

Clothes and Personal Care

Clothes and personal care are important categories where you have to make distinctions between your wants and needs. The decision is personal – things like the latest fashion, massages, manicures, and expensive health care products may be extremely important to some and not at all important to others (and there is a spectrum of everyone in between).

This is one of the categories that most clearly distinguish a frugal approach from a minimalist approach. With a frugal approach, you would simply cut out most expenses in this category, except buying simple clothes you must have to function and maintaining basic hygiene. With a minimalist budget approach, you can decide how important the things in this category are to you and make tradeoffs with other categories. If you put a value on having a new outfit every month, you can put less value on eating out or going on a vacation. However, as with every expense on your list, you must ask yourself if the expenses in this category are really adding value and happiness to your life. Are you willing to sacrifice them for something more important, or reduce the frequency of making these purchases?

You can use the following techniques to save money on clothes and personal care:

- Before you go shopping for new clothes, review your current wardrobe and donate what you don't wear or sell the items to consignment stores. To minimize adding clutter to your life, you can

- implement the "one in, one out" rule described in Chapter 4. You can also trade the clothes you don't use with friends and family.
- When you do go shopping for new clothes, use the same techniques as for grocery shopping: make a list and stick to it, and if you think you might make impulse purchases, bring only enough cash to spend the amount you intend.
- Consider the cleaning costs when you buy new items. Dry cleaning costs can add up if you have a lot of clothes that require it. In addition, you may become hesitant to wear something if it's too difficult to clean, resulting in an expensive item doing nothing in your closet.
- Take care of your clothing and follow the care instructions on the tags. It's not money well spent if a piece of clothing gets ruined the first time you wash it.
- Buy out of season to take advantage of sales and steep discounts.
- Don't overlook thrift stores. In addition to selling deeply discounted gently used clothing, thrift stores also sell new items, with tags, that others have donated. Thrift stores can be especially useful if you are looking for a piece of clothing to wear for a one-time occasion or to experiment with a new style.
- Even if you enjoy wearing expensive name brand products, consider buying your basic clothes – socks, t-shirts to wear under shirts, tank tops – from inexpensive stores.
- Focus on simple and functional – trendy clothes are quickly out of style, and do you really have to make a fashion statement while working out?
- Saving on personal care items, such as toiletries or makeup, involves combining some of the techniques for saving on groceries and clothes: examine what you already own and use it up before buying new things. When you do buy, since most personal care items have a relatively long shelf life, try to buy in bulk when possible to save money, but check the expiration dates to make sure you can use it up in time. While expensive name brand products may be important to you for some items, consider using generic brands when possible. As with any purchase, ask yourself if the item you are buying is really serving a purpose in your life.

Health Insurance and Medical Expenses

In most cases, we do not get to pick our health conditions and how much they cost to manage, so medical expenses are difficult to reduce or simplify. However, there are still several things you can do to ensure that your approach to health-related spending is in line with your minimalist budget. To simplify and reduce your health care and medical expenses, consider the following:
- Review your health plan to make sure it's right for the number of your medical expenses and any specific medical condition coverage that

you need. Make sure you understand your health benefits, what is covered, and what the copayments and deductibles are:
- If you are in relatively good health and have a health insurance policy (and have some decision-making power over what type of insurance it is), consider switching to a high-deductible policy. This will lower your monthly insurance costs. You can put away the extra money toward savings, which can be used toward the deductible if needed.
- If you have health issues that need treatment, a health plan with higher premiums and more coverage is appropriate. You should also compare prescription drug coverage among health care plans.

- If you have a spouse, check if it's more cost-effective for one of you to be covered by the other's insurance under a family plan.
- Seek work that provides health insurance coverage or assistance.
- Research medical cost-sharing networks that you may qualify for. These can save you a significant amount of money, and they can be based on your faith, professional affiliation, and other qualifications.
- If you take medications, ask your doctor if you can switch to generic medicines or less expensive medicines that can treat the same condition. You can also ask for free medication samples. Don't neglect to take your prescribed medicines, as this can cause additional health issues and health care expenses.
- Get routine health exams and health screenings – these can detect issues that will cause significant health problems and expenses down the road, so you can take preventative and corrective action now.
- Have an emergency fund. Even with good health care coverage, you may have to deal with deductibles and expenses that are not covered by health insurance. Make sure you have money set aside to spend on emergencies, as well as to cover for any lost income if you are unable to work.
- Avoid the emergency room for non-life-threatening issues. Go to your doctor or a walk-in clinic when it's not an emergency – this is much more cost effective and wait times at a walk-in clinic are often lower than at the ER.
- Use a Health Care Savings Account (HSA) or Flexible Spending Account (FSA). These are savings accounts that allow you to deposit pre-tax money, as long as you use them for medical-related expenses. Because the money is not taxed, your dollar can go a lot further by using these accounts.
- When you get a medical bill, review it carefully to make sure you understand all the charges and there are not any errors in the billing. If you cannot afford to pay the bill, you can often negotiate the cost with the medical provider or get a low-interest payment plan.

- As one of the most important but often overlooked strategies - take care of your health! That's a topic for a whole other book (or a thousand of them), but the benefits of living healthy is a great investment into reducing your health care costs, improving your outlook on life, and allowing you to lead a life where you are able to do things that make you happy.

Entertainment

If you are used to expensive activities to entertain you, you may have developed an association between fun and spending money. But activities do not have to be expensive to be fun – in fact, living on a minimalist budget will help you realize that fun can be found in simple things.

Think of the activities you do now for entertainment and decide how well they fit in your budget. If you are enjoying what you are doing now – great. However, it's important to consider the opportunity cost of your activities – both from financial and time investment perspectives. Opportunity cost means you are no longer able to spend this money, and this time on something else.

Make a list of simple and inexpensive entertainment activities you might enjoy in place of your current ones. Here are some suggestions and thought starters:

- There are a number of ways to save money when you go out to a restaurant for entertainment. See the "Restaurants" section of this chapter for some ideas on this topic.
- If you like going out for drinks for entertainment, save money by going at "happy hour," which most bars offer. You can also check for special deals and events at your local establishments.
- If you enjoy going to sports venues, attend a local or an amateur game instead of a professional one. High school and college games, as well as minor league games, can often be attended for just a fraction of the price of seeing a professional team play.
- Many nature-related activities are free or inexpensive. If you have a park nearby, you can go for a hike, ride a bike, or rent a canoe or kayak. You can also observe wildlife, go bird watching, or use nature as your inspiration for another hobby such as painting or photography.
- If you enjoy movies, you probably know that movie theaters are very expensive. Save money by attending a matinee (early afternoon showtime), or by going to an independent film theater, where the prices are lower. You can also rent movies for free from a public library, or rent them very inexpensively from Redbox.
- If you enjoy attending live music events, search online for free concerts in your area. There are regular events in most major cities. You can also look for live music performances at local bars and coffee shops.

- If you enjoy reading, there are a number of ways to read the content that interests you for free. There are always public libraries, some even offering digital books you can check out. Many information sources on the internet are free – news publications, how-to blogs, travel journals. You can also find many free digital books online – for example, on sites like Project Gutenberg and ManyBooks.net. If you read a lot, you can also join Kindle Unlimited, which offers a huge amount of free titles for a small monthly fee plus a free trial.
- Take a class or attend a lecture. Many organizations and community establishments offer free or inexpensive classes to both adults and children. You can learn about cooking, painting, photography, a new sport, and many other topics. Some home improvement stores offer DIY classes, which can help you save money on home repairs. You can also use a class as an opportunity to spend time with friends and family or to meet new people.
- Volunteer for a cause that interests you. You can use your time to improve your community and help people and animals. By volunteering at events, you also get to attend the event for free.
- If you find yourself with a lot of spare time on your hands, also consider this time as an opportunity to make money. You can look for a gig or a side job on places like Craigslist or Indeed.com. If you have a hobby, think of ways you can turn that hobby into profit – by selling something that you make, or by working as a coach or consultant for people who would like to learn your skills.
- There are many ways to spend time with friends and family that don't involve going out to restaurants or expensive venues. You can organize a barbeque or a game night, play board games, play sports, or pick some of the suggestions on this list and do them together.

As discussed earlier, in deciding on purchases in the entertainment category, focus on buying experiences rather than things. Physical objects tend to clutter your life and may not add much value to it unless you use them frequently. Experiences are something that you can remember and share with others, something that can deepen a relationship and make a positive impact on you as a person.

Focusing on experiences and consumable items is also a good approach when purchasing someone else a gift. You will avoid adding clutter to someone else's life and instead give them a nice experience. Giving someone gourmet coffee, fancy candy, a gift card for a movie theater or a spa can make for a thoughtful gift and will certainly be appreciated more than an object that they may or may not use.

End of Chapter Exercise

Imagine you just won $1000 (after taxes).
What would you do with this money?

- ☐ Put it toward your current bills and debt obligations

- ☐ Save it for a rainy day
- ☐ Buy yourself something nice or plan a vacation
- ☐ Donate it or give it to someone else
- ☐ Save it in a retirement account

There is no right answer to this question. Examine your answer for how well it aligns with your own values and with what you have learned about the concept of minimalist budgeting.

CONCLUSION

There are trade offs in life, and you have to make a conscious decision about how you want to spend your money. Using a minimalist budget is not about depriving yourself. Rather, it is about differentiating between your needs and your indulgences and cutting out unnecessary expenses and clutter from your life. It's about prioritizing what you want in life and directing your money to where it will matter most, instead of spending it on trivial things that don't matter. A minimalist budget allows you to assess how much money you have coming in and going out, and how to align this cash flow to your goals in life.

The exact implementation of the minimalist budget concepts described in this book will vary for everyone. We all come from different life situations and financial backgrounds. We all have different priorities and things we value. But the principles guiding minimalist budgeting are applicable to any level of income and with a wide variety of financial goals.

Living on a minimalist budget can be an incredibly powerful tool for your life. It uses intentionality and decision-making as a path to finding contentment and accomplishing your financial goals.

Thank you so much for making it through to the end of this book. I hope it was informative and able to provide you with all of the tools you need for your Minimalist Budget journey. The next step is to start trying these techniques and find out what works best for you. Lastly, if you enjoyed this book, I ask that you please take the time to rate it on Amazon. Your honest review would be greatly appreciated. Thank you!

DESCRIPTION

This book is an informative and comprehensive guide to minimalist budgeting. It introduces you to the concept of a minimalist budget, explains the strategies and techniques associated with it, and teaches you how to apply minimalist budgeting in everyday life.

The first chapter of this book explains what a minimalist budget is about and also what it's not. This part of the book discusses how a minimalist budget can improve your life, and how critical your mindset and attitude are to your minimalist budget approach.

In chapter two, you will learn how to define your financial goals and priorities. In addition, this chapter discusses how to find motivation and inspiration to follow through with your minimalist budget goals.

In chapter three, you will learn about specific steps to create, implement, and maintain your own minimalist budget.

Chapter four provides you with a toolbox of minimalist budget tools, as well as tips and tricks to make budgeting easier and more effective.

Chapter five discusses how to deal with financial setbacks and changes that you may experience while following the minimalist budget. This part will also help you with controlling compulsive spending and establishing new, positive habits.

In chapter six, you will learn how your partner, kids, and friends can play a role in your minimalist budget approach. Both positive and negative aspects of this interaction will be discussed. This chapter also shows how a minimalist budget can positively impact your relationships and vice versa.

The bonus chapter offers you specific strategies and ways to save money in various categories of expenses, all while helping you to simplify your financial life and reduce clutter in your possessions.

At the end of each chapter, you have an opportunity to apply what you have learned to your own life through a simple exercise.

After reading this book, you will have a good understanding of minimalist budgeting and practical approaches to applying it to your life.

MINIMALIST LIFESTYLE

How to Become a Minimalist, Declutter Your Life and Develop Minimalism Habits & Mindsets to Worry Less and Live More

**By
Jenifer Scott**

© Copyright 2019 by Jenifer Scott - All rights reserved.

This book is provided with the sole purpose of providing relevant information on a specific topic for which every reasonable effort has been made to ensure that it is both accurate and reasonable. Nevertheless, by purchasing this book you consent to the fact that the author, as well as the publisher, are in no way experts on the topics contained herein, regardless of any claims as such that may be made within. As such, any suggestions or recommendations that are made within are done so purely for entertainment value. It is recommended that you always consult a professional prior to undertaking any of the advice or techniques discussed within.

This is a legally binding declaration that is considered both valid and fair by both the Committee of Publishers Association and the American Bar Association and should be considered as legally binding within the United States.

The reproduction, transmission, and duplication of any of the content found herein, including any specific or extended information will be done as an illegal act regardless of the end form the information ultimately takes. This includes copied versions of the work both physical, digital and audio unless express consent of the Publisher is provided beforehand. Any additional rights reserved.

Furthermore, the information that can be found within the pages described forthwith shall be considered both accurate and truthful when it comes to freely available information and general consent. As such, any use, correct or incorrect, of the provided information will render the Publisher free of responsibility as to the actions taken outside of their direct purview. Regardless, there are zero scenarios where the original author or the Publisher can be deemed liable in any fashion for any damages or hardships that may result from any of the information discussed within.

Finally, any of the content found within is ultimately intended for entertainment purposes and should be thought of and acted on as such. Due to its inherently ephemeral nature nothing discussed within should be taken as an assurance of quality, even when the words and deeds described herein indicated otherwise. Trademarks and copyrights mentioned within are done for informational purposes in line with fair use and should not be seen as an endorsement from the copyright or trademark holder.

INTRODUCTION

Congratulations on purchasing this book and thank you for doing so.
You've picked up this book for a reason.
That reason is that you are ready to make a change in your life. You're ready to be free of what's weighing you down. Free from the home that is full of unused items taking up space that you can't stand to see the mess any longer. Free from the urge to constantly keep buying, buying, buying and feeling like it's never enough.
That change is about to take place now, a change for the better, a change for a completely new way of living. Welcome, to the minimalist lifestyle.
Minimalism may seem to be a new concept to you as you're just starting out on this process, but this concept has actually existed for a long time. Evidence of this lifestyle is seen almost throughout Japan, and in the Western world, several prominent individuals are already reaping the benefits of minimalism and experiencing the joy of living with less. The reason why this concept is growing in popularity and gaining more traction in recent times is that people are starting to wake up to the fact that materialism does not equate to happiness. That filling your life with the latest gadgets, fashion trends, furniture or trinkets is not going to bring you the happiness that you seek.
People are starting to wake up to the fact that *true happiness* has been right in front of them all along, in the things that matter most, which are relationships, health, love and all the other things that cost you nothing. These are the things that were forgotten along the way as the consumerist lifestyle slowly took over (and continues to take over). Constantly being exposed to ad after ad, always encouraging us to buy more, subliminal messages telling us we won't be 'happy' or 'complete' until we have this or that has gone on for far too long.
It is now time to get connected once again with the little things in life that matter. The values that you hold most dear. It is time to reconnect with the true things that bring happiness, and it starts right here with decluttering your life and making way for a new life as a minimalist.
There are plenty of books on this subject on the market, thanks again for choosing this one! Every effort was made to ensure it is full of as much useful information as possible. Please enjoy!

CHAPTER 1
Hello, New Minimalist You

When was the last time you took a good, long, hard look at your life? All the material possessions you have accumulated around your home. Have you ever looked at your surroundings and thought to yourself, *how on earth did I accumulate SO much stuff?* Not to mention the amount of money you have spent buying a lot of stuff which you don't need (yikes! Let's not go down that path just yet). If you're tired of seeing the mess and clutter that surrounds your home, and maybe even several other aspects of your life, then it's high time to do something about it.

You are about to embark on a journey that is about to change your life in ways you couldn't previously imagine. The liberation, the freedom that you're going to feel, not to mention how much *lighter* everything is going to seem when you declutter some of the mess you may have gathered over the years is going to feel like a weight off your shoulders. You are about to venture into the world of minimalist living.

Wait, What? What Is Minimalism?

While this may be a concept which has been gaining popularity in the western world, minimalism is actually a practice which has been around for a long time. The Japanese are prime examples of people who have mastered the art of minimalist living, and the rest of the world is now catching up because we are finally starting to realize just how beneficial this kind of lifestyle can be.

Have you ever been to Japan? If you haven't a quick Google or Pinterest search will reveal how the Japanese live in small, confined spaces with very minimal possessions within this environment. Their homes may be small, yet it doesn't look cluttered and claustrophobic.

But first, what is minimalism? Joshua Fields Millburn and Ryan Nicodemus, authors of *Minimalism: Live a Meaningful Life* defined minimalism as "*a tool to rid yourself of life's excess for focusing on what's important so that you can find happiness, fulfilment and freedom.*" That certainly sounds promising, especially when we're all in pursuit of happiness in one way or another. Nobody ever wants to be unhappy, and while we know that we need to work on happiness internally, we also need to work on it externally, which means creating an environment around us that helps us *focus* on what's important in our lives. Minimalism, according to Millburn and Nicodemus, is an approach that can help with this.

A minimalist lifestyle is meant to teach us that we do not have to turn to material things to find comfort and happiness in our lives. That *we can be happy* even without having these material possessions around us. We don't always need the latest gadgets, the latest fashion trends, or even the latest car models to keep us happy. That happiness, as cliché as it sounds, does come from within after all. We can find happiness in the company of our family and friends. We can find happiness in our pets, find happiness is pursuing the activities that we love, watching a favorite movie at the end of a long day, perhaps even happiness in the careers that we embark on. Happiness is a subjective concept and living a minimalist lifestyle is going to help you connect with what it means *for you* to be happy again.

Just to be clear, there is nothing *wrong* with owning material possessions. Not at all. Living a minimalist life is simply living with *only what you need* to keep you fulfilled and happy. Nothing more. You are still going to have stuff in your life and your home. You're just not going to have *so much* of it, that's the difference. We have become far too consumeristic and materialistic, and it is time to change all of that. In the pursuit of keeping up with this constant, on-the-go and hectic lifestyle, we have forgotten that there are other aspects of our life which need looking after. Our health, relationships, personal growth and mental health have taken a backseat as we race for what else we can buy, who has what new item and finding reasons to constantly make new and unnecessary purchases we don't need.

Does Minimalist Living Come with Benefits? Why Should I Do This?

Yes, it does, which is why this concept is quickly gaining traction and popularity. As human beings, we're wired to be motivated to make a change for the better if we know that there is some benefit in it for us.

Understandably, the thought of getting rid of most of what you have accumulated over the years can be a daunting thought. Some people have a very strong emotional attachment to certain possessions that they own, even if they may not have used or touched those items in years. Yet, they find it difficult to part with these items. *What if I may need it one day? I could possibly use it again. There may be an occasion where I'm going to need this, so maybe I better hold on to it. I can't get rid of this; it's special to me.* Those are just some of the thoughts that run through a person's mind when they think about whether or not they just keep or toss an item.

The benefits of living minimalist, however, is far more than the physical changes that you see happening around your environment. These are changes that you experience are also going to be felt from within, and those are the changes which are more powerful than anything that takes place in your external surroundings. Minimalism brings you right back to what matters the most by reminding you that you don't need to constantly rely on materialistic belongings to feel like a fulfilled and happy individual. The benefits that you are going to feel and see happening within and around you include:

- **You Will Become More Motivated** - With a clear purpose in your life and without the unnecessary distractions taking away your focus, you will once more be able to see your purpose and what you want to accomplish in your life.
- **Your Mental Health Improves** - When you once more begin to focus on yourself, it reminds you of what you have been neglecting all along. That *you matter more* than any material possessions you

could possibly buy, and when you start to focus on yourself again, your mental and physical health starts to shine because you're working on becoming a better you.
- **You Will Feel A Sense of Relief** - Clearing away the clutter in your life is going to feel like a big weight has been lifted off your shoulders. Suddenly, you have room to breathe again once more. We often don't realize just how much we are affected by the clutter and accumulation of possessions around us until we get rid of it and feel much better when we've tossed out a few items.
- **You Are Teaching Yourself A Valuable Life Lesson** - Believe it or not, you'll be teaching yourself a valuable life lesson when you start seeing those material possessions are not responsible for bringing you happiness. Living as a minimalist is going to remind you every single day to be happy and grateful for the things that you already possess in your lives, and that if something is not necessary for your survival, then you probably don't need it after all.
- **Your Relationships Improve** - When you learn to be happy with what you have instead of constantly competing with everyone around you, your relationships with the people who matter most especially will start to improve for the better. The need to feel jealous over a friend or family member who has the latest car or smartphone model, or perhaps even purchase a new home or a new clothing item no longer exists, because you have no room in your life for trivial things that don't really matter.
- **There's Now Time To Be More Efficient** - You are able to concentrate better, your priorities more in focus, you find yourself feeling lighter, happier, and able to work a lot more efficiently and make more productive use of your time because you have fewer things around you that distract you.
- **There's More Space Around Your Home** - This is going to be the benefit that you're going to be able to visually observe the most. The fact that your house suddenly seems a lot more spacious when it doesn't have unnecessary piles of stuff cluttering every available corner. You will feel lighter, more relaxed, and even a sense of satisfaction and having freed up all this extra space around you. You begin to feel that you have more room in your life for the things that matter.

Defining Your Purpose

As with anything else that we pursue in life, we all need to have a purpose. A reason *why* we're doing what we do. What motivates us, what pushes us to want to succeed, we all need a purpose that drives us to become better.

People choose to embark on a minimalist journey for a variety of reasons. It is a very personal experience, and it could mean different things to different people. Some people do it for the betterment of their mental or physical health, others do it to create more harmony in their surroundings and fluidity in their life, some do it because they're tired of living with so much clutter in their home, and then there are those who choose to do it because they want to reduce their carbon footprint on earth by going with the minimalist approach. Your reason does not have to be the same as theirs, you could do it for your own personal reasons. It doesn't matter what that reason is, as long as *you can clearly define it*, because this reason is going to be the driving force and the motivator that is going to help you stick to this new regiment in your life.

The initial stages of this process are going to be the hardest for some (maybe even all) of you who are reading this book right now. The very idea of tossing out or donating most of your possessions and clearing the clutter is going to make some of you want to turn around and run in the other direction. This is why defining your purpose, finding a strong enough reason to motivate you, is so important. It is going to help you get over the hurdle at the start of this process that is going to challenge you the most. But, like everything else, once you've started, it's eventually going to get easier as you go along and start reaping the benefits and the rewards that await you.

Who Is Minimalism For?

The answer is, *everyone*. That's the beauty of this concept. Minimalism is an approach that everybody can practice because it does not force you to add here to any strict set of rules. It is completely personal and motivated by your own goals. This is not a concept that is going to force you to be miserable, having to get rid of some of your favorite things in life. It's not going to force you to toss out your favorite pair of jeans or ask you to get rid of your car or downsize your home (unless you want to). There is nothing *forced* about practicing this way of living at all. It is about doing what is best *for you,* and to teach you it is possible to be happy with fewer things instead of more.

One of the biggest challenges you are going to face is having to change your mindset, but we'll talk about that in another chapter later on. Yet another problem with this materialistic world that we live in is that we are constantly surrounded by advertisements and commercials. All subliminally telling us that we *must have* or *need* something. It's on the radio, on television, and absolutely on social media. It is inescapable. Every day, all we need to do is log onto any one of our social media accounts and within the first 5 minutes, you'll have definitely seen more than 2 ads at the very least as you scroll through your newsfeed. Heck, we're even surrounded by ads when watching a video on YouTube or simply checking our emails. This constant exposure is working on our psyche without us even realizing it, which is the reason we end up with a lot of unnecessary items in our life which are not necessities or essentials for survival. That's because these commercials are portraying the notion that we *need* these items in our lives to be happy or feel fulfilled. But do you *really?* Think about the last time you bought something because you thought it might make you feel happier. Did it? How long did that happiness last?

Retail therapy is another trap word which leads us to believe that spending money and making purchases we don't need equates to happiness. Again, this type of happiness is short-lived, and it will never last no matter how much you think it will. Sure, it can alleviate your stress and make you feel a burst of happiness for a short span of time, but once that happiness fades, you're left with something you're most likely never going to use, less money in your bank account which you could have saved, and more clutter around your home — all while still being unable to fill that empty void within you. Why? Because you are relying on external factors to provide you with the kind of happiness that you seek, instead of seeking it from within.

But that is about to change *right now*.

10 Reasons Why A Minimalist Lifestyle Is Going to Be Good for You

When you think about minimalism, what is the first image that pops into your mind? Is it just an empty room with plain white walls, maybe just two or three pieces of furniture? Well, only if you want it to be. Minimalism is about finding an approach that suits you and your lifestyle the best, something which you can be happy with. No one person is going to have the exact same experience or the same way of living when it.

If you need a little more convincing that a minimalist lifestyle is going to change your life for the better, here are 10 reasons that highlight just how beneficial this approach can be:

- **Reason 1: Do You Want to Be More Productive?** Believe it or not, your material possessions, everything that you own and have in your home right now, is taking up a lot more of your time than you realize. How much time do you spend clearing up your home? How much time do you spend on your tech devices aimlessly browsing through social media or other distracting websites? How much time do you spend arranging and rearranging stuff around your home or your office workspace whenever you feel things are getting too messy? The more you own, the more time you end up wasting on doing unnecessary cleaning and clearing. Valuable time which could instead be spent on working towards achieving your goals, or doing something to better yourself. All the material possessions demand a lot more of our time to upkeep then we realize. Do you want to make the most of your time more productively? Go minimalist.
- **Reason 2: You Hate Cleaning.** Some people love it; others detest it. If you're in the latter category, then you're going to love this minimalist lifestyle because less stuff means less cleaning! Since minimalism is only about keeping what you really need in your life, you're going to realize just how much simpler life is when you have

fewer things to clean around your home. This is by far absolutely the simplest way to cut down your cleaning time.

- **Reason 3: You Want to Increase Your Savings.** Buying less material possessions means more money for you to put aside into building your savings nest egg. Especially if you've gotten into the habit of making purchases with your credit card. It's time to stop accumulating debt and stuff around the home by simply *buying less and saving more*. Minimalism is going to encourage you to spend money on fewer things, and how to instead spend money on *quality things* that are going to last you much longer. In the long run, this will save you a lot more money down the road.
- **Reason 4: You Want to Be Stress-Free.** We don't realize just how much stress the things in our life can cause us, and how distracting they can be too. When one of your tech devices breaks down around the home, you get stressed. When your clothing items get ruined, you get stressed. When you come home after a long day at work only to find a mess waiting for you at home, you get stressed. We don't realize just how much our external physical environment can contribute to the way that we feel until we really think about it. When you reduce the amount of clutter in your life, the distractions and the stress that you feel is going to be significantly reduced, which in turn will help you feel more relaxed and lead to a more stress-free life.
- **Reason 5: You Want to Do Something Good for the Environment.** From individuals to big corporations, it seems that everyone is concerned with going green these days to preserve our precious environment for the future. You too can do your part for the environment by choosing to live a minimalist lifestyle because by relying on fewer resources, you are thereby reducing your carbon footprint impact and the amount of waste that you produce in the environment. Being environmentally conscious has been the reason that some people choose to become a minimalist, and if this reason is good enough to fuel you, then, by all means, go for it.
- **Reason 6: You Want A Change in Your Life.** Do you feel it's time for a big change in your life? We all reach a point sometimes where we're tired of the routine that we have now because it no longer brings us any joy or contentment. Many people actually desire for change; they just don't know what to do sometimes. If you've had this same desire but felt at a loss about what to do, why not try something simple like adopting a minimalist way of living to start? It is a gradual change that you can introduce into your life in stages, which makes it a great option for those who *want* to change things up, but don't want to do anything too drastic which they might regret later on. Think of this approach as spring cleaning your home to start with.

- **Reason 7: You've Realized You've Become Far Too Materialistic.** Sometimes, it just hits you like a bolt of lightning. The realization that your life is not where you want it to be, or hoped it would be. When that realization hits is when you know that something needs to be done to make a change for the better. If it has dawned on you that you may have become far too caught up in the materialistic lifestyle that you have lost touch with everything that once mattered to you, this could be a time when you start to adopt a minimalist approach to living.
- **Reason 8: You Want to Improve Your Relationships.** Having so much going on in your life can cause you to neglect the relationships that you have in your life. You're not doing it on purpose, but it just happens without you even realizing it. By reducing the amount of clutter, you've got going on in your life in every aspect (not just your home environment), taking away those distractions will help you reconnect and focus once more on the people who matter in your life and what's important. The less time you spend on the materialistic aspects of your life, the more time you have to spend on the ones who truly enrich your life and give it meaning.
- **Reason 9: You Want to Find Your Purpose Again.** Feeling like you have lost your way in life is not a fun emotion to experience. Nobody wants to feel that way if they could, because it makes you start to wonder and question what you've done with your life so far. When not dealt with productively, this can lead to a lot of negative thoughts which could cause you to spiral into unhappiness, maybe even depression on more serious levels. Living life as a minimalist is going to teach you how to appreciate the things in your life that you value most. To look beyond just making the next purchase that you think is going to make you happy and instead, focus on being happy with what you already have.
- **Reason 10: You Want A Much Simpler Life.** It can be exhausting trying to live a life where you are constantly trying to Keep Up with the Joneses. Trying to always compare yourself with the people you know, or always trying to one-up them to show that you are living a better life, or you can afford more. It is mentally draining to stay on that kind of path for a long time, and if you're ready for a life that is so much simpler but a lot more meaningful, then it's time to start living life the minimal way and witness just how much your life is going to change for the better when you're not always pursuing the wrong things.

CHAPTER 2
What's Life Like As A Minimalist Anyway?

Remember that image of what minimalism is that was pointed out in Chapter 1? The stark white walls, minimal pieces of furniture around the home? That is an example of what a minimalist myth is. Living a minimalist lifestyle doesn't mean you need to toss out almost all your belongings and live with barely anything like a hermit. It is mainly about re-evaluating what your priorities are so you can eliminate all the things that don't matter in your life. This includes the material possessions around your home, bad habits, behaviors, relationships, even beliefs that don't serve you any good. If something doesn't add any benefit, or even value into your life and who you are as a person at this moment, then you could probably live life without it. *That's* what being a minimalist is.

Why the minimalist lifestyle approach is now being adopted and embraced more is because many people are starting to realize that there is a limit to the happiness that these materialistic possessions can bring. For example, buying a car which costs $20,000 might make you very happy, but buying a car that is $100,000 isn't necessarily going to make you five times happier what you were when you bought the $20,000 car. A watch which costs $30 is going to work the same as a watch that costs $300. They both tell time and that's what they're there for.

Having fewer possessions does not mean your life is going to be any less satisfying. Less stuff could, in fact, make you happier than you ever were before because you learn to appreciate what you have. Minimalism teaches us that it is not about the quantity, but rather it is the quality that matters more. That it is better to have a few treasured possessions that last a lifetime instead of piling your home and life with numerous items that are not bringing you any significant benefit. In the pursuit of happiness, there are many roads and paths to take, one of these roads to live minimally and focus on only what matters in you.

Busting Through the Myths of Minimalism

Minimalism is essentially an ethos; that is what this concept is at its core. It focuses on filling your life with a sense of purpose, a tool to give you the freedom you have been seeking all along, a way to finally cope with what has been overwhelming you by decluttering your life. It is meant to help you unblock the mental clutter that you may have been struggling with.

As you are preparing to embrace this new way of life, it is time to bust through the inevitable myths and misconceptions that have come to surround what it means to live this lifestyle. The sooner you break through the misconceptions, the easier it will be to transition into this new life. Here's what a minimalist lifestyle *is not* about:

- **Myth #1: It Means You Can Only Own A Set Number of Things** - Minimalism is a very personal, individual experience. No two people are the same, and no one is going to live the same life, with the same number of belongings, or live life with the same set of circumstances. Being a minimalist doesn't mean you can only own a certain number of items to your name because not everyone is going to *have the same* number of items. No rule says you only get to keep 10 t-shirts and that's it. Or that you can only have 5 pairs of shoes in your home. This kind of rule does not work, since some people may require more than 10 shirts or 5 shoes, while others could make do with less. It is about finding what works for you. Whether you have 50 or 100 things, it *does not matter*. If the 100 items are functional, serve a purpose and are bringing your life some benefits, then go ahead and keep it.

- **Myth #2: It Means You Can Only Keep What's Practical and Functional** - A minimalist lifestyle is not meant to strip you of joy. If you own one or two items that bring you joy or happiness, but don't necessarily serve a practical or functional purpose, it is perfectly okay to keep them. Minimalism is about being happy with what you have in your life, and it is meant to teach you that you don't need an *excess of stuff* to be happy. Keep what's practical and functional to help you survive comfortably, but if something brings you happiness, you don't have to toss it away. This lifestyle is meant to bring you joy, not strip you of everything that makes you happy. Adopting this minimalist way of living but being unhappy at every moment is not what this journey is about.

- **Myth #3: It Means You Have to Live in A State of Deprivation** - There a Swedish word that described minimalism, and that word is *lagom*. This word defines minimalism is being "enough, being adequate, being sufficient, and being just right." *Lagom* has also been translated widely as "perfect-simple," "moderation" and "in balance." What you will notice about these descriptors is that none of them connote deprivation. One of the most common myths and misconceptions that surrounds a minimalist lifestyle is that you have to live a life of simplicity, depriving yourself of most material possessions. That is not an entirely accurate picture. It isn't about depriving yourself, but rather making your life more functional by only keeping what's practical and serves a purpose.

- **Myth #4: It Means I Have to Decide What Needs to Go Immediately** - Remember in Chapter 1 that it is going to be a daunting task. The idea of decluttering your life, well, where do you even begin? How do you decide what should be kept and what should be tossed out? Take it easy, slow it down, because deciding what should stay and what should go is not something you need to do right this minute. Sure, you've decided that you want to live life as a minimalist, but that doesn't mean you should immediately start going around your home tossing out all the things which you could live without. This is a myth because it is perfectly okay to take your time with this process. The clearing and decluttering can be done over the span of a few days, weeks, even months if you need to. It's about what works for you, always remember that.

- **Myth #5: It Means That You Can Only Own Black and White Items** - Don't believe everything that you see in the pictures. Yes, there are black and white images that represent what minimalist homes look like. Yes, they look absolutely beautiful, especially the homes with white, wide open, airy spaces which are filled with natural sunlight. However, those are just a representation. In movies and in pictures, those representations do not spell out what your life needs to be like. You don't need to have only black and white possessions to be able to dub yourself a minimalist. Have any color scheme you want. Have multiple color schemes if you want. It is your life, and the choice is entirely up to you. Those pictures and movies are merely there to serve as inspiration, if you like what you see and it works for you, go ahead and model your life after it. But if it doesn't? No problem. Your home and your life should be a reflection of *who you are*, not strip you entirely of your belongings and your personality. If bright, loud colors that pop is who you are, then bright, loud colors it is.

- **Myth #6: It Means You Should Only Live in a Tiny Home** - The size of your home does not matter, which makes this a complete myth. Of course, if you love smaller homes and you genuinely want to live in one, you should. But if you have a perfectly comfortable home that you think you should move out from just because you're not choosing to be a minimalist, that's not being practical. That's because smaller homes do not necessarily work for anyone. A single person may do well in a smaller home and be perfectly content, but if you have a family with kids, a smaller home might only make things more cramped and make everyone uncomfortable. Again, go back to making it *work for you* (this should be your mantra going into this new life). The size of your home does not determine your life as a minimalist. Big homes, small homes, it doesn't matter. You can still get them decluttered either way.

- **Myth #7: It Means You Can't Spend Money Anymore** - Well, you will be spending less money as a minimalist, but not because you *can't*. It's because you're inevitably making fewer purchases, which is going to lead to spending less money anyway. Minimalism is going to teach you to be intentional about your spending, not curb your spending entirely. The reason this is a complete myth is that it is *impossible* to live life without spending a dime. There will be moments when you need to spend money, that's unavoidable, but being conscious of your spending is going to be the difference and the change in your life right now. Minimalism is going to change a lot of things in your life, and your mindset about your spending is one of them, which will be discussed in another Chapter later on.

- **Myth #8: Minimalist Don't Have Any Style** - Don't let the downsizing your wardrobe bit fool you. Just because you're only keeping the bare essentials, it doesn't mean that your style has to be sacrificed. Not at all. If all the clothes you already own are style and suited to your personality, there isn't even going to be that much difference in your style, except that you'll only be keeping the clothes that you wear and use often and donating the ones you no longer use for need. Being a minimalist also does not mean that you have to only buy drab and simple clothing. You can continue to buy the clothes that fit in with your personality, except now you're only going to be buying them when there's a genuine need for it. You're not going to be rushing to keep up with the latest trends anymore because there is no real need for it, but that doesn't mean that your style is going to be downsized to boring in any way.
- **Myth #9: Minimalism Is Something That Can Easily Be Defined** - Now, this is a myth is because minimalism is a philosophy. Hence, it is not something that can easily be defined. Sure, you can explain what minimalism is, but *defining it* is a whole other story. It is a concept that does have consistent themes to it, but because this lifestyle is something that is going to be a different experience for everybody, it is, therefore, hard to define it easily. Each person is different, which means that their approach and their ideas to minimalism is doing to differ. The themes may be consistent, but defining them altogether? That's not entirely possible.
- **Myth #10: Minimalism Is Not A Sustainable Lifestyle** - It is only not sustainable if you don't want it to be. That is why one of the consistent themes of a minimalist lifestyle is to *make it work for you*. Because if it doesn't work, then yes, it is not going to be sustainable. You won't be happy, you won't be reaping the benefits of what this concept is meant to offer you, and because you're unhappy, it won't be long before you give in to the temptation to revert back to your old way of life. Minimalism can be a sustainable lifestyle if you make the necessary changes to suit the way that your life is now.

Jumping right into the minimalist lifestyle is not going to be easy, and you shouldn't expect it to be. Like every major change in your life, expect it to be somewhat difficult as you go through the initial adjustment period and get used to the new way of doing things. Don't worry too much about the myths and misconceptions of living life as a minimalist; take it one step at a time and give yourself time to adjust to the process. You'll get there eventually, and remember that there are no forced concepts or rules with minimalist living. Only make changes that you feel comfortable doing because you should never feel deprived or unhappy in any way.

How Minimalism Is Going to Change Your Life

No more fancy, extravagant, over the top purchases that you barely use or don't even really like at the end of the day, cluttering up your home just because you felt the need to buy it at the time. A minimalist keeps it simple. They only keep the essentials which are needed for a comfortable, happy life. Aside from all the money that you are going to save by making fewer purchases, another change that you are going to see in your life is that you will no longer be living above your means.

Yes, there is a way for you to finally get out of living paycheck to paycheck cycle because as a minimalist, you will no longer be caught up with the consumerist way of living. Our wants always seem to surpass what we can afford, which is why turning to minimalism is the way to get out of this never-ending cycle of constantly feeling like you're struggling to keep up no matter how much money you may be earning. The more you earn, the more your wants seem to "suddenly" increase. Minimalism going to teach you to live comfortably with what you have and putting a stop to that desire to always keep up with the latest trends and fads because you no longer feel that desire to seek happiness in materialistic possessions.

The life of a minimalist is going to affect your life in several stages. As you begin to ready yourself for this new lifestyle, you're going to learn the difference between what is essential in your life, and what isn't. You're going to be able to distinguish what's important and what isn't. Where previously you would simply make purchases on the spur of the moment, this time, you're going to give each purchase careful thought and consideration, asking yourself, *do I really need this? How is this going to benefit my life? Is this a necessity or can I survive without it?* This is the part where you begin moving away from the materialistic life that you were once so caught up with. Not only is the change going to affect your physical environment, but you will also notice a shift in your mindset and the way that you think moving forward.

The areas of your life in which minimalism is going to inflict a change include:

- **Your Home** - This one is going to probably be the biggest and most noticeable difference in your life. The clutter is going to diminish, and you're going to observe that your home is going to be filled with significantly less stuff and more space. Every available corner of your home is no longer going to be filled with items that you don't use or don't even remember having. Tackling the decluttering of your home is going to happen in small stages, but once it's done, you're going to step back and see a big difference in your home. Take before and after pictures and compare them side by side to see the change right before your eyes.

- **Financially** - Before minimalism, you might have been making steady income every month, but somehow it never seemed to be quite enough to cover everything that was needed. You might have found it hard to save enough each month, and as you begin to take stock of your life, you'll be shocked at just how much you were spending on a lot of unnecessary purchases. You may not have necessarily been living an extravagant life, but you may not necessarily be living frugally either. Once you begin this new lifestyle, you're going to start keeping track of where and what precisely your money is being spent on, with regular reviews on whether there are unnecessary expenses being tacked on. If there are, and they are non-essentials, then it's time to remove them.
- **The Time You Have on Your Hands** - Clutter isn't just around your home; it's in your life too. Before you adopt a minimalist approach, your calendar may have been full. So full that you found it difficult to have any time for yourself. Social gatherings, business meetings, family commitments, you always seem to be running from one event to the next. Minimalism is going to help you reclaim all that lost time so you can finally *make time* for what's important - *yourself*. As you begin decluttering other aspects of your life, minimalism will teach you (in keeping with the whole theme of the process) to only accept the invitations and commitments that are important. The ones that matter and the ones that bring you happiness. You will learn to decline the invitations that you don't necessarily want to go to. Your time is yours to determine what you want to do with it.
- **Your Health** - Because you would have decluttered your calendar and made more time for yourself, you now have the benefit of redirecting that extra time into doing something good for yourself. Such as taking care of your health. With more time on our hands, you'll be able to invest in time to exercise, and prepare meals at home, which are much healthier than resorting to fast food or take out (which you previously might have done far too much off because you were pressed for time, rushing from one appointment to another). With more time on your hands, you could even start spending the weekend meal-prepping for the week if you're not keen on cooking after a long day of work. Not only is cooking your own meals at home going to be much better for your health, but it is also much better for your wallet too, another wonderful side-effect of minimalism.
- **The Relationships in Your Life** - The honest truth is, not every relationship in your life is important. Even the relationships that you *think* are important. With minimalism, you're going to learn how to invest time and energy into the relationships that truly fill your life with meaning, like the ones with your family, significant other, husband and friends whom you have known for years. In doing so,

you will find that you become a much better friend and listener because you're more invested in the relationship.
- **You Learn to Appreciate Your Own Company** - With fewer distractions in your life and more time to focus on yourself, you'll learn to appreciate being in your own company. Minimalism will teach you to reconnect with yourself, to find happiness within yourself again and learning to be happy and content with life as you know it. You'll come to realize that you don't need to be out shopping, spending time with people or spending countless hours browsing your social media newsfeed to find some semblance of happiness. You'll come to realize that you're capable of being perfectly happy sitting at home with a good book and a warm cup of coffee on any given day.
- **You'll Find You're Much Calmer** - Another happy side effect of minimalism is that life will become a lot less stressful when you don't have so much going on in your life. We often think that we need to be busy, that we need to fill out lives at every waking moment in order to feel happy and fulfilled. But nothing could be further from the truth. Decluttering is going to free up not just your life, but your stress levels too because when you've got significantly fewer things to worry about, what is there to stress about?
- **You'll Be More Productive at Work** - That's right, being a minimalist is also going to spill over into your career too. Once you see how beneficial decluttering your home can be, you'll immediately want to declutter your office space too. Removing the distractions from your work environment, even if it is just within your cubicle, is going to make you a lot more productive because you will no longer have distractions pulling your focus away from what you should be focusing on, which is work. You'll be able to get more things done in a day, you'll be able to work through your tasks efficiently, and as a bonus, your boss is going to be very happy with you because of it.
- **Your Priorities Will Change** - Another big shift in your life is going to be the difference you notice in your priorities. As you begin unpacking your life, removing all the elements that are unnecessary and not actively contributing to your happiness, your priorities are going to change in a good way. The things that you once thought matter will no longer seem so important, while the things that you have forgotten or might have previously taken for granted are what you reconnect with again. Everything about your life is going to change once you start living life as a minimalist, but don't worry because this change is going to be for the better.

CHAPTER 3
Where It All Begins

You're almost ready to begin your new minimalist lifestyle, and in this chapter, you're going to be covering the basics about getting started on this new transformative way of life. To recap, what we have come to understand so far is that minimalism is not a one-size-fits-all solution since each person is going to be undergoing their own unique experience. There is no one way to approach this concept and thus, you have to work around finding solutions that are going to be suitable for you.

If we take a good, long look at the world around us, there are actually plenty of prominent individuals who are already practicing minimalism in some form that we can draw inspiration from. Facebook founder Mark Zuckerberg is one such example, adopting a minimalist approach when it comes to his clothing options. Zuckerberg is always seen donning a simple t-shirt and jeans, and even his t-shirts are often the same color scheme. The late Steve Jobs was another prominent figure who adopted a minimalist approach to his clothing choices, opting for basic black t-shirts and a simple pair of jeans. Efficient, and cost-effective. Other celebrities or successful individuals who have chosen a minimalist approach to living include Warren Buffett, who, despite his wealth, has been living in the same home that he purchased way back in 1958. Keanu Reeves is another celebrity who has opted out of a lavish lifestyle for a much more simple, minimal approach, choosing instead to live in a modest home and often takes public transport just like any other average citizen.

Making the Transition into Minimalism

Now, this is going to be where the most challenging part of the whole process begins. The transition out of your old lifestyle into your new one is where a lot of people struggle the most. As with everything else, it's going to take time to make the necessary adjustments, so don't be too hard on yourself if you find that you're struggling in the beginning. You're about to change almost everything in your life as you know it, a transition period is to be expected. Nobody can turn their lives around completely without facing difficulty at some point along the way.

To keep yourself from feeling discouraged as you begin this big life transition, the following exercises will be good advice to keep in mind:

- **Baby Steps** - Avoid the urge and temptation to immediately jump right in there and start clearing and decluttering your entire life and home all at once. This is a major project, especially when it comes to your home, and you cannot expect it all to be done in one day. It just simply is not possible. Instead, expect the process to span over a few weeks (depending on the size of your home especially), and remember that there is no reason to rush. The more you try to rush the process, the more discouraged you may find yourself when at the end you're completely exhausted, tired, and start to wonder why on earth you decided to begin this monumental task in the first place. This is going to be like climbing a hill, pace yourself and take baby steps. You're not in a race with anyone.

- **One Area at A Time** - When it comes to your home, instead of trying to clear everything all at once, aim to tackle one area at a time instead. Do it in stages or sections, depending on how busy your schedule is and work your way from there. Again, you're not in a race with anybody, so it's perfectly okay to take your time working through this process. Aiming to clear off small sections bit by bit will make the entire process seem a lot more manageable and doable. Some items may require some thought before you decide whether to part with them or keep them and if you rush yourself through the process, you could end up tossing something that you might regret later on. Eventually, before you know it, you would have cleared off your entire home and completed the home environment phase of your minimalist journey.
- **Make a Daily List** - Given that decluttering is an ongoing process, what will help you along the way is to have a daily list that you could work on. Making a list is great for this process because it will help you stay organized and it is much easier to keep track of what's been done and what hasn't. Each day, write down the decluttering goals that you hope to accomplish by the end of the day and it will give you something to focus on. For example, if what's on your list today is to clear out your bookshelf, then focus on that and see how much you can accomplish by the end of the day. Having a visual list that you can look at helps you feel more productive during this process too. Humans are very visual creatures, and we often need to see something right there in front of us before our minds can catch up and start believing in it. When you see a list in front of you that reminds you of what needs to get done, it automatically fuels your motivation because it's reminding you of a goal to work on. If you don't manage to finish a task that is on your list, not a problem, push it to the next day. There is no need to put any added pressure on yourself, baby steps. Remember, baby steps.
- **Having Your Own Rules to Follow** - Wait, what? I thought there were no hard and fast rules in minimalism? There aren't, but there are *personal rules* which you can enforce for yourself when you start to transition into this lifestyle. These rules should only be for yourself and your benefit because you are the one who is living this life now (unless you've got your family involved). The set of rules you can start enforcing for yourself should be both simple and practical. One example of a rule could be that each time you make a purchase other than the essentials like food, groceries and other monthly supplies, you should remove one item from your home. If you were purchasing

a new rug, for example, it should be to replace an old rug which you are going to remove from your home as soon as you've made the new purchase (to avoid clutter). Minimalism is not going to stop you from making any new purchases but is going to help prevent you from accumulating clutter around your home. Another example of a rule that you could set for yourself is to only replace an item in your home if it genuinely needs replacing.

- **Start On a "Free" Day** - Beginning the transition into minimalism is best done on a day when you have no prior obligations and commitments going on. This will leave you with the necessary time to really focus on the process when you're not thinking about other tasks that you need to take care of. Once you have decided that you would like to embrace this new lifestyle, look at your calendar and consider which day would be best for you to commit to getting started with the process. Beginning on a weekend would be a good place to start since you most likely do not have to worry about any prior work commitments or arrangements on that day. You want to commit your time to only focusing on making the transition on this "free" day because it's going to take a lot more out of you than you initially realize. Take a day where you can process everything that is happening, and focus on what needs to get done for the day without having to worry about your next business meeting or errand that needs to get done.

Bad Habits You Need to Start Getting Rid Of

Transitioning into minimalism is not just going to be about decluttering and changing up your environment; it's about making changes in other aspects of your life too. As you leave a lot of things behind moving forward, one of these is going to be bad habits that you should start getting rid of to make your new life as a minimalist easier.

- **Give Up Filling Up Your Wardrobe** - If a priority for you is to save yourself a lot of time each morning getting ready and dressed for the day, then one of your goals would be to work on decluttering your wardrobe first. Downsizing it and keeping it simple will save you *a lot* of time getting dressed in the morning because when you only have a few options on hand, the decision-making process is much quicker. Jobs and Zuckerberg chose a minimal wardrobe for a reason. They did not care that people might see them as wearing the same outfit over and over again. They cared about being practical and functional because they knew there were bigger goals to focus on. When it comes to downsizing your wardrobe, make it easier on yourself by focusing on keeping only the pieces which are considered essential staples and clothing items that make you look and feel good when you wear them. Items which you may not have worn or touched in years can be donated, and items which are too worn out to be donated can be tossed or repurpose if you know what to do with them. By making a commitment to simplifying your wardrobe, you're going to find you're a lot more efficient not just in getting dressed in the morning, but in your shopping habits too, which will slowly adjust to fit your new habits and priorities.

- **The No Duplicates Rule** - Have you previously been guilty of perhaps buying the same item more than once? Or maybe purchased an item only to find that you already had the same item in your home, you just forgot about it. One example would be the same blouse or shirt, but in several different colors which you purchased at the time because you thought they looked good. It turns out, you only use perhaps one or two of those items and the rest lay forgotten in your closet. As you start to transition into minimalism, start enforcing the no duplicates rule when you're decluttering and the next time you're about to make a purchase. Ask yourself why do you need several pieces of the same item? Are they going to serve a functional and practical purpose? Minimalism is all about keeping things simple, practical, beneficial and efficient. Now, with this no duplicates rule, it would depend on the context. You don't need multiple copies of the same book for instance, but if you were to adopt Jobs or Zuckerberg's approach to clothing, then you might have to have duplicates of the same t-shirt and jeans to last you the week (see what is meant by there is no hard and fast rule in minimalism?).

- **Avoid Making Comparisons** - Minimalism is going to teach you how to stop comparing yourself to others, and this is something you should start working on as you begin the transition into this process. Comparison will only serve to leave you dissatisfied and unhappy because no matter what it is never going to be enough. Someone is always going to have something better, or own something grander, or dress better. It's a never-ending cycle. You're going to constantly feel inadequate if you're always looking over at someone else's greener grass. So don't. It is time to stop the comparison and start focusing on your own life. Embrace and be grateful for everything that you have in your life right now and free yourself once and for all from the burden of constant comparison.

- **Give Up Procrastination** - We all know it is a bad habit, yet many of us still end up doing it. Procrastinating and delaying things, putting it off to the last minute and when the time comes to finally do it, you feel rushed and stressed because everything seems to be piling on all at once. If you really think about it, there is no real reason to procrastinate something, is there? Things still eventually have to get done anyway, all you're doing is postponing the inevitable and in doing so, you're creating a bigger workload for yourself because there will be other tasks which need attending to. Maybe you've thought of spring cleaning your home for a long time to get rid of some of the mess that has been piling up, but you've been putting off for some time now because clearing your home is a lot of work. However, before you know it, you're looking around at the clutter that seems to have tripled in size and you're wondering *how did it come to this?* That's what procrastination can do, and that's why it is a bad habit that needs to be dropped as you make room for bigger and better changes. If you've been putting off clearing and decluttering your home and your life, then now is as good a time as any to drop that bad habit once and for all as you begin to prepare for the minimalist way of living.

- **Giving Up the Addiction to Social Media** - Ah yes, another one that many are going to struggle with is to learn to let go of the social media addiction that has you spending countless, aimless hours on your phone. While it is okay to check up on your social media accounts maybe once or twice in a day, spending far too much time on social media than you should is when it starts becoming a problem. Social media does not serve any functional purpose, other than to take away your focus from other, more important tasks, expose yourself to more advertisements encouraging you to make purchases, and comparing your life to the lives of others that you see coming up on your social media feed. All the habits that you want to avoid as you start to embrace minimalism because it isn't going to be about the materialistic lifestyle anymore. It isn't going to be about comparing yourself to others anymore, and as for the ads that you see, you're going to have to block out their subliminal messages encouraging you to make unnecessary purchases that you don't need. In your new minimalist lifestyle, it is time to set some boundaries for the amount of time that you spend on social media.
- **Give Up Always Having to Say Yes** - Giving up this bad habit is going to help you free up a lot more time on your calendar. Believe it or not, you may think you're doing something good by saying yes all the time to the people around you because you don't want to hurt your feelings, but if by saying yes you're *hurting yourself*, that's not something that is going to be sustainable long term. Especially as you prepare to become a minimalist. As you learn to downsize and only maintain the things that are important in your life, you're going to have to get used to sometimes having to say no, especially when you're biting off more than you can chew. Filling up your calendar to a point where you have no time for yourself now has to become a thing of the past as you start to work on minimizing and downsizing the non-material aspects of your life.
- **Give Up the Excuses** - This is going to be an especially useful habit to dump as you begin clearing away the clutter in your home and work space. There will always be a reason not to throw something away. There will always be a reason why you should say yes to a social

event — a reason why you should maintain a certain relationship in your life. The excuses will always be there *as long as you want them to be.* In holding onto these excuses, you're only making the transition into minimalism much harder for yourself, so it is time to ditch the excuses and start thinking practically about what is best for you and your life from this point forward. It is time to put yourself and your happiness first because after all, the whole reason you are making this entire lifestyle change (which is a huge upheaval from what you are used to) is that you want your life to change for the better. Holding onto excuses only means that somewhere down the road when things get too challenging, you'll find plenty of excuses why you shouldn't continue living as a minimalist unless *you break this habit right now.* By getting rid of excuses *to hold onto your excuses,* you're putting yourself one step forward towards being successful at this new lifestyle.

Practicing Mindfulness Meditation

A lot of change is going to be taking place in your life over the next several weeks the minute you decide to embark on a new life as a minimalist. It will be a time of self-reflection, to take a look at what gives your life a deeper meaning, and assessing the things in your life which hold value. Living life as a minimalist is going to give you plenty of time to reflect on everything that has happened in your life so far which has led you to this point, and given all the change that's taking place, it is a good time to spend a few quiet moments meditating on everything that's been going on so far.

Meditation and self-reflection are actually interlinked more so than we realize. These two concepts have certain aspects which intertwine with each other, but the end result is the same, which is to help you reconnect with yourself once more. It gives you a chance to reflect on your life and what is it that you value most, which also links back to minimalism's principles of teaching you to find happiness and joy in the simple things in life. If you're wondering how meditation is going to help you with transitioning into your new lifestyle, the answer is it is going to help you develop an awareness of not just yourself, but with the world around you too. Meditation, when practiced long-term, helps bring a sense of inner peace and balance, enhancing your mental clarity which will, in turn, enable you to sharpen your focus and block out all the distractions that are taking you away from what truly matters.

Meditation and self-reflection are two important tools which are going to help you during this transition period, and you should be taking advantage of it because of the following reasons:

- Meditation helps to improve the relationship with yourself, as well as with other people in your life. We're often surrounded with far too much negativity in our lives, bombarded with images from social media about ideals of perfection that are often unrealistic and only serves to make us question and doubt ourselves. We turn to materialism because we think it is going to bring us a sense of fulfilment, believing what we see in advertisements and on social media. But by turning to meditation to reflect on your life, not only will you rebuild that lost connection with yourself, the outward relationships you have in your life will start to improve too as you become more mindful.

- Meditation and self-reflection teach you how to live in the present, which is also what minimalism endeavors to do. Meditation teaches you how to slow your thoughts and connect with your surroundings, to consistently learn to check in with yourself and how you are doing.
- Feeling overwhelmed is a by-product of a stressful life. Sometimes we feel stuck, unable to move forward because our thoughts somehow cannot seem to connect the way that we want them to. Meditation is a way to help you clear away the mental blocks which may have been preventing you from getting the most out of life so far. Meditation is a process which teaches and trains you how to empty your mind and clear your thoughts, which is exactly what you need.
- Meditation helps to make you more attuned to your emotions, which can help with your feelings of self-worth and happiness when you are reflecting upon your life. It helps you to view the world with a renewed perspective, concentrating less on the negative aspects. Exactly the right frame of mind that you need to get into as you begin the transition into your new minimalist lifestyle.
- Meditation can help to increase your self-discipline, which is a tool that you will definitely need, especially at the start of the minimalism process, to help you navigate those challenging moments. Mindful meditation is an exercise which requires you to sit alone in a quiet space, uninterrupted for an extended period and once you learn how to block out the noise and focus on your thoughts. That act of having to train yourself to sit in quiet contemplation is where you begin to work on increasing your self-discipline too as you resist the urge to give into the noisy chatter that is threatening to break your concentration.

The first 21 days of any new habit or change that you go through is going to be the most difficult stage. If you can make it through this though, through the initial uphill part, then the rest of the way is going to be as easy as running downhill from that point on. Things will only get easier as you move forward, and during this transitional stage, that is something you need to constantly remind yourself of. Get through the hard parts because it isn't going to last for long, and the effort is going to be well worth it in the end. Before you know it, this new way of living is going to be as easy for you as brushing your teeth in the mornings.

CHAPTER 4
The Rulebook To Living With Less

The rules of minimalism may be arbitrary, but there are certain do's and don'ts that minimalists have in common to help them sustain and be successful in this lifestyle, which is what you are going to explore in this chapter.

No one can deny that material goods have consumed us all. All you need to do is look around at the possessions you currently own. The latest gadgets, cars, new pieces of furniture that you maybe didn't really need, new clothes you haven't even gotten around to wearing yet. No surprise, especially since we're constantly surrounded by advertisements from the moment we wake up. On our mobiles, on the radio, on television, YouTube, browsing the internet, even walking into the local grocery stores and supermarkets you'll see ads plastered everywhere encouraging you to buy, buy, buy.

The mindset that purchases and materialistic goods will bring you the happiness that you seek is exactly the kind of mindset that minimalism aims to bring you out of. The moment you shift out of this way of thinking, you will find that life becomes more meaningful because you're now shifting your focus to on the things that matter. Minimalism is the movement that is needed to counter the rise in consumerism before we lose track entirely of what life should be about. Relationships, health, happiness, friendships, family, those are the real things in life that matter.

It is going to be difficult to part with a lot of your material possessions. Some people, in fact, are going to find this stage extremely difficult when it comes to which of their possessions they are about to get rid of. It is going to be uncomfortable and for some, it is even going to be a sad process. Change rarely ever comes easy, and you are going to have to prepare yourself both mentally and emotionally for this stage of the process.

What *Not* to Do as A Minimalist

Minimalism may not have any hard and fast rules, but there are certain things that those who live their lives this way do and don't do. First, let's take a look at what people who live their lives as a minimalist *don't* do:

- **They Don't Hold onto the Past** - Because minimalists are willing to make the necessary changes which are needed if it means it is going to improve their lives for the better. Not everyone has the willpower and discipline to remove almost everything that they own in favor of a new way of living, *and* resist the temptation to give into making new purchases. Cutting things out of your life can be difficult, and minimalists, and you must be ready to let go of the past before you can move forward for a fresh start.
- **They Don't Force Others to Follow Their Path** - Because the choice to live a minimalist lifestyle is a decision that you have made *for yourself*. You did not *have* to make this choice; you *chose* to do so instead. As a minimalist, you can tell others about your new

philosophy and approach to life, but don't expect them to conform and to be like you. It is up to them to live their lives the way that they want, even if you may not necessarily agree with it. Avoid forcing your ideals and your notions about what you think they should or shouldn't do because that's how you will end up alienating the people in your life.

- **They Don't Give into Temptation** - Because it took a lot of effort for them to get to this point, even though they may make it look easy. Every minimalist out there right now started off where you are today, having to make peace with the knowledge that they will now have to resist all their old temptations and be disciplined so that they don't revert back to their old ways and unhealthy habits. Minimalists have trained themselves to be disciplined enough to only buy what they need, and they focus on product quality rather than its aesthetic appeal.

- **They Don't Avoid Their Feelings** - Remember how the initial stages of this process are going to be the most difficult and challenging for many new minimalists? This is why. Some possessions around your home will be items that you've owned for a long time, and though they may not be useful, practical or functional, some of these items will hold a certain sentimental value. A lot of people are attached to their belongings for numerous reasons, and having to part with them is going to be a very emotional process. Those who have mastered the art of minimalist living had to go through that process too, and what they *didn't do* was, they did not try to avoid their feelings. As painful as it may be, you must learn to confront your feelings and deal with it head on, not just in the decluttering process, but in life in general. The suppressing of emotions has never boded well for anyone, and it isn't going to be helpful to you here if you choose to do the same.

- **They Don't Try to Be People Pleasers** - Because you cannot please everyone. It is simply not possible. Even if you think you may have done it, there's one person you're forgetting about - *yourself*. How many times have you found yourself so focused on trying to please everyone that you forgot to ask yourself if you're happy doing what you're doing right now? Too often, most likely. Minimalists understand that there is no necessity to be a people pleaser only to lose yourself in the process, and that is how they have managed to successfully declutter the non-materialistic aspects of their life by keeping their social circle simple and only focusing on the people and the relationships that matter.

- **They Hold onto the Notion of Being Deprived** - Because they know that you're not "deprived" when you have everything that you need for your survival and to live comfortably enough. If you already have what you need, you will never be deprived. A lot of people are guilty of holding onto a lot of unnecessary items because of the all too common "just in case" or "what if I need it next time" fallacy, which is why they fear being "deprived" if they are without this item. If you haven't used it until this point, you're unlikely to need it anytime soon, which means that it is okay to be without this item and yes, you will survive either way.

- **They Don't Fixate on One Mindset Alone** - Because of your mindset is resistant to change, then the transition to become a minimalist is one that you're going to struggle with immensely. Life is always going to be full of change, some of it good because you find it easy to cope, and some of it bad because you struggle to get through it. Change is inevitable, and if you're fixated on just one type of mindset, expecting everything else to conform according to what you think it should be, minimalism is going to be a very difficult change for you to adapt and accept.
- **They Are Get Confused Between Wants and Needs** - Because minimalists have successfully managed to distinguish between needs and wants. When an urge pops up, they stop to think *do I really need this? Or do I just want it?* Not every urge is going to be a need, and that is something that you too will learn to distinguish over time. It took these minimalists time too to finally be able to separate desires from necessities.
- **The Don't Expect Overnight Miracles** - Because great change always takes time. If you're impatient and hoping to see results almost instantaneously, all you're going to be left with is a lot of disappointment at the end of the day. Minimalists know that this lifestyle is a habit and that it takes work each day to keep that momentum going. They know seeing the results of this change is something which could take anywhere from weeks, perhaps even months before they can see or feel any real difference. Patience, in this case, is really going to be your virtue.
- **They Don't Make Items A Priority** - Because they know that relationships and life experience will always mean more than items ever will. No item will ever be able to fill the lonely void you may experience without meaningful relationships in your life, and no item will ever be able to bring you the kind of lasting, meaningful happiness that you seek. Which is why minimalists embarked on this journey, to begin with because they know that making items a priority will never be the right path to take and so, they decided to go with an entirely new approach. They don't form personal attachments to their belongings, because they know this will only make it much harder to get rid of.

What You *Should Do* as A Minimalist

This is going to be your new way of living, and you are going to have to make a commitment to stick to this way of living if you want to see a real difference and a change in your life. Whenever we introduce something new into our lives, whether it is a new way of eating, a new routine, or a different way of doing things, it is going to take some time for you to get adjusted before it becomes a habit and a regular part of your life. So again, if it feels tricky and difficult in the beginning, that is okay. Don't be too hard on yourself, and give yourself some time to adjust to this new way of living.

Now that you know what you *shouldn't* be doing as a minimalist, here's what you should be focusing on instead:

- **Make Mindful Purchases** - No more buying on a whim, those days are going to have to be put behind you now. Minimalists still need to shop (they're not completely cut off from the real world, after all), but what they do differently from the rest of us is that they practice *mindful shopping*. This means that they think long and hard about each item before they purchase it, weighing the pros and cons and whether this item is a necessary or essential purpose. They factor in the functionality and practicality of each item, and in what way it is going to enhance their life. It sounds like a lot of work to do before making any purchase, but once you get used to the process, you'll be able to go through the motions without even really thinking about it.
- **They Fix Instead of Buy** - Minimalists no longer immediately toss out an item or piece of clothing if it's broken or torn. They choose to fix their items instead of immediately resorting to making new purchases. Because they focus on buying items which are durable, this process is often successful, saving them a lot of money in the process and valuable time having to shop around for a suitable replacement.
- **They Borrow, Not Buy** - If something can be borrowed, why spend money buying? Especially if you're only going to use the item once or twice and then hardly ever (or never) after that. That's what minimalists do to save themselves time and money again. Borrowing from friends and family will be one of the first options that they would consider, and that is what you need to start thinking about too, once you start living this lifestyle.
- **They Choose High-Quality Items Instead** - Minimalists usually choose to go for the items which are of higher and better quality, even if they may come with a slightly heftier price tag. That's because minimalists shop with the focus of buying items that are going to last much longer, perhaps even several years. This saves them a lot of time and money compared to if they were to buy the cheaper items, but only to have it break down after several uses. It makes much better financial sense to purchase a one-time more expensive item,

but have it last you almost a lifetime. That's just one of the many ways that minimalists help to minimize their expenses.

- **They Look After Their Items** - Since they have so few possessions, looking after each item carefully is not as hard Is that they start to treasure everything that they have as you may think. Minimalists find it easy to care for the possessions that they currently own because each item that they own is treasured, something that they chose to keep when everything else was either tossed out or donated. So looking after them really happens almost instinctively without even having to think much about it.
- **They Are Always Grateful** - A by-product of living with only a few, very treasured possessions is that they come to treasure everything that they have. Becoming a minimalist has put a lot of things puts a lot of things into perspective and cultivating an attitude of gratitude if you will. Minimalism is in part about the search for happiness and contentment, and about helping you realize that those two qualities do not reside within materialistic possessions. This gratitude is exactly what helps them appreciate and be happy with the life that they currently have. When you are content with what you have in your life, it won't be long before that constant urge and desire to have more fades away over time.
- **They Purge Regularly** - With minimalists, decluttering is not just a one-time process. They make it a habit to carry out regular reviews and purges of their belongings, just to make sure that the clutter is not piling up again without them realizing. They could do this every couple of months, maybe even twice in a year, but minimalists purge regularly and comb through the inventory of their belongings. Anything that hasn't been used in a while must go. Anything that does not serve a practical or functional purpose must go. Clothes that you kept during the first round but realized you haven't worn or touched yet must go. They go through their belongings every now and then and eliminate everything that is not necessary. This is how they maintain that minimalistic lifestyle they built in the beginning.
- **They Have Learnt Not to Feel Guilty** - We all own items that we don't necessarily use or want, but we've kept them around because we feel obligated or guilty. These include birthday gifts, random presents from family or friends, souvenirs you may have picked up on your travels, basically anything in your home that is not essential for your survival. These items continue to remain with us because they could be expensive, sentimental, still in good condition, perhaps even all of the above. Minimalists though have learned to let go of that guilty feeling because they have come to realize that those are *not good reasons* to keep those items around.

Experiencing the Freedom of Living with Less

This experience can be a lot more liberating than you may think. Living as a minimalist, it's not about downsizing all your belongings for the sake of clearing away the mess in your home alone. No, it is much more than that. It is about clearing your entire life and redefining it to have more purpose and meaning than it once did before. You will be amazed at how this experience can bring you a sense of peace.

As a new minimalist, your first goal is to make a commitment to yourself. You need to make a commitment to fully embracing this new change wholeheartedly. Why? Well, simply because you owe it to yourself to live a better life. Having goals throughout this entire process is the key to helping you achieve the most out of living life as a minimalist. This lifestyle philosophy may not have a lot of rules, but there is *one rule* that everyone should abide by, and that is to set up personal goals for yourself as you begin every new journey in your life. Whether it is a new career, a new personal project, a new relationship, anything, setting goals is the key to a successful outcome. Goals help you follow through and remind yourself why you got started in the first place. You know why you chose to begin living as a minimally. You have your reasons, and these reasons must form a concrete foundation, so whenever you start to ask yourself why you began this journey when it gets to the challenging parts, these reasons will be part of your goal setting which will remind you not to give up.

The number one rule of successful goal setting is to have a purpose. Not just any purpose, but a clear purpose and a focal point. Your purpose must be so clear that whenever anyone asks you why you chose to get into this minimalist way of living, you are able to answer without even having to think too much about it. When you have your purpose as clear as day right in front of you, it makes it hard for you to lose sight of the finish line. And that is why you need to define your purpose before you even begin to attend making a list of goals for yourself.

The best way to set clear and defined goals for yourself is to reflect on your current lifestyle. What is it about your current lifestyle that warrants such change? Why do you want to begin a new life as a minimalist? What about your current lifestyle is unsatisfactory right now that is driving you towards this change? Giving your current lifestyle some deep thought and reflection will help you pinpoint exactly what it is you want and hope to improve. It will help you be clear about what you hope to achieve by living as a minimalist. Make it one of your goals to make no excuses. Yes, it may be difficult at some point, but everything in life is not without its challenges. Another goal when you start adopting this minimalist lifestyle is to take it slow and take it small. Don't attempt to be over ambitious right out of the gate, setting overarching goals and then when you fail to meet those goals. You end up feeling disappointed.

Your Minimalist Lifestyle Will Eventually Become a Habit

The general rule is that for something to become a habit, you need to stick to the routine for about 21-days or so. The initial 21-days is when you're going to have to put in most of the hard work into the process and to be disciplined and not give up halfway through when the going gets tough. Stick it out for the first couple of days and minimalism will eventually become a habit that is ingrained and a part of your life. However, you must be consistent. *You must.* Make it a consistent and daily routine, not something that is done a few times a week because that makes it much harder for it to form into a habit. The more effort that you put into making this routine, the easier it will be for it to become a habit. The first 21 days are the most crucial part of the process, and if you don't give it your all during this stage, you're unlikely to achieve the successful outcome that you're hoping for.

What will help make the transition easier is to have positive affirmations. It helps to have little reminders and positive affirmations as to why you started this journey in the first place. It may seem like a pointless exercise and it is easy to brush off "the power of positive thinking" as another ideal that is only preached about but has no real basis, but you'd be surprised at just how effective it can be. Write little positive affirmations on post-it notes and stick them around the places where you are not likely to miss them around your home. Write little motivational phrases to help keep you going and remind yourself not to give up.

Another great strategy that you're going to find useful is to build new habits on a pre-existing habit. Let the old habit will act as an anchor (remember not to choose a bad habit, though). Choose a habit that you don't plan to get rid of. For example, if you already prefer to dress in a simple manner, and already do so on most days, then when you commit to this new minimalist lifestyle, build on that by continuing to choose simple, practical and functional items of clothing to keep in your wardrobe as you work on eliminating the rest.

How Do I Know I'm Doing This Right?

Each day, track how well you did with adjusting and keeping up with the changes and meeting the goals that you set out for yourself. When you keep track of your progress each day, it makes it easier for you to track which areas may be in need of some improvement. Writing down your progress makes it easier for you to see just how far you've come, and therefore, you are more likely to follow through than if you were to just go through each day going with the flow. Tracking your progress a good exercise which keeps you responsible and accountable for how well you are doing, and when you have a strong desire to succeed, it becomes much easier for you to stick to that commitment then you have something that reminds you of just how well you are doing.

Either way, you are doing great just by choosing to start in the first place. Be kind and don't be too hard on yourself, and take everything as it comes one day at a time. You don't need to try and do too much too soon, pace yourself, work through things one and a time and you will eventually get there.

CHAPTER 5
Can I Minimize Other Areas Too?

The answer is, absolutely! Minimalism is not just about decluttering your home environment or your workspace at the office. *Every* aspect of your life can benefit from the concepts and principles of what it means to live life as a minimalist. Keeping it simple and down to only what you need to comfortably survive is something that can translate to a lot of other areas in your life, including your finances, technology, health and the way that you shop or make purchases from now on.

Minimalism and Your Finances

Quite possibly one of the most exciting benefits to look forward to in your new life as a minimalist is how much money you're now going to save when you're not constantly splurging and spending unnecessarily. This is exactly the kind of lifestyle that you would need, in fact, if you were longing to get out of the cycle where you live from one paycheck to the next. Living a life where you're constantly counting the days until your next income boost, only to have the amount flit away before you're even halfway through the month is no way to live. It is stressful, mentally exhausting having to live with that kind of worry, and it is a cycle that is never going to end. Unless you do something about it, that is.

Observe other minimalists around you (if you know of any) and you will notice that one thing they have in common is that they don't live above their means. They don't own the latest of everything, and they don't try to keep up with what the current trends are when everyone else around them is succumbing to the temptation. That's because these minimalists realized something long ago, and that is our wants will always surpass what we can afford. Think about it. As your paycheck gets bigger, do you end up saving more? Or do you find that for some inexplicable reason, your "wants" and "needs" suddenly seem to grow right along with your pay rise and you're back to living from paycheck to paycheck, despite the increase. That's because *our wants will always surpass what we can afford* (write this down and stick it somewhere to remind you of it).

Living a minimalist lifestyle is how you get out of this cycle once and for all. No more will you have to constantly feel like you're struggling to keep up with your expenses, no matter how much money you're earning. You're going to learn how to live comfortably with what you have, and practice minimalism long enough, your materialistic desires will soon ebb away.

To begin downsizing your finances, there are several things which you are going to need to go through. First, you need to make a list of all your expenses — every single one down to the last penny. When you're done, take a look at the list and observe which areas or expenditures are deemed "unnecessary" that you could probably start cutting out of your life. Maybe it's that $3 cup of coffee that you're spending on each morning on your way to work. Cut that out, because making coffee at home will save you a lot more money, and it tastes just as good too. Maybe it is your "monthly ritual" of buying one new pair of shoes each month after payday to "treat" yourself. Cut that out, because you've already got what you need. Observe your expenses with a critical eye and start crossing out the ones that you don't need for survival.

The next step is to work on eliminating recurring debts each month. This includes credit cards, student loans, car loans, mortgage payment, cable bills, gym membership (do you even use the gym as regularly as you would like?), and miscellaneous monthly subscriptions to name just a few. Some people may have different debts of course, depending on their lifestyle, but it is now going to be your goal to eliminate those debts one at a time. Start with your most manageable debt, which for example could be your credit card. Pay them all off, and then cut up your credit cards, so you are no longer tempted to keep using them. Then work on the next debt and the next. Gym memberships are another thing which you could probably do without, especially when you could exercise for free at home. If you don't frequent the gym often enough to make it worth the dollars you're spending, then it's a safe bet to say you could probably cut that out of your life and reinvest that money somewhere else. Miscellaneous expenses like cable bills and Netflix subscriptions, for instance, are also examples of items that are not essential for your survival because you could make do without them. In the spirit of now only living with what you need to survive, if something is not considered a necessary expense for your survival each month, eliminate it and put the money that you saved there into your savings account.

This is going to require a lot of sacrifices (maybe even a *huge* sacrifice) for some people to have to cut out the little luxuries in life they have become so accustomed to. It's going to be challenging, and it is okay to find a compromise towards working on this aspect, so you don't feel so completely deprived. Instead of buying a cup of coffee each morning on the way to work, maybe cut it down to once or twice a week to start until you're completely comfortable weaning it out of your life. It is okay to treat yourself occasionally because minimalism is not meant to strip you of joy. It is simply meant to teach you to spend *most* of the time living life in a simple manner instead of making extravagant and unnecessary expenses a part of your everyday routine. If, every now and then, you do feel like treating yourself, by all means, go for it. It is important to reward ourselves once in a while to keep our motivation going too.

One of the perks of living in the digital age that we do today is that there is an app for literally almost everything. In this case, that's good news because it can help to make your budgeting process a lot easier, perhaps even fun depending on the app that you're using. Budgeting apps are useful to help you keep track of your finances and spending habits on the go, with notifications and reminders to help you stay on track. There are several options to choose from, so pick one that you think works best for you and start taking control of your finances right now.

Minimalism and Your Shopping Habits

As you begin your new life as a minimalist, you will no longer be making purchases the same way you once did. Minimalists have a very different, more efficient way of shopping, as you would probably have already guessed by now. They only shop for want they need, and very rarely do they ever shop for what they *want,* if they ever do at all that is (it is entirely up to you). Now that you are adopting this new approach to living, you are going to have to change your spending habits entirely.

In line with reassessing your finances, you are now also going to have to start creating a strict budget for yourself which you are going to live by each week. It is very important to stick to this budget (unless there is some sort of emergency) and avoid deterring from that budget or giving in to your temptations the way that you may have done previously. What you are most likely going to be spending on weekly is your groceries, and if previously grocery shopping was done without a list, then you will understand just how easy it is to be carried away and end up spending more than you initially thought that you would, especially when there is a reduction in prices for certain items. Creating a budget is a very important step in the reinvention of your shopping habits, and you should try to avoid ever going shopping without a list in hand to help keep you on track.

How often did you stop and think before you made a purchase prior to deciding that you now wanted to become a minimalist? Hardly ever? Or never? That's how most of us end up with a lot of unnecessary items, sometimes duplicate items around the house that we end up storing away and forgetting about. Now that you are about to adopt a minimalist approach to living, every purchase must be accompanied by two actions before you open your wallet and hand over your money. *Stop and think.* Even if the purchase is something as small as a candy bar, for example, you need to stop and think about whether this purchase is necessary and if it is deviating from your budget for the week. For the bigger, more expensive items, even more, thought needs to be put into is. Ask yourself why you're making this purchase. Think about how buying this item is going to help you long-term. Consider if this item is a necessity or a luxury? If you can make do without it, then the honest answer is you probably didn't need it, to begin with. If you can begin training yourself to think this way, you will see what a significant difference it makes and how your spending habits are going to be so different from here on out.

Another way in which your purchasing habits are now going to change as a minimalist is that you will no longer only be focusing on "cheap" items, thinking that it's okay to purchase them because they are cheap enough. They may be on the cheaper side, but how long do they last? Once they do wear out or break down, don't you have to spend even *more* money having to replace them with something else? Making frivolous purchases are now going to have to become a thing of the past because minimalists shop with only one agenda in mind - *looking for items of quality.* Durable items which last much, much longer than the cheaper ones do are going to be so much better long-term because, for one thing, you don't have to keep spending money every few weeks or months having to replace them when they break down. Secondly, higher quality, durable items can often be fixed, which is significantly cheaper than having to buy entirely new items. It is now going to be all about quality and durability when it comes to making purchases.

You're also going to have to do your research whenever possible when making non-grocery item purchases. Whenever possible, do as much research as you can before making any major purchase especially, because this will help you determine which stores will give you the best value for money. Doing research will also let you know if there are alternative options to what you want to purchase, for example, whether it might make more sense for you to DIY the items at home, or if perhaps some of your old items could be repurposed. There are solutions for almost anything these days, which a quick Google search online will reveal. Doing your research will minimize the number of impulse purchases that you make too, which is something you want to get rid of as you begin anew as a minimalist.

Minimalism is going to teach you many things, among them learning the difference between items which are essential, and items which are not. As you learn how to slowly move away from the materialistic lifestyle you were once so consumed with, making purchases will get easier over time and it won't seem so hard to forgo the temptations that once use to persuade you into making purchases that you did not need.

Minimalism and Your Health

Downsizing your life is going to remove a lot of things, one of them is the stress that previously seemed to follow you everywhere you went. A big part of why this consumerist lifestyle was so bad for us is because of all the unhealthy habits and obsessions which it led us to cultivate. Downsizing your life is going to free up a lot of the burden that once weighed you down and took up so much of your time that you ended up having *no time* to focus on what mattered most, which is your health. The consistent pattern that emerges with minimalist living is the theme of keeping things simple and easy to manage, something which could translate into your fitness and nutrition too.

When you start to declutter the unnecessary events and social appointments that you did not necessarily want to attend in the first place, you will have a lot more time to start getting into a healthy workout routine again. You don't need expensive gym memberships either, because you could easily work out in the comfort of your own home, or simply go for a jog in the park, which is free. If jogging is not your style, there are plenty of other workout options which you could find to suit you. At home DVDs or apps that you can download to your phone and follow along too have made it easier than ever for us to take care of our fitness and get in the recommended exercise that is needed to stay healthy. Workouts these days are even tailored to suit your busy schedule, with options that allow you to workout anywhere from 5, 10, or 15 minutes if you're pressed for time.

When you start to create a lot more free time for yourself because you're not constantly rushing from one appointment or errand to the next, you now have the option of preparing more nutritious food at home instead of having to rely on takeout all the time. With your new budget and grocery list in hand, you can take control and make mindful purchases of the food items that you consume. Cooking and preparing your meals at home will always be the choice that makes the most sense, and the choice that is best for your body because you know exactly what is going into your food.

Minimalists are happy with the simple life that they lead because they are not stuck in the *I don't have enough time* mentality. Everyone has the same 24-hours in a day, and minimalists have discovered a way to maximize their time and make it more efficient by cutting out all the unnecessary clutter that they did not need. In doing so, they freed up time for themselves to focus on what matters the most, one of which being their health and nutrition. By eating right and working out several times a week, you will notice quickly how much better your body and your mind feels, and you will be glad you embarked on this journey to change your life for the better.

With the money that you are now saving by eliminating gym memberships and takeaway food, you will now have a little extra wiggle room in your finances to redirect it where it matters, such as towards better healthcare insurance for one thing. Health insurance is essential, especially given the rising medical costs each year. The company that you work for may offer some sort of medical coverage or health insurance, but you should still get your own coverage just in case because you may leave your job anytime in the future to pursue other interests or better career options.

Minimalism and Technology

Technology can be both a good and bad thing, depending on who is using them. Technology can be a beautiful thing because it allows us to stay connected to the people who matter most, no matter where in the world they may be. Family members, friends or lovers who may be on the other side of the world are now a quick phone call or social media app message away. We can easily reach out to the people in our lives on the go, no matter where we may be as long as we have an internet connection on our hands. Or, technology could be a bad thing because it is the cause of us spending countless hours lost in a sea of Facebook posts, Instagram stories and Tweets about the latest happenings. One minute you're checking your phone and the next 3 hours have gone by without you even realizing it.

Minimalists are still living with technology because this lifestyle doesn't require them to be complete hermits, but it is *how* they use this technology that sets them apart from everyone else. Like with all the other aspects in their lives, minimalists limit their use of technology down to the bare minimum, and that is what you need to start doing too as you begin to prepare yourself for this new life. How do they limit their use of technology when it seems that technology is so crucial for everyday survival?

By only focusing on what's important, that's how. Our phones are constantly beeping or pinging each day with an endless barrage of information. From social media updates to emails and what is happening in the news lately, little do we realize that this constant flood of information is disrupting our ability to focus. Remember how social media can cause us to feel unhappy and discontent because we end up comparing ourselves to who seems like they are doing better? That's not doing you any favors, and that is exactly why minimalists keep their social media checking down to the bare minimum because they don't want to be distracted by things that no longer matter. You can still maintain your social media accounts because it is a means of keeping in touch with the people in your life, but instead of checking it every hour or several times a day, limit it to perhaps two or three times a day. Instead of spending an hour or two merely browsing your social media feeds, downsize it to perhaps just 10 minutes or so to get your daily fix and then move onto more important things that matter.

Another way in which minimalists keep their technology usage down to a minimum is to eliminate the gadgets that they don't need. Some people, for example, have more than one phone and perhaps more than one iPad or tablet too. Do you really need multiples of these items? They also do not carry all their gadgets with them at all times, because it distracts from living in the present. If you're on the go and out of your home, then the only device that you're going to need is your mobile phone to be contactable. All the other gadgets do not need to come with you, so leave them at home and focus only on one device at a time.

Minimalists also set designated hours during a day which are "tech-free" hours, meaning that during these hours, there is strictly no technology usage at all. This approach could be employed when spending time with family and friends, or when spending quality time with yourself, reconnecting, meditating, exercising, or simply doing something good for your own benefit. Having technology around will always be distracting, and minimalists approach this hurdle by putting the phones on silent, or putting them away for the time being so they can be more focused on the task at hand and present when they are in the company of others. Even when you're working at the office, having your phone next to your computer as you click away at the keyboard can be very distracting. Putting your phone on silent is not going to be of much help here, because as soon as the screen lights up, your focus will instantly shift from what you're doing to wondering what notification just popped up on your phone. Minimize your use of technology at work by tucking your phone away in your desk drawer during these designated hours where you need to focus on a task. You'll be a lot more productive that way.

Even your computer can be used minimally with more efficiency, and it begins with using your computer with intention. To effectively minimize this area (which seems almost impossible since we spend several hours in a day dependent on our computers for work), you can maximize your time efficiently by eliminating anything on your computer that is not actively contributing to your productivity. When you're able to focus on the task at hand without being distracted, you work through it much quicker, finish faster and thus you minimize the amount of time that you spend on your computer. Who would have thought? Start by first cleaning out your desktop by removing any unnecessary files and folders that you do not use daily or for important work purposes. Save them somewhere else, or delete them entirely if you don't need it anymore. Having a less cluttered, minimalistic view of your desktop will immediately make getting work done a lot more efficient. Uninstall any apps, games and programs that are unnecessary and only serve as a distraction from what your work. Working in full-screen mode is also an effective way to block out distractions, so open up that Word document that you're working on in full-screen mode, so it's nice and big in front of you, making it much easier for you to focus on.

CHAPTER 6
Shifting Your Mindset

In everything that you do, your mindset makes a difference. No matter what situation you may be facing, what challenges you may be going through in life, the minute your mindset shifts is the moment when things will change. How you perceive situations will ultimately shape the reality around you. For life to be better, you need to believe that it *is possible* to change for the better. What we don't realize is that our thoughts have more power over us than we realize, and all you need to do is observe how damaging a negative mindset can be to witness the power of your mind.

A negative mindset will always be an anchor in your life that weighs you down. Minimalism is meant to free you from that old life, but you need to shift your mindset in order for you to get to that point. Yes, minimalism is going to be an upheaval of almost everything in your life, from your belongings, to your social calendar, relationships and now your mindset too. The first thing we need to change is the way that we think about minimalism. It isn't just about downsizing your possessions and decluttering the mess you have accumulated around your home, and it often gets misunderstood because this is the image that immediately pops into most people's minds as soon as they hear the worlds "minimalism." We now need to shift out of that way of thinking and start to understand that minimalism is more of a state of mind than anything else. Yes, it is about decluttering the material objects from your mind, but it is also about *making room* for the more important things in your life, like your health, relationships, friendships and especially family time.

Most people spend their lives constantly working, working, working trying to earn more just so they can keep up with their wants and buy even more stuff. They think that if they were to earn XXXX amount of money, they would then be happy, only to realize when they are earning the amount that they wanted, they're not truly happy at all. This mindset of thinking that we need "stuff" in our lives to make us happy on top of everything else is exactly the reason why many will spend the rest of their working lives forever trapped in this cycle. It is only with a shift in your mindset, the realization that simplicity can bring you more happiness than stuff ever could is when you begin to experience real change.

Signs That You Need to Start Changing the Way You Think

If you've ever wondered whether your mindset has held you back from accomplishing a lot of things in your life, the answer is it probably has. The fact that you're feeling unfulfilled, that there's more you could have done (or wish you had done), means that your thoughts and perceptions have probably held you back on some level. Which is why it is so important to make a real mindset change *before* you begin your journey to become a minimalist because it is the only way you're going to benefit from all the change that is about to take place.

Let's talk about mindset first in general. Has your mindset been the anchor that held you back all this time? The answer lies in how many of the following situations you find you can relate to:

- **You Mostly Feel Unhappy** - When your mind is stuck on negativity most of the time, or more wired to focus on the bad than the good, you find that you spend most of your waking hours feeling unhappy, miserable and wishing that things could be different. Negativity is a force so strong that it blinds you to all the good things that you have going on in your life, and it makes you forget that you have a lot to be grateful for. This inability to see the silver lining and count your blessings will be the cause of a lot of the unhappiness that you feel. You end up comparing your life to those of the people around you, and the grass will always seem greener on the other side than it actually is. If this sounds a lot like what you're going through now, then you can be sure that it is time for a change.
- **Letting Go Becomes a Struggle** - It is going to be a real struggle for you to declutter the way minimalism requires you to if you find it hard to let things go. Letting go is not an easy process, but when you tend to hold onto to something more than you should, then you're going to find this process a challenge every step of the way. People who find it difficult to let go often struggle attaining emotional freedom, and they hold onto the past more than they should using it as reasons to hold them back from accomplishing future successes. These people might also show a greater tendency to hold onto their belongings for years, unable to part with it because there's always a reason why they should keep it around. Unfortunately, as you make the transition towards a minimalist lifestyle, you're going to have to learn to let go of a lot of things, and that can only be accomplished if you're willing to change your mindset.
- **You're Constantly Making Excuses** - Does this one sound all too familiar? Excuses seem to flow all too easily for just about everything. *I want to be a minimalist, but..... I want to change my mindset, but....* There's always going to be a 'but', a reason why you can't, won't or shouldn't do something. People who allow that to happen are the ones who prefer to make excuses because it is simply easier than making any real effort to change. Whenever someone suggests doing things differently than what you may be used to, you immediately feel put off by it and start thinking of excuses to get out of doing it. This mindset has got to change if you want to experience all the benefits from this new lifestyle that you are about to immerse yourself into.
- **You Criticise Far Too Often** - Not only do you criticize yourself, but you also do it to the people around you. That's because a negative mindset is wired to look for the flaws and mistakes more so than

anything else. Do you do this more often than you should? Do you find yourself being more critical instead of praising yourself or others for their efforts, or commending them on their effort? It is certainly time for that mindset to change if you've found yourself nodding along in agreement as you read this.

- **You Lack Motivation** - Do you lack the desire to do even the smallest and simplest of tasks? Even if it is something as small as perhaps catching up with a friend over a cup of coffee? Lacking motivation is a clear sign of a negative mindset, and if you find that you feel demotivated, tired or drained of energy all the time, this is why. You bail out of plans at the last minute, and you cancel social engagements because "you weren't feeling up to it." This mindset has got to change if you want to *see any real change* happening.

How many of the scenarios above did you find yourself relating to? One? Two? Maybe even all of them? Minimalism is here to teach you to focus on what matters the most in our lives, but that cannot be done if you're holding onto your old thought patterns. The fact that you *want* to change, and *want* a new way of living is a good start, and you need to now use that desire for change to fuel you as you work at overcoming your mindset. You can only truly embrace minimalism and all that it has to offer if you train your mindset to start thinking like a minimalist too.

A shift in mindset is something that is going to happen subtly and happen gradually over time in little ways. You might not even realize that it's taking place until one day it just hits you how much things have changed. How much *you* have changed. Especially when you look around your home and at your life since you decided to adopt this new approach to living, it is only then that you will start to realize just how big of a difference a simple shift in the state of mind can be.

What *Is* A Minimalist Mindset?

People often misunderstand and think that by decluttering the possessions they own; it is the end of life as they once knew it. Don't think of it as an end, but rather a *new beginning*. You have been given the opportunity right now to be "born again," to not waste your life pursuing the wrong kinds of happiness. You are about to awaken to the realization that has been right in front of you all this time, which is that you already have everything you need to be happy. You just forgot about it somewhere along the way. The way you perceive it is going to be the defining difference, and if you choose to see it as the end of an era having to part with your belongings, then that kind of mindset is going to prevent you from seeing everything that you are about to gain.

Clutter surrounds our physical space, and we're often so distracted, consumed or overwhelmed with everything that is happening in our lives each day that we forget there is the other kind of clutter that we also need to deal with — the *mental clutter*. Everyone is living with some form of mental clutter, and it starts to become a problem when it is exacerbated by what is known as mental hoarding. In your physical space, you accumulate and hoard in the form of buying things. In your mental space, you accumulate and hoard when you start to hold onto bad memories, negative thoughts, failures of the past, and present worries that you seem to struggle to forget. This is a very real problem which needs to be addressed, especially since mental health is often overlooked and not talked about enough the way that it should. Compounding all these thoughts in your mind over time with no effective way of dealing with it can take a real toll on the body, and often leads to conditions like anxiety and depression. Yet, many people still feel uncomfortable addressing the very real issued that come with not taking care of your mental health, and minimalists have realized that the only way to renew your mind, to remain calm and focused in the midst of chaos, is to declutter the mind along with everything else.

Here is what it means to live with the mindset of a minimalist:

- You are learning how to choose quality over quantity, and to be grateful for what your life is currently filled with.
- You are learning how to be responsible for your own decisions. Financial decisions, career decisions, social decisions, relationship decisions, any decision that you make you are now going to be accountable for, and you are learning how to *choose* the decisions that will bring about the most value for you.
- You are learning about self-discipline, especially during the hard times when your every impulse is urging you to give in to the desire to buy that item you've been eyeing for so long.
- You are learning to choose what is important to you every day, choices which will ultimately result in long-term happiness.
- You are going to learn how to live in the present instead of constantly worrying about the future as you begin to realize that the present is something that you *do have control* over and worrying about what is yet to happen is not benefiting you in any way.

Removing the mental clutter that is currently blocking your mind is a necessary part of the process because a shift in the mindset cannot happen when your mind is blocking the change from happening. Imagine you were driving down the road and there was a big boulder blocking your path. There is no way to move forward unless you first find a way to remove the obstacle that is blocking your way.

How the Minimalist Mindset Is Going to Change the Way You See the World

As you embrace a life where you live with less and live each day in a simple manner, grateful for what you have, you're going to see the world in a different light altogether. Minimalists call this the *minimalist mindset shift*, and here is how it is going to change the way that you think and view life as you know it:

- **You Begin Valuing Experiences More Than Belongings** - The belongings that once mattered so much to you that you had a hard time parting with will no longer seem so important. As you begin to commit to a life where you learn to live with less, you start placing more value on life experiences instead of worldly possessions. You would, for example, value the time that you spend with your family, husband, children or friends more than ever, because it has become clear that *this* is what fills your life with meaning more than a new purchase ever will. That you would rather "clutter" your mind with wonderful memories instead of the actual stuff. New adventures, travels, experiences, shared stories and treasured memories will become more valuable to you than all the belongings that you own in your life.
- **Shopping No Longer Matters** - For those that used to avidly believe in retail therapy as a cure for what "ailed" them in the past, this is going to be a dramatic shift in the mindset. But this is exactly what is going to happen once you've committed to becoming a minimalist. As you fully embrace and immerse yourself into minimalism, you will become a lot more intentional and mindful about what occupies your space, when you open your eyes and come to the realization that you already have everything that you need to live happily and comfortably, your mindset shifts towards other priorities which do not involve shopping and making new purchases. Joshua Becker's once said that *maybe the life you always wanted is buried under the stuff that you own,* and it couldn't be more apt in describing this situation.
- **You're More Mindful About What Surrounds Your Space** - Once you're done decluttering and minimizing your home and your life, you'll realize that clearing up all that mess was no joke. It took a lot of effort and hard work on your part and the memory of that is exactly what's going to keep you from reverting back to your old habits. Because you don't want to have to go through the entire purging process again, sure, technically you could, but *why would you?* It was hard enough work that first round, and doing all that again is not going to be a productive use of your time. The remainder of how much work and effort you put into that first round is exactly why your mindset is going to shift to make you more mindful about what you're allowing into your home and your life.
- **Owning Less Becomes a Priority** - As "stuff" takes less precedence in your life, your mindset will gradually change to where owning less now becomes your priority instead. That's because once you fully immerse yourself into the living with less lifestyle, you will see just how beneficial, time-saving and productive it can be, so much so that you won't *want* to revert back to your old way of living. This is one example of how your focus will shift and change, where

material possessions now become less of a priority and having "stuff" no longer matters to you as much as it once did.

- **You Prioritize What Activities You Spend Time On -** Decluttering your life and spending time on activities which are going to be more beneficial for your mind and body are now going to take priority over attending social gatherings or functions that you had no interest in, to begin with. As you start living the life of a true minimalist, if something is not going to align with your values, then they no longer take priority. If a task or commitment is going to take away too much time from doing something that you value, you're going to find it much easier to say no because you now recognize that time is your precious and most valuable resource. The minimalist mindset teaches you how to be intentional with how you're spending and investing your time, and your priorities are going to shift as a result of that.
- **You No Longer Equate Happiness with Objects -** The reason why minimalists are happier than so many others even though they live with less is that their mindset has shifted to where they no longer equate their happiness with objects. They longer believe that having stuff is going to be the reason for their happiness, and therefore, they don't base their happiness on that any longer. They realize that true happiness comes from the relationships they have in their life, or spending their time in activities which fuel their passion and align with what they value the most. This is how they find joy in living a simple life.
- **You Realize That You Don't Need to "Own" Things to Enjoy Them -** Another big shift in your mindset that is going to result from minimalism is the notion that you need to "own" something before you can enjoy them. That was a big part of why you ended up with more things than you should because you *thought* you needed all of it to indulge in the things that you enjoy. Minimalists realize that this is no longer true. They don't need to own exercise equipment to still benefit from it, because there are plenty of other alternatives like running outdoors, working out in groups at the park, or even downloading workout apps to follow along with. They realize that they don't need to own the latest car model to get where they want to go, because there are always alternatives like carpooling, riding a bike or taking public transport. Minimalism shifts your mindset from thinking *what do I need to buy to do this* to *what alternatives do I have if I don't own this?*
- **You Are Going to Be Aware of Your Time -** You may not have given much thought to how you were spending your time pre minimalism, which made it easy for the minutes and hours to just slip by. Without realizing it, several hours and past and you're left wondering where did the time go. As you remove all the distractions

that once crowded your life, you'll come to an awareness that time is your most valuable resource. From this point on, you're going to be acutely aware of just how you're spending your time. Are you spending more time than you should be investing in relationships that you shouldn't? Do you spend far too much of your time online in an unproductive manner? The deeper you go into your journey as a minimalist, the more importance you are going to place on doing things that benefit you, and if something isn't beneficial, then you won't be inclined to waste as much time on it anymore as you once did.

- **Fear No Longer Controls Your Mindset** - The fear of being deprived and living in scarcity that you were once so afraid of is no longer going to be what controls your mind. Once you have embraced minimalism and rid yourself of the "just in case" mentality, you will realize that all those fears which you were holding onto in reality had no basis at all. You will realize that there was nothing to fear because there are always solutions to every problem. In the event that you do find yourself without an item that you need, you now know that it's okay because you do have options to choose from. You could borrow what you need, or make do with what you have if it is good enough and fits in with what you need at the time. Minimalism will shift your mindset to lose the belief that you must hold onto a whole bunch of things which you may or may not use because of the "just in case" factor and instead, teach you to get creative with your solutions because you will realize there is no value in holding onto something that you're hardly ever, or never, going to use.
- **You Are Going to Rediscover Yourself** - When the material possessions are no longer around to serve as a crutch that is distracting you, only then will you be able to take a long, hard look at yourself as you reassess your life. It is only through getting rid of all the things that do not matter that you start to see clearly for the first time in a long time, what does matter. In doing so, you're going to reconnect with yourself and rediscover things about yourself that you may have forgotten for a very long time because you were so distracted and couldn't see that it was right there in front of you.

As with everything else, a gradual shift in your mindset as you immerse yourself into the minimalist lifestyle is a change that is going to happen over time. The best thing you can do is to let go of your old thought patterns and let this change happen gradually on its own. Don't resist it, don't try to fight it off, but rather embrace it just as you are embracing this new lifestyle.

CHAPTER 7
Goal Setting

Deciding to make a change in your life is a step in the right direction. Maintaining though is the next part of the journey that needs working on. How do you maintain this new lifestyle that you have committed yourself to? By setting goals and avoiding mistakes, which is what we will be exploring in this chapter.

What Is a Goal?

If you've got a desire and a vision to achieve something, a goal is what's going to help turn that vision into a reality. The goal is what fuels you to put in the necessary effort required to turn that desire you have from a vision that only exists in your mind into something tangible that becomes part of your achievement. For example, if you have always envisioned living a much happier, simpler life with less stress and clutter filling up your environment, the life of a minimalist, then having goals is how you take the necessary steps towards making that vision happen. Goals push you towards taking action because they require you to make plans, and these plans need a commitment from you, calling for you to stick to these plans and see them through until the end. It's like making a promise to yourself that you need to keep.

Goals are reminders as to why you got started in the first place, and these reminders are going to be the very thing that helps you stay on track and keep moving forward. Why did you want to become a minimalist? What outcome do you hope to achieve by choosing to live this kind of life? What is your long-term and short-term vision that you're hoping to see manifest by taking the necessary steps and embracing minimalism? These are all the things you would have thought about before embarking on this life-changing process, but without the necessary action steps motivating you to get started and get moving, there's nothing concrete for you to focus on. Without a focal point, the chances of you losing sight of why you started in the first place are much higher, and when you've forgotten your 'why', it becomes much easier to give up and revert back to your old ways.

Setting goals for yourself will give you perspective and help shape the next few decisions that you make from this point moving forward. Every decision will affect your life in one way or another, no matter how small or insignificant we think that decision may be. Buying a candy bar, for example, may seem like a tiny decision, but that one decision could cause you to deviate from the weekly budget that you have set for yourself, resulting in a slight overspend for the week. *Every* decision is going to matter, even more so when it comes to the big choices you have to make, such as what items you need to remove from your life, or what relationships you will now choose to invest less time in.

Can Goals *Really* Make a Difference in My Life as A Minimalist?

Yes, it can. Especially if you are new to this process and just starting to discover what life as a minimalist is going to be all about. Goals make a difference because it forces you to think about what's important in your life, what it is you value, and it is going to help you live this new life with a greater sense of purpose. Pre minimalism, you may have spent a lot of time wondering what you're doing with your life, feeling unhappy, disgruntled and perhaps even a little lost because you forgot your sense of purpose along the way. You wanted to get more out of your life, but you did not know how to do it or what needed to be changed. That's because you had no goals to focus on, nothing guiding you down the path that you needed to go. Goals can change all of that.

A goal is going to help you make the decluttering process *significantly* easier. When you set goals for yourself before you begin, having them by your side as you start to remove the excess stuff that you no longer need will make the decision process move much swifter. When you find yourself holding onto one of your items and staring at it for an awfully long time, wondering if you should toss or keep, take a look at your goals again. If this item isn't in line with the goals that you have set for yourself, then there is only one decision to be made. Toss, done and moving onto the next item. See how much more efficient the process can be? Compare that to if you didn't have a goal to focus on. You could spend hours pondering over whether you should get rid of an item or not, going back and forth for days even because you can't quite make up your mind. All of this is precious time which could be used more productively, and goals are here to help speed things along.

Where and How Do I Get Started Setting Goals as a Minimalist?

That's the question that a lot of new minimalists will often ask. In the interest of simplifying and streamlining their lives to make it more efficient through minimalism, *how do you get started creating efficient goals that fit in with this new life?*

As with everything else in minimalism, you want to try and keep your goals simple too. After all, the whole reason you chose to begin this new lifestyle in the first place was that you wanted to step away from your old life where too much was happening and causing you to feel overstressed, overworked and overwhelmed. Therefore, it makes sense to keep your goals within the similar theme of this whole new approach, and the simpler it is, the easier it will be for you to create habits that are likely to stick.

- **Step 1: Start by Identifying the Goals and How It Fits in With Your Lifestyle.** The beginning of any new life change is where most people find themselves struggling. Identifying your goals in this stage will be key because it will help you prepare for what's ahead, and they kind of goals that you set will either help you or hinder you in your attempts to live like a minimalist. With each goal that you set, think about how it is going to interact with your life and why it would be a good fit. It is important that you be able to answer the question very clearly and definitively because you must know the reason why you are setting this goal. If you are in doubt, then it might not be a goal that is necessary right for you and this change that you're about to go through. To make real progress, you need to think long and hard about what you want your future to look like moving forward. Do you want to live a life where you feel free, happy and healthy, no longer consumed by the desire to constantly compare yourself to others? If yes, how is the goal that you just wrote down going to interact with this vision and make it a reality? Start thinking about the big picture and how to use goals as a tool towards achieving your desired outcome.

- **Step 2: Observe What's Holding You Back.** Of course, this isn't going to be the first time in your life that you would have attempted to set goals for yourself. Most people start every new year with goals and resolutions of what they want to achieve by the time the year reaches an end. Some are successful at making those goals come true, while others are not as successful as the enthusiasm from the start of the new year starts to die down and fade away once they go back to the daily grind of life. Here's where you need to do a little bit of self-reflection, and look back at the past goals you have tried to set but never quite carried out. What factors contributed to this and kept you from turning those goals into reality? What was holding you back? What could you have done differently to change that? The self-reflection part of the process is important because you don't want to be making these same mistakes as you try to set new goals for yourself as a minimalist. Remember, this lifestyle is going to be a *big* change and completely different from the life that you are currently living now. It's a big commitment, and the last thing you want is to get halfway through the process and abandon it. Reassessing what stopped you from carrying out goals in the past will help you confront anything that you might have been afraid of. Perhaps you were worried about the change, or you may not have been ready to get out of your comfort zone just yet.
- **Step 3: Start to Visualize Your Success.** Visualization is the part of goal setting that often gets overlooked, but it is just as necessary as being very clear from the beginning about what your goals are. You must be able to visualize your success with great clarity, see your goals manifest in your life in great detail. Try to even visualize what success is going to feel like for you. The more details you can put into your visualization exercise, the better because it gives you a very clear mental picture of what you should be working towards. It also helps

you give your goals deeper thought about how it is going to impact and interact with the lifestyle that you have now chosen for yourself. This is going to be closely connected with Step 1, where you need to start thinking about the bigger picture. Dream about what your life would look like as a minimalist, what your home is going to look like with just the bare essentials, and what life is going to feel like with fewer relationships and commitments cluttering your social calendar. Being able to visualize helps to create a sense of calm, and when you're happy with the vision you see in your mind, you'll be excited and eager to start living the life that you see. The more you visualize, the more attainable your goals will seem to be.

- **Step 4: Making an Action Plan** - Action plan is a must when you are setting goals for yourself. An action plan helps to break down that goal into smaller, more doable tasks that you can work on one by one, setting deadlines for each task even. For instance, if your goal was to have your study area at home cleared out by the end of the week, make an action plan to spend 10-15 minutes over the next 7-days sorting through the items and decluttering anything that you don't need anymore. By the time you reach the end of the week, you would have finished your goal without even realizing it. Without a proper action plan in place, achieving goals can often feel like a struggle, because you don't know where to begin or where you should even start. Minimalism is all about simplifying your life, and that includes the goals that you set for yourself. Have a goal, and break it down into smaller, simpler, action steps that seem far less overwhelming and much easier to start working on.

The Minimalist's Guide to Goal Setting Strategies

Now that you know where to begin with setting out your goals, the next step is to look at the strategies to keep your goals simple. *Minimal.*

- **Start with No More Than 3 Goals** - Always keep in mind that your aim right now is to go for simplicity and avoid clutter. Which means you're going to want to avoid having too many things on your plate at any given time, including goals. To successfully carry out your goals as a minimalist, aim to have no more than 3 goals that you're working on at any given time. Limiting the goals that you can choose to focus on has the added advantage of making you more mindful towards the kind of goals you are selecting to work on. Since you can only pick 3 at a time and finish those before you move onto newer goals, you really want to make those goals count, so your time and effort does not go to waste. Time is always going to be your most valuable resource, never forget that, so be very selective about how you choose to spend your time. A good tip would be to make your goals inspiring enough that you get excited just thinking about them,

so you look forward to the change instead of being hesitant or worried about it. A goal should be so exciting that you can't wait to get started on it and motivated you enough that you want to push through the challenging parts.
- **Manage Your Expectations** - Setting reasonable expectations for your goals is important to avoid disappointments. Often we get carried away setting goals and we can't wait to see the outcome that when it takes longer than expected to achieve, we find ourselves feeling discouraged or disappointed. Setting reasonable expectations is how you avoid falling into that cycle which may cause you to feel demotivated and perhaps even want to give up because you think it's not working out quite like you hoped. Be patient; some things take time, especially big things like making an entire lifestyle change. It is okay to have goals with deadlines attached to them but make those deadlines reasonable.
- **Shift Your Focus** - Instead of thinking too much about the outcome, why not shift your focus towards the process instead? In the wise words of Ralph Waldo Emerson, *it is not the destination that matters, but the journey instead.* And Emerson was right. You're about to embark on a new and exciting journey, something you have never done before. Yes, there are outcomes that you hope to achieve at the end of it, but avoid being so focused on the outcome that you lose sight of the journey that you're taking to get you there. The little habits, the positive changes for the better, the improvements that you're going to feel both physically and mentally are all part of this journey, and if you're too focused on just the outcome, you miss out on these little moments that also matter just as much.
- **Spread Out Your Tasks** - Trying to do everything all at once is how you end up overstretching yourself. Understandably, you want to get the clearing out portion of the process over and done with as soon as possible so you can get to the part where you start to enjoy your newfound clutter-free life, but trying to do too much too soon will only exhaust yourself. You need to give yourself time to accomplish your tasks and your goals, which is why you needed to set those reasonable expectations in the first place. Depending on the size of your home, clearing it out in a day or two is not going to be possible, unless you've got a lot of free time on your hands and several people to help you. Give yourself a couple of weeks to declutter your home, tackling different sections at a time and making it a goal to finish one section before moving onto the next. This will help prevent you from feeling too stressed or worried that you're not meeting your goal deadlines. Use your time wisely and it will not be wasted, *and* you will still get things done without feeling the pressure.

Common Minimalist Mistakes to Avoid

When you're new at anything, mistakes along the way are to be expected. This includes when you're starting out your new life as a minimalist. Mistakes, however, are sometimes the best way for you to learn, so don't be too hard on yourself if it happens. The best way to minimize the mistakes that occur is to prepare beforehand by arming yourself with the knowledge about what these mistakes are so you can avoid them when the time comes.

- **Mistake #1: Putting Pressure on Yourself to Be Perfect** - Minimalism is not about perfection, and if you are expecting it to be, you're only putting unnecessary pressure on yourself to achieve an unattainable concept. Minimalism is not meant to be a process that is going to stress you out, or something that you're going to regret later on. It shouldn't be a process that is forcing you to constantly think about how and what you could do better. Minimalism is not about pursuing perfection; it is about pursuing happiness and balance in your life once again. Life is never perfect, and that is what makes living each day so exciting.
- **Mistake #2: Being Too Strict with Yourself** - Minimalism is not a binary choice, and that is one mistake that often gets made. Minimalism can be what you want it to be. You can still be minimal while living in a big home if it works for you, and there is certainly no rule that says you need to toss out almost everything that you own before you can be considered a true minimalist. Some minimalists have more possessions than others, but that doesn't make them any less of a minimalist. This lifestyle is going to be entirely personal and tailored to suit what works best for you, so you don't have to be too strict on yourself. If there's an aspect of minimalism that doesn't work well for you, you can choose to adapt and modify it into something that does work. No need to make yourself miserable over the process, because this is meant to be a change for the better, not worse.
- **Mistake #3: Getting Rid of Stuff Doesn't Mean You Can Buy More Stuff** - Another rookie mistake which often gets made is the idea that by decluttering the old stuff from our lives, we can buy new stuff because we now have more space. That is not what minimalism is about. You need to now learn to live with less and live with only what's important, that's the whole point. Decluttering is not a window of opportunity to go out and buy more new stuff just because you have all this extra space in your home. It is okay to have empty spaces around your home, not every nook and cranny needs to be crammed full of stuff.
- **Mistake #4: Thinking That Being a Minimalist Means You Will Automatically Be Happy** - You will, but not in the way that you think. Getting rid of the clutter in your home and your life does not equal automatic happiness, and thinking that way will only lead

to disappointment. Minimalism doesn't work like that. Material possessions won't make you feel happy and fulfilled the way that you hoped, but neither will tossing everything out. Happiness is something that comes from within, and it's not about how much or how little you have. Minimalism teaches you to be *content* with what you have and to find happiness in the things that matter more than material goods. For true happiness to exist within you, you need to be happy with who you are and what you already have and to stop looking externally for a solution.

- **Mistake #5: Trying to Avoid Making Purchases Altogether -** Minimalism is not an extreme, and if you genuinely have a need for something, you shouldn't restrict yourself from buying it. Minimalists shop less, but they still do shop and buy the things that they need to survive. It's not that they have now decided to avoid shopping altogether, they have just changed the way that they now make purchases based on their priorities.
- **Mistake #6: Feeling Obligated to Keep Certain Items -** There's no real need for you to keep something around if it isn't adding value to your life. If you're using that approach towards decluttering, you're going to still be holding onto a lot of unnecessary items, which then defeats the purpose of minimalism in the first place.
- **Mistake #7: Thinking Minimalism Is Going to Fix Your Problems -** Minimalism is not a quick fix for happiness, and it is not a band-aid or magic formula that is going to make all your problems just go away. Going into minimalism thinking that it is going to help fix the problems you have in your life is only going to leave you feeling disappointed. The problems will still be there until you do something to fix it. Minimalism is meant to make life easier for you by removing the clutter and distractions, but it won't remove the problems, and doing it because that's the outcome you're hoping more means you're doing it for all the wrong reasons.
- **Mistake #8: Waiting for the "Right Time" Before You Get Started -** There will never be a "right time" or "perfect time" to get started, and if you're always going to be waiting on that before you make a change, you're going to be waiting for a very long time. Perhaps even not going through it at all. You need to make it the "right time" for yourself based on your schedule, and just start by putting one foot in front of the other until you slowly gain momentum. Waiting for things to be perfect before getting started is how a lot of people let opportunities in life pass them by because they didn't seize the moment. There will never be a right time; it is up to you to *make the time right*.

CHAPTER 8
Success Tips For Your New Way Of Life

Now that you have learned about the minimalist way of life and how it benefits you, it is time to start putting a plan in place. Below is a step-by-step guide to help you embark on your journey towards minimalism.

Step 1: Set a vision

Setting a vision and a plan is important because you don't want to find yourself falling back into your old habits. As Sue Grafton puts it, *"Ideas are easy. It's the execution of ideas that really separates the sheep from the goats."*

Try to envision what your life would be like when you apply this lifestyle and determine in your mind that this is really what you want to happen. Always start with the 'why.' Perhaps you intend to declutter to ensure you are able to focus on the important things in life. Perhaps, you are choosing this lifestyle to save money. Whatever it is, determining your 'why' is important because this is what you will fall back on every time you hit a roadblock.

After considering the 'why,' you need to think about your 'how.' How do you envision yourself transitioning into this lifestyle? Some people prefer to do this area by area, and some prefer to go full-on, cold turkey. This is ultimately your choice. Choose something that works best for you and that you think is achievable. Try not to set too high an expectation that will discourage you when you are not able to cultivate the habit.

Lastly, think about what you are trying to achieve as a minimalist. Set measurable goals that will encourage you on your journey, and consistently act as a reminder of why you have chosen this life. It could be as simple as saving a few hundred bucks a month to, seeing how your home is transformed room by room. It could also come in the form of time, where you have an extra hour a day to spend on your hobbies.

Step 2: Change your perspective

In order to change your lifestyle, your mindset has to change first. A minimalist mindset is simple - everything fits, and almost everything is black and white. Set rules to help you make decisions, and commit to them. If there are things that you do on a daily basis, try to develop a routine that will help you accomplish these activities with minimal effort and time as possible. Old ways may feel comfortable, but they may not be the most effective.

Another example of shifting your mindset would be to choose what you want to keep instead of what you want to get rid of. Many people feel like they have to discard a lot of things when they choose to live as a minimalist, but a change of perspective would help, when you think about what you should keep instead if helps you take on a more positive perspective and reduces stress of being separated from your beloved things.

Step 3: Simplify

Decluttering your mind is also a part of being a minimalist. Minimalist living is simplifying your life also through the way you think. In your process of eliminating things, ask yourself if it is possible for you to discard it. You are allowed to be honest with yourself. How far can you go in cutting these certain things from your life?

The next question you can ask is, "Can I delegate it?" People tend not only to hoard things but tasks as well. Sometimes, we take ownership of something and continue to feel responsible for it although our roles have progressed. Assess if this kind of 'work' should still be your responsibility. If not, delegate.

Lastly, if there is something that is not worth your time, outsource help. Hire someone else to do the job so you can clear your head and spend time to focus on something more important. Time is money, and if you feel that your time is worth more than what you can pay someone else to do, hire help.

Step 4: Apply to all areas

Unless all areas of your life are decluttered, you are not considered a minimalist. Physical, mental and emotional are almost always aligned. Therefore, you can start getting rid of physical clutter first before trying to declutter every other part of your life. We will explore more later in the chapter, but below is the list of areas you can start with.

Areas to declutter

Physical

The most obvious way to determine whether you have a problem with hoarding is to look into your living space, but being able to identify it also means it is the easiest to declutter and the first place you should look into when embarking on your minimalist way of life. The most common physical spaces to declutter is your wardrobe, the bedroom, your office and the kitchen.

The wardrobe is the most common area where people accumulate access. Keep what you love and donate the rest. A bedroom is for sleep, and where your body recuperates from your day. So, get rid of disruptive noises, namely the television. Hint, getting rid of the television declutters two areas of your life, the bedroom, and your mind. In your office, try to arrange your things in binders instead of piling it on.

Below are some tips on how you can declutter these physical areas in your home:

The closet

1. The first thing you can do is to first decide how much you really need. Honestly, you only need a few items for each occasion and

putting a number to each category can help you decide whether to keep or bin your clothing items.
2. Get rid of any clothing item that is damaged. If it is torn or has huge holes, it's time to let it go.
3. If you haven't worn it in over a year, chances are you won't be wearing it ever again. Put it in the 'donate pile.'
4. Choose the items you absolutely love, or cannot live without. Tally it with the number of clothes that you need, and see if you have more to spare. If not, get rid of the rest.
5. You only need enough undergarments to last you for the week. Those really old and worn-out ones that are comfy but you cannot bring yourself to wear belong in the 'throw bin.'
6. Decide what shoes you really need and keep the ones that you wear often. Shoes do not last long in the closet and they deteriorate quickly if not worn - ironically. Ideally, keep those that are versatile and can be worn with any clothing item.

The kitchen

1. The most obvious thing to clear out of the kitchen are expired goods. This is not only for the minimalists but for those who want to avoid visiting the emergency room. You'd be surprised how many homes have expired goods in their fridge or cabinets
2. Throw away anything that is broken. This can range from dishes to appliances. If it is chipped, cracked or unusable for over a year, it's time to throw it away.
3. Like in the previous exercise with your closet, determine how many items are essential to your kitchen, and donate or bin the rest.
4. One of the common guidelines you can use is to keep 1 mug for each person living in your home, and a few more extra in case you have visitors.
5. If you have any appliances that are not in use or duplicates of necessities like measuring cups or blenders, donate or sell them.
6. Invest in high-quality items. A good stainless steel or heavy-duty cast-iron skillet will serve you well for a long time. This can also prevent you from spending more.

The living room

1. Go digital. Put all your movies and music that are still in its cases to your computer. This way, you can get rid of its plastic cases and recycle them. This saves you a ton of space in your living room.

2. Donate books that you no longer read. It is understandable that books may be sentimental to some people. However, if they are not important to you and you don't intend to read them anymore, donate or sell them. You can also participate in book exchanges. Better yet, visit your local library to read and clear out all your books.
3. Get rid of things that you don't use, need or like. Most living rooms are filled with souvenirs, toys or packaging that we thought were nice some time ago. If they aren't functional, beneficial or spark joy, get rid of them.
4. Throw away or donate your throw pillows. Throw pillows were a thing some time ago (maybe they are still a novelty in some households), but they take up a lot of space and most of them end up not being used. Donate pillows that you no longer need in your home.
5. If you have kids, and they have a mountain of toys, use the same guide as the above. Throw away those that are broken, no longer spark joy, and think about how much your children actually need. Most kids outgrow their toys. If they do not age appropriate, donate them.

The bathroom

1. Some people collect toiletries from their travel and most of them are kept unused for a long time. Use whatever you have before buying more. Make it a point to finish using your current toiletries before being tempted to buy a different brand or range.
2. Go through your medicine cabinet and check the labels. If they are expired, throw them out. Different countries have different regulations on how to dispose of medicines. Be sure to check yours before disposing of any drugs.
3. Donate all unused towels. Keep a few extra and donate the rest. Towels last you a long time and it'll be long until you need a new one.
4. You only need one of each of your appliances like hair dryers, curling irons, shavers, or straightening irons. If you have extra, donate them.
5. Ideally, your powder makeup should only last you up to 2 years, and your lipsticks a year. If you have some that are older than that, throw them away.

The above discussed are tips on how to declutter the physical spaces in your home. It may not apply to you in entirety but rest assured that a little goes a long way. Next, we will look into minimizing digital and mental clutter.

Digital

One of the most easily gathered, but less obvious clutter in our lives are digital. Try to minimize time on the phone, or turn off notifications at times where you intend to rest. Sometimes, unfollowing or unfriending unnecessary people on our social media does wonders for us mentally.

On your computers, organize your desktop and delete files that are no longer in use. Sometimes, closing tabs and programs that you are not actively using can also clear your mind and allow you to focus on what you need to be doing. You can also choose to make use of certain websites that allow you to access content and stream online instead of downloading. While it may be impossible to totally disengage from everything digital, doing a digital or social media fast once a while will help you be more aware of the present and your surroundings.

Below are some things you can begin doing to declutter digitally:

Unsubscribe from emails that you don't read

Unsubscribing from newsletters or notifications from companies or brands that we don't need will not only reduce digital clutter but also mental clutter. We don't need to be flooded with promotions that don't apply to us, or information that is irrelevant to us. When you feel that they are relevant again, you can always re-subscribe.

Organize and clear your email inbox

Most of us have unread emails that date back for years. Clear them out and try to organize your emails by sender or by categorizing your folders.

Organize and clean up your Desktop

Placing files on your desktop for easy access is always tempting. However, whenever you turn on your computer and the first thing you see is clutter, the 'easy access' can in time, turn into disruptive excess. Organize files in folders instead and delete the ones you no longer need.

Uninstall software that you don't use

If you no longer need a particular software, uninstall it to clear up space in your computer. This also helps you find programs that you actually need easily.

Delete unused files

There is no argument here. If you no longer need it, delete it to make room for what you actually need.

Turn off unimportant notifications on your mobile
Unsolicited notifications can distract you from the present, drain your mental energy and also your batteries. Take 2 minutes to turn off unimportant notifications from applications that you use rarely.

Clean your browser by deleting cookies, plugins or cache
Although the intention for cookies and cache is to store information to help you load pages faster, they can quickly add up act adversely. It is important to clear out cookies and cache to clear up space and save computing power.

Organize your files in folders
It is a given that organizing your files in folders will ensure easy access. You will also save time looking for the particular files.

Mental
Sometimes, we unintentionally collect mental clutter by setting unnecessary expectations on ourselves based on what others are doing. For instance, the perception that you absolutely have to own your own home is a mental burden that you may not need. If it is currently too far-fetched or not in your capabilities, then rent and be okay with it. There is no point putting unnecessary pressure on yourself.

Scheduling regular meditation or 'me time' is vital to your mental health. It allows you to reflect, identify unproductive thoughts and declutter. This will result in mental clarity and better ability to focus on the important aspects of your life.

One of the most common mental stressors for people is money. Worrying about money is one of the major sources of migraines and headaches. If you have a debt, focus on paying it off before setting any other financial commitments or goals. Declutter your financial ins and outs, and try to set simple goals like spending less than you earn, or saving up to 20% of your salary each month. The less time you spend worrying about money is more time spent on things that you enjoy.

Some mind clutter is also often related to our past. We tend to think about the mistakes we've made, opportunities we didn't take and those who have hurt us. Take time to address these feelings, deal with them and let them go. If you can fix them, do it. If not, best to forgive yourself, forgive those who have hurt you and move on.

One of the things therapists encourage patients to do is to write their thoughts and feelings down. They may or may not be reasonable or rational, but writing them down can help clear its recurrence in your mind and decreases your mental burden. Putting it down on paper helps you visualize your thoughts and you can begin to make sense of them. At the end of it, you can make an informed decision of whether or not to keep these thoughts or give them a place in your mind.

Sustaining Your Minimalistic Lifestyle

Now that you have a plan and are ready to set things in motion, you need to ensure you're in for the long haul. Remember that it takes time to get into the groove of a lifestyle change and you will need to be prepared to tackle minor discouragements and setbacks along the way and ensure that you stay on track.

As long as you are prepared with a system in place, you should have no problem sustaining your minimalistic lifestyle. Below are a few rules you can use as guidelines when setting your sustainability system.

90 Days Rule

When clearing out your spaces, look at each item and think about whether you have used it in the last 90 days. If you haven't, it is unlikely that you will use them again. Choose to bin or donate them. If you can set a benchmark of fewer days, the better.

Weekly Reflection

Review your progress and run a health check on how you're doing as a minimalist. It is always good to reflect, declutter, and refocus on your priorities. The more often you reflect, the less likely you are to find clutter; be it physical, mental or digital. This also ensures that you are running on a clear focus on priorities.

Quality vs Quantity

Choose to buy high-quality things that last you for a longer time, compared to quantity. This will reduce the need to eliminate things in your life and actually save you more money in the long run. It also saves you the time you spend repairing something that often breaks or needs more maintenance than a low-quality one.

When it comes to food, whole food is better than processed. Invest time cooking and save money buying fresh instead of processed and packaged foods. This also contributes to better and stronger immune system.

Tradeoff

Whenever you decide to buy a new item, you have to swap and get rid of the item that you already have. But before you decide to buy something, question whether you need it. If you already have something that functions the same, resist!

Be flexible

Sometimes along the way, you discover that the plans or systems you put in place may not suit your needs or goals. It is okay to recalibrate and reset new plans or goals. This is why constant reflection is needed. A few changes could take place before you finally find something that you are comfortable with.

One step at a time
Trying to declutter your entire home at one go is not the best idea. Try to set a timeline to clear out specific areas in your house first, and see how well you do. Attempting too much at the beginning could cause massive discouragement and fallout. You could start with one room and arrange items into three (3) piles: Keep, Throw or Donate.

Create a schedule
When planning to sustain your lifestyle, it is important to think about scheduling regular clear-outs. It's one thing to clear things out, and another thing to *keep* things out. To ensure that the clutter does not creep its way back in, it's important to set time for regular review of the items in your home.

Travel Light
The two main rules that minimalists abide by when travelling is to bring a small bag and differentiating between needs and wants. Try not to bring a big bag during travel unless you want to fill it up. This could either mean bringing excess things for travel or bringing home more than what you intend to.

Next, think about where you're going and what are the essentials. For instance, if you're going to the beach, you need flip flops, bathing suits, sunglasses and shorts. Wants include extra dresses, inflatables, costume jewelry and heels.

Redesign your home
This doesn't mean major renovation, but it could be rearranging furniture and clearing out things that are merely decorative, and collect dust over time. If you find ornaments or souvenirs that have years of dust resting over it, it's time to let them go.
Designing a home that is simple and clean can help you feel calm and better sustain the minimalist lifestyle. You are less likely to continue accumulating things you don't need.

Cook with less
As mentioned earlier, whole foods are always better. You can whip up a good meal with ten ingredients or less, saving you more money and cutting down on waste created by the packaging of the processed foods. Better yet, plan your meals and have a shopping list, so you don't come home from the supermarket with extra things you bought on impulse.

Cultivate edifying hobbies
Often times, people end up spending money on things that don't edify them or add to their growth. Think about what you enjoy doing and fill your time with useful hobbies that will grow your talents or skills, or something that you actually enjoy doing. If you have to invest your time on something, it better be for something that's good for you.

If the hobbies are free, that's a bonus. Free hobbies will help you live a more minimal life. Hobbies like outdoor sports like yoga or running helps you clear your mind, maintain wellness and also accumulate fewer things.

Be grateful
Lastly, in your reflection, remember to be thankful for the things that you have. Be thankful for the luxury of being able to travel, donating excess, spend time with your hobbies and being able to create a clean space for you and your mind.

Conclusion
In your journey towards minimalism, always remember your end goal and be kind to yourself. As mentioned earlier, a lifestyle change takes time. Remember your purpose and do what works best for you in order to achieve it.

CONCLUSION

Thank for making it through to the end of this book, let's hope it was informative and able to provide you with all of the tools you need to achieve your goals whatever they may be.

This is an exciting journey you're about to embark on, and hopefully, you're just as eager to get started after reading through the chapters of this book. The transition into the lifestyle of a minimalist can be a deeply fulfilling experience. It may be daunting to think about living life with just the bare necessities and only a few worldly possessions to your name, but once you fully immerse yourself into the experience, you will wonder why it took you so long to get started in the first place.

This is going to be a unique experience for each and every one of you, but the ultimate goal is going to be the same - *to declutter your life, find your focus again, that happiness cannot be found in material goods and rearrange your priorities to remind yourself about what's truly important in life.*

Rearranging your life is going to put so many things into perspective, and it is up to you to use this newfound focus and hopefully extra time on your hands in a more productive manner. Go after the goals you have been pushing aside for so long, reconnect with old friends and strengthen existing relationships, commit to your health, your passions and explore new interests you've never had the opportunity to before. The world is yours for the taking; all you have to do is to start living your life the way that it was meant to be lived.

No more will you have to be a slave to consumerism; this is the start of a brand-new beginning. Take each day as it comes and open your heart and your mind to new possibilities as you go forth and begin your minimalist lifestyle.

Finally, if you found this book useful in any way, a review on Amazon is always appreciated!

DESCRIPTION

How would you like to live a life that is *simple*?

How would you like to live a life that is *free*?

Free from the stress, worries and anxieties that plague most of us each day as we spend countless hours, day in and day out, trying to keep up with the never-ending demands of a materialistic lifestyle? Free from the constraints of living paycheck to paycheck? Free from the mess and clutter that surrounds your home to a point you don't know where certain items are kept anymore?

How would you like to live a life that is lighter, happier and more focused on the things that matter most in life? Relationships, life experiences, passion, joy, happiness and all these priceless parts of life you somehow forgot about along the way?

All that you long for can be yours, and all it takes is one change in your life — the change from becoming a *consumerist* to a *minimalist*.

Did you know that on average, almost all of us own more than what we actually need to survive? And more often than not, this excess of 'stuff' is unnecessary. How many items have you purchased in the past thinking that you need them, only to find that you never use them? How many items do you have around your home that you forgot you even purchased? This accumulation of items is not doing you any favors, and in fact, all you're doing is cluttering up your home and adding more mess onto your already busy, hectic life. You're spending hard earned money which you could put to much better use on things that you don't even necessarily need.

It is for those very reasons and more that minimalism is now gaining popularity as people start to realize *you know what? I don't need all this stuff at all.*

Minimalist Lifestyle: How to Become a Minimalist, Declutter Your Life and Develop Minimalism Habits & Mindsets to Worry Less and Live More is step-by-step guide that will show you how to transition from the life that you know, into the life of a minimalist with insightful advice and helpful strategies that are easy to follow and apply. Explore:

- What it means to live life as a minimalist
- The rules of living with less
- How to minimize other aspects of your life (finances, health, relationships and more)
- What it takes to make the mindset shift
- Why it is important to set goals for yourself as you begin this new lifestyle
- *And more...*

Start your simple, stress-free approach to living today with all the tools that you need to help you get started off on the right foot from Day 1. Isn't it about time that you started to worry less and live more?

MINIMALISM FOR FAMILIES

For Families Who Want More Joy, Health, and Creativity In Their Life by Decluttering Their Home, Learning Simple and Practical Budgeting Strategies to Save Money & Worry Less!

By Jenifer Scott

© Copyright 2019 by: Jenifer Scott- All rights reserved.

This book is provided with the sole purpose of providing relevant information on a specific topic for which every reasonable effort has been made to ensure that it is both accurate and reasonable. Nevertheless, by purchasing this book you consent to the fact that the author, as well as the publisher, are in no way experts on the topics contained herein, regardless of any claims as such that may be made within. As such, any suggestions or recommendations that are made within are done so purely for entertainment value. It is recommended that you always consult a professional prior to undertaking any of the advice or techniques discussed within.

This is a legally binding declaration that is considered both valid and fair by both the Committee of Publishers Association and the American Bar Association and should be considered as legally binding within the United States.

The reproduction, transmission, and duplication of any of the content found herein, including any specific or extended information will be done as an illegal act regardless of the end form the information ultimately takes. This includes copied versions of the work both physical, digital and audio unless express consent of the Publisher is provided beforehand. Any additional rights reserved.

Furthermore, the information that can be found within the pages described forthwith shall be considered both accurate and truthful when it comes to the recounting of facts. As such, any use, correct or incorrect, of the provided information will render the Publisher free of responsibility as to the actions taken outside of their direct purview. Regardless, there are zero scenarios where the original author or the Publisher can be deemed liable in any fashion for any damages or hardships that may result from any of the information discussed herein.

Additionally, the information in the following pages is intended only for informational purposes and should thus be thought of as universal. As befitting its nature, it is presented without assurance regarding its prolonged validity or interim quality. Trademarks that are mentioned are done without written consent and can in no way be considered an endorsement from the trademark holder.

INTRODUCTION

Congratulations on purchasing Minimalism for Families and thank you for doing so.

The following chapters will discuss everything you need to know to develop a mindset of minimalism and build a minimalist lifestyle your entire family can follow. First, we'll talk about what minimalism is and what it can look like in the life of an entire family. We'll go through specific strategies for explaining minimalism to your family members and convincing them to jump on board. We'll talk about methods you can use to declutter your home, as well as specific tips and tricks for each room in your house. Finally, we'll talk about how to deal with family members who remain unconvinced and resistant to your vision of minimalism, as well as how to maintain a lifestyle of minimalism for the long-haul.

Throughout this book, I have tried to provide an easy-to-follow process for developing a minimalist mindset and building a minimalist lifestyle. You can absolutely read through the entire book before taking action, but I designed this book to serve as a guide to walk you through the process. Use this book however you learn best!

I hope this book is extremely practical and useful to you and that it provides you with much-needed encouragement and motivation along the way. As you'll come to see in the following pages, minimalism is an incredibly worthwhile mindset and lifestyle. It will help you and your family learn how to focus on the things that truly matter in your life, like spending more time with each other. It might be a bit painful and difficult at first, but I'm willing to bet that your entire family will eventually come to see the value of it.

As you go through the pages of this book, keep in mind that the guidelines I have written out here are only the opinion of one person. I obviously do not know you or your family. Feel free to take the tips and ideas I've outlined and adjusted it to fit the needs of your family.

There are plenty of books on this subject on the market, so thanks again for choosing this one! Every effort was made to ensure it is full of as much useful information as possible. Please enjoy!

CHAPTER 1
Definition

There's a reason for Walt Whitman's quote, "Simplicity is the glory of expression." In today's busy society of consumerism, with ads running rampant throughout our daily lives, simplicity is something that can be incredibly hard to achieve. We're constantly bombarded with ads, begging us to buy the latest gadgets or the newest upgrade to things we already have. We're tempted by the shiny new toys that promise more happiness, higher status, and ultimately better lives. Our money is constantly being pulled in all different directions, and we're left struggling to make ends meet, looking around and wondering where it all went.

In much the same way, our time is also pulled in different directions, taking our attention off of what's truly important to us and placing it on things that don't matter as much in the long run. As we scurry about from work to soccer practice, to the church, to the gym, to the grocery store, and back home to start the process over again, our lives slip by all too quickly and, once again, we're left standing around, wondering where all the time went.

In such a world, it's hard to see a viable solution. How do you avoid wasting all of your precious time and money on worthless "stuff"? When the whole world is doing one thing, it's extremely difficult to learn how to swim against the tide.

But it can be done!

Simplicity is the cornerstone of the philosophy of minimalism. It means subtracting all of the things that don't add happiness and joy to your life and learning to live with less. It means not trying to fill up all of the empty spaces with trinkets and baubles, even if they're sentimental or valuable. It means saying no a lot so that you can say yes to what really brings you joy.

I don't know what your story is, maybe you just started out in your adult life. Maybe you just got married, and as you merge two people's belongings for the first time, you're finding that you could use a little bit of a trim to cut off a bit of the excess that's starting to build. Or, maybe you're a mom of five, with a large house of your own, a husband, two dogs, and a garage full of unused, outgrown stuff (and an attic…and a basement…), and you find that you spend a lot more time cleaning and taking care of all of that stuff than you do spending time with and taking care of your family.

Whatever end of the spectrum you're on, it's not too late (or too early) to get started on your journey to minimalism!

"But I'm that mom with five kids and ten hundred animals! I've got stuff coming out of my ears! There's no way I'll ever be able to start living a minimalist lifestyle, much less sustain one. Also, my kids would stage a rebellion. Surely it's not possible for me!"

I have to be honest; I'm not exactly where you are. I'm probably somewhere in the middle of the "stuff spectrum." I only have two kids, a husband, and one dog, and my house is about the size of a shoebox. But I promise you, no matter what your life looks like now, living a minimalist lifestyle is absolutely possible. It might take a little bit more work on the front end and a little more intentionality to sustain, but it is possible, and it's absolutely worth the effort.

Before you get down to all of that hard work, though, let me tell you what I mean when I talk about minimalism.

What is minimalism?

To me, minimalism is about trading all of the excess junk that piles up so easily for more of what brings me joy: spending time with my family and friends, writing, sleeping, and experiencing life. It's about teaching my kids to live simple lives so that we can experience the beauty of the world together. It's about working with my husband to build the life we want for our family instead of fighting with him about all of the junk that needs to be taken care of.

For those of you who are new to the idea of minimalism, it's also important to note what minimalism isn't. Minimalism isn't about living like a monk, with absolutely nothing to your name except the clothes on your back and a tiny, windowless room to sleep in. It doesn't even have to be about living in a tiny house and owning just the bare minimum to survive (Although a tiny house might be a great option for you. I know my husband and I are considering it!).

The main idea behind minimalism and the guideline you should hold onto as you work to implement minimalism in your family's life is to figure out what brings you joy and adds value to your life and to let go of anything else. Minimalism is a mindset and a lifestyle. It's not a project to be completed in a weekend and put back on the shelf for next time. It's a chance to reconsider what your priorities are and to design your life (and your stuff) around those priorities. And although minimalism usually starts by getting rid of excess physical clutter, you'll likely find that it leads to getting rid of all of the clutter in your heart and mind as well.

It's a Trade

Like I said earlier, minimalism isn't about setting unrealistic limits on what you can own. It's about making a trade. Everything costs something, so when you choose to accept something into your life, you're also choosing to let go of something else. When you choose to accept busyness and clutter into your life, you choose to let go of money, time, and experiences. However, you can also choose to let go of the clutter and busyness and welcome back the money, time, and experiences you lost.

It means living intentionally

The process of trimming down all of your stuff naturally leads you to ask questions. Do you really need this knick-knack? Does this bring me joy? By asking yourself these questions, you start to become intentional about what you own and the things you do. It all needs to serve a purpose—the purpose you've set out for yourself and your family.

It means living within your means
When you choose to live a minimalist lifestyle, you learn how to say no to much of the excess you're bombarded by every day. You have the mindset that helps you say no when you're tempted to buy something you probably don't need. Minimalist living means that you live off what you make, and anything extra will just have to wait until you've saved up for it because going into debt to get it isn't an option.

It means learning to tell the difference between a need and a want
Do you really need that new shirt? Does your three-year-old really have to have all of the Paw Patrol dogs and their vehicles? If you have enough shirts to last until laundry day and if your three-year-old has a few beloved toys to entertain him, the answer is no. They are not needs. You might still decide to buy them, but you can do so knowing exactly what you're doing. You're indulging a want—which is not always a bad thing. Minimalism doesn't mean you can never get something you want. What it does mean is that you need to know the difference between a need and a want, and you need to know that you have a place for what you buy. If you indulge in your wants too often, you'll only be building the clutter right back up again.

Advantages of having a minimalist lifestyle
There are so many advantages to minimalism—advantages that go beyond and far deeper than the initial advantage of having a clutter-free home. As I said, minimalism is a trade, a trade of your excess stuff and busyness for more simplicity, deeper relationships, and greater joy. All of these things lead to enormous benefits that you'll be so grateful for at the end of your life that you won't even come close to missing the "stuff" you let go of.

Financial Freedom
As you trim down your belongings and learn to live within your means, you'll find that your money starts to free up as well. You no longer have to buy more and more stuff to "keep up with the Joneses," as it were. You'll be able to get out of debt and live a life full of rich experiences with those you love.

More time
I don't know about you, but even in my shoebox-sized home, I spend an inordinate amount of time cleaning. It feels like I'm constantly picking up toys, vacuuming dog hair, doing laundry, washing dishes, and making beds.

And I work, so all of that has to be done outside of my working hours, which is the time I should be spending with my family.

I clean so much because we have too much stuff! Even though we've been on this minimalism journey for a long time now, we're not perfect at it, and in this season of our lives, it's become incredibly difficult to maintain (So, see, you don't have to be perfect at this! I'm writing a book on minimalism, and I'm not perfect at it, either!). My kids have far too many toys (courtesy of well-meaning grandparents who live nearby). I have far too many clothes (courtesy of my recent influx of maternity clothes and subsequent need for clothes that fit my post-baby body). And my husband has far too many hygiene products (courtesy of his strange need to constantly have mousse in his hair and body spray all over his body—even at night. Gotta love him!). We also really love board games, so we have an entire shelf in our closet devoted to all of them.

Needless to say, there's a lot to keep up with, even in my little home. Minimalism can certainly help with that. If my kids had just enough toys to keep them entertained, if I had just enough clothes to last until laundry day, and if my husband had just enough hygiene products to keep himself clean (meaning, only one can of each product instead of five), imagine how much less time I'd have to spend keeping toys organized, folding laundry, and putting hygiene products back in their proper place? That's a lot of time.

Less stress

With less stuff comes less stress. Less time spent cleaning up stuff means more time I could spend on other things that need to get done. Studies have shown (UCLA Center on Everyday Lives and Families 2001-2004) that managing a house full of stuff leads to higher levels of stress and anxiety for mothers. In the study, women associated with a clean and clutter-free home has a successful and happy family.

Excess clutter not only affects mothers but the children as well. Excess stuff means excess stimuli, which leads to greater distraction. Not to mention, when their mothers are stressed, kids often become stressed as well.

Better relationships

This is a huge one. I know I joke about my husband's surplus of hygiene products, but if I can be honest for a moment, there are days when I want to take his mousse bottle and stab him with the pointy end. The tip might break off before it could do much damage, but the sentiment is still there. In a small house with two very young children, even one excess bottle of mousse out of place makes a room look cluttered and disorganized, which drives me a little crazy.

It drives me crazy because I look at that bottle of mousse, and I know that it's insignificant. It's only one bottle of mousse. But it's one bottle of mousse and one load of laundry and one meal to cook and one pile of toys to put away until it adds up and up and up, and all of my time has gone. It's a maddening reminder of all of the things I have to complete each day just to maintain a livable space (much less a homey and welcoming space), and it stresses me out immensely.

Then, I'm snapping at him and the kids (despite my best efforts to hide my frustration), refusing to tell him what's wrong because, in my mind, he should just know to pick up his own things. My three-year-old is wondering why mommy's upset, and my infant is crying in his chair because I just can't figure out what's going on with him. It's a horrible cycle, and my relationships with my husband, my kids, and even my dog suffers because of it.

Read this carefully: Minimalism is not a magic pill to fix all of your relational ills. In fact, it might initially add conflict that might not have been an issue before (We'll talk about how to handle that in a later chapter.).

However, if you can get over the initial hard work to declutter your home and can consistently build habits to maintain a minimalist lifestyle, it will improve your relationships. You'll have more time to spend with your loved ones. You'll be less stressed about spending that time with them. And you'll be able to experience life with your family in a way that wasn't possible when your home was too cluttered for you to even breathe.

Healthy boundaries

Choosing to live a life of minimalism will mean that you have to say no to some things. Whether it's declining to take on more work for your boss or having a conversation with eager-to-spoil grandparents about the number of toys your children have, maintaining a minimalist lifestyle requires you to develop strong boundaries with those around you. Just remember: setting and enforcing boundaries doesn't make you rude or mean. It means you're honest with others about what you can do and accept. You'll even be able to avoid feelings of resentment toward them that might arise when you do something that violates your boundaries.

So set the boundaries you need to have for your family and be confident in enforcing them. Having boundaries for you and your family is extremely healthy and will make your life with others much more pleasant and honest. There are so many more benefits to living a minimalist lifestyle that I simply don't have time to go into in this chapter. As you continue reading this book and getting ready to implement minimalism in your family's life, keep these benefits in mind. It can be a long, hard journey (as I've already shared, my family and I are still not perfect at it.), but keeping all of these benefits in mind will give you something to look forward to and motivate you to keep on keeping on.

CHAPTER 2
Mindset Of Minimalism

It might seem ridiculous to think that minimalism can actually work for an entire family—especially one with a couple of young kids. Between all of the sports gear—participating in multiple sports at a time builds character, right? —clothes, school supplies, and toys that constantly pile up, cutting it all down to only the things that are necessary (and keeping it that way) seem an impossible task.

It might be crazy, but the mindset of minimalism is actually most valuable in the context of a family. Minimalism is about replacing all of the clutter that sucks all of your time, money, and energy with the relationships and experiences that really mean the most. And what relationships are more important than family?

None of that takes away from how difficult it can be, though. Believe me; I'm well aware. So how do you get your entire family on board to becoming a minimalist family?

Developing a mindset of minimalism

Most of this book will be about the practical steps you'll take to implement minimalism in your home because the method you use is absolutely important to your success. But understanding and developing a minimalist mindset is every bit as essential to your success. If the steps you take for an example is the car that gets you to your destination, the mindset is the gas that fuels the car; both are necessary if you plan on getting anywhere.

Understand that minimalism isn't just about organizing all of your stuff better and making it look better. Minimalism is about actually reducing the number of possessions you have and getting rid of it all. If you want a book about the organization, this won't be the book for you. This book (and minimalism in general) is about changing your heart and mind in relation to your possessions. It's about developing a mindset that values experiences and relationships more than possessions and that designs a life that reflects those values.

The very first thing you have to do to get started on this journey is developing a mindset of minimalism for yourself. It's hard to convince others to do something you aren't convinced of yourself. If you read the first chapter of this book and found yourself longing for the kind of life described here, you're well on your way to a mindset of minimalism.

Why are you doing this?
One of the first things you need to understand to develop a mindset of minimalism further is why you're doing this in the first place. What is the one reason that stands above all the other good reasons you could have for taking on this journey? What will be the motivator that drives you through the hard times of starting a minimalist lifestyle?

But don't just think about it. Take out a sheet of paper and actually write it down. Start by writing all of the reasons you have for wanting to get rid of all the clutter in your life and home and live a minimalist lifestyle. Then, narrow it down to just one overarching reason. If you want to get really into it, write it down by itself on a sheet of paper and hang it up on your wall or your refrigerator. You can even decorate it if you're into that kind of thing. The point is: to make your reason both extremely important to you and highly visible. That way, when the going gets tough, you can look at the beautiful sheet of paper hanging on your wall and tell the tough to get going. Sorry, my humor is a bit cheesy at times.

What's the purpose of your home?
It's time to take out another sheet of paper. We're doing practical here, folks, not just thoughts swirling around your head. This time, I want you to think about the purpose of your home. What do you want your home to mean to those who step into it? Is it shelter? Is it a place to enjoy friends and family? Personally, I want my home to be just that: a home. I want it to be somewhere my family and those who visit can go to feel at home. I want it to be calm, beautiful, and comfortable. I want it to be cozy and for people to immediately feel safe there. I want it to be a place where people can be together and experience life together.

If you have the purpose of your entire home written down, start doing the same thing with each room in your home. What is the purpose of your living room? Your kitchen? Your dining space? Your kids' rooms? Your bedroom? For me, I want my living room to be a place for people to relax and spend time together (on super comfy couches). I want my kitchen to be a place where delicious meals are produced that provide nutrition for my family and hospitality for guests. I want my dining space to be a place where people gather to talk about everything and nothing, to connect with each other through conversation and games. I want my kids' rooms to be a place where my kids can go to express themselves through their unique interests and hobbies and to spend a few moments alone when they're feeling overwhelmed. And I want my bedroom to be a place for my husband and me to relax and connect with each other every day.

In short, my home and all of the rooms in it are all about connections, relationships, and experiences.

What purpose do you want your home and its rooms to serve?

What happens next?
Now that you're clear on your own reasons for choosing a minimalist mindset, it's time to start getting into the practical steps you're going to take to start implementing minimalism in your family's life. These first steps are all about bringing your family on board with you and developing a mindset of minimalism within your family as a whole. They're also about becoming more deeply in tune with your underlying desires and purpose in order to cut out the indecision that leads to cluttered homes and lives.

Lead by example

One of the qualities of an effective leader is that they "walk the walk" long before they ever expect anyone else to do it. If you really want to lead a minimalist lifestyle with your family, the first thing you have to do is start minimizing your own stuff. Sometimes it's easy to start minimizing your family members' things. After all, it's all of your kids' toys you have to pick up, or it's all of your husband's (clean) shirts that keep piling your laundry basket high. Your stuff isn't the problem!
Yeah, right. Sorry, sister...or brother. It's easy to see everyone else's stuff and think that's got to go. But if you haven't gotten your family on board yet, that's a sure way to make sure they're never on board. No one likes to wake up one day and find that their belongings are suddenly gone.
However, if you start the process with your own stuff, your family will start to see how you're able to live (happily) with fewer things. They might start asking questions on their own about why you got rid of so much of your stuff. They might even initiate their own "clutter purge" without you having to do much besides answering their questions.
By giving your family members a chance to initiate their own induction into the world of minimalism, you'll be empowering them to take ownership of it. When your entire family is able to take ownership of this new mindset, you'll find that it'll be much easier to sustain a minimalist lifestyle.
Not to mention: if you start the process of minimizing your belongings only with your own stuff, you'll be familiar with the process and able to help your family members get started. The process of minimizing can be a daunting one, so serving as a trailblazer for your family can be a great way not only to get everyone on board but to give them a real-life example to follow.

Hold a family meeting
Once you've been leading your family by example for a little while and have the process down for yourself, it's time to hold a family meeting. In this meeting, share with them your reasons for minimizing your own stuff, as well as the purpose you wrote out for your home. Share why this lifestyle choice is so important to you and how doing it with your own stuff has already changed the way you live. Explain to them what minimalism means to you—and what minimalism does not mean.
If I were you, I'd go into this meeting with notes prepared. It might seem forced and a little bit silly to be so formal about a family meeting, but minimalism can seem like a radical lifestyle choice to those who don't understand it yet. It's important to be prepared to answer any questions your family members ask. It's also important that you're able to explain it in a way that's easy to understand. And if you're like me, writing it out beforehand will make sure you're able to accomplish both goals, even if you get a little flustered.
It's also important to explain it to them in a way that they'll understand and appreciate. If you have young kids (not toddlers or babies, but kids who are old enough to understand what's going on), remind them of how much time they have to spend cleaning their room right now. Remind them of the times

they've been grounded because they didn't clean their room when they were asked to. Paint a picture for them of what it would look like if they had fewer toys in their room, fewer clothes in their closet, and less clutter to keep up with. They'd be able to spend more time outside, hanging out with their friends, or participating in the activities they want to be part of. They might balk at the idea of losing their toys, but it probably won't be too hard to persuade them to give it a try. You might even compromise with them by having them put away most of their toys but keeping them in storage for an agreed upon trial period. If they find that they miss their toys at the end of the trial, they can get some of them back. Just make sure that the trial period is a long enough time that they're able to really get into the routine of having less clutter.

Once you've explained what minimalism is and why you think it's important, ask your family members for their input. Answer their questions and concerns, and if they put up a lot of resistance, try to find ways to compromise with them. Minimizing might have to be a long process of weaning your family off their clutter. But that's ok. Remember that this is about enriching your relationships with your family, not causing division and conflict with them. If taking it slower than you'd like is the cost of avoiding division, it's well worth it.

Find a way to motivate them

Once your family has agreed on the extent and timeline of the minimizing process, it'll be time to start decluttering your house. The initial decluttering will likely take several days and lots of decluttering sessions that will likely give your kids a sour taste for the whole idea, even if they initially agreed to it in the family meeting.

So, find ways to make it fun for your entire family. Offer a reward for participating, like taking them out for a special treat after a long day of decluttering. You could even plan a vacation as a reward for your entire family when the entire house has been decluttered. During your decluttering sessions, play upbeat, fun music that will boost everyone's mood and make it a fun time instead of a boring one.

Another trick you might want to use, especially while working with your kids to get rid of their toys, is to focus on what they want to keep instead of what they want to get rid of. Have them put the things they want to keep in a pile, then simply get rid of the rest without making it a big deal. Keep their mind on the positive side of minimizing, and as much as possible, avoid focusing on the things they're losing.

Teach them to think about others

As your kids go through their things, have them consider what they might be able to give away to another kid who needs toys. Let them know that there are kids in their own neighborhoods and towns who don't have any toys to play with. Then, when you get ready to get rid of the toys for good, research where you can take them, so they'll be given to kids who need them and take your kids with you to drop them off. Being able to see where their toys are going and know that their small sacrifice will help someone else is a great way to motivate your kids, as well as teach them to help other people.

Let them choose

As much as possible, let your kids choose what they want to keep, as long as it's within the guidelines you've set in place (more about that in the next chapter). Allowing your kids to make their own choices about what they want to keep will not only earn brownie points for you but will give them a sense of ownership in the process and responsibility for their belongings.

Getting your family on board with minimizing can be difficult, especially when you have kids. It's hard to convince someone to part with their beloved possessions, but if you're prepared to answer their questions, compromise when possible, and find fun ways to motivate them, it'll be a much smoother transition. Part of your preparation should include setting guidelines for the belongings your family chooses to keep, as well as for how your family will treat those belongings, all of which we'll talk about in the next chapter.

CHAPTER 3
Factors To Consider

It's pretty easy (and can even be fun, once you get in the groove of things) to do the physical work of decluttering your house. What's hard is keeping it decluttered once it's all gone and you start to return to a normal routine. School work starts piling in "we might need this someday" folders again, toys start finding their way home via well-meaning grandparents, and various odds and ends seem to slip through the cracks in your front door. In a shopping bag. That you're carrying (but you needed it!).

Coming up with guidelines for your family is probably the most boring part of this whole process, but it's also one of the most important things you can do to make sure that the clutter stays gone. The first and most important guideline you can set for your family is that of gratitude.

Be thankful for what you have

If you choose to have a list of your guidelines out for your entire family to see on a daily basis (which you should do, by the way), the very first one on that list should be this one. I don't know about you, but I have a preschooler who has gotten in a phase where he can be very ungrateful for what he has. My parents bought him a toy one day, and the next day, he tells me that toy's old and he needs a new one. Despite it being somewhat cute in his three-year-old little boy voice, it's also infuriating (As are most things with a stubborn three-year-old, I'm finding—cute but infuriating.).

You wouldn't know it at that moment, but he's actually very good at saying thank you when people do something for him, though. But that's another story.

My point is: I never in a thousand years would have consciously taught my child that kind of behavior. Perhaps I did it in my own behavior sometimes, but I think it's also just a natural inclination we all have. We want to be better, have more, and do cooler things and that drive isn't always a bad thing. It's also what helps us become better people and do better things with our lives.

Left unchecked, though, it can also lead to entitlement, discontentment, and clutter.

So, it's important to teach our kids to be grateful for what they do have so that they're less likely to want to keep getting more and more. One way to start teaching your kids to be thankful is to share your gratitude with each other every day. Whether it's in the morning, at dinner, at bedtime, or some other time, go around to everyone in your family and have them tell one or two things they're thankful for. The trick is that it can't be something generic (my family, my house, my toys, etc.). It has to be specific, and they have to say why they're thankful for it. And of course, this isn't just for your kids. You and your partner should participate, too! We adults can become just as ungrateful and discontent as our kids can, and we need to train ourselves to focus on what we do have as well.

Another way to do this is to change your "I want..." statements to "I have...". Anytime you find yourself, your partner, or your kids saying, "I want...", stop them and have them rephrase it to say, "I have...". If you hear your kid say they want a new toy, have them say something they already have. Or if you hear yourself say, "I want this beautiful new coat," stop yourself and remember the coat you already have. It probably works just as well as it did last year when you were just as excited about it as you are now about this new coat.

Follow the Rule of Replacement
It might not always be possible, but as often as you can, follow the guideline of "one comes in, one goes out." When you're able to remove something from your house every time something else comes in, it's easy to see how this guideline helps keep clutter from piling up again.

Of course, you probably won't be able to do this with everything. You might need two of something for a particular reason. However, you should try to do it as much as possible. For example, you can use this guideline with your kids. Every time they ask for a new toy, have them think about what toy they already have that they would be willing to get rid of to make room for the new one. Doing this will kill two birds with one stone, so to speak. It will help control the clutter that accumulates, and it will also help your kids learn to make wise choices about their belongings. It might turn out that they don't really want that new toy after all.

This also works well for small items, like hair or beauty products. Every time you buy a new set of makeup, throw your old one out. Don't keep both just because your old one has a tiny bit of your favorite color left.

It can be used for your calendar, too. If you or a family member wants to add something to the calendar (an event, a sport, etc.), make that person choose something to get rid of. Of course, their choice should be something that affects them. If your son wants to start playing baseball, he can't choose to get rid of his sister's soccer from the calendar. That wouldn't make any sense. He has to choose something that affects him, like not playing football or swimming with his friends every week. You can't add more hours to the day or days to the week, so instead of piling your calendar full of stuff and finding yourself running around like a chicken with its head cut off and never having time to just be with your family, stick the "one comes in, one goes out" rule with your calendar as much as possible.

Use it or lose it
If it's not being used and it's not adding beauty and meaning to your life, it has no place in your home. Once a month (week, season, whatever works best for your family), take time to evaluate what's being used and what's been sitting on the shelf for a while. If it isn't being used, find a way to get rid of it. Again, giving your unused belongings away is a great way to teach your kids about helping others and being grateful.

For example, as you bring out clothes for a new season, go through them. If you didn't wear it the year before, it's probably safe to get rid of it. So, do. Wield those decluttering shears often and with enthusiasm!

A place for everything and everything in its place

I'm a smidge OCD about this, and I know my husband hates that about me. But honestly, it's how I stopped losing all of my belongings and started actually knowing where everything is (most of the time). It's also a good guideline for maintaining a minimalist lifestyle. If you don't have space for it, it's hard to keep. So, don't try. If you don't have space for it, you probably don't have a need for it.

This guideline can also be used to manage the number of toys your kids have. Designate a space for each child's toys. Anything that fits in that space and doesn't require the owner to solve a jigsaw puzzle every time they need to close the lid (drawer, etc.) can stay. Anything else has to go. That way, he can keep practically anything he wants to keep, as long as it fits within his designated space.

Items used must also be put away

Clean up time! My three-year-old hates it. But if I don't make him do it, his toys litter the floor and create tripping hazards for anyone in the house. It's actually dangerous. My husband also hates this one. Just ask him.

But it's important! And you're not a nag for insisting on it. Well, I guess you can become one, and that's not good either. Again, our goal here is to create fewer sources of conflict, not more. But families do have rules and one of them should be that, at the end of the day, anything that was taken out during the day has to be put away. Everyone is responsible for their own belongings, another time to cultivate that sense of responsibility in your kids.

There are ways to make it a little more fun, though. Make it part of the getting-ready-for-bed routine, a fun family game with a small prize at the end if you have to. One game could be for everyone to gather their own items and race to see who finishes first. The first person to finish receives the small prize (5 minutes extra to stay up, for example). Another game could be to have everyone gather someone else's items. Whoever gathers the most items wins and receives the prize.

Finish what you start

The final guideline I would suggest (though you may come up with different ones for your family) is that any project that gets started must be finished. This is the guideline that points directly at me. I'm horrible about starting a project and then quitting in the middle. I get distracted by a shinier project (I'm ADHD, forgive me!). I run out of time. Whatever the reason is, I almost never finish the projects I start out to complete.

Most of the time, this happens because I start a project off with far too much energy and enthusiasm. My eyes were greedier than they needed to be, and I just got tired, and the project fell to the wayside. Be realistic from the start about how long a project will take and how hard it's going to be. If you go into something expecting that it's going to be hard, you'll be much better prepared mentally, and you'll be able to prepare yourself physically as well by getting a good night's sleep the night before, taking breaks, eating well, etc.

When you're planning to take on a large project (like decluttering your entire house for the first time), it's important to break the project down into manageable chunks. Start small with a single room or even a single closet in that room. This is hard for me because I'm kind of an "all or nothing" kind of person, but that doesn't usually work out, even for me. There's no way I can declutter my entire house in one day, and I'm willing to bet you won't be able to either.

So, start off small. Even if you build to taking on larger tasks as you go, starting small will ensure that you get your projects finished. Finishing projects feels really great, and as you finish more and more, your momentum and motivation to finish will grow as well, allowing you to take on those bigger projects.

Take some time to decide on the guidelines you want to have for your family and introduce them to your family meeting. Keep in mind that your family members might not be so enthusiastic at first, so be patient and willing to compromise if you have to. Also keep in mind, though, that these guidelines are essential to maintaining a minimalist lifestyle and keeping your house decluttered. Compromise where you must, but don't be too willing to bend.

CHAPTER 4
Things That Clutter

I'm sure you've noticed this phenomenon in your own home, so I don't really need to remind you. But in case you haven't noticed, clutter is annoying. It piles up in your home, making it look disorganized and full of junk. Sometimes my house looks like I'm a toy hoarder. It piles up on your calendar, leaving you hurried, harried, and exhausted. And it piles up in your relationships, infringing on your boundaries and leading you to deal with people you have no business dealing with.

Clutter is so annoying because it piles up and steals away your time, energy, and money. Instead of being able to spend it on the things that actually matter to you, you're forced to spend it on all of the tiny little things that constantly add up.

The tricky part about clutter, though, is that we often become so used to it that we don't even realize it's there. It just piles up quietly until one day, you're looking around your house and wondering where in the world it all came from. Then we get the decluttering bug, which might help tone the clutter down for a moment. But for the most part, accumulating clutter is second nature to us and happens almost subconsciously.

When we think about clutter, we usually think about physical clutter, the little odds, and ends that pile up throughout our houses. However, clutter can accumulate in other areas of your life as well.

Clutter on your calendar

Aside from physical clutter, one of the more vexing types of clutter is the clutter that piles up on your calendar. You bite off more than you can chew for your job. You have meetings scheduled through the next 20 years, it seems. Your daughter is in both drama and choir, both of which have performances on the same weekend. Your son is also in choir, but he can't make it to this weekend's performance because he's traveling with the baseball team. He's also on the basketball team. And maybe even in the band. Your partner's job requires him to work odd hours, so you're always trying to coordinate schedules with him. And you have this friend who constantly wants to call and talk for three or four hours at a time.

It's all too easy for your calendar to become cluttered. As your kids grow older, you want them to be involved in things at their school. It's part of the high-school experience, right? But when you add all of that to your already full calendar of work, friends, and other familial obligations, you'll quickly end up with very little time to spend on things that really matter to you.

Clutter in your mind

You might not think about it much, but your mind can become just as cluttered as your house. If you've ever felt like your brain might be turning to mush inside your head, then you've felt the mental exhaustion that comes with having too much clutter floating around in your mind. In some ways, we can't help this. Our minds are constantly working, telling our body what it needs to do, reminding us not to do things that could get us killed, and otherwise performing tasks that are necessary for daily survival.

That's already a lot of stuff, and it never stops, not even when you're asleep. But then you add onto that all of the extras we pour into our minds, and they can quickly become a constant whirlwind of activity. Mental clutter is distracting, keeping us from being able to focus on things that are important to us. And, when we're unable to focus, we're more likely to be thoughtless and hasty in our decisions, leading us to make poor choices that could affect our relationships, our time, our careers, our energy, and other areas of our lives.

Clutter in your relationships

Have you ever kept up a relationship purely out of a sense of duty or obligation? It's that person who is constantly needy, calling you at all hours of the day, sucking up your time and energy for their own needs. Or it's that person who's constantly negative and critical and who makes it difficult for you to be positive when you're around them.

When my husband and I were dating, he had a friendship like this. The guy was a strange person. He was constantly negative and extremely needy. I sometimes felt like my husband had two girlfriends. And one (not me) was a very bad girlfriend! He also hated me because he thought I was a bad influence on my future husband (not true, by the way!). My husband continued being friends with him because he felt bad that this guy didn't have many other friends. Meanwhile, his real girlfriend (me) felt uncomfortable and even felt slightly ignored in favor of the friend. Eventually, my husband did stop allowing his friend to take my place, they drifted apart, and our relationship was better for it.

In trying to be a nice guy, my husband continued a relationship that threatened to harm other relationships that were important to him. It's incredibly easy to do. Once you have a relationship with someone, it's difficult to end it. No one wants to be the person who stops being friends with someone. It's even more difficult when the toxic relationship is with a family member like a parent, a sibling, or even a grown child. However, relationships that do nothing but take up your time and energy and harm the other relationships in your life should be let go, regardless of how hard it is. Perhaps you can keep the door open to renewing the relationship in the future (in the case of close family relationships), but it might be that you need to take a good, long break from them in order to declutter your life of the relationships that are causing you harm.

Clutter in your house

Physical clutter is easily the most visible type of clutter you can have, and interestingly, it's often a sign of how much clutter you have in the other areas of your life. A cluttered house can contribute to a cluttered mind. It can also be a sign of a cluttered calendar and relationships that need to be let go because both will eat up the time you could be spending managing the clutter in your house.

Clutter in your house is all of the stuff that piles up throughout the years, most of which you use once or twice then put away in the garage, never to be used again. It's the clothes you keep because you'll fit into it again, "one day." It's the multiple layers of kids' artwork that covers your refrigerator because each one is precious, and you can't find it in your heart to throw it away. It's the equipment for the sport your child no longer wants to play.

Physical clutter is absolutely the most visible, but it's also probably the easiest to manage, and it can be a first step in learning how to minimize the clutter in all of the other areas of your life.

Decision Fatigue

One of the most damaging results of physical clutter is something called decision fatigue, and it's a type of mental clutter that's directly related to the physical clutter you choose to keep. Decision fatigue is something that happens when you give yourself too many options. For example, when you have a closet full of clothing options, it can actually take you longer to choose something to wear than if your closet only contained the essentials.

Studies have also shown that decision fatigue has an especially damaging effect on kids. It puts their minds on mental overload and leads to all kinds of bad behavior. Having too many options for clothes, food, and yes, even toys, is damaging for kids, so decluttering your home and learning to live a minimalist lifestyle will have huge benefits for your kids, as well as for you.

How to get started with minimalism

Living a minimalist lifestyle is a process, one that takes a lot of work and a lot of patience to start and to maintain. Like with anything, though, the only thing you can do is start with step one and keep taking one step at a time. It might take a long time and a lot of frustration (That's where the patience comes in!), but if you just get in there and get started and continue moving forward, you'll eventually get to where you want to be.

To put it as simply as possible, that first step is to pick one area of your house and just start moving things out. Make it something small: a closet or a bookshelf, maybe. Or if you're more ambitious and have more time on your hands, start with an entire room. Whatever you do, make it something manageable, something you can get done in one session.

Then just start getting rid of stuff. If possible, try to find a good home for it all, like a donation center or a Goodwill. However, if you don't have something like that available to you, don't waste your time trying to find the perfect home for it all. Throw it away or have a bonfire night. We'll talk more about the whole process in the coming chapters, but for now, keep the first step in mind: pick one small, manageable area to get yourself started and get it done in one session.

CHAPTER 5
Questions To Consider

Ok, so clutter is annoying. We agree on that. If you're still reading this book, I assume you are at least intrigued by the idea of minimalism and are curious to see how this whole idea could play out in your own family. You may have even started thinking about the guidelines you want to set for your family and planning the meeting you'll have to get them on board.

That's all well and good, and you're at a great place to get this whole thing going. But how do you actually go about clearing out the overflow of useless stuff piling up in your home? How do you decide what things you want to keep and what you could get rid of? What do you do with the stuff you decide to toss? These are all great questions, and I'm so glad you asked them! We'll be taking a look at all of that in the next several chapters. In this chapter, we'll look at the overall strategies you can use to declutter your home, and in the following chapters, we'll walk through each room in your home, considering the things that probably should stay and the opportunities for minimizing the clutter.

Learning to ask the right questions

One of the first things you'll have to learn in order to start on the journey to minimalism is how to ask the right questions. If you haven't done it already, you should seriously stop reading right now and take a few minutes to consider your reasons for doing this, as well as the purpose you want your family and your home to have. Both of these will inform your answer to pretty much every question you go through in this process, so it's definitely to your advantage to be extremely clear on them.

What questions should you ask?

Remember the first step in the decluttering process? Pick one spot and get it done in one session. Great. Except where do you get started? How do you decide what you should keep in that one spot? Well, you ask a bunch of questions. As you stare at your overflowing closet, catch-all room, or bookshelf, have a list of questions scrolling through your mind. Start pulling things out until it's completely empty, then go through each individual item and seriously consider your answers for that item:

What purpose does this item have?

Everything in your minimalist home should have a specific purpose. There can be little decorations and things to improve the aesthetics of your home, but for the most part, there should be a practical purpose for everything.

Am I currently using it, or will it be used in the coming months?

If you have a future purpose for it, make sure that it will actually be used for a specific purpose. For example, don't keep your too-small clothes because you think you'll be able to fit in them again. By the time that happens, you'll likely want new clothes! A new wardrobe is a great reward for getting to your goal weight, so don't keep a bunch of old stuff that just adds to the clutter! On the other hand, if you're decluttering your garage in the winter and come to your son's baseball gear, certainly don't get rid of all of that! If you plan on registering him for baseball again in the spring, he'll definitely use it again. Perhaps you can get rid of a few of the baseballs or the extra bats and gloves you have lying around that are too small for him. But if it's the right size and he wants to play again, by all means, it should be kept!

Do I have more than one?
No one needs ten empty notebooks (I'm pointing at myself on this one.). Obviously, you should have more than one shirt and pair of pants. However, there are a lot of things in our homes that we could get by with only one. For example, keep only one pair of each type of shoe you need—work, sandals, boots, etc.—instead of accumulating several pairs of each. Or, who needs twenty different wrapping paper designs? Keep one roll for Christmas (maybe two) and one or two for birthdays/generic gifts. If you're minimalists, though, you might not have too many gifts to wrap in the first place, since you'll want to keep your kids' toys to a minimum as well!

Does it simplify my life or complicate it?
My husband is a technology guru. He loves it! And I love it, too! In fact, I'm writing this book on my beautiful MacBook that makes me incredibly happy every time I open it. I know that's goofy and a little materialistic (a lot materialistic), but that's the way it is! Anyway, my husband, though, is kind of obsessed with finding new and unique ways to store and watch our movies. It's great because he's getting a lot of our movies where we can watch without relying on the internet. However, it can also make things quite complicated when it doesn't work the way it's supposed to. One of the questions you should ask yourself about each item is, "Does this make my life easier or more complicated?" Hopefully, when we get it set up correctly, the movie stuff will make life simpler. But for now, it definitely makes it more complicated. If something in your home makes your life more complicated, it might be better just to throw it out.

What do I really need during this period of my life?
This is kind of similar to the second question about if something is being used or not. Again, don't keep your too-small clothes just because you plan to fit into them again someday. Another example would be keeping a curling iron after chopping all of your hair off. Nobody with a pixie cut needs a curling iron, so if you have a haircut like that, throw out the curling iron (Pro tip: no one really needs a curling iron at all. A thinner (1" or so) flat iron can actually curl hair beautifully!)!

Could I borrow it?
If you use a particular item, but only on very rare occasions, is it possible that you could borrow it from someone else who has that item? For example, if you almost never use your kitchen aid, but you have a friend who has one, could you find a new home for yours and borrow your friend's on the rare occasions you want to use it?

Do I want to leave this for my family?

This question could be interpreted in one of two ways. On items that are more sentimental in value, you should consider if it's something you would want to pass down to your kids or their kids someday when you're gone. Things like family heirlooms or particularly special clothes or blankets might mean something to your family members after you pass away. On the flip side of this question, one of the less romantic aspects of leaving things for your family is that when you pass away, someone is going to have to figure out what to do with everything you own. When my grandfather passed away, bless his heart, it was a job to clear out his and my grandmother's home because they had accumulated so much stuff! So, as you consider each item, you might also think about your kids: is it important enough to keep that if you passed away suddenly, you wouldn't mind that your family had to clean it up. Morbid, I know. Forgive me. But it's kind of a good thing to consider, too. No one wants to leave a mess behind for their grieving family to deal with.

Strategies for the cleanup

There are several methods you can use to organize your decluttering sessions, so in this section, I'll go through some of them so you'll be able to choose which will work best for you! But first, you should decide what kind of cleaner you are. Some of us, myself included, will be all-or-nothing kind of people. We want to get it all done as quickly as we can. If you're one of us, you might want to set aside a Saturday or even a whole weekend to devote to decluttering your entire house in one fell swoop. It can be incredibly tiring, but at the end of the day (or weekend), I find that it's also incredibly satisfying. Everything's done, and I can move on with my life and with making sure that it doesn't get so cluttered again! Doing it this way does have its challenges. First of all, setting aside the time to get it all done might be next to impossible if your family is very busy. Second, if you're not able to get it all done in the time you set aside, you might lose the momentum you had and never find the time or motivation to finish the job.

You might prefer to take a more slow-and-steady approach. You can tackle a small area every day or every few days until eventually, you have a decluttered house. Because each task only takes an hour or two, it'll be relatively easy to find the time. The challenge here, of course, is that your recently decluttered areas don't become re-cluttered before you're able to declutter the rest of the house. I also find that it's not quite as motivating. But that's just me.

Whatever type of cleaner you decide you are, one of these methods will likely be right up your alley.

The Minimalist Challenge

This method is great for those of you who aren't quite sure you want to jump all in. It starts you off at a slower pace, but as your momentum increases with each project completed, so does the pace. It makes getting started simple and relatively effortless.

It works like this: on the first day of a given month, choose one thing in your house to get rid of. On the second day, choose two things. On the third day, choose three things. And you get the point. It might sound agonizingly slow, but by the time the 30th day of the month rolls around, you will have gotten 496 items out of your house. That's no small number!

The trick with this challenge is to stay consistent. Don't miss a day because you'll end up behind and off schedule, which could make it hard for you to finish the challenge. Also, you don't have to start on the first day of the month, but it'll be easier to keep track of the days if you do. I wouldn't sacrifice the motivation you're feeling right now, though, in order to start at the beginning of a month, especially if you're only a week or so into a new month.

The Packing Party

This one sounds kind of fun to me, though I've never tried it, and it might sound absolutely crazy to you. However, it's a straightforward and low-risk way to get started because you actually won't be getting rid of anything right away. You do the decluttering first and worry about finding new homes for everything later. It also gives you a ton of free space instantly! Super cool.

The Packing Party is just what it sounds like: you start by packing up everything you own—except maybe the essential furniture like beds, your couch, and your dining room table and chairs. Label everything clearly so you would know what's in each box, and over the next few weeks, unpack only the things you need. As you go through the weeks, you'll find that you spend a lot less time going to your boxes because the things you use are already unpacked. Everything else is basically useless. Do this for about a month, then decide what you want to do with all of the things that are still in the boxes. Some of it might still be worth keeping, even if it stayed in the box for the entire month. For example, seasonal things like sports gear and Christmas lights could be kept, though you might want to minimize the amount of gear or lights you own. However, if you're able to leave most of the boxes unpacked, all the better! It'll be so much easier just to put the boxes in your car and drive them to a donation center!

The 12x12x12 Method

This method is great if you have an hour or two here or there to spend decluttering. It might not get your entire house decluttered very quickly, but if you spend a few hours doing this a couple of times a week, you'll chip away at all of the clutter until it's eventually clear.

During each cleaning session, you'll choose a total of thirty-six items in your house and sort them into three categories: things to put away, things to give away, and things to throw away.

In the "things to put away" category, you'll choose twelve items that you use on a regular basis. Once all thirty-six items are divided into their categories, these items have to be given a logical home. If you need to put it away because it's only used during a particular season, label the box clearly so it's easy to find later. Organize these items as you put them back, and when you get through every area of your house with this method, you'll not only have a decluttered house but an organized one as well.

The 4-(or-5)-Box Method

This method makes taking on one section of your house (a closet, a chest of drawers, etc.) quick and easy. All you do is get four or five boxes and label them: Give Away, Put Away/Keep, Throw Away, Not Sure, and (optionally) Sell. Then, set your boxes up next to whatever junk collector you plan to tackle and start going through each item. Quickly decide where each item belongs and toss it in the appropriate box. Rinse and repeat until the entire space is cleared, even of the items, you plan to keep. You'll replace those items later.

Once space is clear, choose a box and deal with it. It might be helpful for you to start with the easiest box to deal with first and move on to the harder ones as you go. Or, you might want to get the harder ones done and out of the way first. Whichever way works for you. You might also choose to simply put your Give Away box out of sight until you have several boxes and can make a trip to your local donation center. The same could be true of your Sell box. My only caution with putting these boxes away instead of dealing with them immediately is that you be careful not to forget to actually deal with them once you have a decent number of items to give away or sell. Otherwise, you're simply moving the clutter around. It's still good because it's out of the way and out of sight, but it's still there, so make sure to actually do something with all of it.

All of these strategies are great ways to get your momentum going and to make the decluttering process a little simpler. If none of these sounds useful to you, do some research to find a method that might work better. Or, simply do it your own way! However you choose to do it, just get in there and get it done!

CHAPTER 6
Important Places And Items

For me, one of the most important places to declutter is my bedroom because it's the place I go to relax on my own. When it's cluttered and messy, I can get extremely grumpy about it. And bless my husband's heart, he does not know how to put his own stuff away. So, I can be grumpy a lot.

I might be wrong for getting grumpy about it with my husband, but I'm not wrong in thinking that a decluttered bedroom is important. We've all known for pretty much as long as we've been around that sleep is not only important but necessary for life to be sustained. If we go without it for long, our very sanity starts to dissolve, and we could even die from exhaustion. Obviously, that's a bit dramatic for this discussion. The vast majority of us will never come close to being this exhausted. But if I have to go just a couple of nights without good rest, I can be extremely grumpy, and I struggle to think straight. I'm sure anyone reading this book has felt that kind of exhaustion.

Getting adequate rest is essential to maintaining the positive energy you'll need to make it through the decluttering process. By decluttering your bedroom first, you'll create a place of calm and relaxation in the midst of the chaos that'll help you get the rest you need. And declutter your own bedroom first! You might be tempted to do otherwise, but if you declutter your own bedroom first, you'll make sure you have the energy and motivation to help them declutter theirs. Not to mention, seeing you in your newly decluttered space is likely to make the transition smoother for your kids. They can see how clean and calm your room looks and how much you enjoy it, and it'll make it less scary for them to make the transition.

The first thing you need to consider when starting to declutter any space in your house is what the purpose of that space is. Go back to Chapter 2 and think about the purpose you've set out for your home and for each room inside. For many of us, our bedroom is where we relax and share alone time and intimacy with our partner. It may also serve as an office or a craft room. If that's the case, make sure that your secondary space is kept neat and decluttered as well and that there's some kind of visual barrier that helps divide the room. If at all possible, though, try to give your bedroom a single purpose.

Once you've determined the purpose you want your bedrooms to serve, you can set about getting rid of anything that doesn't serve that purpose. Should you have a TV in the bedroom? Probably not, since there have been many times I've found myself going to sleep way too late because I got caught up in a TV series, and I'm sure you've done the same thing. Should you keep the laundry basket right across from the bed? Not if it reminds you of all of the chores you still have to do. If your bedroom's purpose is to serve as a place of rest and connection with your partner, everything that distracts from that purpose has to go.

Then get started! Choose one of the methods we talked about in the last chapter and get to it. If you want to try the Packing Party, go to the store and grab some boxes, tape, and a marker (If you don't have these things already—don't add another Sharpie to your collection just because you can't think of where they might be! We're decluttering, here, not re-cluttering!). And get to packing. Put everything in a box except the absolute essentials, like your bed frame and the linens on your mattress. When you're done, put the date on the box, as well as a note about what's inside and put them to the side, preferably out of your bedroom, but somewhere you can see them every day. Enjoy your fully decluttered bedroom, and only unpack things you absolutely need. After a few weeks, revisit the boxes to see if there's anything in them that you missed, then decide what to do with the rest.

That method sounds particularly fun to me, but if you think that's just too much, pick another method! However, you choose to get it done, just make sure that you completely declutter the room so that you can enjoy a calm, relaxing oasis while you tackle the rest of the house!

Decluttering the Furniture

How many pieces of furniture do you have in your bedroom right now? Personally, my bedroom is tiny, and I have 7 pieces of furniture crammed in that space. Like I said, never beat yourself up too harshly if you come to a season where minimalism just isn't possible. I'm writing a book about minimalism, and even I have had to accept the season I'm in right now.

However, the more furniture you keep in your bedroom, the more surfaces there are to catch clutter. So, take as much furniture out as you can. If you have to keep a dresser in your room to store clothes, make sure you keep the top clear of clutter. But if at all possible, store all of your clothes in your closet or put your dresser inside the closet. It may not be this way now, but there was a time in my family's life when my husband and I had four simple pieces of furniture in our bedroom: a bed (obviously), two wall shelves, and a simple, clean-cut desk. A note about those wall shelves: The wall shelves actually serve as our bedside tables. Instead of keeping regular bedside tables there, with their extra clutter-accumulating shelves and drawers, we opted for a single surface on which to place only the essentials.

Decorations

Decorations are great. Believe me, I'm a decoration kind of girl! However, there's a balance between carefully placing just enough decorations to be tasteful and throwing so many decorations on your walls and surfaces that your room looks more cluttered. I know it's a hard concept to grasp, but white space is actually a good thing.

When deciding how many decorations to keep and where to put them, remember that less is more. Instead of covering a dresser or bookshelf with photos and trinkets, choose only one or two high-quality photos or decorations. Again, remember the purpose of your bedroom and choose your decorations accordingly.

Clothing and Linens

The thought of going through all of your clothes and linens might make you more stressed out and overwhelmed than the clutter itself. However, it can also be one of the most freeing parts of the whole decluttering process. Too many clothes only lead to continued decision fatigue (Chapter 4), so read this section, plan out how you want to do it, and get going. Trust me; you'll be glad you did.

- Quality over quantity
  - Owning a week's worth of the best clothes you can find (the ones that fit you best, that are made out of the best material, etc.) is so much better than owning a month's worth of mediocre clothes that don't fit you right and are cheaply made. It's ok to wear the same things from week to week. It's simpler, it's faster, and it's just plain easier than having to choose from a vast selection. Not to mention, if you only choose the clothes that look the absolute best on you, you'll always look amazing.
- Plan a capsule wardrobe
  - If you haven't heard of it before, a capsule wardrobe is an amazing thing for families who are trying to live minimalist lives. Essentially, it's a wardrobe that consists of only the...essentials, typically no more than 40 items total, including everything from winter to summer clothes, accessories, and pairs of shoes. The beauty of a capsule wardrobe is that each piece of clothing you own is high quality and is interchangeable with other pieces to create a variable wardrobe with only a few pieces. For example, a pair of jeans can be dressed up with a black blouse and a pair of black flats or dressed down with a t-shirt and a pair of tennis shoes. If you can fill your wardrobe with interchangeable pieces like this, your wardrobe will be small but efficient, which is exactly what it should be if you want a minimalist lifestyle!
- Be careful when you go shopping
  - We all know how tempting it is when you go shopping and you see a good sale. Before you go shopping, you should have a list already made out of what you need, just like you would for groceries. You should also have a good idea of what kinds of styles you like best and that work best for your lifestyle. That way, when you come across a great sale, you can evaluate if you truly need the item or not. If you don't need it, don't get it! If you do, great! You've managed to save money while still only buying the things you need.
- Don't fall for all of the trends
  - Every season, the fashion industry churns out a few trendy items that are "in fashion" that particular season. And they're usually cute and great and make you feel like you fit in. But

don't fall for it! Stick to your capsule wardrobe, full of high-quality pieces that work for you. Don't mess with it by trying to add all of the trendy items of the season. You'll end up right back where you started with a closet that's bursting at the seams.

Here's a couple of methods you could use to decide what clothes to keep and which ones should be given a new home:
1. The Last 2-Weeks
   - For this method, you'll take out everything you've worn in the last two weeks and pack up the rest. Over the next 30 days, use only the clothes you kept in the closet to see if you miss anything that had been packed away. If you didn't miss it, chunk it! Or, more responsibly, give it away.
2. The LUK Method
   - Every item in your wardrobe should adhere to the LUK rule: Do you like, use, and know each item? For example, if you have three pairs of jeans, but only one makes you feel amazing, just keep that one. If you have two pairs of tennis shoes but only use one for your daily exercise, just keep that one. And if you have five scarves but tend to forget that you even own three of them, keep only the two you remember. It's a simple method, but it gives you three easy-to-remember questions to ask of each item in your closet. If you don't like, use, or know it, toss it!

As far as linens go, I want you to first get it all out in one giant pile. Just plop it down in the living room floor and start sorting through it all, getting rid of any damaged linens or towels you come across. No one needs to keep all of those stained, hole-filled linens and towels in their home! Personally, I avoid using those like I avoid the plague, even though I know they're perfectly clean. There's just something nice about using a plush, soft, giant towel after a shower. Again, we're looking for quality over quantity, so only keep the linens and towels that are high quality (or that at least aren't just plain bad).

Once you've gotten rid of the dingy, stained, and hole-filled linens and towels, decide how many of each item you need to keep for your family. For most, having one towel per person, plus a few extra is enough. Hang the towels up after they've been used and use them for a couple of days. If something comes up and you're a day late doing laundry, start using the extra towels. Otherwise, one towel per person should be plenty. Sheets are kind of the same way, though you'll probably want an extra set of sheets for each bed, that way you don't have to get all of the sheets washed and dried before bedtime. So, keep two sets of sheets for each bed in your home. Pro tip: fold and store your sheets inside the matching pillowcase. That way, the entire set is stored together, and your linen closet is better organized.

Baby's Room

For the next little bit, we'll be going through each of the other bedrooms you could have in your home, namely, your kids' rooms. Each age group will have different needs, so we'll start with the easiest age group to declutter. It's the easiest because babies don't get much say in what goes in their rooms, nor do they actually care. Therefore, you get to make all of the decisions and don't have to fight a toy-hoarding 8-year-old every step of the way.

Furniture

Obviously, there are a few pieces of furniture that are essential to have in a baby's room, such as a crib. Some would say a diaper changing table and a comfortable chair are essential, though if money's tight, you can honestly do without both. You can't, however, do without a crib, and really, unless money is so tight you honestly can't buy the other two pieces, you'll be glad you invested in a changing table and a chair. However, other pieces of furniture like a full-sized dresser or bookshelf are completely unnecessary.

When you're deciding on a crib, try to think into the future. Do you plan to have more than one kid? If so, you could invest in a high-quality crib that will last through each of your future children's babyhood. Or you could get a crib that converts into a toddler bed if you plan only to have one child or want each of your kids to have a new crib. Either way, you plan to do it, do your homework on each potential crib to make sure it's safe and high-quality.

Gear

There are so many different kinds of baby gear out there! It's astonishing. As you start making these purchases, remember that your child will go through different stages. Purchase only the things that are necessary for each stage and donate everything they've grown out of as you go to avoid accumulating clutter. For example, a newborn doesn't need a high chair. Your baby won't really need one of those until he's ready to start eating baby food, so don't make that purchase before you really need to. Also, a toddler doesn't need a baby swing, so donate your old one! As I said, there's a lot of really cool gadgets out there that will claim to make your life easier. Don't fall into the trap! Purchase only the essentials for you and your lifestyle and forget about the rest!

Clothes

How often do you do laundry? Once a week, twice a week, every day? How often you choose to do laundry has a direct impact on how many outfits you need to have for your baby. Some minimalists recommend 3-4 outfits for a newborn, but let's be real: their newborns are either perfectly neat and never spit up, or they wash laundry at least every day, and who really has time for that? That's like being a prisoner to your laundry room! Personally, I try to wash laundry once a week, but it usually ends up being twice a week. If that's more your style too, you'll probably need at least 8 outfits, though it wouldn't be a bad idea to keep 10-14. That way, your baby has something clean to wear when he spits up all over his first outfit! Don't try to buy clothes for the future. Stick to the size your baby is currently wearing.

Books and Keepsakes

Babies and toddlers don't really need an entire library full of books. It may cause you to want to pull your hair out, but they generally like to listen to the same ones over and over again. So, keep a small library of about 8-15 books that your children really love.

As far as keepsakes go, start early by creating a space to store your baby's keepsakes, and add to it sparingly over the years. Maybe have one labeled box for each of your children's keepsakes. As they grow, you might have to add a box, but try to keep the number or keepsakes to a minimum.

Young child's room

Perhaps the most difficult age for decluttering comes during the toddler and preschooler phase, especially if they aren't already used to a minimalist lifestyle and have a lot of toys. If your preschooler is anything like mine, each of his toys is precious to him, even if he hasn't even looked at it in weeks. But try throwing it out, and he's on the floor in tears. Gracious.

However, it's also the time you can start teaching them why your family is choosing to live with less, and they can start helping you decide what belongs in their room and what can go. If you're able to get your toddler or preschooler on board, it can be fun to work with them.

As you start teaching your young child about minimalism, a few ground rules can be helpful:

- Everything needs to have a home. If you and your toddler or preschooler can't find a good home for it, it may not belong.
- Be generous. Young children might be selfish sometimes, but they can also be hugely generous and find great pleasure in giving to others. Teach your young child to be generous by helping her pick out toys to give to someone else and then taking her with you when you go to give them away.
- Family cleanup time is for everyone. Optimize your child's room so that it's easy for them to participate and help with family cleanup time. Make their toy storage easy for them to use (low to the ground, simple, etc.) and teach them how to clean up their own belongings.

Older child's room

At this age, your child is likely ready for some more independence. Let them take responsibility for the cleanup by giving them some guidelines and let them have at it. Provide support and guidance as needed, but otherwise, let them take charge. Perhaps give them a specific space where they can put as many toys as they can reasonably fit and allow them to choose which toys go in the space and which ones have to find a new home. As far as their clothes go, allow them to take part in choosing what they want to wear. At this age, style might start to become important to them as they start going to school and wanting to fit in with their friends. Within reason, let them choose what clothes they want to keep in their wardrobe, but make it a simpler wardrobe with fewer items. Keeping about 10 outfits for each child is a pretty fair amount for the average family.

Teenager's room

If your persuading your preschooler to give up his toys was hard, convincing your teenager to give up some of their clothes could be just as difficult. Teenagers thrive on individuality and often place their identity in their clothing style and other material possessions they own. Before insisting that they have to declutter their entire space, talk with them about the advantages of a minimalist lifestyle in a way that will motivate them. For example, it will give them more time to spend with their friends or financial freedom to save up for a car. If you know there's a specific goal your teenager really wants, use it to help motivate him. If they're still hesitant, try to get them to declutter a single space in their room, like their closet or their desk. The key here is just to be patient and allow them to have as much independence with the process as possible.

CHAPTER 7
Furnitures And Other Items

As you move throughout your home, the next space you may want to consider decluttering is your living areas. These spaces are likely where your family goes to spend time together, and it's probably pretty cluttered, especially if you have young kids who like to keep their toys out. That would be my kid, by the way. It's great fun.

Anyway, before you get started going through your living spaces, get yourself set up. Choose the method that works best for you so far. If it's the four-box method, get four boxes out and label them. If it's the packing party, assemble several boxes and have a marker and tape ready to go. Decide where you might want to put the boxes or where you want to donate your giveaway box. Having all of this in mind before you even start will help make sure you actually get the job done instead of putting everything in boxes, only for them to remain where you left them for weeks.

So, get your boxes out, put on some comfy clothes, and let's get to work!

Furniture

Ah, the living room. A place to sit back, kick off your shoes, and binge-watch some Netflix after a long day. Or a place to sit down with your family, pull out a favorite board game, and go at it with some friendly competition. Whatever you and your family tend to do the most in your living room, it likely revolves around the furniture in the space. Everyone has their own spot on the couch. Do you play board games on the dining room table or on the coffee table? Do you have bookshelves filled with hundreds of books?

Whatever furniture you have in your living room, if it feels at all crowded or cluttered, it's probably too much. So, what pieces do you actually need in your living spaces and which ones could probably be moved or even disposed of?

To make these decisions, you have to consider your space. How big is it? What is its shape? Where are the doorways and windows? You also have to think about the room's purpose. Go back to chapter 2 and look at the purpose you laid out for your living spaces. What pieces fit with that purpose and which ones aren't entirely necessary? How many seats do you really need at the dinner table? Enough to fit a small army? Probably not. Enough to fit your family and maybe a couple of guests? That's more like it.

As you go throughout the room, ask yourself questions about each piece of furniture that's already in the room: is it necessary? Does anyone actually use it? Could a smaller piece serve the same purpose as a larger one? Does it look right/fit well in the space?

Bookshelves

I love books. I'm a reader and a writer, and I just love them. I own hundreds of books. But I only have a single shelf for my books. Strange? Impossible?

Not really. I went digital. My husband and I both have Kindles, where 95% of our books are stored. Only the really important ones are kept in paperback. Hence, only one shelf for hundreds of books. It's great.

In the past, bookshelves have been a necessity to store books, CDs, DVDs, etc. However, with the advent of the digital age, we now have the option of storing such items on computers and tiny little boxes that attach to our televisions like Apple TV, Fire TV, Roku, etc. Kindles, Nooks, and Kobo e-readers can hold hundreds upon hundreds of books on a device that easily fits in the palm of your hand. Movies can be stored and watched on apps such as VUDU and iTunes Movies. Walls lined with bookshelves have become a thing of the past, so take advantage of it! Start building your digital libraries instead of continuing to hold onto your physical ones and get rid of those shelves!

Decorations

Here's a new concept for many of us: not every space has to be filled! In fact, there's something relaxing about white space. It looks clean, fresh, and calm. As you go through your living spaces, I'd actually recommend that you start your new minimalist lifestyle without any decorations at all. Give yourself time to feel and enjoy the empty spaces and clear surfaces. Then you can add a few pieces here and there that really add beauty to the room, instead of just adding clutter.

Coffee Tables

Do you really use your coffee table to hold a cup of coffee? Better yet, does a cup of coffee need a space as large as a coffee table? If your answer to these questions is no, you will probably do well to find a smaller solution to your drink-holding needs. A small end table between two chairs or at the end of the couch could serve you well.

Electronics

I believe I told you about my husband's obsession with electronics? It's especially bad with the TV in the living room. There are wires going everywhere; he's always taking cords or the Apple TV and moving them to another part of the house. It drives me batty.

Besides driving me batty, the television situation also contributes to a lot of our family's struggles. Our young son has gotten addicted to watching TV, something we woefully regret allowing to happen. My husband and I get into fights over where the HDMI cord is to the Apple TV or why he spends so much time trying to put all of our movies on this server thing (Sorry, I'm not an expert in electronics, you guys.). I find myself binging far too often on Netflix shows. I try to tell myself it's just for the noise. Except then I get sucked into the show, and all of my productivity goes out the door! It's a problem.

If you're anything like my family, you probably have many of the same issues. Your husband or wife may not spend too much time putting movies on a server, but it could be watching sports instead of playing with the kids, binging on a favorite show instead of getting the laundry done. Whatever issues your family faces when it comes to electronics, it could be easily fixed by simply getting rid of it. Believe it or not, television is not a necessity. It's hard for me to believe it too sometimes. But it's not.

If you're really dedicated to this idea of minimalism and to spending more time with your family, I highly recommend getting rid of the TV. Whether you chuck it out altogether or put it away for a time, having no TV can be incredibly beneficial to everyone in the household.

Even if you decide that going radical and chunking out the TV isn't for you and your family, you could likely pare down your electronics quite a bit. Does everyone in the house need an iPhone, an iPad, and Kindle? Probably not. Limit your kids to one device each (depending on their age). Designate an area in the living space as a charging station, where devices should be kept unless they're being used. Place time limits on device usage and hold to them strictly. No child needs to be glued to a device for hours upon end. As a mom dealing with this with my own kid, believe me, you want to set limits!

Sentimental items

It can be really, really difficult to say goodbye to an item that holds sentimental value. They hold fond memories for us and make us feel safe and comforted. They help us remember family members and loved ones who have passed away and left something special for us to keep. Many times, getting rid of such items can feel a bit like chopping your own hand off: painful, unnecessary, and just plain horrible. However, there are a few things you should keep in mind:

The value isn't in the item itself. It's in the memories and character of the person the item reminds you of. You don't need a specific item in order to honor and remember a loved one. That person is forever in your heart and mind.

Life isn't about living in the past. It's about being present in the moment and looking toward the future. Holding onto sentimental items that only add to the clutter and disorganization of your home means that you're holding onto the past too tightly. It's good to remember what has happened and the people you've loved in the past, but it's unhealthy to hold on too tightly.

You could take photos of sentimental items and keep them in a photo book. If you don't need the item, you just don't need it. That doesn't mean you want to forget about it, though. Hold onto it by taking a photo of it instead of keeping it in your house to add to the clutter.

Keep a single box for really important things. Sometimes you just can't let go of something, and that's ok. Either find a truly useful way to use it in your home or put it in a single box where you house all of your keepsakes that are too important to lose. Just be very selective about what goes in the box and keep it to a minimum.

Special spaces for the kids

In many homes, toys kid's belongings tend to start trickling out into areas they don't belong. My three-year-old has toys in every conceivable corner of our house. As you start decluttering your house and reorganizing it for maximum efficiency, you may consider setting aside a specific area of your home for your kids' toys and activities. I'm as big a fan of independent play as any busy mom, and it can be useful to have a stimulating, fun area for your children to play in that doesn't creep out into the entire home.

If you decide you want to create a space for your children to play, be sure to consider the design of the area carefully. Instead of going at it with all kinds of closed-ended toys, invest in good, educational, and open-ended social options like dolls, crayons, play dough, and puzzles. A chalkboard wall is a great option, especially for younger kids. It gives them a chance to write on the wall with immunity, and what child doesn't want to do that?

You should choose items that promote sharing and teamwork. Encourage your kids to share with each other and work together to solve puzzles or play games.

You should choose items that promote creativity. Create an art table, where all of their art supplies (at least the ones that can't really cause a lot of damage if left unsupervised) are easily accessible. Keep only a few toys in the space, so they have to be creative and innovative with their play.

Finally, as with any area of your home, you should consider your purpose for the area and for your kids. Is it for them to be independent, creative, and willing to share? Then your space should reflect that purpose, and everything that goes into it should do the same.

A special note here: if one of your goals is for your children to be independent and responsible, make sure that everything in the space is both accessible to them and safe for them to use without constant supervision. If you have young children, this space might be in the living room, where they can still be supervised while playing independently. However, if you have older kids, they might appreciate a little more privacy and independence, so set up their space in their bedroom if you feel comfortable.

Again, however, you choose to do this, it's important for children to have space for their imagination and independence to grow along with them—without infringing upon everyone else's space and your sanity!

CHAPTER 8
Confessions And Steps

Quick confession: I hate cooking. Well, hate might be a strong word. It's more like I hate planning meals for the week and grocery shopping, both of which have to happen in order to cook. Once both of those things have happened and I have everything neatly laid out and ready to go, I actually enjoy cooking, especially when I'm alone in the kitchen with a glass of wine and my favorite TV show playing on my iPad. But let's be real: I have a three-year-old and a newborn. That never happens.

Instead, there's usually a little boy clinging to my leg or opening all of the cabinets behind me. Or a baby is crying because he dropped his pacifier. Or a husband is trying to tell me something about his day. It's often loud and chaotic and not exactly relaxing.

But it's also a great place for my family to hang out and spend time together. As long as the dangerous items are out of reach, it's a relatively safe place for my three-year-old to play while I'm watching. He likes to "help" me cook, which usually only makes a huge mess but is super cute and sweet. My husband likes to sit at the table while I cook, talking to me about something interesting that happened that day or working on a project he has going. So as hectic and crazy as it can get, I do enjoy the kitchen, even if I don't often get to cook in my perfect set of conditions.

I imagine that your kitchen is probably very similar. Lots of people refer to their kitchen as the heart of their home. It's often where the kids work on their homework, where families sit down to eat a meal together, and where the delicious smell is constantly inviting everyone in the home to come to enjoy the fun. It can also be an extremely stressful place, as papers pile up on the counter, the trash can starts to smell because your son forgot to take it out last night, and appetizers for the part you're hosting start burning on the stove.

You may not always be able to control how many people follow you into the kitchen (nor would you really want to). You might not always get the recipe just right or have a perfectly clean trash can. Try as you might, you just can't control other people, and sometimes your child will forget to take the trash out. However, you can control what items belong in your kitchen and where they are placed. Decluttering your kitchen could be just the solution you need to make one of your most hectic, memory-filled spaces a calm and relaxing place.

First Steps

As always, when you first get started decluttering a new space, remind yourself why you're doing this in the first place. Why do you want your home and your lifestyle to be minimalistic and simple? What is the purpose of your kitchen? After you've reminded yourself why you want to do this, it'll be so much easier to find the motivation to push through the hard work.

Next, it'll be easier to declutter your kitchen if it's clean and everything is put away. So, make sure it's in its normal, clean state (not it's normal, dirty state, mind you!). All of the dishes are clean and put away in their proper place. All of the counters are clear of papers, food, and any other items that don't belong in the kitchen. The stove, sink, and counters are wiped down, and the floors are swept and mopped.

Decide how quickly you want this done. Do you have a day to tackle it all at once? Or do you have an hour here and there to declutter one or two cabinets at a time? Whatever choice you make, just make sure that you have enough time to get it all done! There's nothing worse than pulling everything out of a cabinet and not having enough time to put what you decide to keep back.

Personally, I think it's easiest to try to do the kitchen all at once. I'm generally more apt to do things that way anyway, but with the kitchen, I think it's especially useful. If it's been a while since you've decluttered and reorganized your kitchen, you likely have similar items in different places. You might also want to move items to a different area of the kitchen. The problem with tackling one spot at a time is that if you do want to rearrange, there's not much room to do it because everywhere else in the kitchen is still filled. That's just my personal opinion, though. Feel free to do it however you want! As long as it happens, that's all that matters.

In your kitchen-decluttering adventures, try to replace items where you might actually use them. For example, keep your oven mitts close to the oven. Place your dishwashing soap under the sink, next to the dishwasher. And put your pots and pans near the stove. Just do what makes sense for you and the way you use your kitchen.

Cabinets and drawers

Now that you have your kitchen ready to go, you can get down to the real business at hand: decluttering and reorganizing your kitchen for maximum efficiency and minimum clutter. You can start at any point in the kitchen, so let's start with the cabinets and drawers. Getting started with this part of the kitchen is great, especially if you only have a few minutes at a time for the decluttering process. You can work on one cabinet or drawer at a time, getting rid of anything that isn't used often or is sometimes forgotten about. You could also choose a category that might belong inside that particular cabinet. For example, if you choose to start with the cabinet next to your stove, you could gather all of the pots and pans throughout the kitchen and arranging them neatly inside that cabinet.

This method is called decluttering by category, and it is incredibly useful for taking note of all of your duplicates. If you have multiple copies of similar items, it is easy to get rid of all but one of them. For example, if you have two or three mixing bowls of the same size, chunk two of them, and keep just one. As you go through each cabinet and drawer, you might as well take the time to wipe down each of them to make sure they're clean. After all, it's not often that you have a chance to get those cabinet shelves clean!

As with all of the space in the house, you will need to ask yourself questions about each item you consider getting rid of. Do you use the item very often? Do you own something else that could serve the very same purpose? Do you like it? Does it still work well? Again, every item in your kitchen should follow the LUK guidelines: you should like, use, and/or know each and every item you own.

There are so many items that a lot of people keep in their kitchens that are very rarely used, especially in the small appliance department. Things like ice cream makers, sandwich grills, bread machines, rice cookers, air fryers, all of them tend to be quickly bought but rarely used. If you happen to be someone who uses one of these small appliances often, keep it! However, if you're like the rest of us and you find that you are pulling these small appliances out from the back corners of your cabinets, you probably aren't using them very often, and they can be thrown in the give-away pile.

Get those counters clear!

Ok, I don't know if you've noticed this in your own home, but the horizontal surfaces in my home are not my friend. I get lulled into thinking they're my friend, but then inevitably, they turn on me. They become the greatest ally to my hoarding tendencies because they hold things so nicely! Also, it's super easy to simply plop your stuff down on the counter and walk away from it. My horizontal spaces are a mess!

In your kitchen, you're definitely going to want to clear off your countertops. So here are some tips that might help you clear your kitchen counters off for good!

First of all, set up a command center somewhere in your home. It doesn't have to be in your kitchen, but if you find that it's where your family tends to dump all of their homework, papers, backpacks, and everything else they own, the kitchen might be a natural place for your command center. That's where my family's belongings generally end up, so that's why I'm bringing up the command center here.

A command center is really whatever you need it to be. It can simply be a place for your family members to place their papers without causing the counters to become cluttered. It could include a family calendar and a list of chores or anything else you think might be useful for everyone in your family to see and have access to on a daily basis. It can (and definitely should) contain a basket for small items like keys or wallets that are usually just dumped anywhere and easily lost.

One thing I would recommend is that, whatever you choose to include in your family's command center, you set it up inside a cabinet, probably a top cabinet if all of the children you want to have access to it are tall enough to reach it (after all, you wouldn't want your toddler to reach in and pull everyone's papers out every day). Your countertops are going to be a clutter-free zone, so don't even start inviting more clutter. Even organized clutter can drive you crazy. Have your small-item basket in the cabinet as well as a paper organizer with each slot labeled with a different family members' name. That slot then becomes the place where that person can dump any papers they have. If you want to have a family calendar or chore chart, attach it to the back of the cabinet door so that it's out of sight but still easily accessible.

Once you have set up a command center in your kitchen that will be natural and easy for your family to use, you can start enforcing a clutter-free zone on the kitchen counters. From this point forward, nothing goes on the counters that do not belong there. Here's a radical idea for you: you might even decide that all of the small appliances that usually live on your counters can be put away. I know, I know. Crazy, right? You should definitely give it a try, though. Having completely clear counters might sound ludicrous, but it is actually incredibly freeing and is a great sight to walk into. I completely get that you might not want to have to get your toaster oven or coffee maker out of the cabinet every morning, but you might also find that you enjoy the feeling of clear counters more than the convenience of having them there all the time. So, I encourage you to give it a try. Put your coffee maker in the cabinet directly above its normal spot, that way it's easy to pull out and put back up. It really doesn't take that much longer, and I think you will find you like it.

What to do with the cookbooks?

Ok, now that you have cleared off all of your countertops and gotten rid of all of your duplicate gadgets and tools that you thought were oh-so-necessary, it's time to go through those cookbooks you've held onto for ages. Let's be honest: most of us don't use cookbooks anymore. We might hold onto them for sentimental value, but we generally don't use them very often. Most of our recipes are found online today. We save them on apps that are extremely useful. There are plenty of really great ones that you can save your favorite recipes too. You can even keep an inventory of the items in your pantry so that you can easily search for recipes that you have the ingredients for. It's great for meal planning. I definitely encourage you to look some up and try them out.

That being said, cookbooks aren't that necessary anymore, but I get it. Your precious great-grandmother used to use this one cookbook for ages and ages. It's been worn by years of helping prepare delicious and nutritious meals for generations of your family members, and now it's been passed down to you, and you feel horrible for throwing it out. That's fine. Treat it like a sentimental item. Keep it and store it where you store your sentimental items. That's fine.

However, we all have cookbooks that hold absolutely no sentimental value. They might have a recipe or two that we like, but they aren't used daily or even weekly. Or usually even monthly. Most of the time not even quarterly. Again, those apps that I was talking about earlier are great for these things. You can find the recipes you like in these books and type them into the app. It takes a minute, but once you've done it, it's there. The ingredients will be compiled, and you can search for them based on what you have in your pantry. And then you can get rid of the cookbook. It's pretty darn great.

If you decide that you have to keep a cookbook, set some guidelines for yourself. Make sure that there are at least five recipes that you all the time in the cookbook. I would still recommend uploading the recipe into an app on your phone, simply because of the clutter cookbooks contribute and how useful those apps can be.

Or, if you are not super keen on the idea of using an app for your recipes, you can also create your own binder where you write down the recipe, type it out and print it off, tear out the page (probably don't do this one!), however you choose to do it. Get a binder and some tabbed dividers. Write the different categories of food on the tabs, and you're on your way to having one single binder for all of your recipes.

I know it might be tough, but getting rid of the cookbooks will free up a lot of space in your kitchen.

CHAPTER 9
Decorations And Decluttering

I know I've said this about a hundred times, or at least it seems like it, but one great place to start your decluttering journey is actually the bathroom, especially if you are hesitant or nervous about minimalism or if you simply don't have the time to get started on a bigger project. The bathroom is great because it's usually a very small room, and you generally don't store sentimental items there. The hardest decision you'll probably have to make is which color lipstick to toss out and which ones actually look good enough on you for you to keep.

For many of us, especially those of us who are women, our bathrooms are filled with all of the beauty products, skin care products, age-defying products, and anything else you can think of. Our medicine cabinets are full to bursting. Believe me, the bathroom is full of things that will be painless to get rid of, so I recommend that you just start chunking. What makes it even easier is that no one wants half-used shampoo, so there's generally no use in trying to gather everything up to give away to someone. Now, if it is completely unopened and you feel led to, I know there are certain places that could use some of the more generic bathroom products like shampoo and conditioner and body wash, and maybe even some makeup. However, most of the things you find in your bathroom, you'll simply want to throw away.

So, get started! Go through your drawers and your cabinets and pull out anything and everything you don't use every day. As far as your makeup goes, take an incredibly critical look at everything in your makeup bag, drawer, or whatever, and decide if it's something you really use and need or if it's something that's in there but you rarely use it or you don't really need it. Cut your makeup to the bare minimum and put away the rest.

If you're feeling nervous about doing this, you might put it in a box, label it, set it in the garage, and live with what you have in your bathroom for a few days, a week, maybe even a few weeks to see if you really even miss what you put away. I'm willing to bet that you won't. Most of the time, when we have a surplus of items in our bathroom, it's because we're searching for that perfect thing to make our eyelashes longer or our hair less frizzy. But we usually end up going back to the same things over and over again.

So, unless your skin is genuinely abnormally dry or your hair is very curly and frizzy, you probably don't need a wide variety of specialty products for every member of your family. Generic, multipurpose products work just fine. I even bought the cheapest shampoo and conditioner I could possibly find the other day, and my family's hair is still clean and soft. I haven't even noticed a difference.

Decluttering

Decluttering your bathroom is really an easy thing to do. All you have to do is start pulling things out and tossing anything you haven't used in the last week. Or, if you're feeling a little bit more ready for your bathroom to be cleared, you can even get rid of everything you haven't touched in the last day or two. That's getting bold right there. Or, you could do this method, but then keep the few items you use once a week or every other week for special occasions. You can store these items in a separate container that belongs under the sink or somewhere that isn't as easily accessible as all of your everyday items. Once you've decided what those everyday essentials are, return them to a place in your bathroom that is out of sight, and/or natural to access.

If you don't have enough storage in your bathroom, you can try to add storage by hanging a cabinet or a few shelves on the wall. But as with the kitchen, you should try your best to keep all horizontal surfaces clear. Your bathroom will be much calmer and more relaxing, and you'll thank yourself for it later when you aren't using your precious, alone, bath time to put away all of the clutter on the countertops. As far as the rest of your products go, you can either toss it out wholesale, or you can gather some of the less-used items and donate them to a local donation center or shelter. They may not want half-used specialty beauty products, but I'm sure they could certainly use shampoo, conditioner, and body wash, as well as some of your gently used grooming products like hair brushes and nail clippers.

A note about medicine: I don't know why people tend to store their medicine in a damp area like the bathroom. It doesn't make any sense to me. Although to be completely honest, I totally did this for the longest time. However, if you do keep your medicine in the bathroom you might find that the kitchen is a more natural place to store the medicine, just don't store it right next to the stove or the oven. So, consider moving your medicine to the kitchen, as long as you know that it's accessible to those who need it and not accessible to those who shouldn't be able to use it, as your toddler. Also be sure to check the expiration dates on your medicines because it's very easy to lose track of, and if you're anything like me, you have a lot of expired medications in your medicine cabinet. Just make sure you follow any guidelines your community might have for getting rid of old medication.

Decorations

Again, I'm a decoration kind of girl. I like to have a vase with a single, simple flower in it or a picture frame or some other kind of decoration to brighten up a room and make it feel like home. It's perfectly fine if you're the same way. However, the bathroom is usually a small space, and adding much extra to that space will immediately make it feel cluttered. So, either do without decorations at all, or if you find that to be boring or un-homey, place one small decoration, perhaps two, and leave it be. In a small space like the bathroom, less is generally more.

Adding in your kids

Depending on the bathroom situation in your home, you may share a bathroom with your kids, or you may (blessedly) have your own bathroom while your children have their own. Whatever the situation is, getting rid of all of the clutter in their bathroom will greatly help them be able to use the bathroom without having things to distract them. They'll be able to use the bathroom without getting into the bathtub toys every time, and they'll also be able to clean the bathroom on their own, depending on their age.

If you have teenagers, the decluttering process might be a little more complicated, especially if your teenager is a female. If that's the case, and your teenager is not fully on board with the minimization process, you might allow them a bit of independence on this. Set some guidelines that you're comfortable with, show them what your bathroom looks like, and then let them decide how they want to follow the guidelines you've set in place. For all of your kids, no matter their ages, minimalism is partly about teaching them the difference between needs and essentials versus extras, clutter, and wants. But for your teens, this is especially true because they'll be on their own in a few short years, and they'll need to be able to make these decisions on their own. So, let them have the freedom and independence to go through this process on their own, only helping them out if they need it.

Again, the bathroom is a pretty easy place to declutter, so don't overthink it. Just throw anything you don't use every day in a box, donate it, chunk it, throw it in the trash. That's really all there is to it.

CHAPTER 10
Aspects To Embrace

If you're lucky enough to have a separate room for your office, consider yourself blessed. Personally, I do not have an office, and I'm sitting in my kitchen, trying to write this book for you. It's going super well. But I would love an office with a door. However, having a home office can also serve as a repository for extra clutter. It's an entire room that you don't really need a whole lot of space in because sitting at a desk with a computer doesn't take up an entire room. Therefore, the entire room fills up with your extra clutter. If you have a large desk, those pesky horizontal spaces will fill up with paper, pens, post-it notes, and anything else that can fit on it.

Again, I truly believe you are blessed if you have one of these rooms, and I certainly would love one. However, it can be a tricky room to control because it's often viewed as an extra room simply for clutter. There might be a desk with a computer and a chair. But the rest is for clutter. So, in order to reclaim your beautiful home office space that many of us would die for, the first thing you should do is just take out anything and everything that doesn't help you get your work done. Take out anything that doesn't relate to your work. Sort everything on your desk. Go through all of the papers and decide whether they should be shredded or kept.

Once you've done the initial cleaning of the room to get rid of the clutter, you can get started preparing your office for continued minimalism and productivity.

What do you really need in an office?

As always, the first thing you need to do after you have cleaned the room is to consider the purpose of your office. What do you do there? Is it strictly for your work and no one else'? Do your kids have their own desk on which they do homework? Do you meet with clients in your home office? Whatever you do in your office, pick out the furniture and other items that are absolutely essential to that purpose, and nothing else.

Furniture

If you work online, and most of your work is done only on the computer, it's likely that you'll only need a small desk and a computer chair. However, if you meet with clients, you might decide that you want an entire living space in your office so that you can consult with your clients in a comfortable, calming environment. Or, if your kids study there alongside you, you might have an extra desk or two that your kid's study on, along with a corresponding computer chair. Of course, along with more desks come the pesky horizontal spaces so you might want to be careful about how much horizontal space you keep in the area.

Electronics
What electronics do you really need in your home office? Do you really need a separate scanner? Have you even used the fax machine behind you since 1998? If the answer to either of those questions is no, pack them up and move 'em out. It's likely that you'll need a printer. Regardless of how much I like working digitally, it can still be useful to have a pen and paper to scratch out ideas, and sometimes it's even necessary for signing papers and returning them.

A great option is that many printers these days come with a scanner attached, which allows you to have both a printer and a scanner without taking up the space that both devices would have used in the past.

Office supplies
Office supplies! We love them! We love to collect them. We love to hoard them. However, most of them are never used, especially if most of your work is done online. So, chuck it. You only need one stapler, one pair of scissors, a small handful of pens and pencils, and maybe a highlighter or two. Depending on your work, you might need a few more specialized items. However, the point here is that you get rid of anything that is unnecessary or that is duplicated. If you already have it, don't keep it. Chunk it. It's easy to accumulate extras over the years.

Mail
Mail is awful. It's either junk mail or it's a bill. I never get good mail anymore. It's sad. However, you might not just want to throw it all away because some of it might actually be important. So, go through whatever mail you have and chunk all of the junk (hey, that rhymes!) and sort through everything else to see if you need to keep it. If you do find something that you need to keep, put it in an organizer that is clearly labeled with the categories of paperwork you might have, such as bills, bank statements, etc.

There are ways to control the amount of mail you get. Most bills can be paid online these days, and it's really very easy to switch from paper billing to electronic. In fact, most companies would prefer you pay electronically. Not only does it reduce paper waste, but it also saves both you and the company time, money, and effort writing the check, paying for postage, and delivering it to the post office. In addition, most banking needs can be met online. It's definitely something to look into, so I highly recommend it. It will help you immensely in minimizing the amount of mail you get.

Papers
If there's anything I hate more than mail, it's papers! Or at least, I hate it just as much as mail because it's basically the same thing since most of my paper comes from my mail. It's so easy for the paper to become cluttered and disorganized because we tend to get in the habit of just stuffing paper anywhere that has space. We rarely take the time to develop the habit of putting the paper where it belongs. Personally, I'm rather good at creating organization systems at the start, but it never fails that I'll come across a

piece of paper that doesn't fit in my organization system, so I stuff it anywhere I can, and from there, the disorganization erupts.

However, the only way to truly master the paper clutter is to simply be disciplined about your organization system. Create it from the start, keep a handful of empty folders available at all times so it's easy to create a new folder when a need arises. Every category of paper that you keep should have a home, so receipts, insurance papers, bills, tax returns, etc. all need to have a separate folder or binder. If at all possible, always put your papers away immediately. As soon as one appears on your desk, find its home. Don't let it linger on your desk.

Personally, I try to keep as little paper as possible. I digitize most of my papers because it's very easy for me to lose physical paper. Like with paper files, I'm fairly good at creating an organization system, but not very good at maintaining it. However, unlike paper files, with digital files, if I look hard enough, I will be able to find it. Paper files are usually just lost. I do need to get better about maintaining organization, though. I would try to choose one or the other: physical or digital. If you try to keep both, you'll end up paying a lot more because you'll be paying for the digital storage service, as well as the supplies to keep or physical files organized. So, choose one, organize it effectively, and be disciplined about sticking with it.

Embrace the digital age

This time period in the life of the world is extremely cool. What used to require stacks and stacks of paper and hours and hours of library research is now done on a single screen with a laptop that weighs less than a bag of sugar and takes only a quick Google search that leads me to all of the resources I could ever need. As I said, it's pretty cool.

I know that a lot of people are a little bit hesitant to completely embrace the digital age, though. It's a little unfamiliar, and a lot of people aren't confident enough in their digital skills, so they choose to remain analog for a lot of their needs. However, if you simply take the time to learn how to do it in the first place, I promise that digitizing your life will make it simpler and much more space-friendly.

Scan old photos that are currently collecting dust in a box in a corner and be excited that you will never lose those photos. Get rid of all of those DVDs and CDs that have been taking up space in your office for ages. Get an Apple Music subscription where you can listen to and even download all of the music you could possibly want. Pay for Netflix or Hulu every month or one of the other great TV streaming services, and I promise you won't miss your giant DVD collection for long. You can even buy digital movies online and build up a movie collection that way. You can also buy a Kindle. They're amazing for storing hundreds upon hundreds of books on a tiny little device instead of lugging around stacks of books that are heavy and take up a lot of space.

Set up your bills so that you receive statements electronically. Choose electronic magazine subscriptions instead of paper ones so that you can get rid of the clutter they create on your desk. Take a picture of the cover of any device manuals you think you might need. As long as you have the model number, I promise you can find the full manual online.

Like I said before, the advances of the digital age are incredibly useful and can make your life so much easier. It might take some time to learn, but I think that you'll find it's worth. Be careful with your digital space, though.

As cool as going digital can be, you also don't want to just throw all of your physical clutter into the computer and create a mess for yourself there. Digital clutter can be just as frustrating as physical clutter. So, start this process right by first creating an organization system for yourself and then starting to add your photos, papers, movies, etc. Whatever storage option you choose (Dropbox, iCloud, etc.) create a home for everything you might put in there and schedule time every week to make sure that it's organized and maintained.

Personally, I like to keep the desktop of my laptop completely clear. It's kind of like a horizontal space in my house. It's the place my eyes immediately go to when I open up my computer, and it's much happier for me if I open it up, see a cute picture of my kids and nothing else. If there are a ton of files cluttering the screen, it stresses me out and that's not good. So, I recommend that you try to keep your desktop as clear as any other horizontal space in your home. If you have to have a folder on your desktop (because it is very convenient), create just one folder to dump everything in that you might need it for and then at the end of the day, go back through that folder and put everything in its proper place.

I don't know about you, but I love that my smartphone has a camera. It's a great camera, too, and it's specifically why I bought the phone. However, it makes it extremely easy to simply start tapping that little white button to take dozens of pictures at one single time, so I have a lot of pictures that are very similar. If you have young kids, it can be incredibly useful because their facial expressions change on a moment-by-moment basis. You might get a really horrible, sad picture one second and a really precious and cute picture the next. You just never know what you're going to get, so being able to take multiple pictures is a great thing. However, it also takes up storage space on my phone or on my computer, so it's important that you regularly go through your photos and clear out the ones that you don't need. Pick out a few of your favorites from those dozens-long duplicate sessions and delete the rest.

Also, be sure that you back everything up. Computers are great. They work great most of the time. But there are times that they crash. Sometimes digital storage options fail, and you could risk losing your digital photos and paperwork. I highly recommend that you not only purchase an online digital storage solution like Dropbox or iCloud but that you also buy a physical hard drive so that your digital files are always backed up on a physical device.

Another area of the digital world that is notorious being cluttered is email. I don't know about you, but I personally have a ton of junk email. Some of it is stuff that I actually enjoy reading and want to be kept up to date one, but a lot of it is useless and just takes up space in my inbox. So, depending on how quickly your email gets cluttered, you should definitely set aside time on a regular basis to go through your emails and decide which ones you want to keep and which ones you can delete.

The digital world is definitely a great one, and it's worth learning how to put your physical paper files into a digital file for a lot of reasons. However, you should always be careful to keep your digital space decluttered, just as you would your physical space.

CHAPTER 11
Humanity

Ok, so far, we've talked about what minimalism is, how to develop a mindset of minimalism that will appeal to your entire family. We've discussed guidelines that you might want to set for your family, as far as what goes into your house, what your home's purpose is, and how to treat the items that remain in your house. We've talked about strategies for decluttering your home, including the 4-box method, the packing party and the 12x12x12 method. We've talked about specific tips for decluttering your bedrooms, your living spaces, your kitchen, your bathroom, and your office. And by this point, I hope that you have gained a greater appreciation for the benefits of minimalism. However, unless you're completely naive, I'm sure you're aware that this process might not be an easy one for everyone in your family. Some people simply like their stuff, and they don't want to be told that they need to get rid of it. Regardless of who is presenting the resistance, I promise you it will come, and it won't be fun. However, I hope to provide you with some tips for dealing with the resistance that will help you navigate it without causing more conflict or stress in your family's life.

The Beauty of Humanity

The beauty of humanity is that every single one of us is completely unique and different. We have our own hobbies, our own interests, our own wants and desires, dreams, and needs. And it's a beautiful thing. It's what makes the world such a diverse and interesting place to live in. However, it can also be a little bit frustrating. If I were, to be honest like I've tried to be throughout this book, my husband and I have very different opinions on what decluttering means. I might want to wholesale chunk out everything we own except for the major things like my computer, our furniture, and a few sentimental items. He, on the other hand, will want to keep about 60% of the stuff that we own. He'll want to keep the duplicated can openers because one works differently than the other. He has a stack of journals that he doesn't want to get rid of, even though most of them aren't even filled. We're different that way, and it can be frustrating. In the past, when we have worked on decluttering our home, we both generally agree that it's something that needs to be done and that we should get started doing it as soon as possible. We agree with the purpose we have for our family. We agree on the purpose of each room in our house. But for whatever reason, we don't tend to agree on how it should be done. He's more of a slow-and-steady person, and I'm more of a get-it-done kind of person. Now, to give him credit, he is much better at maintaining a decluttered house than I am. I tend to purge it all, get it out, be done, and then allow clutter to start trickling back into the house rather quickly. He, on the other hand, is much better about resisting the new forms of clutter. So, the point is, we're all different. We all frustrate each other, and it's just something you're going to have to deal with.

Through this chapter, I hope that you can find some strategies that will help you to do that.

Find your people

Before you really start confronting your resistant family members, I would recommend finding people who are already on the same page as you. It can be incredibly helpful and relieving to find other people who think the same way as you do. They can often help you decide how to approach your less-than-enthusiastic family members, and they'll be people you can go to when you feel frustrated, defeated, and a little bit crazy. So, I definitely encourage you to join a Facebook group or find people in your community who are already on the minimalism journey because you'll find that they are a great source of ideas and encouragement. If your family members can't be that for you in this particular area of life. However, I would caution that you don't use the Facebook group or your friendships as a place to harp on the negatives and the frustrations your family might bring. The other people in your home have a right to their own thoughts and opinions on things and you shouldn't use your platforms to bash them for disagreeing with you, no matter how frustrated you might become at times. So, ask for encouragement, ask for support, vent a little bit about your frustrations if you have to, but always come back to something positive about your family members because they deserve your respect, whether you agree with them or not.

Remind them of the benefits

Personally, my idea for simplifying our home is specifically for my family to have a better life. In our highly cluttered and busy home, it's difficult to feel connected with any of them truly. I'm constantly cleaning or being frustrated that I just cleaned and it's already dirty again or telling my kids to go clean their rooms or being frustrated with my husband that he has left dirty laundry on the floor. Simplicity is for my family. I want to be able to connect with them better, and I believe that owning fewer things will help us to do that. For your kids, I would recommend just kind of constantly bringing it up in everyday conversation. Slide in a comment every once in a while, about how great it is that there's not too much stuff to clean up because it means you'll be able to get to the park earlier or spend more time at the pool that afternoon. Remind your family that minimalism is about being able to live your life in a way that is more fulfilling. Consistently highlighting the benefits of minimalism, especially to your kids, will start to erode some of the resistance they may have to the idea at first. They'll eventually come to see that there even though they may have lost some of their toys, they've gained a lot of time and a lot of happiness because of minimalism.

Be a role model for them
One of the best ways to teach anything in life is to model it. So if you find that your family members just simply are not interested in this whole minimalism journey, I think the best way you can convince them to jump on board is simply to show them what it looks like and how much simpler it can make your life. I know it's easy to get down and frustrated when the people you love don't support you in your vision for your family's life. It's easy to blame them when you want to have a simpler life, but their bedroom is still full of clutter and junk and is always dirty. But try to simply do your best, declutter the areas that won't affect them, and enjoy those spaces. Let them see what a minimalist lifestyle can look like and how much happier it makes you. A lot of the time, your family will see how much less stressed you are and how much time you have, and they'll be interested just because of your example.

Don't chuck someone else's stuff.
Whatever you do, don't just start chunking everything out, regardless of whose it is. Sure, sure, you may have bought that toy, so technically, yes, it's yours. But your child won't see it that way. That toy is his. There is no faster way to squash whatever enthusiasm was starting to build than to throw out someone else's belongings. It's a hostile thing to do, and it will make your family members upset. Rightfully so. They have a right to their feelings. They have a right to be part of the process, so respect that.

Of course, there will be times that you have to set guidelines. For example, when you are going through your 8-year old's room, you might designate a specific area that can contain toys and anything that doesn't fit in that specific area. That's ok. You're still allowing them the independence to figure out what can fit in that space and make a decision about what will need to go. You're still giving them a choice about what toys they want to keep and which ones they want to give up.

It's a respect thing. You probably wouldn't like it if someone just started throwing out everything you own. Don't force minimalism on anyone. Sure, it's kind of hard to be a minimalist if no one else in your family wants to live that way but do your best. Continue to maintain your minimalist lifestyle as best as you can in your own spaces, with your own stuff, and model how much it helps you.

If you try to force it on your family, minimalism will not last. People don't just make these life changes because someone else tells them to do it. They do it because they really are behind it and they believe in it. So, if you really want to have a sustainable lifestyle change, you need to focus on the long game, model minimalism for your family, and just be patient with them.

CHAPTER 12
Recap

Who reading this has money problems? Raise your hand. It's fine. The person sitting behind you in the coffee shop isn't going to care. If you didn't raise your hand, I'm pretty sure you're lying. Because we all have money problems. Or most of us, anyway. Money is a dirty five-letter word that somehow has the power to ruin people, marriages, and even entire communities. It makes the world go around, and for some people, it can also cause the entire world to stop. It's a small word and a relatively simple concept, but it has incredible power. It's a little bit astonishing what money (or, more accurately, the desire for money) can lead people to do.

I could go on, but that's not what this book is really about. It's about you and your family and setting you up to live a minimalist lifestyle in every aspect of your life, including your finances. And guess what? In this chapter, we're going to take a deep look at what a minimalist budget can look like.

A reminder of what minimalism isn't

I don't know what you think of when you first think of the word budgeting, but for me, it makes me think "tight." It makes me think of the phrase, "tightening our belts." It makes me think of all of the things that I can't do or won't be able to do in the coming months because I haven't saved up for it. Budgeting doesn't really sound all that great most of the time. In fact, it kind of sounds like a negative view of minimalism.

Minimalism means doing without. It means having less, which can sometimes sound scary to those of us who grew up in a capitalist society. But just like minimalism isn't only about doing with less, budgeting isn't only about doing with less. It's about living within your means. It's about learning to use what you have to live a purposeful, fulfilling life. I promise you can do it on a budget.

I know it might often seem like money is incredibly important, but it's really only one resource in our lives. There are many other resources that need to be managed and used wisely. So just like minimalism isn't about starving yourself, punishing yourself, or living without anything to make life comfortable, neither is having a minimalist budget about any of those things. Both are about figuring out exactly what you need and living within those needs instead of living to excess.

A good example of this would be deciding to buy a dryer after your old one gives out. Dryers cost a lot of money, especially if you want to get a good one that will last a long time. And you can certainly dry your clothes without a dryer. All you have to do is set up a clothesline in your backyard (if you have a backyard—in your laundry room if you don't), lug out all of your wet clothes along with a bag of clothespins, and hang them out to dry. Of course, you have to be able to know that it's not going to rain and that your clothes won't get soaked all over again.

So, technically, yes, you could do without a dryer. Does it belong in a minimalist budget, then? Well, that depends: does the drying process without a dryer sound like way too much hassle? Will it leave you prisoner to the laundry in a way that will sap your other important physical resources like time and energy? It might not cost any money to dry your laundry this way, but that doesn't make it free. So, you have to decide: is the extra time and energy spent worth the money you save by not buying a new dryer?

The Purchase

For many people, shopping is a practice of mindlessness. They go into a store and simply wander the aisles, looking for something they might want without any real plan or intention in mind. Advertisers love this kind of shopper. However, part of learning to live on a minimalist budget is learning how to become a more mindful consumer. Here are some tips to help you do just that:

Don't go shopping when you're emotional, bored, or hungry

In other words, don't go shopping when you're not on your A-game. Any other time, you'll be much more vulnerable to the work of advertising. If you're hungry, an ad for a yummy, juicy hamburger is likely to send you running to the nearest fast food restaurant. If you're frustrated because your kids' clothes are already starting to get too small, an ad for the latest trends in children's clothing will tempt you to head on into the clothing store. If you're bored and simply looking for a distraction, you'll wander into a retail store without any thought as to what you might need, and you could easily end up with a cart full of things you never needed in the first place.

Many of us who have grown up in Western society has been taught that problems are most easily solved when you buy something new. You will look more stylish, your status will be raised, you'll have more friends if you have the latest clothes, etc. Ads are designed to promote those kinds of messages. So, be careful not to go shopping when you are in a compromised mental state.

Go in with a plan

This is especially true for grocery shopping, though you can make a plan when you go shopping for anything, including clothes, furniture, etc. Try your hardest not to make decisions spontaneously. Build a meal plan for your family, take a look at what you have in your pantry already, and then make a list of everything you have to have in order to follow the meal plan. Everything else in the store that might tempt you can be left on the shelf.

Look at other options

If you are looking to make a bigger purchase, it's always a good idea to stop before you buy and take a few minutes, at least, to research what your other options might be. For example, if you need to buy a new computer and you have your eyes set on one, in particular, don't buy it immediately. This is even easier to accomplish with the advent of smartphones because you don't even have to leave the store to do it. You can simply take a few moments, look at the websites of a few other retailers, and see if this is truly the best option for you. You could even look into marketplaces that sell used computers or items like Craigslist or Swappa. That way, you could even end up getting exactly what you want for a much lower price because somebody has already used it. For smaller purchases, like at the grocery store, you can still follow this guideline. Instead of grabbing the first thing on the shelf, look around a little bit to see what is cheaper or what might be on sale.

Don't get bogged down
At the same time, it's sometimes possible to spend too much time and energy looking for those other options. In a minimalist budget, that isn't good either because time is just as important a resource as money, so you should use it wisely. If you need a bag of potatoes, for example, and there are several different kinds to choose from, simply grab the cheapest one that will work for you and move on with your life. For bigger purchases, do your research, look for cheaper options, but don't spend days and days doing it. Give it a good thirty minutes or so, and move on. So, keep the other resources in your life in mind as you make your purchasing decisions. Sometimes the time it takes to do something yourself or to research other options is worth more than the money you might save. So, learn how to balance saving time and saving money.

Deciding what's important and cutting out the rest

Once again, minimalist budgeting is not about simply financial budgeting. It takes into account your other resources, like time and energy. The goal of a minimalist budget is to find a balance between needs and wants and to divide all of your resources between them effectively. Obviously, we need to be smart with the money we have and spend it responsibly. However, you should factor in your other physical resources into your budget as well.

Time
I'm not sure if you've ever thought of it quite like this, but time is actually the most unforgiving resource available to you. Money can be made, borrowed, or even stolen (probably not a great idea, though!) when things get desperate. You can always sell your house or cut down on your monthly subscriptions. Of course, there does come a time when money can simply run out, and there's not a whole lot that can be done. So, budgeting money and being smart about how you spend it is still important.

However, time is actually much less forgiving. When time passes, it's gone. There's nothing you can sell or borrow that will bring the time back. What's worse: none of us know when our time will simply be over. We can run out of it in a moment.

So, instead of starting to build your budget with money, you should start with time. Everyone has the same amount of time: 24 hours a day, seven days a week. Decide what things are most important to you and where those things should fit in your week. You might find it helpful to spend a few days or even a full week keeping track of where your time is spent. Keep a small notebook with you and write a short note every time you change activities. I know it sounds like a lot of work, and it kind of is. But if you can do it for at least a full day, it'll be extremely helpful for you to determine which activities to keep and which ones you can stop doing. You'll probably be surprised how much of your time is spent on things that don't matter to you.

It might be tempting to look at your journal when you're done and beat yourself up over the time you consistently waste on unimportant things. Resist the urge because you'll only be wasting more time. Simply acknowledge it, take a look at the things that do matter to you, and figure out how you can be doing more of those kinds of things.

Energy

The other non-monetary resource that we have to learn how to budget is our energy. We only have a finite amount of energy, and we have to learn how to use it wisely. Kind of like time, it's easy to spend energy on things that don't really matter that much to you. I know I spend an inordinate amount of my time and energy cleaning our house. There's not really a whole lot I can do about that except to learn to be ok when things aren't exactly perfect in my home. At some point, the house does have to be clean. It does have to be safe for my family to live in, so I can't just let it go forever.

However, I could learn how to understand that life is a little messy sometimes and let my kids' toys stay in the living room until our nightly clean-up time instead of trying to pick up after them throughout the day constantly. Cleaning like that only saps the energy I should have used to play with them or to take care of other things that are important to me. After a day of cleaning up after every single mess my kids make, I'm way too tired to do things like connecting with my husband when he gets home from work or enjoying a meal with my family at the dinner table.

When you start thinking about all of the things you do throughout the day, take note of the unimportant things that sap a lot of your energy and try to figure out how you can lessen the toll it takes.

Creating your budget

Once you've identified and set apart the things in your life that are non-negotiable, you can start taking a look at the things you can move around. It's a pretty simple principle: if it's not one of your non-negotiables, find a way to either reduce the resources you spend on it or get rid of it altogether. For me, one of my non-negotiables is playing with my kids and making time for them. Constantly fussing over how clean the house is throughout the day gets in the way of that. So, I have to learn how to be ok with a bit of a mess during this phase of my life. The mess can wait, but my kids won't always be little and want me to play with them.

The same principle goes for the items you spend your money on. When creating your budget, you don't have to trim it down to the bare minimum you need to survive and save every penny over that. Not only is that not practical, but it's also unenjoyable. If you enjoy traveling, set aside a little bit of money every month to save up so that you can take a trip every few months or so. If you really love books, it's ok to spend a portion of your money on books. However, if you find that you spend a lot of money every month on things that don't matter to you, stop paying for it! Of course, be responsible! If you're in debt, you can't really decide that paying off your debt doesn't matter to you and then just stop paying for it. That's a good way to get in trouble with your credit! But, if you find that you're spending close to $100 on television services when you know, you'd really rather be out walking with your family, cancel the services! Do everything you can to spend your money on things that truly matter to you.

Creating a minimalist budget isn't nearly as scary as you might think. It's not about living on the bare minimum and saving every penny you possibly can for that future "rainy day." It's about taking all of your resources into account and spending your money on things that will serve you and your values. I strongly encourage you to consider building your budget with this mindset because I think you'll find that your entire life is more well-rounded and enjoyable.

CHAPTER 13
Reasons And Guidelines

Yay! If you've made it through to this chapter, you've at least started decluttering your home. Your family at least knows what your plans are (and hopefully, they're on board). You've set some guidelines for the items in your home and have determined why you're doing this.

Now it's time to start thinking about how you're going to maintain your new minimalist lifestyle, and unfortunately, this is the hardest part of the whole deal. It's incredibly easy for clutter to make its way back into your life. In fact, I can promise you that no matter how hard you try, it will happen. Minimalism won't keep the clutter away, but it will give you the tools you need to know how to deal with it. And giving yourself a clean slate by decluttering your house at the start will make the clutter-creep much more manageable.

The problem is, you have to be consistent about maintaining it, which can be difficult to do. If you let it go for very long, clutter has a sneaky way of accumulating rather quickly, and before you know it, you could end up with another mess on your hands.

The good news is, it can be done if you work to develop good habits and routines that will help you and your family keep your home clutter-free. Here are some tips for making that happen.

Remember why you are doing this

As always, keep your reason for doing this at the front of your family's mind. You could even write it out and put it somewhere where it will be visible to everyone in your home. If you're intentional about remembering why you want to have a minimalist lifestyle in the first place, it will be easier to find the motivation to maintain it for the long haul.

Make your house guidelines clear and visible

Just like your reason for doing this should be visible to everyone, the guidelines for your home should be visible as well. When something new comes into your home, you can hold it up against the guidelines to determine if it can stay or if it should find a new home. This also makes sure that everyone in the family knows and is clear on what the guidelines are. If you have young kids, take time to review the guidelines often to help them remember what they are and why your family has them.

Ask questions of everything you buy

Every time you go to buy something new, take a few minutes to ask yourself a few questions:
- Will I want this next month?
- Do I need this?

- Will it bring me joy?
- Can it replace something I already have?
- Am I willing to get rid of something else in order to have this?

Train your children to ask these questions, too. Maybe even add one more to it: would they be willing to spend their own money on it? Learning to ask these questions consistently will cut down dramatically on the number of new gadgets and toys you ultimately decide to buy. And you can be sure that the ones you do decide to buy will be used and enjoyed.

Make space for things that will leave

Somewhere in your home, ideally where it will be easily accessible to everyone in the family, room set a box out where people can place the things they no longer need or want. That way, as they come across the things they want to get rid of, they can immediately get it out of their home, instead of deciding to wait until they have time to decide what to do with it. Taking away that extra layer of effort will definitely help them (and you) maintain a decluttered home.

Sweep through your house every day

At the end of each day, do a quick sweep through your house to put everything back where it belongs. Have your family members join you by picking up their own belongings and returning them to their proper place. Your home doesn't have to be perfectly picked up at every moment throughout the day, but it does help to go to bed with a picked up home so that you can wake up with a clean slate for the next day.

Don't stock up on things

I know this might sound counterintuitive. Stocking up sounds like a good idea, especially when the items are necessary, and the price is low. It's hard to pass up on a really good deal! The issue is, if you stock up on things too much, they can start accumulating and will only get lost in a house that is way too full. Again, minimalism isn't just about saving every penny you possibly can. It's about learning how to live in a way that is fulfilling and that you honestly enjoy. If coupon-clipping and stocking up on sale items only lead to more stress and clutter, don't do it! Save money by buying the off-brand laundry detergent or whatever the item is.

Learn how to borrow

Sometimes you'll have an item in your home that serves a purpose that can't really be duplicated by another item but that you only use on rare occasions. If you know someone who also owns the item, it might be possible for you to get rid of yours and simply borrow theirs on the rare occasions you need it. There's no sense in you storing an item that is only used once in a blue moon, so try to see what items you can borrow from someone else.

Get rid of the clutter magnets

Some items in your house are just magnets for clutter. Keeping extra storage containers, for example, is just asking for them to be filled with new forms of clutter. It never fails: an empty, purposeless drawer will eventually become filled. If you have a desk or table that always seems to be covered in clutter, would it be better for you to just do without that piece of furniture? If you can get by without it, do it. Simply don't allow yourself or your family a place for clutter to accumulate.

Limit the number of possessions your family can have

If you and your family struggle to control the number of possessions you have, it might be a good idea to set a limit on yourselves. Count your possessions from time to time to see if you've exceeded your limit. If you have, it's time to cut back on a few of your possessions. I wouldn't be super strict about this. Counting your possessions every single day can be an unnecessary and draining task that will only bring frustration and conflict. However, doing it from time to time can be a good, objective way to determine if your family has too much stuff.

Stop going shopping

For a time, at least, set a ban on shopping. Decide what the essentials are that you will continue to buy and then simply stop buying anything that doesn't fall into that essential category. Items like food and toiletries will still have to be bought, but clothes, books, movies, etc. can all wait until the ban is over. This is a good way to give your budget a bit of a break as well as your newly-decluttered home.

Stick with your community

Hopefully, by this point in your journey, your family members have all decided to jump on board with you. If that's the case, you might not feel like you need a community of like-minded people you joined back when you were on your own in the minimalism journey. You may have since found the support and encouragement you needed then, but it's still a great idea to stay in touch with the people who helped you at the beginning of the journey. They'll continue to be another source of encouragement and accountability as you work to maintain the habits of minimalism. They'll help you stay motivated when the going gets tough. So, stay connected to the online communities and blogs and continue to educate yourself about minimalism and strategies for continuing on the journey.

Resist the temptation to make impulse purchases

Every time you go shopping, you're at risk of making an impulse purchase. Advertising companies and retailers spend inordinate amounts of money on ads designed to convince us to buy things we really know we could do without. And they're really, really good at it. They're so good, you often won't even realize you bought into the ad's promises until you turn around and the purchase is made. I've said it before, but I'll say it again: always go into a store with a plan. Have your grocery list, your list of clothing needs, etc. in hand any time you walk into a store. If you come across something you think you need/want that isn't on your list, write it down and walk away. When you're finished shopping, think about it again: is it really worth going back and finding it again now that you're done shopping, or would you rather check out and go home? If the answer is yes, it's worth it, go for it. If the answer is no, I'd rather just be done, then great! Either way, you resisted making a purchase on impulse by giving yourself time to think about it and get over the initial excitement of it.

Declutter your schedule

I know it's hard to do, especially if you have kids in school, a full-time job, and everything else going on in the world. However, minimalism doesn't work well with a busy life. You'll find yourself constantly running and never taking the time to follow through on the habits you're trying to build. It's hard to be consistent about following your family's guidelines when everyone's too busy. Decide what's absolutely necessary and worth the time and energy and simply stop doing all the rest.

Set goals with your family

Work with your family members to set goals for your home. If you and your family can have a specific and appealing goal in mind, it will make it that much easier for everyone to stay motivated. Plan a family vacation after your home has been fully decluttered. Or pay off as much debt as possible with the money you save during a shopping ban. Making goals that your entire family can get behind will help motivate them to continue.

Practice thankfulness

When we learn how to be thankful for the things we have in our lives and in our homes, it makes it much easier for us to resist the urge to accumulate more. If you already believe you have enough and are thankful for everything you have, you won't feel the lack that leads to impulsive purchasing decisions and clutter-creep. Institute a daily moment of thanks with your family. Take a few minutes every day, whether it's at bedtime, at the dinner table, or as you drive your kids to school every morning, to talk about everything you're thankful for. Have your kids do the same. If they're not sure where to start, have them come up with at least three things in their life that they're thankful for.

It can be simple things, and, in the beginning, you might even allow repeats. However, as you and your family get in the habit of saying what you're thankful for, tighten up the ropes a little bit. Everyone has to come up with something unique and thoughtful. Three of your kids can't say "I'm thankful for my family" every day. That's cheating. If they get stuck, you might prompt them to think about why they're thankful for their family or what specific person they're thankful for at that moment. Teaching your kids how to be truly thankful for everything in their lives will be a great lesson for them to learn, not only during their years in your minimalist home but throughout their entire lives.

A note about gifts

One of the most difficult parts about living a minimalist lifestyle is what to do about gift-giving holidays. It doesn't matter if your family is just starting out on the journey or if you're old pros at it and have lived this way for a while. Gift-giving holidays can present a unique set of challenges that you'll have to learn how to best navigate for your family.

A minimalist mindset and holidays

Holidays and birthdays can be tough. I don't know about you, but it kind of hurts me to think of my kids not getting gifts around the holidays. It's silly and honestly a little bit dumb, I know, but I remember having so much fun around Christmas and my birthday as a kid, trying to guess what new treasures I would get and then ripping open the wrapping paper to see if I was right. And it's kind of difficult to think about not letting my kids have that experience.

However, if I take off my rose-colored glasses and look at my childhood experience objectively, I remember actually feeling disappointed at the end of the gift-giving segment of the day. I would have all of my brand-new toys sitting all around me, but I would already have a countdown running in my mind for the next holiday. Mind you, gifts are not bad things, and I promise I wasn't an abnormally ungrateful, self-centered kid. I was simply a normal kid growing up in Western society. I may have been normal, but that doesn't mean it was the best experience or that I was right for feeling that way. And it doesn't mean that I want my own kids to grow up with those kinds of expectations and attitudes.

Instead, I would like for my kids to have the experiences and memories that truly important and meaningful in my own childhood. Those memories weren't about the gifts I received; they were about the family I got to be around. They were about the traditions of my faith that surround the holiday. They were about being reminded that my family loves, values, and celebrates the day I was born. So, I would encourage you to adopt a mindset around holidays that puts the focus back on the true meaning of it instead of what kind of new, cool toys and gadgets your kids will be getting.

Unfortunately, not everyone in your family will understand why you want to limit (or even completely stop) the gift-exchange tradition. I know my own parents love to give my kids gifts, and they weren't very thrilled when I told them I didn't want them to buy any more toys for my boys. However, you simply have to stand firm. Give your extended family ample notice, especially if they tend to buy gifts throughout the year as sales arise or they find something they think will be particularly enjoyed. If your extended family really wants to buy something, have them give you and your kids' experiences. Tickets to a baseball game or a concert might be a great idea. It's true that holidays can be a little tricky to navigate with extended family members, but I promise it can be done, and you'll be glad you did it.

By working with your family to learn the habits of minimalism, you'll eventually come to find that it's not that difficult to maintain. Simply stay mindful, stay consistent, and stay patient with yourself and everyone in your family. Easier said than done, I know! But believe me, it's definitely worth the initial struggle!

CONCLUSION

Thank you for making it through to the end of Minimalism for Families. I really hope it was informative and was able to provide you with all of the tools you need to achieve your goals, whatever they may be.

In this book, we discussed everything you need to know to develop a mindset of minimalism and build a minimalist lifestyle your entire family can follow. First, we talked about what minimalism is and what it can look like in the life of an entire family. We went through specific strategies for explaining minimalism to your family members and convincing them to jump on board. We talked about methods you can use to declutter your home, as well as specific tips and tricks for each room in your house. Finally, we talked about how to deal with family members who remain unconvinced and resistant to your vision of minimalism, as well as how to maintain a lifestyle of minimalism for the long-haul.

I hope this book was extremely practical and useful to you and that it provided you with much-needed encouragement and motivation along the way. As I'm sure you discovered throughout the pages of this book, minimalism is an incredibly worthwhile mindset and lifestyle. It will help you and your family learn how to focus on the things that truly matter in your life, like spending more time with each other. It might be a bit painful and difficult at first, but I'm willing to bet that your entire family will eventually come to see the value of it.

As you went through the pages of this book, I hope you kept in mind that the guidelines I have written out here are only the opinion of one person. I obviously do not know you or your family. Feel free to take the tips and ideas I've outlined and adjusted it to fit the needs of your family.

The next step is to get started developing a mindset of minimalism in your family and building a minimalist lifestyle that you can all follow! Purchasing and reading this book was a great start toward that goal, but now it's up to you to take what you learned here and use it. Throughout this book, I tried to provide a step-by-step process that's easy to follow so you can use this book as a guide for developing a minimalist mindset and building a lifestyle of minimalism.

Finally, if you found this book useful in any way, a review on Amazon is always appreciated!

DESCRIPTION

When you think of Minimalism, what comes to mind? It is worth noting that minimalism is about trading all of the excess junk that piles up so easily for more of what brings me joy: spending time with my family and friends, writing, sleeping, and experiencing life. It's about teaching my kids to live simple lives so that we can experience the beauty of the world together. It's about working with my husband to build the life we want for our family instead of fighting with him about all of the junk that needs to be taken care of.

One of the aspects worth noting is that in order to start on the journey to minimalism is how to ask the right questions. If you haven't done it already, you should seriously stop reading right now and take a few minutes to consider your reasons for doing this, as well as the purpose you want your family and your home to have.

In other words, Minimalism is a mindset and a lifestyle. It's not a project to be completed in a weekend and put back on the shelf for next time. It's a chance to reconsider what your priorities are and to design your life (and your stuff) around those priorities. And although minimalism usually starts by getting rid of excess physical clutter.

It is worth noting that minimalism involves a lot of issues that are relevant in life. For instance, It might seem ridiculous to think that minimalism can actually work for an entire family—especially one with a couple of young kids. Between all of the sports gear—participating in multiple sports at a time builds character, right? —clothes, school supplies, and toys that constantly pile up, cutting it all down to only the things that are necessary (and keeping it that way) seem an impossible task. Thus, you need to create some more time and grasp some more aspects of minimalism.

In a nutshell, in this book you'll learn:

- What is minimalism?
- Advantages of having a minimalist lifestyle
- Developing a mindset of minimalism
- Strategies for the cleanup
- Aspect on:
    1. Furniture
    2. Bookshelves
    3. Decorations
    4. Coffee Tables
    5. Electronics
    6. Sentimental items
    7. Special spaces for the kids
- You need to create some more time and learn more on:
    1. The Beauty of Humanity
    2. Find your people

3. Remind them of the benefits
4. Be a role model for them
5. Don't chuck someone else's stuff.

You will also have a golden chance of understanding why minimalism is a trade. In that, like I said earlier, minimalism isn't about setting unrealistic limits on what you can own. It's about making a trade. Everything costs something, so when you choose to accept something into your life, you're also choosing to let go of something else.